MY DARLING CLEMENTINE

Also by Jack Fishman

THE SEVEN MEN OF SPANDAU

MY DARLING CLEMENTINE

The Story of Lady Churchill

by

JACK FISHMAN

with an introduction by

ELEANOR ROOSEVELT

DAVID McKAY COMPANY, INC.

NEW YORK

MY DARLING CLEMENTINE

COPYRIGHT © 1963 BY JACK FISHMAN

LIBRARY OF CONGRESS CATALOG CARD NUMBER: 63-17288

MANUFACTURED IN THE UNITED STATES OF AMERICA

VAN REES PRESS • NEW YORK

TO LILIAN, MY WIFE

*from whom I learned to appreciate
how much any man owes to his wife*

Contents

List of Illustrations

Photographs are reproduced by courtesy of U.P.I.: P.A.-Reuter; Pictorial Press; Radio Times Hulton Picture Library; and John Hill Productions.

Author's Preface

Marriage is the greatest earthly happiness when founded on complete sympathy.—DISRAELI

WINSTON CHURCHILL is the statesman the whole world recognizes. Clementine Churchill is the diplomat few know.

This book—this tribute to her—began on a bomb site in the East End of London, during the blitz days of 1940, when I was a newspaper reporter covering the tour, by the Prime Minister and his wife, of bombed areas.

People who had lived through the night were cheering this man to whom they looked for leadership and hope. But it was the woman beside him—or, at least, one pace behind him—who held my attention. What kind of woman could share his life, could be his wife? The question remained unanswered a long time. I watched her on many occasions seated in the Distinguished Strangers' Gallery of the House of Commons, when her husband held the floor of the Chamber below; I covered part of her blitz tour with Mrs. Eleanor Roosevelt.

Through the years, I constantly added notes and anecdotes to a file I kept at home marked "Clementine." I gathered stories and facts from people she met; people with whom she worked, and who worked for her; Ministers and their wives; Members of Parliament; relatives, friends, literally hundreds of people—known and unknown—whose paths had crossed hers. I went to many who had already written of Winston Churchill and asked them to view various events again from a different aspect—his wife's.

To persuade her to write her own story, or to write a book about her, has been an ambition of mine since those early war days. Her husband is the most written about man of our times, but largely because she has avoided the limelight, this is the first book ever to be written about her, and her place in the Winston Churchill legend.

This does not pretend to be her life story and is in no sense a full biography, for to tell her story would occupy almost as many volumes as those written by her husband on his own incredible life.

She may never tell her own story. Some years ago, I initiated a proposal for her to write her autobiography. At first, she was intrigued with the idea, then she decided to leave the writing in the family to her husband and to her son Randolph.

At the time of this approach to her, I was acting on behalf of Kemsley Newspapers, of which I was an editorial executive. I even prepared a draft outline of the manner in which I thought her story could be told—based on the notes and anecdotes I had collected over the years.

The canvas of her life is so large that I suggested the storytelling be concentrated on revealing her point of view of a number of incidents in their lives. Because her life is so much bound up with his, I wanted to see historic moments through her eyes; wanted to record some of her share in them. I never stopped hoping she might, one day, be persuaded to write her version of the Churchill story, and I continued collecting useful material from sources all over the world.

Finally, I decided to write this tribute to her, based on my "Clementine" file—a file that now fills a very large cupboard and contains almost 600,000 words of notes. From these I have chosen approximately 200,000 to present the story of a unique marriage and of the woman married to the world's most unique man—a woman who could have basked in her own limelight but chose to walk in his shadow.

Clementine Churchill has played a bigger part in history than most realize. She has the right conception of woman's power. She knows that companionship and understanding are the strength and foundation of true marriage. She knows, too, that a woman's real influence is behind the scenes, and that this is especially true in the world of diplomacy and politics.

The wife of any man eminent in public affairs must, of necessity, be a somewhat shadowy figure, ever present, but never too much in the foreground. That the ability to submerge her own vivid personality is one of Clementine Churchill's special talents is shown by the thousands of newsreels and press photographs taken of her husband throughout their married life. Whatever her personal achievements—and they have been many—she has contrived to remain, first and foremost, Winston Churchill's wife. She has never tried to be anything else.

To make her marriage a success, she has had to be armed with infinite patience, for she has had to live with a husband who at one moment can be a roaring lion, at another a lively fox terrier, and again, a brooding teddy bear.

My sincere appreciation is due to those who helped, cooperated, and advised, and in particular to Lady Churchill's cousin, the Hon. Mrs. Sylvia Henley, for guiding me on a number of points in the first chapter; to the Dowager Marchioness of Hillingdon; General Lord Ismay; Lady Limerick of the British Red Cross Society; Mrs. Doris Moss, Chairman of the Woodford Conservative Association; Gerald O'Brien of the Conservative and Unionist Central Office for giving me access to their files; Sir Tom O'Brien; General Sir Frederick Pile; the Dowager Marchioness of Reading; ex-Detective Inspector Walter H. Thompson of Scotland Yard and Mrs. Thompson, who was a wartime secretary to both Mr. and Mrs. Churchill; Miss Ruth Walder, National General Secretary of the Y.W.C.A.; and Colonel Barlow Wheeler, Sir Winston's constituency agent.

Acknowledgments and thanks are also due to General H. H. Arnold; Constance Babington Smith; the Earl of Birkenhead; Lord Beaverbrook; Bernard M. Baruch; John Spencer Churchill; Sir Winston Churchill; General Mark Clark; Lady Diana Cooper; General Dwight D. Eisenhower; General Sir Leslie Hollis; Lieutenant General Sir Brian Horrocks; H. Montgomery Hyde; Major General Sir John Kennedy; Field Marshal Viscount Montgomery of Alamein; Elizabeth Nel; Vic Oliver; Mr. Mackenzie King; Elliott Roosevelt; Samuel I. Rosenman; Robert E. Sherwood.

I have drawn on innumerable documents, diaries, and memoirs, and my indebtedness to many of these is recorded in the Bibliography.

I am also grateful to the Y.W.C.A. and the British Red Cross Society for allowing me to use extracts from their reports and files, and for permission to quote from some of Lady Churchill's correspondence.

Finally, I wish to record my deepest debt of gratitude to another unique woman who is also part of this story and who helped to make several of its chapters possible—the late Eleanor Roosevelt. She was the only person I ever hoped would contribute the Introduction to this book. With typical generosity, she not only granted me permission to use a section of our discussion on Lady Churchill as an introduction to this tribute to her, but she also gave me invaluable information and advice for use in other chapters.

Mrs. Roosevelt's own life story has been written. I am glad that she was able to help me tell some of the Clementine Churchill story.

Jack Fishman

MY DARLING CLEMENTINE

Introduction

by Eleanor Roosevelt

LADY CHURCHILL has always had a very keen sense of the responsibility she carried. Her husband was Prime Minister at a most crucial time in England, and she knew that in the first place she must make life as easy as she could for him at home, with as much attention to detail as possible, to ensure that his life would be comfortable and lightened of any burdens she could remove.

In those days, we understood and admired the kind of courage and tenacity her husband was beginning to put into words that expressed the spirit of the people in Britain after Dunkirk.

My husband thought Mr. Churchill typical of John Bull and considered him to be a man with whom he really could work. The bond between them strengthened every time they met. Their friendship grew with their respect for each other's ability.

Mrs. Churchill, as she then was, had to endure many anxieties. She had, of course, long periods of anxiety during the war when he was away; then, when she did accompany him, she had her own duties.

I remember when she was in Quebec with the Prime Minister on one occasion, and I was there with my husband. My husband and Mr. Churchill were meeting over certain questions that had to be decided, and I remember Mrs. Churchill had to do a great many things that were her responsibility and not in any way connected with his work, except that they were things people appreciated and liked her doing, because they brought them closer to both her and her husband. Everything she did, whether it was addressing meetings or making a broadcast, she did remarkably well.

She was more or less propelled into public life, as I was. When this happens, you learn to develop ideas of your own as well as developing the initiative and ability to act on them.

In many cases the need for doing things will in itself develop an ability to do them. You might not have this ability naturally, but it comes because you have to do it. This is a capability that may be in any woman, although it might lie dormant forever, if you didn't have to bring it out to meet special situations. It is, I suppose, like a man who doesn't know his own courage or his own strength.

A woman, no matter what she may have in her, can fall by the wayside and fail unless she carries responsibility and is aware of her responsibility. As far as I was concerned, it was much easier than it must have been for Mrs. Churchill.

The wife of the President of the United States can, to a large extent, do whatever she wishes, really. There are certain duties—you must be a hostess—but outside of that you make your own life. But I don't think this is true of a woman in England who is married to a prominent political figure. She almost automatically must take part in the political work of her husband. She really hasn't the separate life that a First Lady can have in the White House. Perhaps, because of this, her sacrifice is, in certain respects, all the greater, because she is willing to make the sacrifice.

But Mrs. Churchill would never have married her husband unless she was prepared to make this sacrifice, and unless she really enjoyed the responsibilities demanded of her, because she would have certainly known beforehand what marrying him might entail.

As for realizing that it could also entail abuse, discredit, and almost political ruin, I think you get accustomed to that. You don't really care much about that, except as it affects the ability of your husband to do whatever his work may be. You develop a sort of philosophical point of view that, after all, these things have to be settled by history; they can't be settled by you. Therefore, you just forget about them.

As my husband used to say, "Nobody should go into politics unless he has a hide like a rhinoceros." Perhaps politicians have to pass along a little of that to their wives.

A wife must have tremendous belief in her husband to bear this kind of thing, because criticism comes to anyone who lives his or her life more or less in the public eye. Much of the criticism may be unfair, but you come to accept it as one of the hazards.

Mrs. Churchill was, I am sure, able to face all the trials she had to face because she achieved an inner calm that enabled her to withstand the strain. This inner calm gave her added strength.

Self-discipline of this kind is absolutely essential. It is essential in a life in which you are liable to be constantly meeting defeats and recovering from disasters. You can face whatever has to be faced if you master your own fears and simply go on.

Mrs. Churchill has always been the perfect partner for her husband. As far as she was concerned, whatever trials had to be faced, she faced, and whatever duties were expected of her, she did.

One cannot live in a political atmosphere without absorbing some of it. You learn to appreciate what is important to your husband; you learn to appreciate many things. You find that good timing is always essential, and you consequently have to choose to say things at what you consider to be the right moment, even though the reaction to what you have to say may be unfavorable and uncomfortable at first.

Lady Churchill has always been very much an individual in her own right. It is a brave thing to have the courage to be an individual. It is also often a lonely thing. But it is better than not being an individual, which is to be nobody at all.

She certainly did not agree with her husband on every issue. Two people must differ at times, on method if not on principle. But whatever differences she might have had with her husband on political matters, she would never air any such differences in public.

My husband never asked me to refrain from speaking my own mind on any issue, and I am sure it has always been the same with Sir Winston and his wife.

A man and woman who are both anxious to discover the truth in a political situation may, through study and argument, influence each other, but the ultimate decision must always remain with the individual.

Some people say that a wife can ruin a husband, if she does not give him stability in the home. It would of course be very hard to ruin a man of the stature of Winston Churchill, very hard. But you could make it more difficult for him to do his work; there is no question about that.

Sir Winston has always been a man to whom the personal element means a great deal; his wife therefore organized her time to first and foremost suit his needs. This planning of time—although never so rigid as to be inflexible—must have contributed greatly to the smooth running of his home and daily life. But then meeting the needs of others is what makes life worth living—especially, perhaps, for a woman.

A man may have to turn at times to someone in moments of great emotional stress. If he turns to his wife, and she happens to be the wrong wife for him, she would not be a constructive force in his life— she could, in fact, be destructive. On the other hand, the right wife can give a man something that helps him, and makes his life.

3

Mind you, I think my husband would have led his life and done the same things exactly, whether I had been there or not. I made it easier. I took certain things off his shoulders, but he would have done it just the same. And I think Sir Winston would have, but life can be made easier and pleasanter, and that is important. A home can be made a haven—or a hell. That happens.

But Lady Churchill is warm, unselfish, full of understanding and real human sympathy, and a very delightful person.

A wonderful person, she always gives the impression of being so welcoming to everybody and so happy to be with any of her husband's friends and with any of the people who came to meet them. She carries her responsibilities in a very extraordinary way.

She has always made the effort to establish an understanding relationship with people in any and every walk of life.

Her capacity to entertain and meet the great and the simple, the distinguished and the unknown with equal charm, graciousness, and hospitality, made a tremendous contribution to her husband's success.

Whenever we were together, we never seemed to have enough time, there were always things to be done, and we went and did them.

The deep and obviously sincere affection that both of them had for my husband and me, we reciprocated. I think the war would have been harder to win without the friendship of our two husbands.

Since the war I have seen them several times, both in America and at their homes. I saw them at Mr. Bernard Baruch's whenever they came to New York. I always tried to be there when they were.

When Mr. Churchill was not reelected after the war, it was a great shock, both to him and his wife, as well as to us all. I thought he would be elected at this time. I know he didn't expect defeat. He had repeatedly said that he would like to stay in office until the men had come back and been rehoused and restarted again. I know my husband felt that Mr. Churchill would be elected the first time, although he did not expect him to be elected more than once after the war. At least I don't think he went beyond that.

My husband often said he felt sure Mr. Churchill would retire from office after the war, but definitely expected him to have his say about the policies to be laid down for the future.

When he was voted out of office, I think to most of us in the United States, and to me personally, it seemed a rather cruel thing to have done, but we didn't try to contact them at that moment—somehow you don't feel that either a man or a woman wants to be sympathized with in a situation of that kind. You just accept what the people have done and that's all there is to it. You just accept it, that's all. It's part of the life of a political person. Sometimes he loses, even though his defeat may seem like ingratitude, but ingratitude is exactly what a person in public life very often does get.

Lady Churchill undoubtedly fulfilled, I think in a very ideal way, all the things that a man in public office could possibly ask or want. She built the right kind of atmosphere around him—an atmosphere that enabled him to work at his best.

A man in public office must be sure his wife and family are ready to accept a mode of life which is unlike any other.

I sometimes wonder whether people realize the price the wife and family of a man in public life have to pay.

In my own autobiography, I said that there was little or no personal compensation for the members of the family of such a man. There is, of course, pride in the man's achievement and gratitude if he is able to help his countrymen and the world.

Love is usually selfish; but when sufficiently disciplined, a family may be glad that a man has the opportunity to fulfil his heart's desire, and they will work with him in every way they can to help him achieve his objectives. But something of the personal relationship must be lost.

It is the price paid for a life spent almost entirely in public service.

Mr. John Winant, who was, during the war, the United States Ambassador in London, once wrote to my husband that he hoped some future historian would recognize and record Mrs. Churchill's service to Britain. I am therefore glad to have been able to assist with this book by telling anything I know, and I am delighted that such a tribute to this great woman has been written at last.

As I saw more of Mrs. Churchill over the years, my admiration and affection for her grew. She has had no easy role to play in life, but she has played it with dignity and charm.

Eleanor Roosevelt

1

Young Man in a Hurry

"Miss Clementine Hozier—Mr. Winston Churchill."

It was as simple as that—the beginning of their love story, their historic marriage partnership.

This introduction took place at a dinner party at the London home of Clementine's great-aunt, Lady St. Helier, in the spring of 1908.

Winston, one of the most eligible bachelors in Britain—hated, loved, unpredictable, tempestuous—hadn't given marriage a thought; he was too busy with his political career and was already feeling his strength, saying, "Sometimes I think I could carry the world on my shoulders."

And he was already President of the Board of Trade and a member of the Cabinet.

Miss Clementine Hozier, aged twenty-three, came from an aristocratic family, but she was poor. She was one of the four children of ex-cavalry officer Colonel Sir Henry Hozier, who became a secretary of Lloyd's. Sir Henry was twenty-five years older than his wife. The marriage broke up, and Blanche Hozier, daughter of the seventh Earl of Airlie, was left to care for their children Kitty, Clementine, Nelly, and her twin brother Bill, on a modest allowance from the Countess of Airlie.

The Hozier children had a rigorous childhood with a nurse who spurred them to housework with a cut of the cane on their bare legs. Apart from occasional visits to Cortachy Castle, the Forfarshire home of the Airlies, Lady Blanche and her children lived in lodgings in London and Seaford.

Blanche Hozier struggled to keep up appearances on her very limited income. The family moved to France when Clementine was thirteen, and there she learned excellent French during the years they resided in-expensively in the obscurity of Dieppe. It was in Dieppe that her eldest sister Kitty died of typhoid at the age of seventeen.

The family returned to England and to the small house at Berkham-sted in which they had lived before. In April, 1900, when Clementine was fifteen, her mother enrolled her at the Berkhamsted School for Girls.

In answer to the application form query, "Has she been a pupil at a school before, and if so, where?" Blanche Hozier wrote, "For three months at the Convent Les Sœurs de la Providence of Rouen, at Dieppe."

Clementine, with her already excellent mastery of French, became Mlle Kroon's star pupil. Mlle Kroon was, of course, the school's French mistress, and her humor, her great love of flowers, and her sparkling personality, had a deep influence on Clementine. She, and her class-mates, remembered Mlle's lessons with vividness—it was no use think-ing of other things, they recalled. If the mind wandered in the slightest degree, one would hear, "Now you fat bolster, wake up and translate the next passage." Sometimes a pupil was "pudding" or "boiled owl." Clementine loved Mlle Kroon, and honored her by winning a silver medal for French.

The Hoziers moved back to London to live in a little rented house at 51 Abingdon Villas, Kensington. Clementine shared a room with her sister and supplemented her dress allowance of £30 a year with the money she earned giving French lessons. She came out at a ball given by Lady Stanley of Alderley for her daughter Sylvia, who was Clem-entine's cousin.

Intelligent, independent, liberal-minded like her grandmother the Countess of Airlie, and passionately interested in politics, Clementine was a lovely girl who had no intention of conforming to the accepted customs of the times of being "suitably married off." *She* was going to do the choosing.

It was her great-aunt, Lady St. Helier—known in those days as "Lady Santa Claus," because of her kind heart and reputation for never refus-ing to help anyone—tall, gracious Lady St. Helier, the finest hostess in society, who was giving the party at her London home at 52 Portland Place, the night that Winston Churchill met Clementine Hozier.

"Lady Santa Claus" had been left £250,000 by her famous husband, who had been a judge of the Probate and Divorce Court. In her role as a fairy godmother, she had taken a small house in the slums of Shore-

8

ditch from which she could work to help the poor. She was elected to the London County Council, and the L.C.C. suburb of St. Helier perpetuates her name. She was to play fairy godmother to the young Churchill and her great-niece.

While independent Clementine had been saying "No" to many of London's eligible bachelors, Winston had been successfully fighting a defensive action against society mothers with matrimonially inclined daughters.

Clementine looked radiantly lovely that night in her white satin princess dress. The dress had been a gift from her grandmother.

The society magazine *The Bystander* described Clementine in a 1908 issue as having "lovely brown hair and most delicately aquiline features, fine gray eyes, and a delightful poise of the head. Her shoulders and neck have something of the grace and distinction and soft strength of early Grecian art; she is divinely tall."

Also speaking of the reigning beauties of the era, Lady Cynthia Asquith described her as, "classical, statuesque; yet full of animation. A queen she should have been; her superbly sculptured features would have looked so splendid on a coin. 'There's a face that will last,' said everyone. How right they were!"

Winston arrived at the dinner party late, as usual. For more than six seasons, he had been the matchmaking mamma's despair. Not that he was oblivious to the charms of beautiful young ladies, he was just too busy. "You see," he would explain, "we Churchills are apt to damp off after forty."

Eyes turned to watch his entrance, not that he was a handsome figure of a man—he wasn't. But the atmosphere of his personality, his very presence was electric. His blazing red hair, and his equally blazing blue eyes, compelled attention.

Even in those days his face was thrust forward as if to defy enemies, and his lips pouted. Although young, he already walked with a slight stoop and would pace the room with restless explosive energy, talking all the time.

Everyone in the room knew of the young Mr. Churchill. Born at Blenheim Palace, the fabulous estate of the Dukes of Marlborough, he had crossed the floor of the House of Commons in 1904 to join the Liberals. He won his first Ministerial post as Under Secretary for the Colonies at the age of thirty-one.

To the Tories he was a renegade and a traitor. He had achieved fantastic political success at an incredibly early age. Even his father, who was considered precociously successful in Parliament, did not attain a Ministerial post until he was thirty-six.

But Winston was a young man in a hurry.

"Some men change their party for the sake of their principles; others their principles for the sake of their party," he said in answer to his critics.

Winston had little time for women, but they were eagerly willing to devote plenty of time to him. Not only was he a target of the husband hunters, but he was also a target of the Suffragettes. Suffragettes just wouldn't leave him alone and seemed to make a particular beeline for the bachelor Cabinet Minister, continually harassing and attacking him at meetings.

"Get away woman!" he once roared at one young Suffragette in Dundee, who followed him about constantly ringing a deafening dinner bell.

"It's no use your being cross," she replied, and went right on ringing the bell as close to Winston as possible.

Added Winston, "I won't attempt to compete with a young and pretty lady in a high state of excitement."

Suffragettes bombarded him with rotten fruit, eggs, coal, and stones. One of them slashed at him with a riding whip, which he managed to take away from her.

Yet, he fell in love with a girl who was a Suffragette at heart, and who passionately believed in "Votes for Women."

Winston and his friend Edward Marsh had devised a pastime for soirée evenings. They would often stand together within sight of the ballroom entrance, watching the ladies arrive, and, using the classic line "Was this the face that launched a thousand ships?" as their theme, would assess the beauty of each young thing as she appeared.

"Two hundred ships, or perhaps two-hundred-and-fifty?" one of them might hazard, studying the latest piece of femininity to grace the scene.

"By no means," the other might reply. "A sampan, or small gunboat at most . . ."

Both unanimously agreed that among the rare few worthy of the full thousand score, were Lady Diana Manners and Miss Clementine Hozier.

Talking to her at Lady St. Helier's, he recognized in the vivacious girl ten years his junior, a spirit equal to his own. He admired her gaiety, her conversation, her independence—so he continued to listen.

Said her Aunt Mabell, the Countess of Airlie, "I think that subconsciously I had expected Clementine to make a romantic marriage. She was a lovely girl; I always kept in mind the picture of her one evening when she was staying with us at Cortachy [Cortachy Castle] and came down to dinner in a white satin dress which she had made herself. It was very simply cut, and her only jewelry was a little string of pearls, but her beauty needed no adornment. She looked like a lily.

"After that I did not see her for a year or more. I heard that she had many admirers, but her own heart was not touched."

There was only one other woman who might have become Mrs. Churchill had she given Winston half the chance. In his youth he had a "crush" on actress Ethel Barrymore, who was then the toast of London.

"I sent a note to Winston asking him to send me a ticket for the gallery at the House of Commons. He sent one by his secretary, Edward Marsh, and he and Winston and I had tea together in Winston's rooms," recalled Miss Barrymore.

Enchanted by her beauty and dignity, he sent her almost nonstop gifts of flowers, and went almost every night to Claridges Hotel for supper, knowing she, too, always went there after her performance at the theater. But he was just one of her army of hopeful admirers and didn't get very far.

Years later when Winston was passing through Washington and she was appearing there, she received a box of flowers from him accompanied by a note reminding her how much he had always admired her.

Strangely, Clementine had much in common with Ethel Barrymore's looks and character, and they met in later years from time to time.

Visiting New York when he was twenty-six years old, Winston "met everybody, but would sit in the midst of the most delightful people absorbed in his own thoughts. He would not admire the women he was expected to admire," said the noted Mr. George Smalley, describing the visit.

Continued Mr. Smalley, "They must have not only beauty and intelligence, but the particular kind of beauty and intelligence which appealed to him; if otherwise, he knew how to be silent without meaning to be rude...it was useless to remonstrate with him. He answered: 'She is beautiful to you, but not to me.'"

With Clementine it was different. It was very difficult in those days for girls to find work, yet somehow she managed to keep bolstering the family's housekeeping money with her French lessons, as well as by reading to an elderly lady for so much an hour. Winston respected her for it.

He admired her, too, because, although he loved flattery and reveled in success, here was a girl who didn't simper, didn't pander to him.

Friends observed that for the first time in his life—after the ladies, in accordance with custom, had withdrawn from the dinner table— Winston was plainly anxious to leave the port-and-men-only conversations on topics of the times, to rejoin the ladies as speedily as possible.

Years later, when asked whether at their first meeting she considered Winston handsome, Clementine answered tactfully, "I thought he was very interesting."

At the same party, an admiral was also attracted to the beautiful Miss Hozier; Winston counterattacked by sidetracking the admiral and out-maneuvering him.

There were other campaigns on Winston's mind at the time—he was busy preparing for a by-election at Dundee, but once he had decided that this was the girl for him, he lost no time. He became a regular caller at the Hozier's Kensington home, courting Clementine, and he made sure everyone knew it.

Lady Blanche Hozier was impressed with the young man who was so nervous in her presence and yet so distinguished a politician with a reputation as a firebrand. His mother-in-law-to-be knew Winston much better than he realized. She had known his mother for many years and was aware that Lord Randolph Churchill had fallen madly in love at first sight with the dark, lovely, intelligent American, Jennie Jerome; Lord Randolph courted, won, and married Jennie against the wishes of both his and her parents. Lady Blanche recognized the tremendous influence of Jennie Jerome on Winston's life.

"My mother," he wrote in later years, "made a brilliant impression upon my childhood's life. She shone for me like the evening star, I loved her dearly but at a distance. She always seemed to me a fairy princess."

Those who knew Winston said he owed a lot to his American grandfather, Colonel Jerome, who in his seventies went to a circus and got so annoyed at the boasting of the professional strong man that he accepted a challenge to wrestle. The colonel threw his man all right, but strained his inside doing it and subsequently died from the effects.

Whirlwind courtships ran in the Churchill family. Winston's father boasted that when he met nineteen-year-old Jennie Jerome, he proposed and was accepted all in three days.

Of their courtship, Clementine said, "He was of a temper that gallops till it falls."

Lady Blanche saw that Winston was an incurable romantic and that a woman in his life could make or break it. Knowing her daughter, she recognized that, although a natural rebel, her disciplined modesty, her discretion, her gift of devotion, plus sense of duty, would make her the right woman for Winston. Lady Blanche was certain that in spite of Clementine's possessing a distinct personality of her own, her sense of dignity would never allow her temperament to create domestic turmoil that would intrude into her husband's public or private life.

Even in those days, when Winston wanted something, he usually got it, and he wanted Clementine.

He asked his cousin, the Duke of Marlborough, to invite Blanche Hozier and her daughter Clementine to Blenheim Palace.

"A female friend, amiable, clever, and devoted, is a possession more valuable than parks or palaces; and without such a Muse few men can succeed, and none can be happy."

Those were the words of Benjamin Disraeli, and young Winston Churchill was certain that his success and happiness were bound up with Clementine Hozier.

One day in August, he strolled with Clementine from the front entrance of historic Blenheim Palace toward Diana's temple—the stone pavilion set among the yew trees by the lake he loved so much.

Within the temple a bas-relief shows Hippolitus offering a wreath of flowers to Diana. The first line of the inscription, which is in Greek and English, reads:

"To thee bright Goddess, these flowers I bring. . ."

It was there he proposed and she accepted.

Said Clementine, "Now I have got you, the trouble will be to keep you."

To which Winston replied, "You will find that no trouble at all, my dear."

His mother, who had known Clementine from a baby, was delighted with the match. Her son was affectionate, emotional, home-loving. She was sure Clementine was the wife he needed.

An excited Blanche Hozier wrote to a friend from Blenheim Palace with the news of the engagement, saying:

"Clementine is to marry Winston Churchill. Yesterday he came to London to ask my consent, and we all three came on here. He is so like Lord Randolph, he has some of his faults, and all his qualities.

13

"He is gentle and tender, and affectionate to those he loves, much hated by those who have not come under his personal charm."

Her mother also wrote to her sister-in-law Mabell, the Countess of Airlie:

"I do not know which of the two is the more in love. I think that to know him is to like him. His brilliant brain the world knows, but he is so charming and affectionate in his own home life."

A few days later Clementine, answering her Aunt Mabell's letter of congratulations, wrote:

> Dearest Aunt Mabell,
>   Thank you very much for your letter. It gave me a great deal of pleasure.
>   I cannot describe my happiness to you. I can hardly believe it is true. I have been engaged nine days now. I cared very much for him when he asked me to marry him, but every day since has been more heavenly. The only crumpled rose leaf is the scrimmage getting ready in time. September 12th has now been settled for our wedding. We shall have only seventeen days away as Winston has to be back in London on October 3rd.

Said Clementine's Aunt Mabell:

"My mother-in-law had the final word. . . .

" 'Winston is his father over again, with the American driving force added,' she wrote in a letter to me. 'His mother and he are devoted to one another, and I think a good son makes a good husband. Clementine is wise. She will follow him and, I hope, say little.' "

Clementine certainly did follow Winston loyally and devotedly, but not in the role of a meek, mild, submissive wife, with opinions she was afraid to voice.

When society heard of the engagement, skeptics said it would never work. "No one can live with Winston Churchill without upheavals," they predicted.

"Clementine is a girl who likes her own way, and Winston will never give in to anyone," they added.

To which Clementine replied, "Being married to him couldn't be easy, but I think it would be tremendously stimulating."

Clementine found her mother-in-law-to-be an incredible, delightful compound of worldliness and eternal childhood. She was warmhearted, witty, sincere, and courageous. Clementine saw in Lady Randolph the pattern of the kind of woman she wanted to become herself.

The Hoziers' modest Kensington home was a little too modest for the kind of wedding reception expected of a Churchill, so once again "Lady Santa Claus"—Lady St. Helier—stepped into the picture.

Clementine and her mother were invited to move into the St. Helier home in Portland Place on September 8,—four days before the wedding. This was to be the home from which she would leave to be married in St. Margaret's, Westminster.

There had already been one wedding in the family a few weeks earlier when Winston's cavalry-officer brother, Jack, had married Lady Gwendoline Bertie, who became the mother of Clarissa—later to become the wife of Lord Avon—Anthony Eden.

Winston held a stag dinner at his house in Bolton Street. Guests included the Chancellor of the Exchequer, Mr. Lloyd George, and the Bishop of St. Asaph.

Clementine also entertained a small party of close friends to tea at 52 Portland Place, and in the evening dined with her mother, Lady St. Helier, and other relatives and friends.

But even as some of the guests departed from the two parties, they were saying, "It will never work out." They were echoing the talk of London society.

Lord Rosebery forecast, "The union will last about six months, with luck." He concluded, "Their marriage will fail because Winston is not the marrying kind."

Know-alls said, "He hasn't any money, and neither has she." And in society, in those days, it was the accepted "thing" to marry for money.

The bridal gown was ready, so were the dresses of the five bridesmaids. "Something Old" was supplied by Winston's mother—lace to trim the bride's cuffs and neckline. London was excited at the prospect of the occasion—it was to be one of the most brilliant weddings of the year.

Now that he had found his Clementine, Winston couldn't wait. A month after he proposed, they married. It was like a royal wedding. Extra mounted as well as foot police were there to control the crowds of thousands spread from St. Margaret's to Whitehall and Parliament Square. It was a Saturday, and half of London seemed to have turned up to cheer. People had waited hours all along the miles of wedding route. At twenty minutes to two, Winston with his best man, Lord Hugh Cecil, arrived at the church, having left Bolton Street at half-past one, and driven by way of Piccadilly and Whitehall. As they stepped from their motor-car to enter the church, the crowd gave a welcoming roar. A smiling Winston walked into the body of the church from the vestry, bowed to relatives seated in the front pew, then leaned over and shook hands with the Duchess of Marlborough.

At two minutes past two Winston looked at his watch. The bride was late. So was Mr. Lloyd George, who arrived at this moment and took the seat next to the best man. Winston, Lord Hugh Cecil, and Mr. Lloyd George were the only occupants of the front bench.

Lady Blanche Hozier, dressed in purple, her hair decorated with some soft, white material, and the wrists of her dress trimmed with white fur, drove in a brougham with Clementine and her twenty-year-old brother William, a Royal Naval lieutenant, from Portland Place to arrive at four minutes past two.

Sixteen hundred guests were waiting at the church. The packed congregation included most of the eminent personalities of the day. Mr. Joynson Hicks, M.P., and his wife were among the first to arrive. "Jix," as he was later known when he was the Home Secretary, had only recently beat Winston in a Manchester by-election. Others present included the Marchioness of Blandford, the Duke of Marlborough, Mr. and Mrs. G. R. Asquith, the Duke and Duchess of Sutherland, Mrs. Beerbohm Tree, and many Members of Parliament.

The bride, when she entered, took the congregation's breath away. She walked down the aisle on her brother's arm, the organ boomed, and many stood on the pews to get an extra good look at her.

The church was decorated with palms and chrysanthemums and arum lilies. The chancel and altar were wrapped in white flowers, chrysanthemums and camellias in a setting of green. The bride, a picture of white in her satin dress and veil of Brussels net, carried a white bouquet of lilies and myrtle and a prayer book bound in white kid. On her head was a simple coronet of orange blossoms.

Nelly, the bride's sister, led the bridesmaids. With her were the Hon. Venetia Stanley, daughter of Lady Stanley of Alderley, cousin of the bride; Miss Clare Frewen (later Clare Sheridan, distinguished authoress and sculptor), cousin of the bridegroom; Miss Horatia Seymour, daughter of the late Sir Horace Seymour; and Miss Madeline White, daughter of Lady White, cousin of the bride. Winston had given each of the bridesmaids necklaces of platinum with pendants of diamonds and a sapphire.

The bride's only jewelry was a pair of diamond earrings—a gift from the groom.

The organist finished the Wagnerian wedding music, the choir sang the hymn "Lead us, Heavenly Father," and the bride's procession moved to the chancel.

Some weeks earlier, Winston had had a political dispute with the Bishop of St. Asaph over education, but the bishop was nevertheless at St. Margaret's to conduct the marriage service. The headmaster of Harrow in the days when young Churchill was one of the school's worst scholars, Bishop Welldon, at that time Dean of Manchester, was present to give the address to his former pupil.

The clergy came down to the chancel. As his bride approached, Winston put out his hand and shook hers warmly.

The ceremony began.

In his address Bishop Welldon uttered prophetic words, "The sun shines on your union today.

"Allow me to remind you how much you may be to each other in the coming days, in the sunny hours and in the somber hours.

"There must be in a statesman's life many times when he depends on the love, insight, penetrating sympathy, and devotion of his wife.

"The influence which the wives of our statesmen have exercised for good on their husbands' lives is an unwritten chapter of English history too sacred perhaps to be written in full.

"May your lives prove a blessing, each to the other, and both to the world."

They were wed, and the signing of the register was witnessed by Jennie Cornwallis West, Winston's mother, D. Lloyd George, and William Hozier. The groom signed himself as Winston Leonard Spencer Churchill. His father was described on the register as "Sometime Secretary for India, Chancellor of Exchequer."

Commented Lady Blanche Hozier's poet friend, Wilfrid Blunt, "It is a good marriage for both of them, for Clementine is pretty, clever and altogether charming, while Winston is what the world knows of him, and a good fellow to boot."

Of the wedding, he said, "It was quite a popular demonstration. Lord Hugh Cecil, Winston's best man, and the great crowd of relations, not only the church full, but all Victoria Street, though that may have partly been for the Eucharistic Congress.... At St. Margaret's I arrived late when all the seats were taken, but Blanche Hozier found me one in the family pew.

"The bride was pale, as was the bridegroom. He has gained in appearance since I saw him last, and has a powerful if ugly face.

"Winston's responses were clearly made in a pleasant voice, Clementine's inaudible."

First to congratulate Mr. and Mrs. Winston Churchill was the Chancellor of the Exchequer; Lord Redesdale; his mother; and the Dowager Countess of Airlie, who were among those present in the vestry.

Even the Suffragettes who had fought and harassed Winston all over the country, called a truce for the wedding day, although in case of any demonstrations, plainclothes police officers occupied seats in various parts of St. Margaret's during the ceremony. They had received warnings that several militant Suffragettes intended to interrupt the service.

The Suffragettes were there all right—cheering with the rest of the crowds.

As the bride and groom left the church, the police couldn't hold back the crowd's enthusiasm, and hundreds broke through, surrounding the car to get a clearer view.

Winston and Clementine bowed and waved to the six-deep throngs on the pavements along their return route up Whitehall and Regent Street to Lady St. Helier's, where the reception was to be held.

Recalling the day, one of the bridesmaids, Clare Sheridan, said, "The outstanding thing I remember is the crowd lining the streets from St. Margaret's to the reception in Portland Place. It was as deep as it would have been for the King and Queen. As we drove past, they shouted 'good old Winnie!' and 'God bless Winnie!'

"Clementine looked absolutely radiant, with a wonderful smile. She looked so beautiful that people were stunned. Winston looked very handsome, too. We bridesmaids wore amber satin dresses and carried cream roses. We also wore large hats of stretched black satin with a row of waxen white camellias."

And Clare Sheridan's brother, Oswald Frewen, wrote in his diary, "Got a pew pretty near the front and despite a large pillar saw the ceremony pretty well. Afterwards went to 52 Portland Place and attended the extremely crowded reception. . . . At Clare's suggestion we strewed the petals of the roses from the bridesmaids' bouquets over the Bride and Bridegroom and their path instead of the usual rice. . . ."

At 52 Portland Place, champagne flowed, guests gossiped, presents lined the tables, dukes and duchesses were there in their dozens as well as counts and countesses, lords and ladies, the even more famous plain

"Misters" such as Mr. Austen Chamberlain, Mr. Balfour, Mr. Rufus Isaacs, and, of course, Mr. Lloyd George.

Wedding gifts included a silver fruit basket, which had come from Lloyd George. Edward Grey sent a bound set of Marlborough's dispatches, while other Cabinet colleagues gave varied books—Mr. Asquith sent ten volumes of Jane Austen—and *Conversations with the Duke of Wellington*.

There were traveling clocks, silver trays, gold, silver, and jewelry for the bride from the Rothschild family and from Lord Northcliffe, who also gave Winston a walking stick. Lady Blanche Hozier gave her daughter diamonds and sapphires and also presented her new son-in-law with three glass perfume bottles.

There were gifts from the Royal Family, and from admirers. Antique silver candlesticks, in fact twenty-five candlesticks in all among the gifts. A Bible came from the deputy Lord Mayor of Manchester; ten cigarette cases; eight sets of salt cellars and twenty-one inkstands. Sir Joseph Chamberlain sent two silver decanter stands. Almost no great name was absent from the wedding-gift list. King Edward's gift of a malacca cane had a massive gold knob, richly chased and engraved "W.S.C., Turf Club."

But the most important present of all was recorded as: Bridegroom to Bride, fine ruby and diamond cluster necklace, with ruby and diamond drop, pair of diamond cluster earrings.

The wedding cake with its ornamentation stood nearly five feet high and weighed over a hundred pounds.

The newly wed Churchills didn't stay long at their own wedding reception. Early in the afternoon, they left to spend the first part of their honeymoon at Blenheim Palace, where Winston had proposed.

Clementine's going-away dress was a smart gray costume, and Winston wore the wedding suit, which the "Tailor's Bible"—*The Tailor and Cutter*—described as "one of the greatest failures we have seen, making the wearer look like a glorified coachman." Winston's taste in clothes never improved with the years, in spite of his wife's efforts.

The honeymooners drove to Paddington Station, where a special reserved coach awaited them. It was uncoupled at Oxford and switched to Woodstock, where they were received by another great crowd, who had been standing for hours to catch a glimpse of them.

They later left Blenheim to spend a week of their honeymoon at Bareno on Lake Maggiore, in Italy, and then traveled to Austria to stay with Baron de Forest, one of Winston's friends, on his estates in Moravia.

Sir Edward Carson—later Lord Carson of Duncairn—wrote in a letter to a friend: "...I suppose you did not come to town for Winston's wedding. I never saw anything so much advertised—nearly as much as 'Eno's Fruit Salts!'..."

And so the story began. As Winston himself later wrote:

> It was in 1908 that I met the young lady of dazzling beauty who consented to be my wife.
>
> On her mother's side she was one of the Airlie's whose country seat is so close to Dundee.
>
> Her father, who was dead, Colonel Sir Henry Hozier, had been a prominent member of Lloyd's, and had written a valuable account of the Austro-Prussian War of 1866.
>
> We had a wonderful wedding at St. Margaret's, with enormous crowds in the streets and everybody gave us presents without the slightest regard to politics.

His "Clemmie," as he called her from almost their moment of meeting, was his ideal. Even his youthful thoughts were of a woman like her.

In his only novel, which he wrote at the age of twenty-three, his hero, Savrola, fell in love with a woman named Lucile.

Describing Lucile, Winston wrote, "her perfect features, her vivacity of expression which is the greatest of woman's charms, her tall figure ...instinct with grace." It described his mother, and it described Clementine.

2

The Voice of the People

THE honeymoon was over, and they set up home at 33 Eccleston Square, Westminster. Winston held almost nightly discussions with friends in his study on the first floor, and Clementine began to experience her first sampling of a husband who enjoyed staying up half the night working or talking.

From the earliest days of their marriage, people made it abundantly plain to Clementine that they considered him a "noisy, shameless, truculent and pushing person."

She alone recognized that no assessment of his character could be farther from the truth. She knew another Winston Churchill—one of the most sensitive of aspiring politicians, who only by the exercise of remarkable courage had mastered a terrible nervousness.

Ambition drove Winston; but it was courage—his own and his wife's —which carried him through to final triumph.

An impediment of speech, which would have deterred lesser men even from attempting to enter public life, made his words almost unintelligible in moments of stress. Winston never allowed that to stop him.

When he rehearsed his speeches with Clementine, she noticed his vocal difficulties were most apparent during his opening sentences. The painful effort of mastering his utterance would make his normally pale cheeks flush angrily. Directly he had managed to establish sympathy with his audience, his speech became almost clear and the fiery patches in his cheeks disappeared.

In those days, only Clementine knew that the accent of brutality in his speech was the mark, not of a truculent nature but of a highly strung temperament fighting its own sensibilities for the mastery of its own mind. Winston was fighting himself more often than his enemies.

At times, when Clementine's was the one loyalty on which he could really count, he had to fight desperately with body and mind to keep his place in the political firing line. Impossible as it may be to credit, it is nevertheless true that the man who was, in later years, to become the greatest human driving machine of the century would frequently return home to his wife physically weak from the simple strain and effort of public speaking. He was exhausted by a tongue that refused to give the standard of eloquence he desired to the torrent of thoughts flooding from his brilliant mind.

Clementine mothered him like a child. In their early years together, one of their closest friends said, "But for the devotion of his wife, I think he could not have held his place so long."

The simile of mothering is not so exaggerated as it might seem. Though no longer young, with shoulders bowed and thinning hair, Winston retained in large measure the roundness, freshness, and playfulness of youth. He might have left the playground only the day before, having been a terror to his school-fellows and a problem to his masters. His pouting, petulant lips suddenly expanding in a broad smile that bordered on a grin, heightened the impression.

To make himself a great Parliamentary speaker and platform orator was the most difficult task Winston Churchill ever set himself.

When he first attempted to address the House of Commons, his vocal handicap with its intrusive sibilance was daunting to himself and an embarrassment to his audience. He was often reduced to an agonizing stammer, and at times there was a fierce, silent struggle to voice the first syllable of a word. He was wrestling with an impediment similar to that which, years later, King George VI was to face so bravely. Sometimes his diction was so hampered that listeners suspected he had a cleft palate.

Often he would look to Clementine, seated in the gallery of the Chamber, for silent, smiling encouragement, as he fought to make his points with clarity. He took heart from her, in his determination to overcome his dreadful handicap, as she helplessly watched one or two sadistically cruel young Members mercilessly mocking his affliction on the very floor of the House.

The young Winston, who found every speech an ordeal and trial of his strength, loved the English tongue and had decided views concerning its use. His creed was, "Short words are best, and old words the best of all." He despised the kind of officialese, which described the poor as "the lower-income group" and homes as "accommodation units." His insistence that every sentence should be well turned and balanced, as well as his overwhelming desire to overcome his handicap, led him not only to rehearse his speeches but always to bring a full manuscript to the House and read from it. Clementine alone listened to him and helped him in the privacy of their home. And with her understanding and aid, the emotion and eloquence that were locked within his heart began to flow.

She would share his mood as, with tears running down his cheeks, he would declaim from a newly written speech some passage dwelling on an incident of pathos or disaster. She would laugh appreciatively at his touches of wit or nod in endorsement of his carefully prepared debating points.

Like an actor performing at a dress rehearsal, he would seek advance acclaim and criticism from Clementine, taking careful note of her shrewdly constructive comments. If she told him, "I would not say that, Winston," he would remove the offending phrase or passage, recognizing the wisdom of her caution.

Clementine told him frankly that many of his early speeches were too impetuous, overelaborate, and frequently harsh and strident. Gradually, he curbed and softened faults and injected the understanding tolerance, which was to make his outstanding speeches models of good temper as well as of grand elocution. He was no longer diffident about showing his emotions, about revealing that sympathy with suffering and misfortune that was part of his natural makeup. With her influence his genius lightened and mellowed.

True, his judgment and temperament continued to lead him astray at times, but he had the wisdom to learn from mistakes. Fortified by his wife's unwavering support and belief in his destiny, he never lost courage, never lost faith in himself.

Constant practice with Clementine strengthened his confidence and developed the ability to fight impromptu verbal duels with crisp wit, biting sarcasm, and great originality of argument.

With Clementine as his most constructive critic and audience of one for rehearsals, he became a heckler of unrivaled talent and usually proved most formidable when apparently off-guard.

There was the time when a Member, in mid-speech, noticed that Winston, on the Opposition front bench, was shaking his head forcefully.

"I see my Right Honorable friend shaking his head," cried the M.P. "I wish to remind him that I am only expressing my own opinion."

"And I wish to remind the speaker that I am only shaking my own head," Winston replied.

Clementine admitted to friends, "Being married to him couldn't be easy." It certainly couldn't be, and wasn't. Careless in personal matters, brooding, sleeping by day, working through the night, uplifted by success, desolate in failure, Winston was, to put it mildly, a handful for any girl, but she handled him gently, tactfully. She nourished him with calmness, constancy, and content. She could humor him magically, make him laugh when he wanted to cry.

Clementine's favorite saying to about-to-get-married friends was, "You must have four children—one for mother, one for father, one for accidents, and one for increase."

A few months after their marriage, she told Winston she was expecting their first child.

He fussed and treated her like a fragile piece of porcelain, and Clementine laughed.

In 1909, their daughter Diana was born.

Lloyd George asked him. "Is she a pretty child?"

Winston beamed. "The prettiest child ever seen."

"Like her mother, I suppose," remarked Lloyd George.

"No," Winston answered solemnly. "She is the image of me."

Even in the House of Commons, he could never resist the opportunity of being the proud father.

Their domestic happiness was plain for all to see, and many who had previously disapproved of the match began to feel that, after all, it might prove to be a good marriage. In the happiness of his home, and with the faith of his wife, Winston's confidence as a politician and orator flourished.

Recognizing that the written word is not necessarily the same as the spoken word, he was never content merely to read speeches after dictating them. First, he would voice the draft aloud; then, when satisfied, send it to Clementine, and she would either make her remarks on a separate piece of paper or go to his study to discuss and listen to his personal phrasing of passages which he felt seemed to need further expansion or clarification.

He tried to imagine, days or even weeks beforehand, the sort of conditions and situations, which could arise in the House when particular issues were debated.

"Guided by this light I prepared and wrote out my arguments with the greatest care, and then learned them so thoroughly by heart that I knew them backwards and forwards, as well for instance, as one knows the Lord's Prayer, and could, within limits, vary the sequence not only of the arguments but of the sentences themselves," Winston confessed.

"Not many people guessed how little spontaneity of conception, fullness of knowledge, or flow of language there was behind this fairly imposing façade," he added.

Curiously, Winston still displays a certain diffidence about the effectiveness of his oratory. A friend said, "He worries about people going to sleep during his speeches and keeps saying, as he works, 'Now I had better drop in a joke to wake them up.' Time after time, as he was coming off a platform after a public meeting, I have watched him turn to the chairman or his wife and say, 'Well, what did you think of that? Was it all right? Was it what was wanted?' He seemed to like somebody around to reassure him. A few words from Clementine on anything that he did or said seemed to give him a very special lift—and he loved those lifts."

The dedication of her own powers to the well-being of the man she loves, so that he may realize to the full the strength and brilliance of his talents—that became her contribution to his greatness. He could easily have been spoiled by adoration, but by standing up to him, by refusing to be overwhelmed, she made sure that despite his genius he kept both feet firmly on the ground.

From the earliest days of their marriage, when to be a political hostess meant more than it does today, Clementine devoted herself to being her husband's wife and to being a skilled and charming hostess, who could put the most difficult guest at ease. Her consideration and patience would balance his frequent impatience; her outward calm would make up for his turbulence.

Social reformers Sidney and Beatrice Webb were among the first guests invited to the Churchills' home.

Beatrice Webb recorded, "We lunched with Winston Churchill and his bride—a charming lady, well bred and pretty, and earnest withal—but not rich, by no means a good match, which is to Winston's credit. Winston had made a really eloquent speech on the unemployed the night before. He is brilliantly able—more than a phrase-monger, I think.

"Lloyd George is a clever fellow, but has less intellect than Winston and not such an attractive personality."

Before lunching with the Churchills, the supercilious Mrs. Webb's judgment of Winston was harsher:

"Restless—almost intolerably so, egotistical, bumptious, shallow-minded, and reactionary, but with a certain, personal magnetism, great pluck, and some originality...more of the American speculator than the English aristocrat...bound to be unpopular...but his pluck, courage, resourcefulness, and great tradition may carry him far unless he knocks himself to pieces like his father...."

Those who came to dine with Winston and Clementine—though they may have been prejudiced against the ambitious young man before—left with warmer feelings and a greater respect for both, having been charmed by Clementine and given an impressive display of Winston's agile mind.

From the beginning of their partnership, she had to learn to live with danger, because he loved danger. He loved a battle and sniffed brimstone at the slightest provocation.

"Politics," he once told her, "are almost as exciting as war and quite as dangerous, although in war you can be killed only once but in politics many times."

Clementine had to contend with a husband like no other; always something of an unknown quantity, something of an enigma, possessed with reckless courage, incredible industry, daring flights of imagination, a dazzling inability to limit himself to the dogmas of party, and a martyr to excitement. She had to live with a man to whom life was a perpetual drama in which he was the hero and his enemies the villains. Politics, to him, was also drama. The gods might hurl him into the wings for a time, but before long he would be back in the center of the stage.

Because of his fearlessness, his boyish zest for adventure, and his indomitable willpower, he had entered life as though he were entering an obstacle race in which life and limb must be risked. His heart rose with the risks.

In order to understand her husband more completely, the young Clementine made it her business to learn all she could from his family, his friends, and his tutors.

From a master at Harrow School, she learned of his first meeting with Winston the schoolboy. "I was," he said, "a young master lately from the University, with possibly a sufficiently full knowledge of the subjects to be taught but with little knowledge of human nature, and least of all boys' nature. I entered a room where there were some twenty boys to try and find out what they knew and where to start. I tried this place and that in the textbooks, going back and back until, in despair—*sotto voce,* as I thought, and certainly with no wish whatever to be answered—I said, 'What am I to do with boys who know nothing?' Quick as a flash of lightning came the reply from a small, fair-haired boy near me, 'Please, sir, teach us!' That boy was Winston Churchill!"

She heard of the occasion when Winston's old nursemaid arrived to visit him at Harrow. The elderly lady was wearing a poke bonnet and looked a very Early Victorian figure. He put his arm through hers and paraded her proudly through the school grounds.

Commented Lord Moran, the Churchills' family physician, "I think the George Medal has been given for less."

Clementine heard, too, of the morning when Winston was having some difficulty with his governess, Miss Smith. He rang the bell for a servant and asked politely, "Will you remove Miss Smith? She is very cross."

From Professor Pearce, at the Marylebone Baths in London, she collected the story of Winston's first swimming lesson at the age of fourteen.

"He was brought to the baths by his nurse with his younger brother," said the Professor. "I am not likely to forget the day that he found he could actually swim.

"He stood for a moment on the edge of the bath; then in sheer exuberation snatched foot rack after foot rack from the cabins and threw them in the water. The superintendent walked in and nearly exploded.

" 'Did you throw those things in the bath?' he demanded. Winston turned and, still smiling, answered, 'Yes, I did.'

" 'Why did you do it?'

" 'I don't really know.'

"The superintendent threatened to lock him up and told the bath attendant to go and fetch a policeman. He then explained in grim tones to the boy that he was the superintendent.

" 'Oh! You are the superintendent,' said Winston quietly. 'Well, I am the son of Lord Randolph Churchill. Please take off your hat when you speak to a gentleman.'

"Fortunately, Charlie could not find a policeman."

Professor Pearce revealed that Winston was a wizard at diving for pennies.

"He once asked me whether I was a Liberal or a Conservative," the

Professor said. "When I told him I did not know, he cried, 'What? You actually pay rent and taxes and yet don't take an interest in politics? Why, if I were a man like you, I should want to stand on a box at Hyde Park Corner and tell proper things! My father is going to be Chancellor of the Exchequer, and probably I shall be the same.'

"After his sixth lesson he could do almost anything in the water and was afraid of nothing. Although it was forbidden, he would creep up to the gallery and dive from the protective railing."

Winston's temptestuous life has evolved amid three impregnable family relationships: first with his mother, secondly with his wife, and thirdly with his daughters; and of these three influences unquestionably Clementine's is immeasurably the greatest.

From the beginning, Winston always considered Clementine's opinions long and carefully, and often followed her advice. Though she would never reveal in public if she was at variance with him on any subject, at home she never hesitated to disagree if she felt he was wrong.

With Winston a political and social outsider during many of the early years of their marriage, life was difficult for Clementine; but she treated difficulties merely as a challenge, never doubting he would achieve to the full his latent greatness. Meanwhile, through the years, she often mothered him like a precocious, unruly child.

To any other woman, Winston would have been an impossible husband; but he has always been able to turn to "Clemmie," to lean on her without hesitation, without fear, in the secure knowledge that she would support his spirit and give him strength to go on.

Safe in her love, he rose to greater heights than he could ever have achieved without her. When he was just a voice, to whom few wanted to listen, she fortified him with her belief that one day he would be heard.

Although at the beginning of their marriage they moved in exclusive social circles, and although he was a distinguished politician, they were poor by the financial standards of the day. Winston had little money. He had to work hard as a journalist and author to pay the household bills. He has always had to earn his living. But, in the happiness of his home, he was able to say, "I had no idea that ordinary life could be so interesting."

No marriage continues through the years without crises, and the Churchills have had more than their share of them.

Clementine has a genius of her own, for none but a genius could cope

28

with Winston's temperament, his changes of mood, and his way of life. Sometimes, in the small hours of the morning, he would restlessly ask her to talk to him or even to sit down and play bezique with him. Clementine became the safety valve for his explosive mind. No wonder that his book *My Early Life* ends with the words: "... until September, 1908, when I married and lived happily ever afterwards."

In fact, their wedding bells did not ring in an era of unalloyed happiness. Trouble was waiting for both bride and groom.

Winston in his role of President of the Board of Trade launched attacks on the House of Lords, was called a traitor to his class, and both he and Clementine were ostracized by many of their acquaintances. Because he was such a radical, he was politically the most hated man in the country.

Less bitter opponents were saying, "If he ever does rise to the leadership of the Party, he won't lead it successfully or for long. The function of a leader is to lead public opinion. Winston follows it—often a little late. Very often he does not know his own mind."

As Home Secretary in 1910, soon after their marriage, he was absorbed in his Home Office work, and although realizing that prison reform was no vote-winner at elections, visited prisons, introduced changes, and conceived at least one new reform a week. In the interests of his work, Clementine took him to hear what John Galsworthy had to say in his new play *Justice*. The play affected him very much and spurred him still more to achieve penal reforms.

One evening, he returned home to inform his wife that prayers had been offered on his behalf in the Home Office. It happened that General Booth had called personally at the Home Office to discuss with him the views of the Salvation Army. To strengthen his argument the white-bearded, fiery-eyed General had knelt and prayed loudly for the conversion of the Home Secretary.

There were renewed hostilities, too, on another flank. The Suffragettes had sworn a vendetta against Winston, which was to continue until unlimited suffrage was finally granted. Sylvia Pankhurst had announced that "in Winston Churchill, the Liberal Government will receive the weight of the women's opposition." Wherever Winston went, the women were also sure to go.

His romance with Clementine temporarily softened the hearts of the most militant crusaders, but the wedding truce was over, and he was once more howled down at meetings.

Yet now there was a difference, for Clementine was seated on the platform with him, and it was no secret that she could not be counted among the enemies of women's suffrage.

Clementine made it plain to Winston that she agreed with the Suffragettes; and she showed her sympathy by being present at every prosecution of their leaders. But though, even in later years, Winston still had qualms about the entry of women into public life, he always permitted his wife to be mistress of her own thoughts. Indeed, throughout a lifetime spent in trying to change people's opinions, he never used his will to compel Clementine to his own point of view.

Whatever interest he had in the question of equal rights for women was fostered by Clementine's keenness on the principle. She tried enthusiastically to win him over to the cause of women's suffrage, but the campaign waged against him by the Suffragettes and their leader, Miss Sylvia Pankhurst, muffled his ears to all her persuasive efforts.

Some of their friends maintained that, in his heart, Winston was not as antagonistic toward the Suffragist cause as he outwardly appeared, and there is at least one incident to support that view.

William Beveridge (later Lord Beveridge), who conceived the scheme of employment exchanges which Winston backed and brought into being, went to Winston for help in the middle of the election campaign in 1910. He walked into Winston's bedroom one morning with a list of the first women divisional officers to be appointed to the labor exchanges.

Winston, who had suffered constantly at the hands of militant Suffragettes demanding equal status for men and women, looked at the list of females now seeking to take equal administrative responsibility beside the male employment officers. He looked at the list hard and long, then announced, "Let there be women!" and signed the order approving the appointments.

Two years after his marriage, Winston was still a target for the Suffragettes. Diana, their first child, had to be specially guarded in her carriage because of the fear that the Suffragettes might kidnap her.

Clementine was with him when three women climbed onto the roof of a hall and throughout his address shouted demands for votes through a ventilator. Clementine, seated on the platform, waved gaily to the demonstrators while Winston spoke.

She went with him everywhere, applauding triumphs, helping him to smile through misfortunes.

Although to see a wife and mother on an election platform was an almost unheard-of thing in those days, she joined him in public because she knew he needed her to do so. In the days before 1914, they set something of a precedent by traveling together to inspect battleships.

In return for her love, Winston proudly showed his devotion to his Clemmie in public. He has done so throughout his life.

With her at his side his stature grew. To their home at 33 Eccleston Square, the famous came. The young Mrs. Churchill was a success as a political hostess.

Lloyd George was always completely at home with the Churchills. Winston and the Welsh Wizard made a wonderful partnership for dinner-table conversation.

"I am all for the social order," Winston said once.

Lloyd George, looking over his glass of champagne, replied, "No! I am against it."

And Winston, wrinkling his nose as he does when he knows he is going to be impertinent, retorted, "You are not against the social order, but only against those parts of it which get in your way."

Lord Esher, confidant of King Edward VII, was another who went to dine with them in their first home. He noted afterward:

"He has a charming double room on the first floor, all books. A splendid library.

"It was a birthday dinner. Only six people. But he had a birthday cake with thirty-five candles. And crackers. He sat all the evening with a paper cap from a cracker on his head. A queer sight, if all the thousands who go to his meetings could have seen him. He and she sit on the same sofa, and he holds her hand. I never saw two people more in love. If he goes out of office, he has not a penny. He would have to earn his living, but he says it is well worth it if you live with someone you love. He would loathe it, but he is ready to live in a lodging—just two rooms—with her and the baby!

"They have a cook now, two maids, and a man. She ran down to the kitchen before dinner to see that it was all right. And an excellent dinner it was!"

Winston had played an influential part in the settlement after the Boer War. South Africa's peace offering to the Crown was the Cullinan Diamond. The Boers knew that it was largely owing to Winston that the gift had been accepted, so they sent him as a souvenir a replica of the stone. Delighted, Winston gave it to Clementine to keep, and every now and again he would proudly ask her to produce it for inspection by his guests.

One day his cousin, Lady Lilian Grenfell, came to lunch. Winston

31

asked Clementine to send for the replica stone. Meanwhile the conversation turned to other topics.

Eventually the butler presented himself at Lady Lilian's elbow, bearing the stone on a salver—a shapeless mass looking like a not very well-strained jelly, which had escaped from its mold.

Lady Lilian eyed it distastefully, and said coldly, "No, thank you."

Although Winston was so unpopular with many of his political colleagues, Clementine knew that those who worked with him respected him. Sir Edward Troup, Permanent Secretary to the Home Office in 1909, confessed to her, "There is no period of my time in the Home Office of which I have pleasanter recollections than the eighteen months when Mr. Churchill was my chief. Once a week, or perhaps oftener, he came down to the office, bringing with him some adventurous and impossible project; but in half an hour's discussion something was evolved which was still adventurous but no longer impossible."

Her own assessment of values in the domestic sphere is practical, down-to-earth.

She was once asked, "Who is the most important person in your home?"

"The cook, of course," she replied.

Attending a speech day at St. John's School, Leatherhead, she told the parents and students why she had once had to refuse a job as a cook.

She said that an old boy of St. John's, the late Sir Leonard Woolley, had asked her to join one of his archaeological expeditions and do the cooking. She had been tempted to accept, but when Winston heard of the proposal he told her firmly, "If you are going to cook for anybody, you can cook for me!"

Two years after their marriage, the Churchills were entertaining guests and the conversation had turned to a weighty discussion of Home Rule and the nationalization of railways when Clementine entered the room with baby Diana in her arms. Immediately, politics forgotten, Winston was down on the floor playing with the baby.

At the age of thirty-five he was sharing with Lloyd George the leadership of the progressive Liberals, he was already the Secretary of State for Home Affairs, he had a baby daughter, and he had his Clemmie.

3

Men Must Fight

Winston was transferred from the Home Office to the Admiralty—to put the Fleet "into a state of instant and constant readiness for war in case we are attacked by Germany," as the Prime Minister instructed him.

During the three years in which, as First Lord of the Admiralty, he was reorganizing the Navy, he was so determined to gain an understanding of his ministerial task that he left Clementine and his family to spend more than eight months afloat.

In those months, he visited almost every ship in home waters and in the Mediterranean, meeting all the captains, commanders, and crews, and hearing all kinds of things, which no official files could have taught him about his job. Throughout his journeys, he slept aboard the Admiralty yacht *Enchantress*—the same vessel on which he and Clementine, in the spring of 1913, sailed on holiday with the Prime Minister, Mrs. Asquith, her stepdaughter Violet, and two other friends. They went sightseeing by gondola in Venice, sailed to the historic palace of Spoleto, and drank beer under giant plane trees at Ragusa.

Now holidays and pleasures were far from his thoughts, and he had made the *Enchantress* his office afloat and left his family to learn his job.

While he was preoccupied with the Admiralty, including the formation of a revolutionary Naval Staff, both he and Clementine encountered ever-increasing bitterness in the political and social worlds. They found themselves unwelcome in many homes into which they had formerly been enthusiastically received. Once, after an attack on her friend Mrs. Asquith, Clementine packed her bags and left Blenheim in protest. But their friend, poet Wilfrid Blunt, remained sympathetic

33

and hospitable. They stayed at his Sussex home one weekend in October, 1912, and it turned out to be a memorable party.

Winston started a political argument with another guest, George Wyndham, which went on from teatime, through dinner, until midnight.

"It was a fine night," said Blunt, "and we dined in the bungalow, dressed in gorgeous Oriental garments; Clementine in a suit of embroidered silk purchased last year in Smyrna, Winston in one of my Baghdad robes, George in a blue dressing gown, and I in my Bedouin robes. . . ."

Noting the change in Winston since his marriage, he added, "Winston was very brilliant . . . he kept his head, and played with George's wild rushes like a skilled fencer with a greatly superior fence. He is certainly an astonishing young man and has gained immensely within the last two years in character and intellectual grip."

Clementine had to accustom herself from the first to Winston's extraordinary capacity for work. When he became First Lord of the Admiralty, Edward Marsh, writing to a friend, said, "He stays till at least eight every day. Even Sundays are no longer my own. We have made a new commandment: 'The seventh day is the Sabbath of the First Lord; on it thou shalt do all manner of work.'"

Also noting the improvement in Winston brought about by Clementine's influence, Marsh wrote, "He is becoming the idol of the Tory party. The sailors seem to like him very much. He has completely changed his character in some ways and has come out with a brand-new set of perfect manners. . . ."

The late Sir Edward Marsh, for years Winston's private secretary, was to become a dear friend to whom he and Clementine would turn in many moments of crisis. Eddie, as they called him, was a great foil for Winston's love of argument, and he also made a great tennis partner for Clementine.

Winston had asked for Edward Marsh as private secretary when taking up his appointment as Under Secretary for the Colonies in 1905. Marsh was not sure whether he would enjoy the honor and sought the opinion of Lady Lytton, who knew the Churchills well. Her sole comment was, "The first time you meet Winston you see all his faults, and the rest of your life you spend in discovering his virtues."

Eddie Marsh took the job.

He was optimistic in his assessment of his chief as a potential "idol of the Tory party," however. At the outbreak of the First World War,

Winston was still battling vicious unpopularity. The warmth of his home and family was almost the only comfort for him anywhere.

Clementine was in the gallery of the House of Commons, when his former Conservative party colleagues screamed "Traitor!" at him and when one overwrought Member threw a large book across the Chamber at his head. She walked with him into a city of hate when they went to Belfast, where he had undertaken to address a public meeting of the Ulster Liberal Association on February 8, 1912.

Threats of violence and a rough reception had been so serious that Winston had been compelled to write to Lord Londonderry, warning him.

"The very grave and direct responsibility which will fall upon you if serious rioting occurs in Belfast on the occasion of my visit makes me sure that you will not seek lightly to widen the grounds of the quarrel. For my own part, I only care about one essential thing. It is my duty to keep my promise to the Ulster Liberal Association and to assert our right of free speech and public meeting...."

Determined to take no chances, the Government in Belfast drafted strong military reinforcements to the area. Five infantry regiments, a cavalry squadron, and a detachment of Royal Engineers were already in the city, and had marched through it to their barracks watched by great crowds.

Clementine had decided to accompany Winston, and no threats of violence or riots could make her change her mind. She left with him for Belfast. Their party also included a secretary and two Liberal M.P.s.

Of their reception, former Northern Ireland M.P., H. Montgomery Hyde, says:

"Hostile onlookers hissing and booing lined the route as they drove from the station in Belfast to the Grand Central Hotel, but no attempt was made to interfere with their progress. But on leaving the hotel in the early afternoon for the Celtic football ground, a more ominous incident occurred. Royal Avenue, through which they had to drive, was now densely packed with people. As the car moved slowly along, men thrust their heads in, shaking their fists and muttering fearful imprecations. At one moment, two of the car's wheels left the ground, but whether this arose from a deliberate attempt to overturn the vehicle or merely from the involuntary pressure of the throng against its side is not clear.

"There is no doubt, however, that it was the most critical moment of this critical visit. It was said afterwards by many who witnessed the scene that, had it not been for the fact that Mrs. Churchill was also a passenger, the car might have been smashed and the Minister seriously if not fatally injured, before the police and military could have got through to his assistance. As things turned out, Mr. Churchill, who has never been lacking in courage, did not flinch, and no harm befell him. And his wife displayed equal courage."

Winston addressed the meeting of several thousand Nationalists at the football ground in heavy rain. Later, as they stepped up the gangway of their departure ship at Larne quayside, dockers pelted them with rotten fish.

Back in London, Clementine admitted to their friend, Lord Riddell, "I was not afraid of being killed, but feared I might be disfigured for life by the glass of the motor being broken or by some other means." She said Winston wasn't nervous and that the opposition and threats seemed to "ginger him up."

Lord Riddell recorded in his diary, "The Suffragettes gave them more trouble than the anti-Home Rulers, as they disturbed their sleep both on the boat and on the train. Winston threatened to smash the face of one of the male tormentors who forced his way into their compartment on the train."

In the summer of 1912, Clementine suffered her first serious illness— an illness that almost crippled her for life and might have, in consequence, altered the course of Winston's life and of history.

For months medical treatment made no headway, and her condition deteriorated. Winston could hardly bear to leave her a moment.

One day a bedridden Clementine said to him, "I am a poor wrecked ship. You must take me in hand as I were one of your battleships. Think my case over carefully, and decide what is to be done."

Winston did. He called in another doctor, who changed the treatment. The crisis passed, and she was cured.

On October 22, 1912, Lord Riddell wrote in his diary:

"Lunched with Mr. and Mrs. Winston. The latter seems to have completely recovered from her serious illness. She said she had steadily got worse and feared she would become a permanent invalid.... Winston is charming in his home life and Mrs. W. a most attractive person, full of charm and vivacity. Little Diana, their daughter, is clever, pretty, and intelligent."

A few weeks later, Lord Riddell reciprocated their luncheon invitation, and, talking of friendship, Winston remarked, "I don't readily take to people. I have few friends, but those I have are very dear to me."

During the meal, Winston explained some of Disraeli's policies to Clementine. Noted Lord Riddell:

"It was pleasing to see the satisfaction Winston took in furnishing the information and the evident delight of his wife in the trouble he was taking. . . ."

Clementine told their host that on a previous evening she and Winston had been involved in yet another clash with the Suffragettes, who attacked them, this time at a theater. Lord Riddell noted, "Mrs. Cornwallis-West, who was with them, went for the Suffragettes and told them they ought to be forcibly fed with common sense!"

By the summer of 1914, war with Germany was an imminent certainty, but Clementine was determined the children should have a holiday, and that Winston should take a short, badly needed break with them from his Admiralty duties.

She took Diana, Randolph, and baby Sarah down to Overstrand, near Cromer in Norfolk, where they were joined by Winston's brother Jack, his wife, and their children John George Churchill and baby Pebin. The families had rented two cottages. Clementine had chosen Pear Tree Cottage, while the other Churchills were at the opposite end of the lawn in a little place called Beehive Cottage. Winston came down and things immediately got organized with the issue of buckets and spades, and plans marked out on the sands for the construction of giant fortresses.

"More sand for the outer defenses!" Winston, with trousers rolled up to the knees, would cry, flourishing his cigar. A wonderful time was had by all until buckets and spades had to be packed away. The call now was for rifles and artillery.

On August 4, 1914, Germany had invaded Belgium, and Britain had sent an ultimatum to Berlin. In their living quarters above the Admiralty, Winston and Clementine sat waiting. Through the open windows they could hear the excited crowd gathered outside Buckingham Palace singing "God Save the King." The chimes of Big Ben began to boom the hour. It was eleven o'clock. Britain's ultimatum to the Kaiser had expired.

Winston dispatched his "war telegram" to all the ships of His Majesty's Navy. Then he left his wife and children and walked to Downing Street to inform the Cabinet.

Winston's brother was called up in the Queen's Own Oxfordshire Hussars. Before he was posted abroad in October, 1914, the two families got together in one of the drawing rooms at the Admiralty to have a souvenir photograph taken. Winston's mother, Lady Randolph Churchill, was seated in the middle, the two daughters-in-law and sons on either side, and the children along the front. Twenty-five years later, in October, 1939, the families came together again for another photograph in the same Admiralty room.

Clementine evacuated Diana, Randolph, and Sarah, with children from other branches of the Churchill family, to an old farmhouse; she remained to share with Winston whatever was to come.

She was to walk with him proudly when, after the war, his enemies never tired of shouting the names of Antwerp and Gallipoli, which they had adopted as convenient terms of abuse. In fact, those strokes of military strategy had been sound in conception. Had Winston's plan to make Antwerp a sea-supplied threat to the rear of the German armies been followed with decisive action, the right flank of the enemy forces would have been affected fatally. The idea of forcing the Dardanelles by a combined sea and land attack was a conception of genius, and few doubt now that if it had been carried through it would have removed the menace of Turkey and Bulgaria, given the British a direct link with Russia, and shortened the war. Had the Dardanelles expedition been sent sufficient reinforcements by Kitchener, Constantinople would have been taken, Russia saved, and the collapse of Austria precipitated. Antwerp and the Dardanelles were bungled by Military Command. Winston had conceived the strategical enterprises; others had failed to support them, but he was made to take the responsibility. It is the author of the play, not the actor, who has to bear the stigma of failure.

Winston, who craved always to be engaged on some momentous enterprise, in which he believed, with the faith of positive fanaticism, that he alone among his countrymen could guide the forces of triumph, was out of office, devoid of power. He was forced to resign his office of First Lord of the Admiralty in May, 1915, although he remained a member of the Cabinet and War Council.

He was to write, "I have never in my life suffered anything that compared in pain with my removal from the Admiralty.

"At this juncture I was sure that if I had been left at my post I could have carried through the great naval and amphibious operation I had launched, and for which I take full responsibility.

"I had as a Cabinet Minister to watch for six hateful months the great enterprise slowly and shamefully muddled and cast away by half measure and three-quarter measures all taken just too late."

Clementine had watched him ceaselessly striving to win the war, fighting a lone hand, pushing and buffeting his way in all directions, struggling for a way to victory, tearing up miles of red tape, treading on corns, standing on no ceremony that delayed results while men were dying on the battlefields. Critics began to call him the "amateur Commander in Chief of Navy."

It was no wonder that many considered him a "troublesome fellow," and made no secret of their preference for a nice, quiet, respectable war with Germany.

So they got him out.

On a wintry evening, before a roaring fire on the hearth of the sitting room in their home, he was crouched in his large armchair, and Clementine could see that neither the fire nor the armchair with its cushioned ease gave him comfort. His heavy brows scowled and his eyes flashed suddenly in anger. "I have nothing to do," he complained. "How terrible it would be to get resigned to a state like this."

His restless, energetic spirit was suffering the wretchedness, the boredom of idleness, and maddened by the knowledge that, for the present, it must be unemployed. "I can do nothing," he said. "None of us can do anything—without power."

Speaking of this period, Winston's great friend, General Lord Ismay, who in the Second World War became his Chief of Staff at the Ministry of Defence, said, "He had conceived the Dardanelles operation, which, if he had been properly supported, would have shortened the war by two years. But he was not supported—he was dismissed—after having been acclaimed as the greatest War Minister since Pitt. He had been denied any further employment by the hatred of the Tories, and he felt his life was broken. That experience had the most tremendous impact on him, an impact that people never realized, and I am sure that the memory of it was at the back of his mind throughout the Second World War.

"I think it must have been, above all, the belief of his wife in him that was his rock during that terrible time, because I cannot imagine what other comfort he could have had. He had to have something and someone to preserve his sanity, because there was no immediate work to be done as he had refused minor office in the Government; there was the Dardanelles—his wonderful conception—he saw that being thrown away; and he was waiting to go to France to take his turn in the battle line. For a man of his dynamic energy, there had to be solace, and someone to support him in those awful moments."

This man who could see the play of life and the clash of material forces vividly, imaginatively; who could leap at his conclusions with an assurance that swept away all doubt; who could burst into battle with a conviction so clear, so burning, that all opposition was stampeded —this man was now discarded, weary, desolate. Only Clementine's belief in him never wavered. He knew it and was grateful.

"The change from the intense executive activities of each day's work at the Admiralty to the narrowly measured duties of a Councillor left me gasping," he said. "I had great anxiety and no means of relieving it; I had vehement convictions and small power to give effect to them. I had long hours of utterly unwanted leisure in which to contemplate the unfolding of the war."

It was at that time, on a Sunday afternoon, at Hoe Farm, in Surrey, where the family had been spending part of the summer, that Clementine asked, "Are these toys any good to you? They amuse some people," and handed him one of the children's paint boxes.

Characteristically, in a flash, he felt a compelling urge to paint. A buried talent was seeking an outlet. Winston Churchill, the artist, was born.

Immediately after breakfast next morning, he bought a paint box, easel, and canvas. The revelation which they brought him prompted him to say, "It will be a sad pity to shut off or scramble along through one's playtime with golf and bridge, pottering, loitering, shifting from one heel to the other, wondering what on earth to do—as perhaps is the fate of some unhappy beings—when all the while, if you only knew, there is close at hand a wonderful new world of thought and craft, a sunlit garden gleaming with light and color of which you have the key in your waistcoat pocket."

Painting, however, was not enough to satisfy his turbulent soul. He was by temperament and training a soldier, and nothing less than the spur and exhilaration of danger could rout the devils that plagued him.

Winston left his desk to go and fight at the front. His mother, Lady Randolph Churchill, was grief stricken and anxious, but Clementine's farewell to him was calm and assured. Her conviction then that a great destiny awaited her husband was as unshakable as it remained throughout the years of his stormy career.

On the night before Winston was due to depart for France and the front line, Lord Beaverbrook went to his home.

"The whole household was upside-down while the soldier-statesman was buckling on his sword," he recorded. "Downstairs his dear friend and secretary Edward Marsh was in tears; upstairs his mother was in despair at the idea of her brilliant son being relegated to the trenches; and Clementine—she seemed to be the only person calm and collected—was confident that Winston would return to her and to the great destiny she was so certain awaited him."

While he was at the front, she decided to cut expenses by taking her family to live with brother-in-law John Churchill's wife and children in their house in Cromwell Road, South Kensington. It was a tight squeeze for everyone, but money was tight, too, for her in those days.

Winston's letters home informed her of his swift promotion from Major to Lieutenant Colonel. She also learned that immediately on arrival at his Battalion H.Q. he had summoned all his officers for formal introductions, and the next day summoned them again to announce, slowly, and with great dramatic effect, "War is declared, gentlemen ... on the lice." He then proceeded to give a masterly biography of the louse, followed by proposals for creation of a committee of company commanders to organize countermeasures for the extermination of all lice in the battalion forthwith. Within days the task was done.

His letters home also told her that his men were calling him everything from Lord Churchill, Viscount Churchill, Sir Winston Churchill to the Duke of Churchill.

He might have stayed in the trenches, might have been killed in the trenches, but for Clementine and friends in Parliament pressing him to return to Westminster—"Your abilities are needed more in England where they will do the most good, than in the trenches where their scope is limited," letters to him pleaded.

Finally, he was persuaded that he hadn't the right to remain at the front, and his decision to return was strengthened by information he received in messages from home. He came back, but it was some time before he was restored to ministerial power—old prejudices against him still kept him from public office.

"My life is finished," he said. "I am banished from the scene of action." Clementine was as optimistic as he was pessimistic.

On July 17, 1917, Lloyd George, Prime Minister again, felt himself strong enough, in spite of great Tory opposition, to bring Winston back into the Government. He appointed him Minister of Munitions.

The family's house in Cromwell Road became, almost overnight, Winston's second war headquarters, with only the remotest resemblance to a home. Prime Minister Lloyd George and other Cabinet Ministers came and went at all hours; official dispatch boxes piled up in the hall and on the stairs, and as soon as one lot of the boxes was cleared another pile appeared. Telephones, and secretaries pounding typewriters were everywhere, and the two mothers and the domestic staff had their work cut out keeping the children out of the way.

Winston didn't help much either. When, one morning, on discovering the children building a crane with a construction set they had been given, he suggested that they make a bridge instead. On finding there were not enough parts for this project, he sent a secretary on a mission to buy additional construction sets, and the dining room was transformed into a workshop. Clementine's complaints about girders on the sideboard, and nuts and bolts all over the carpet, got her nowhere. The result was the total occupation of the dining room by a bridge some fifteen feet long and eight feet high, stretching from wall to wall. Finally, yielding to protests about the loss of the dining room, he transferred the bridge to the hall, where visitors, including Cabinet Ministers, had to stoop under the raised center section of the bridge to get through the door.

During the remainder of the war, Winston directed the supply of arms to the Forces; but trouble still had a way of finding him—though perhaps it was the other way round. With Clementine and their friend Edward Marsh, he visited a munitions factory outside London. Shortly after they had begun their return journey, an automobile carrying a convalescent out for her first airing hit their car broadside, turning it completely over.

Eddie Marsh recalled, "There was I, with Clementine sitting on me in what struck me at the time as a remarkably becoming attitude. I felt inclined to ask her, as a man in one of Gilbert's plays asks the lady who has fainted in his arms by arrangement, 'Is that comfortable?' hoping that she would reply, as the lady does in the play, 'It is luxurious!' We were neither of us frightened till Winston began banging on the glass over our heads. 'Don't do that,' we said irritably—but he explained that he wanted to get us out before the car caught fire (which it didn't), so we forgave him."

Winston, a great lover of music-hall songs, could not stop singing "Keep the Home Fires Burning," which, by that time, had become *the* war song. It had become almost an obsession with him, and he was like a happy schoolboy when Clementine told him that as a surprise it had been arranged for him to lunch with the composer of the tune. The luncheon had been arranged at the home of Lady Randolph Churchill, and an extraordinary meal it turned out to be, for the conversation became almost exclusively a memory test on titles of old songs.

The composer of "Keep the Home Fires Burning" was a young man in Royal Flying Corps uniform, Ivor Novello. While Clementine, Lady Randolph, and Eddie Marsh listened, Winston and Ivor swapped titles of obscure songs across the table like a couple of enthusiastic collectors trading stamps. Winston displayed a fantastic repertoire dating from his Sandhurst days. Ivor knew them all—except one. "Do you know *you* ought to be in a home?" asked Winston.

Poor Ivor was flummoxed. He could not understand what he had said so tactlessly that called for such a drastic rejoinder. Then he realized with relief that "You Ought to Be in a Home" was yet another obscure song title dredged up by Winston's incredible memory.

On the morning of November 11, 1918, Winston and Edward Marsh were looking through a window of the Admiralty at the figure of Lord Nelson in Trafalgar Square when, once again, Big Ben chimed eleven o'clock. Armistice had been signed. The war was over, and the church bells throughout London joined in the general thanksgiving. As they rang out jubilantly, Clementine, radiant, excited, ran in to share the moment with her husband. Together they left the building and drove through the cheering thousands in Whitehall to see the Prime Minister. Some of the more enthusiastic celebrants clambered onto the car and stood, yelling, on the running boards.

Winston had been one of Prime Minister Lloyd George's war-winning team, but the fighting was over, and with its ending Clementine joined her husband in the political shadows. The public's gratitude, adoration, and limelight seemed to be reserved exclusively for their war leader, David Lloyd George.

At the beginning of 1919, Winston was Secretary of State for War, dealing with the great problems of demobilization. The situation in Russia was also, at this time, a frequent topic in the Churchill home. One afternoon a guest—newly arrived from eastern Europe—joined them for lunch. It was Lieutenant General Sir Adrian Carton de Wiart. He had returned with a firsthand report of the offensive launched against the Bolsheviks by Denikin—commander of the White Russian troops. Denikin was advancing so fast that it looked as if he would reach Moscow.

Whenever Clementine was present at discussions with military or political colleagues or informants, her role was mainly that of the good listener. But if her own shrewd assessment of a conversation differed from Winston's, she gave her opinions. Its clear grasp immediately commanded respect and often obviously influenced him.

General de Wiart's luncheon with them to discuss the Russian revolu-

43

tion provided an example of this. Of the meeting, the General says, "I returned home to report, and Mr. Churchill, who was then at the War Office, asked me to lunch. Mrs. Churchill and Jack Scott, his secretary, were the only other people at the lunch. It was the first time I had met Mr. Churchill. I was immensely flattered by the idea of discussing with so great a man what was at that moment an important situation. Mr. Churchill wished me to get the Poles to join in Denikin's offensive, but I repeated Pilsudski's warning [Poland's Chief of State, General Pilsudski, had told him that Denikin would fail and soon be pushed back in the Black Sea]. I remember Mrs. Churchill saying, 'You had much better listen to General de Wiart.'"

Winston did listen, and within weeks Pilsudski was proved a good prophet, and the White Russian forces were back in the Black Sea.

In January, 1921, Winston was appointed Colonial Secretary, with the Middle East as his chief concern.

Throughout the changes Clementine was constantly at his side, confident and smiling whatever her inward thoughts might have been. It was a time when Winston was in need of every ounce of her comfort and support, for politically he was in eclipse. Indeed it was already being said that he was "growing old and was a politician with a past and no future."

That was something she would never believe.

44

4

Arrest Winston!

THE fortunes of politics played havoc with their early married life.

Few who honor the name of Winston Churchill realize how intensely that same name was once hated and despised. While Winston jutted his chin more determinedly in defiance of his enemies, Clementine displayed her pride in him for all to see as she endured with him the catcalls and jeers of rowdy political meetings; and lived with her family virtually as social outcasts.

For more years than most people care to remember, Winston and Clementine walked together through their public and private lives, almost friendless. She was the only person who saw the two faces of Winston Churchill. The public one was for all to see; the other turned only to her for consolation and the strength to continue. How many women who envy Clementine Churchill her place in history would have envied her in the days when the cries were, "Arrest Winston!"—"Try him for treason!"?

Claiming that he had made war on the Soviet Republic without the approval of the electors, the Scottish Independent Labor party, with the approval of other Socialist circles, demanded in August, 1920, "the arrest and impeachment of Winston Churchill." The Newport, Monmouthshire, branch of the National Union of Ex-Servicemen passed the following resolution:

"That this meeting of Ex-Servicemen calls upon the Prime Minister to immediately bring to trial Mr. Winston Churchill on the charge of high treason, as much as he secretly gave help by way of British troops to Admiral Koltchak, an adventurer, without explaining the truth of the whole gamble to the country."

Winston absolutely denied the accuracy of the statements contained in the allegations made against him, but the mobs continued to yell for his blood.

Clementine listened to them again demanding his political destruction, when, as Chancellor of the Exchequer in 1928, his policies raised the cry once again—"Churchill must go!" from hundreds of M.P.s and influential men outside the House of Commons. They accused him of being "the evil influence in the Cabinet which had intimidated the Prime Minister and his other colleagues," they labeled him a "dangerous and distrusted political renegade." They shouted "Will the greatest limpet that has ever clung to the Treasury bench renounce his last political refuge?" The cries of the mob and his opponents couldn't waver his wife's supreme faith in him.

He thought he had done well at the Colonial Office. He had achieved settlement of Middle East problems in 1921; brought into being the Irish Treaty of 1922; his speeches were winning greater Parliamentary acclaim than ever before, and he seemed about to reap a reward in public opinion and public popularity. Then, inexplicably, at that point his career went into a decline. The resignation, in 1922, of Lloyd George's great First World War Coalition Government brought Winston's first General Election disaster and Clementine's first public trial of strength. Three days before the opening of the campaign in Dundee, Winston had an attack of appendicitis. The operation, performed only just in time, made active electioneering impossible for him.

"My wife and a few friends had to keep the battle going as well as they could," said Winston. "The tide flowed fierce and strong against us. Meetings were everywhere interrupted and disorderly, not through the efforts of individuals, but far worse—from general discontent and ill will."

At four previous elections he had easily held the Dundee seat, but by 1922, postwar reaction and disillusion was rampant.

In his election memorandum Winston declared, "I stand as a Liberal and a Free Trader." But Dundee wasn't convinced that he really was a Liberal, for, in the four years since the end of the First World War, he had publicly advocated the idea of a Center party to be composed of moderates from both Conservatives and Liberals.

With political fortunes going against him, illness denied him the opportunity of defending his policies and actions.

As he lay bedridden in a nursing home, the entire weight of the election campaign fell on Clementine. She arrived in Dundee with her little daughter Diana and opened the campaign for his reelection by addressing two meetings the first evening—one at which she faced a rowdy, threatening crowd in the Larch Street Hall, the other preaching to the converted at a ladies' meeting in the club rooms at the Liberal and Unionist Association's headquarters.

Just before she arrived at the Larch Street meeting a quantity of "electric snuff" was released by troublemakers in the crowded and stuffy hall. The meeting was off to a rough start, and efforts to retain order met no success. Windows were hurriedly flung wide to clear the atmosphere.

Clementine's entry was greeted by hoots and some subdued cheers. She bowed to the audience and smilingly took her seat on the platform. A fresh supply of snuff was released by someone and the platform party were among its first victims. Clementine was overwhelmed by an almost uncontrollable bout of sneezing.

She rose to speak, and, finally mastering the urge to sneeze, said, "I'm glad to see that you are all alive and kicking in Dundee." She was immediately interrupted by about a dozen hecklers, and there was temporary pandemonium again. She stood, calmly waiting for the noise to stop. When order had been restored, she added, "I only wish that my husband had not been prevented by his illness—"

A voice interrupted. "Oh! Is he ill?"

"He has been very ill," answered Clementine. "If he had not been very much better I would not be here tonight. I hope he will be here before the end of the week. I don't think it is very sporting of you to ask such a question. My husband has had the great honor of representing this great city for fourteen years.

(Voice: "Fourteen years too long.")

"He is much handicapped by not being able to be present at this election," Clementine continued, "but I feel a great deal of confidence in that the great majority of the men and women of Dundee will not take advantage of that fact; and I should not be a bit surprised if he got a much bigger majority at this election than ever before."

There were groans and hisses; and a voice yelled, "Don't be daft!"

"At any rate, I would not like to see the voters who came out for him all these years letting him down when he is ill," she went on.

A barrage of incoherent questions followed, to which Clementine, raising her voice, replied, her words ringing through the hall, "Do you think this is a good advertisement of the proceedings of an open meeting?" She gave as good, and better, than she got, and finally departed the undoubted victor.

Earlier that evening, she had launched her appeal for support to the women electorate at the other local mass meeting. Regretting Winston's absence, the meeting's chairman announced, "We miss him at every turn of the way; we miss his dominating convincing powers of argument and persuasion, but Mrs. Churchill has powers of argument and persuasion, which even her husband could not surpass."

Urged Clementine, "It is really the women of Dundee, who are going, to a great extent, to settle this election, and I appeal to them to help my husband."

Two nights later, at a gathering of almost 4,000 people in Caird Hall, Dundee, she faced and handled pandemonium created by a section of the meeting. The hall had filled hours before, and a queue stretched on and on round to the Green Market.

Clementine rose to address the meeting, but, before she could speak, some women near the front of the gallery, two of whom were carrying babies in their arms, proclaimed themselves to be Communists and started to shout almost incoherent arguments at the tops of their voices. They screamed and waved their fists at her, and Clementine just stood there, waiting for the storm to subside.

She began again. "A great many people," she said, "throughout the country—and I am told some of them live in Dundee—think and say that the unemployment in the country—"

"What about a bob a week for a baby?" interrupted a woman from the gallery. Hissing started.

"I am rather inexperienced, and unless the lady is quieter my speech will take much too long," countered Clementine. "A great many people, I say, think that the prevailing unemployment and distress is caused by the shortcomings and wrongdoings of the late Government—"

The hecklers chorused their agreement.

"—and, as my husband was a member of that much-abused Government, and he is the only member of the Government that you here in Dundee can get at, some of you say, 'It's all Churchill's fault—let's put him out.'"

("Hear! Hear!")

"That is what some people say; now I have a chance, and I want to tell you what I think. I want you to consider whether this unemployment and distress is really the fault of the late Government or is rather, in great measure, caused by those men who profess to lead the working

48

men and women of the country, but who very often give them very bad advice?"

Her voice, at this point, was drowned by shouts, boos, and hissing. Once more she waited for the outburst to die a little and then proceeded to review the industrial situation since the 1918 election.

"Until then," she said, "Labor was represented in the Cabinet. But, in the autumn of that year, Labor withdrew its Ministers and went into Opposition. Shortly after the election, a threat of a coal strike clouded the industrial world, and before this strike there was the great railway strike in 1919, which greatly hindered the revival of trade and threw many out of work. Now it is known that the railway men secured nothing by the strike that they could not have had by negotiation.

"The good sense of the railway men and transport workers prevented a disastrous general strike, but the three months' idleness in the mines lost fifty million tons of output and thirty millions in wages, while unemployment was increased enormously."

An interrupter screamed, "What about Mesopotamia? Your husband was responsible for all the millions spent there."

"Most of the millions there were spent *before* my husband took over control," emphasized Clementine.

The gallery howled her down. She waited patiently with a smile until the hall was reasonably quiet again.

"The latest evidence of this unhelpful attitude," she went on, "was seen in the reluctance to cooperate with the Cabinet to produce measures and schemes to cope with unemployment."

Applause and jeers greeted this.

"Now, the late Government, so abused and despised, had stood between the community and all these threats. By constant work, impartial attitude and fairness, and yet by its alertness, it had guided the ship of State safely so far through all those dangerous shores and quicksands."

Cheers and protests.

Disregarding a query from a woman heckler in the gallery, asking, "Does your bairn live on a shilling a day?" Clementine said she could not believe the citizens of Dundee would vote for the Socialists, or for Mr. Pilkington, who was simply splitting the Liberal vote.

A woman cried, "Your supporters should be ashamed to support you, the way you are keeping down the working classes."

"*You*, my dear lady, need not support me," replied Clementine.

Communists in the hall started to sing "The Red Flag," and there was pandemonium again.

49

The following morning the local *Dundee Advertiser* headlined the meeting—"Mrs. Churchill Again in a Storm," and the *Glasgow Herald* declared, "Although she has not by any means encountered smooth water, Mrs. Churchill has proved herself a 'bonny fechter' on behalf of her husband. Facing an enormous audience in the Caird Hall, she got the best hearing of all the speakers, mainly as the result of admirable tact and determination in handling the obstreperous interrupters, who were Communists...."

At yet another meeting, Clementine faced, for the first time, the cry, "Your husband is a warmonger!"

Defiantly she stood up to defend him, "He's not a warmonger!" she cried. Then she asked the packed hall, "Will you trust my husband once more?"

"Never again!" "He is incapable!" shouted people from the audience.

"This is the first time in my life," said Clementine, "that I have heard my husband described as incapable." The meeting ended.

Two days before polling day, Winston arrived to join the battle. He had to be assisted from the train and practically carried to his room up the stairs of his hotel. He nevertheless insisted that he would address an important meeting himself.

"If you are going to speak," said Clementine, "you must sit down—you are not fit enough to stand for an hour."

He promised to follow her advice.

The hall at which he was to speak was besieged long before the time advertised for the commencement of the meeting. Ten thousand people clamored for admission to the hall, which could only accommodate 5,000, with the majority standing. The doors opened, and the rush for admission was such that the police had to draw their batons.

Winston entered by a back door, leaning heavily on his stick and gripping Clementine's arm. As soon as the crowd saw them, they were received with cheers, hissing, and booing, and the demonstration continued for some time. The meeting's chairman announced that the candidate would remain seated during his speech because of his still weak, postoperative condition. The unsympathetic, hostile crowd shouted, "Stand up, Winston!" "You'll be at the bottom of the poll!" shouted one interrupter.

"If I am to be at the bottom, you might let me have my last dying fling," cried Winston. "I won't go on any longer than you wish me to," he said, and strove hard to catch some of the insults and questions hurled at him from all parts of the hall. It was hopeless. Finally, provoked to the limit, Winston forgot he was an invalid. Shaking his fist, he angrily cried, "If about a hundred young men and women choose to spoil the whole meeting, and about a hundred of these young reptiles choose to deny to democracy, to the mass of the people, the power to conduct a great assembly, the fault, the blame, is with them, and the punishment will be administered to them by the electorate."

Winston tried to continue the meeting. Then, rising from his chair and leaning heavily on his stick, he surveyed the hall, and, with the color mounting in his face, lifting his voice above the boos and shouting, he announced, "Ladies and gentlemen!—I thank you most sincerely for the attentive hearing you have given me, and I think you have indicated in a most effective manner the devotion of the Socialist party to free speech. It has been shown very clearly that a handful of rowdies can break up a great meeting and prevent ten times their number from transacting their public business. But, ladies and gentlemen, we will not submit to the bullying tyranny of the featherheads. We will not submit to be ruled by the mob." He resumed his seat amid renewed cheers and boos. A few moments later he rose, waved, and bowed repeatedly to all parts of the hall. Then, turning from his chair and leaning once more on Clementine's arm, left. The meeting had lasted thirty-five minutes.

On polling day, Winston and Clementine were at the count, moving from table to table watching the assortment of ballot papers grow. The mountains in favor of both his opponents were clearly dwarfing the comparatively insignificant accumulation of voting papers supporting him.

The result was soon obvious. Clementine, who had worked ceaselessly and tirelessly throughout the campaign, stood beside him at the bottom of the steps leading to the platform from which the result, and his defeat, was declared. They did not go on to the platform. The postwar Coalition Government collapsed.

Winston was now out of Parliament. To jeers and boos, Clementine took his arm and they stepped into a taxi and drove to their hotel. There was nothing left to do but go home.

Commenting on his defeat, the *Observer* wrote at the time, "Dundee was more than a bombshell. It was like an electoral landmine exploding with shattering din and fantastic sequel. The circumstances were such that Mr. Churchill, on personal grounds, has, we believe, the generous sympathy of the country. Stricken by illness at the beginning of the struggle, late in the field, not fully restored even then, yet assailed by Communist rowdyism, he was cruelly handicapped. The burden of the

51

task fell on his devoted wife, but, in the dour circumstances of Dundee, the odds were too great."

On their return to London, Winston went to Buckingham Palace to hand back the seals of his office. He emerged again, no longer a Minister of the Crown, but the words "Right Honorable" were prefixed to his name to denote his membership of the Privy Council.

"I am without an office, without a seat, without a Party, and without an appendix," said Winston to Clementine. And, added, "If Dundee doesn't want me, I'll have to try somewhere else."

He was exhausted and still suffering from the aftereffects of his illness. Clementine decided on convalescence. "We're going to Cannes," she announced.

As he climbed slowly back to health, Winston confessed he was "getting used to sitting in armchairs in front of the fire and going to sleep." He didn't fool Clementine. Every afternoon he would put up his easel on the beach or at some countryside beauty spot, and paint, with Clementine sitting close by. They rarely spoke as he painted, but he liked her there. Soon he settled down to work, writing the first volume of his *World Crisis*. Although he was no longer in any way connected with the Government, threatening letters still reached him from Ireland, and, in consequence, both he and Clementine continued to live under constant guard. He daily grew stronger, and she observed his growing impatience at being out of things. The time had come to return to London.

Suddenly, Parliament was dissolved, and together they stepped back into the political arena, to battle for Winston's election as a Liberal Free Trader at Leicester. His opponents used the publication of his book, *The World Crisis,* as ammunition in the campaign, reviving the accusation of his responsibility for the "Dardanelles disaster," in spite of the expedition having been triumphantly vindicated at a meeting of senior naval and army officers.

Winston counterattacked his accusers. "The Dardanelles might have saved millions of lives. Don't imagine that I run away from the Dardanelles. I glory in it."

Clementine also hit back on his behalf. At an election meeting in Leicester, she flayed critics and rallied supporters with, "Perhaps your Free Trade swords have grown rusty with lying by for so long, but you must get them out and polish them up and fight for this really great cause. My husband has been described as unfit to represent the working class in Parliament," she declared. "Someone has got to speak up about him, and who, if not his wife?

"There was a man at one of his meetings who said my husband was not fit to speak for the working classes. Well, I am not a politician, but I must say my blood boiled when I heard that."

And, listing some of his efforts on behalf of the working classes, she said, "With the single exception of Mr. Lloyd George, my husband has been responsible for the passing of more legislation for the benefit of the working classes than any other living statesman. When he was at the Board of Trade in 1909, he framed the Sweated Industries Act; he was responsible in a large measure for the system of Labor Exchanges, and also for the Coal Mines Regulation Act, designed to make the mines as safe as possible for the miners to carry on their work. Then there was the Shop Hours Act. I mention these things," said Clementine, "because it always vexes me when I hear people saying that Mr. Churchill is fitted principally to take part in wars.

"A great many people think he is essentially military. I know him very well, and I know that he is not that at all; in fact, one of his greatest talents is the talent of peacemaking."

With her as his chief election aide again, Winston fought the battle of votes. Arriving at a great mass meeting in Essex, a brick smashed through the window of their car, narrowly missing injuring them both. Violent crowds did everything but rush them on the platform, and Winston described it as "the worst crowd I have ever seen in England in twenty-five years of public life." He failed to gain the Leicester seat, too. Both of them were now under constant fire. He was out of favor, and Clementine felt the sting of social unpopularity.

One morning, as they were driving past the Houses of Parliament, Winston turned to her and said, "It's difficult, after one has been nearly a quarter of a century in that place, to know that one has no longer any right there."

"The opportunity will come," she answered.

5

The Chancellor's Lady

THEY waited impatiently for another chance. It came. The Abbey Division of Westminster faced a by-election.

Winston, who had been a Conservative, then a Liberal, decided to contest the division as a "Constitutionalist and Anti-Socialist candidate."

The constituency, which includes the Houses of Parliament, the seat of the Government, Buckingham Palace, all London's principal clubs and theaters, with areas varying from St. James's Street and the Strand to Soho, Pimlico, and Covent Garden, is one of the strangest and most remarkable in the world.

The poorest and the richest are there.

In this novel constituency they campaigned and won all manner of support—dukes, jockeys, prizefighters, actors, actresses, businessmen, and restaurateurs.

Clementine persuaded the chorus girls at Daly's Theater in Leicester Square to sit up all night, after the shows were over, addressing envelopes and dispatching election leaflets.

"It was," said Winston, "incomparably, the most exciting, stirring, sensational election I have ever fought."

It certainly was.

Even in the very cosmopolitan Abbey Division, the two of them faced, and met, nonstop trouble.

Traveling from one meeting, the driver of their car made a wrong turn and found himself in a cul-de-sac. A large crowd closed in. A man jumped from the crowd onto the running board of the car, and the fight started.

Winston's personal detective sent several attackers sprawling. The mob eventually gave way, and the attackers' ringleaders were chased down the street.

Back in the car, Brendan Bracken, M.P. for North Paddington and one of the Churchills' closest friends, was found to have been stabbed in the thigh during the scrap!

Clementine, working from a luxurious house in Lord North Street filled with priceless Gainsborough paintings, organized and led an army of canvassers ranging from peeresses and beautiful society girls to theater chorus girls.

On the eve of polling day a great car procession, with Winston and Clementine in the leading vehicle, wound its way through every street in the constituency until the small hours of the morning, sounding their horns, whirring rattles, and shouting "Vote for Churchill!"

The vote count was held at Caxton Hall.

As the last packet was being carried to the table, someone shouted, "You're in, Winston, by a hundred!"

Clementine embraced Winston excitedly and kissed him, and on-lookers cheered. Churchill was back in politics.

His opponent's officials went across to the returning officer and demanded a recount.

The result—his opponent was declared elected by a small majority!

Now it was the turn of Winston's agent to demand a recount, and the final answer was reached. Winston had been beaten by forty-three votes! He was out again.

Clementine had helped wage a tremendous fight, but they had lost. This time there was no deep bitterness—it had been a fair battle and they had got close to victory. Neither of them was downcast. Both were convinced their political fortunes were about to change. They hadn't long to wait. Parliament was dissolved again.

The autumn, 1924, election, which became known as "the Red Letter Election," brought a red-letter day for the Churchills.

Winston was invited to stand at Woodford in Essex. He was returned with a majority of 10,000.

Said Winston, "It makes me earnestly hope that I have now found a resting place amid the glades of Epping, which will last me as long as I am concerned with mundane affairs."

A few days after the election the new Prime Minister—Stanley Baldwin—sent for him.

Winston walked out of No. 10 Downing Street, and moved with Clementine and the children into No. 11, next door—he had been appointed Chancellor of the Exchequer. The tide had turned in their favor again.

A happy, smiling Winston, accompanied by Clementine, their son Randolph, and daughter Diana, stepped out of No. 11 on April 28, 1925 for a great day—the presentation by the new Chancellor of the Exchequer of his first Budget.

As the family appeared in Downing Street, waiting crowds cheered, and Winston, gripping the little traditional red dispatch box containing the Budget secrets, promenaded with his family down Whitehall to the Houses of Parliament. People stopped, buses stopped, cars stopped— everything stopped for the Churchills and the little Budget box that day.

Clementine took her seat in the Distinguished Strangers' Gallery to witness the scene in the crowded Chamber of the House. Showman Winston put on a great performance. In the middle of a sentence he broke off, filled a glass before him with what was unmistakably not water, and, raising it, announced, with a grin and a typical Churchillian touch, "It is imperative that I should fortify the revenue, and this I shall now, with the permission of the Commons, proceed to do."

With that pronouncement, he looked up, raised the glass to Clementine in the gallery, and drank a toast to her. Her laugh echoed through the Chamber above all others.

As wife of the Chancellor of the Exchequer and hostess of No. 11 Downing Street, Clementine found new scope for her own remarkable personality.

It is said that the devoted wife of an outstanding public man is liable to be a somewhat shadowy figure, for it is in the nature of the role she has chosen that she should be ever present but never too much in the foreground. Yet, more than one Minister's wife has sought to gain the reputation of being a power behind the throne, a buttress for her husband's brilliance.

Clementine decided to be neither, but instead a little of both. The art of not being overshadowed, yet never stealing the limelight, became one of her special achievements.

Her self-appointed task was to bring a sense of normality into the home life of her abnormal husband.

Her reputation as a hostess had already been established. Now, as the Chancellor's Lady, she was in her element and at her best. She introduced personal touches into historic No. 11, bringing a new warmth to the usually formal, cold rooms of the house. She made it a home.

She also made it a social center. Winston loved to entertain, and whoever the guests, and whatever the subjects for discussion, he liked Clementine to be at the head of the table facing him. Her subtle role and influence were obvious to everyone who dined or lunched with them. She was ever ready to take over when one of his moods threatened to turn table talk at a meal into disaster. She could melt conversational ice with the warmth of a smile.

That Winston worshiped her was plain to everyone. Millions idolized him. She gave him someone to idolize. She is the only person who has ever known really how to handle him, but it has never been by any attempt at domination.

He had his life—she had to make her own. To a large degree, she had to learn to lead a separate existence. Wrapped in his own world, Winston could, though in the same house, leave her very lonely for a great deal of the time. Their temperaments, completely different—their marriage would never have worked had it been otherwise—found a clear appreciation of each other's role in their home and public lives.

Above everything else, she considered his creature comforts. Comforts which to others are luxury, but which to Winston are the breath of his existence, leaving his thoughts unfettered. She organized their home, letting the staff carry out her orders in their own way; but always personally watching over his foibles and wishes.

She fashioned a rule for living for both of them—a pattern for making the best use of time, allotting specific activities to specific hours each day. She found it necessary to plan in advance whatever needed doing, though, at the same time, wisely allowing sufficient flexibility for the unexpected. She believed implicitly in this plan for daily living and made her daily schedule pivot around her husband, her work, and her family. She would start each day knowing what she wanted to accomplish with it, beginning with instructions to secretaries and staff to ensure that everyone knew exactly what duties were expected of him and knew what part he was required to play in the day. Without this basic routine, the machinery that has run the Churchill home through the years could never have contended with the countless unpredictable things that happen within its walls.

Like Winston, she also believed in relaxation as a vital necessity to good health, and that the best relaxation is change. To conserve energy, she found it essential to live sensibly, regulate living and habits, and keep a careful balance between activity and relaxation. She followed this code of living and did her utmost to see that, as far as possible, Winston followed it, too.

Without question, it is this pattern for living that has carried Clementine and Winston so successfully through the immense turmoil of their lives.

The public vision of her has always been of a controlled, calm person. In fact, by nature, she is excitable, vivacious, bubbling. But she managed to achieve an inner calm, enabling her to work undisturbed by everything around her, and to concentrate on matters in hand.

The willpower that gave her the strength to stay outwardly and inwardly calm became, perhaps, her greatest asset, although at times this disciplined rein on herself has temporarily broken, but it would be incredible and inhuman if it had not. In the main, she succeeded in maintaining a peace within herself in spite of all the tensions and crises around her. Without this control she could never have withstood the terrifying wear and tear on her nervous system. With all the strains and stresses with which she has had to contend, it is miraculous that her outbursts of irritation and impatience have been so comparatively few.

Like Winston, her powers of concentration are remarkable. When she is talking to you, you are conscious that during those moments it is you and only you receiving her undivided attention with no distracting impression that she is thinking of the next person while speaking to you.

She always attached tremendous importance to general care of health and to conserving energy, and her stamina and energy for a woman of her responsibilities was remarkable. Her tennis was of tournament class, and one of her favorite tennis opponents was Sir Edward Marsh, one of their closest and dearest friends throughout his life.

During Winston's "misunderstood years," Eddie Marsh was staunchly loyal. Said Eddie to Clementine, commenting on Winston in office, "It is true to say that those of the officials who saw most of him, liked him best. When he has been unpopular with his subordinates, as has undoubtedly happened, it is because they were not long enough with him at a time to realize how little 'vice' or substance there were in his occasional asperities.

"I myself never much minded having my head bitten off, because I knew that instead of throwing it into the wastepaper basket, he would very soon be fitting it back on my neck with care and even with ceremony."

When Edward Marsh became seriously ill, Clementine nursed him back to health at Chartwell. He wrote in his diary:

"With Clemmie and Winston. If only there were a God I could thank for those who love me."

When later he was stricken with pneumonia, a letter arrived from Chartwell. It read:

My dear Eddie,

I was much concerned to read in a press cutting, which coupled our names, of your illness. . . . Randolph tells me that you are recovering alright, but that you had to have two nurses. I am indeed sorry for this calamity and wish I had known about it before.

We shall be down here a great deal now and if you like to come and pay a visit, pray let us know. You could rest comfortably here. Clemmie says you *must* come. Just—vegetate—as I do.

Love from
W.

Eddie Marsh accepted the invitation to convalesce again at Chartwell.

Both at their Chartwell home and at No. 11 Downing Street, Clementine made an outstanding success of her duties. She made a personal impact on the social and political scene. But, on one occasion, the Chancellor's Lady put the Chancellor on an embarrassing spot.

She had gone with a number of her friends on a visit to Paris—a shopping spree, for, among other things, some new dresses. On her return, Winston went to Victoria Station to meet her. She arrived with just some hand baggage, which was put into the car. Her heavy baggage had been registered and sent ahead to London.

On reaching Downing Street, she asked Winston whether he was using the car; if not, she wanted to send the maid and another member of the staff to the station to collect the registered baggage. Winston was not going out again, so off went the two messengers.

When they had located the baggage, a Customs officer asked whether they contained anything to declare.

"I have no idea what is inside them," answered the maid, "so perhaps you had better open them yourself and see."

The Customs officer was about to do so when he noted the labels, the name on them, and that they were addressed to Downing Street.

"Never mind," he said, changing his intention of examining the cases, and, chalking clearance markings on them, passed them through unopened.

The following week the friends who had journeyed with Clementine to Paris came to lunch. During their conversations, one of them asked Clementine how much duty she had paid on the new dresses she had brought back from Paris.

59

"I didn't pay any at all," she answered.

Overhearing this, Winston inquired why not. She explained what had happened when her maid had gone to collect the baggage from the station and about the obliging Customs officer.

She had thought no more of the incident at the time.

Winston immediately requested the bills for the dresses. When she had found them, he instructed his secretary to telephone the Customs and Excise and ask for an officer to come round to No. 11 the following day. The officer duly arrived, examined the bills and the dresses, did a swift calculation of duty due, and the Chancellor of the Exchequer's wife paid up.

She was upset at first at her forgetful oversight in not dealing with the duty liability from the outset, knowing how particular Winston always was about payment of duty on anything he, or any of the family, purchased abroad. It had been a slip on her part in all the excitement of her homecoming. A few days later they both laughed about it all, and her unintentional smuggling episode became a family joke.

As the months and years passed at No. 11 Downing Street, Winston's popularity and following increased. He presented five Budgets to Parliament, but Clementine sensed an increasing resentment and fear of his aggressive personality among many who purported to be their closest friends and political colleagues.

Newspapers started to turn on him viciously. "His life is one long speech," declared one newspaper.

Clementine listened to his critics ask, "At what age does a politician cease to be a promising young man and become a middle-aged disappointment? At what period are we obliged to confess that the mischances and indiscretions have accumulated to such a total, that failure has become a habit with him?

"Mr. Winston Churchill has been before the country for some twenty-five years and has now reached respectable age of fifty or so. Despite much personal charm and a very creditable amount of industry, it is not unfair to say that, having regard to the time at his disposal, he has mismanaged more public business than anyone else of whom we have any recollection."

The cold wind of change was beginning to blow against them again.

In 1929, Baldwin's Government went to the country. Clementine went down to Woodford for the fight. Accompanied by Diana and Mary, she mounted the gaily decorated motor wagon being used as a platform and spoke to a mass meeting in the marketplace at Epping.

"My husband is away at Liverpool speaking to two big meetings so I am at home keeping shop for him."

She then invited the Irish M.P., Sir Robert Lynn, to talk. In the course of his speech there were several interruptions, and one man called out, "What is Winston—Constitutionalist, Conservative, or What?"

Clementine asked to be allowed to answer the question.

"My husband, in his later years, returned to his old Party. His father was Lord Randolph Churchill, who endeavored to start a Party which he called 'Tory-Democrat,' so it was natural that his son should join the Tory party.

"Some twenty-five years ago, however, he left that party on the question of Protection and joined the Liberals. He remained with them until 1924, when Mr. Asquith put the Socialists into office. He then sought election as an Independent at Westminster, and although that was a strong Tory stronghold, he was only defeated by a few votes.

"He was asked by the Epping Conservatives to represent them as a Constitutionalist, and did so. Now, however, he was assured that the Party did not include Protection in their program, and he was a Conservative. He had always been a Free Trader, and always would remain so."

Another interrupter called out, "What about his previous defeats?"

Never lost for a quick answer, Clementine replied, "It is no disgrace to be defeated."

She asked the crowd to give three cheers for Winston, and they did.

Later, adding his words to hers in answer to the cries of "Turncoat!" Winston himself replied:

"A policy is pursued up to a certain point; it becomes evident at last that it can be carried no further.

"New facts arise which clearly render it obsolete; new difficulties, which make it impracticable. A new and possibly the opposite solution presents itself with overwhelming force. To abandon the old policy is often necessarily to adopt the new.

"It sometimes happens that the same men, the same Government, the same Party have to execute this volte-face. It may be their duty to do so because it is the sole manner of discharging their responsibilities, or because they are the only combination strong enough to do what is needed in the new circumstance.

"In such a case the inconsistency is not merely verbal, but actual, and ought to be boldly avowed.

"Few men avoid such changes in their lives, and few public men have been able to conceal them. Usually youth is for freedom and reform, maturity for judicious compromise, and old age for stability and repose."

He was reelected, and the Conservatives as a party weren't. Once more, the Socialists emerged as the largest party, and resumed power with Liberal support.

A story told by Lord Baden Powell, father of the Boy Scout movement, reminded Clementine of Winston's ability to bounce right back at a moment of apparent defeat.

He recalled days in India when Winston led the polo team of his regiment to victory in a great polo tournament, scoring two goals with a dislocated arm strapped to his side.

Said Lord Baden Powell, "Winston delivered one of the finest orations ever pronounced on polo at the dinner that followed the victory. He had, until then, made one short speech in public.

"After this, someone moved 'that this be enough of Winston.'

"The motion was carried—naturally enough with one dissent—and they put young Winston under an upturned sofa to be kept there for the rest of the evening, and the fattest subaltern in the regiment sat on top of the sofa and him.

"After a few minutes, Winston wriggled out from under the sofa's arms, and, grinning up at the company, spoke prophetic words:

" 'It's no use sitting on me—I'm India rubber!' "

Nervous of Winston's personality and bounce, Baldwin swore he would never include him again in any future Government he might form, and Baldwin kept his word.

Winston and Clementine went back into the wilderness.

A friend inquired, "Don't you think No. 10 Downing Street would be a lovely place to live?"

"No, I don't," replied Winston. "I've lived next door to it long enough to know."

6

Living with Danger

FROM the early days of their marriage, whenever the call and demands of work took Winston overseas, Clementine insisted on going with him if it was possible. She knew he liked to share his official life with her and that he valued her opinions and comments. So in March, 1921, when he departed on a Middle East tour, he was accompanied by Sir Hugh Trenchard (later Lord Trenchard), Sir Archibald Sinclair—his Parliamentary Private Secretary—and Clementine.

At that time Winston was combining the joint offices of Air Minister and Colonial Secretary. The visit to Egypt was to decide whether an increase in air installations there would relieve some of the pressure on army garrisons in the area, and he also hoped to simplify policing of the Suez Canal zone by the introduction of an improved air patrol system.

Clementine was under no illusions about the trip—it would be no picnic, no Cook's tour. She was well aware that Russell Pasha, head of the Egyptian Police, had warned, "Churchill is in the greatest danger; trust no one, black or white, throughout your journey." So far as she was concerned, the warning was all the more reason for being at his side.

Winston and his official party traveled overland via Paris to Marseille. In those days the Paris-Lyons-Marseille Express was one of the worst and most uncomfortable rail journeys in Europe. She didn't like the journey, but knew Winston was enjoying it, and that was good enough for her. Before boarding ship for Alexandria, Winston felt like indulging in a little painting. Immediately after lunching on bouillabaisse, the two of them set out by car along the Marseille coastline to a spot overlooking the town. Up went the famous Churchill portable painting table, and he continued to paint the beautiful view almost until sailing time, with Clementine keeping him company.

A tremendous crowd of Egyptians and Arabs watched the ship dock at Alexandria. As the Churchills and their party walked down the gangway, the noisy dockside seemed abnormally silent. Suddenly the silence was shattered, and as Winston and Clementine walked toward the waiting Air Force car, police, using long thin canes, drove shouting, threatening demonstrators back until the cars moved off. In defiance of the hostility around them, they insisted on riding in the back of an open touring car. With Sir Archibald Sinclair, they drove through the streets along which Egyptian nationalists, voicing their opposition to Britain, yelled insults and threats. The Egyptians stared at the impeccably dressed Englishwoman seated at the side of her husband in the car, who, in spite of the menacing crowds, showed no fear—unafraid for herself and unafraid of anyone.

On reaching the hotel in Alexandria and tidying up in their rooms, they went down to lunch. After they had eaten, Winston, who didn't believe in wasting time, started his tour of inspection at a large R.A.F. camp outside the city. Serious complaints had reached Whitehall of conditions in a number of camps, and he was going to see for himself. Clementine was particularly insistent on inspecting the married quarters. The officer in charge didn't seem too happy at her interest, but, acting as her husband's aide on the one subject on which she was the foremost expert in the party, she looked everywhere, at everything, examining bedrooms, kitchens, not missing a thing. Any point deserving attention she pointed out to Winston, who, in turn, dictated a note to his personal secretary for future action. Married quarters were the servicemen's wives' domain, and Clementine made certain Winston got the woman's point of view on the accommodation provided.

Outside the aerodrome, demonstrators marched about screaming "À bas Churchill!" and "Iskut (shut up), Churchill!" Native police breaking up a "Down with Churchill!" demonstration were stoned and forced to take flight. Reinforcements arrived and fired on the crowd. At first it was believed that three people had been killed, but casualties turned out to be nine rioters injured with bullet wounds, and twenty police injured by stones. When the party returned to Alexandria, the men held a dinner conference. Clementine, exhausted from the long day in the heat, preferred to retire to her room. As she lay resting on the bed, she became conscious of someone moving about the adjoining room. It was supposed to be unoccupied. The room next to their suite had been reserved for the storage of boxes containing official documents. She realized it would be useless rushing downstairs to summon assistance—the intruder could be gone by the time they returned—and so could important papers. There was only one thing to do, and she did it.

She opened the door of her room and yelled. "Quick! Quick!" she shouted. "There's someone in the next room!"

Her cries for help were answered by their personal detective. He rushed to the room, but the door was locked. The intruder could still be heard rummaging about inside. The detective stepped back and charged the door. It didn't give. He ran back and charged again. This time it smashed open to expose an Arab disappearing through the window. Before the detective could draw his revolver, the man had vanished somewhere on the roof. Clementine and the detective checked the contents of the room and were relieved to find that the seals of all the boxes were still unbroken. The incident was over by the time Winston, hearing of the disturbance, hurried to Clementine. It was agreed that the detective should sleep in the room with the boxes to prevent any further attempt, and a bed was put in there for him.

When, a few days later, they visited the famous jail known as the Citadel, news came of a demonstration in the quarter through which they were due to return, and for the next half hour they were virtually prisoners in the jail. Although Winston had nothing to do with Egyptian affairs, as far as the country's nationalists were concerned, he represented Britain, and the danger to both him and Clementine grew with every hour they remained in the country. It was decided to maintain absolute secrecy for their departure from Alexandria. Arrangements were made for them not to leave from the station but to join the train at a point along the line. They slipped away from the hotel by car early one morning and took a roundabout route along obscure thoroughfares, heading for the rendezvous. The King's personal train was to take them out of Alexandria. It was garishly painted pure white, and that included the locomotive itself. There was bunting around the boiler door, and flags waving from the cowcatcher. Despite all attempts at secrecy, Egyptian nationalists still managed to discover the route, and, as they boarded the train, angry mobs appeared on both sides of the line, screaming abuse and hurling stones at the carriage windows. One large stone shattered the window beside Clementine, and glass spattered all over her. Miraculously, she was unhurt. Her reaction was to calmly and meticulously brush the pieces of glass from her clothes. More stones hurtled through the broken window. Throughout the attack, Winston, unperturbed, sat smoking a cigar. The perspiration on their faces was due to the heat of the day, not the heat of the mob. Clementine snapped on a fan in the royal compartment and began to read while Winston busied himself with a dispatch box of papers. As the train slowly approached a crossing, more stones were flung at the windows by Egyptians beside the railway track. Some tried to jump the train and cling to the doors. Window after window was smashed, glass splinters were everywhere. Clementine stopped reading—she wasn't scared—she was annoyed. Attendants in red uniforms started to sweep up the glass, the train went on, and she went back to her book. This woman who could charm anyone, could also freeze to a block of ice with a look that would make an Arab intruder shiver in the noonday sun.

The remainder of the journey was uneventful until, about five miles outside Cairo, the train suddenly, and unexpectedly, slowed to a halt. Beside the railway line stood a number of open cars. Two British staff officers appeared at the carriage door and informed them that tremendous crowds were awaiting their arrival in Cairo. What kind of "welcome" the crowds were anxious to give, the two officers didn't make clear. It was therefore decided that the Churchills and their party would leave the train and proceed by car to the city. It was just as well. When the train steamed into Cairo station, mobs broks through police cordons to storm it. Winston and Clementine's entry into Cairo that day could have been their final exit.

When they reached Cairo's Semiramas Hotel, General Allenby, conqueror of Damascus, and Russell Pasha, Chief of the Egyptian Police and greatest enemy of international drug smugglers, were waiting. Both emphasized the seriousness of the threats to their lives. Following the stoning of the train at Alexandria, there was no question of their warnings being taken lightly. Nevertheless, they decided that the next day, they would, for the first time, act like typical tourists and treat themselves to a visit to the pyramids. Two of the guides asked them to sponsor a race between four natives to the top of a main pyramid and back. Clementine was appointed starter and judge and, at her signal, the four natives commenced to scale the pyramid like monkeys. They climbed at an incredible rate, and she presented the winner with a money prize.

Another commercial-minded native then offered the hot and weary visitors some "freshly brewed" English tea. Only Sir Archibald Sinclair drank the tea. The following morning, he became quite ill—almost certainly from the tea—and the inspection tour continued without him.

They visited a large R.A.F. camp close to Cairo. Again Clementine requested to see the married quarters, and again the request seemed unpopular. She crossed to an N.C.O. standing to attention, and asked, "Are you married?"

"Yes, I am," he replied.

"Do you live in the camp's married quarters?" she asked.

"Yes, Ma'am," the N.C.O. answered.

"I hear that the married quarters are causing some dissatisfaction. What is the matter with them?" she inquired.

"They are bad, Ma'am—that's all," replied the N.C.O.

"Mr. and Mrs. Churchill do not wish to hear all your private domestic troubles," one of the accompanying camp officers interjected. Winston looked at the officer without saying a word. The officer visibly paled.

Disregarding him, Winston asked the N.C.O., "Will you conduct us personally around the married quarters?"

It was agreed that the complaints about housing were far from unjustified, and cutting straight through red tape, orders were immediately issued to remedy the grievances.

The following morning, Colonel T. E. Lawrence—Lawrence of Arabia—joined them for a visit to Sakkara, site of the famous excavations, which was a two-and-a-half hour camel ride across the desert from the pyramids.

Lawrence was introduced to Clementine, and she studied this strange man about whom she had heard so much from Winston—this man who had been of such tremendous help to the Allied cause during World War I, and who had, by his leadership and personal magnetism, prevented Arab forces from joining Germany. She saw before her a shy, slight, awkward, untidy little man, and she swiftly put him at ease with her own warm personality. She penetrated his reserve, and they were soon laughing and talking animatedly together. She was deeply impresssed with the sincerity with which he talked about his adopted people, the Arabs. Lawrence made no attempt to hide from her the risks of the visit to both her and Winston and warned that their lives would be in jeopardy every moment in Egypt.

"The Egyptians are convinced that Mr. Churchill's visit is to inferfere with their internal affairs. They are bitterly resentful of British policy," he told her.

Their arrival at the pyramids was greeted by a magnificent turnout of local sheiks mounted on Arab horses. There were also a number of camels belonging to the Egyptian Camel Corps. Clementine mounted the wooden saddle on a large bony camel that had been decorated for the occasion with a vivid purple shawl. Winston mounted his animal and was like a schoolboy reveling in the novelty. At a command, the camels swayed to their feet and, accompanied by the escort of Arabian sheiks and their stallions, the party galloped off. It is hard for any novice camel rider not to look ridiculous first time out, but somehow Clementine contrived to look well dressed and well in command of everything.

Once you mount a camel you go where the camel goes. A cord runs from the saddle to the camel's right nostril but pulling it sometimes only brings a dirty look from the camel—and nothing else.

Clementine looked at Winston incongruously astride his camel and noticed he was slipping to one side of the saddle and was anxiously looking for something to hold onto. There wasn't anything. Suddenly, the cavalcade came to an abrupt halt—Winston had fallen off! There was complete confusion. Sheiks dismounted and rushed to him. The strappings of his beast obviously hadn't been tightened enough, so they had slid round, toppling him off into the sand. The Arabs begged him to continue the journey on one of their horses. He wouldn't. They also offered Clementine a horse. She politely, and graciously, refused, equally determined to continue by camel.

Said Winston defiantly, "I started on a camel, and I'll finish on a camel."

Colonel Lawrence, convulsed with laughter, exclaimed, "You know what happened, Winston, when that camel of yours knew you were going to ride on its back and they were putting on the saddle and tightening the girth, he blew himself up with pride, but when he got out in the desert and found you were the same as any other man, pride went before the fall. He just decided to get rid of you as speedily as possible, so he let out the air, the saddle girth loosened, and off you came."

Throughout the two-and-a-half hour rocking, swaying, bumping, camel journey, Clementine never once complained, determined to stick it out with the rest of the novices. But when it was time to return to Cairo, she didn't mount her camel again—she went back by car. For days she didn't stop chiding Winston on how easily the mighty are fallen and how simple it was for an Air Minister to be brought down to earth.

Back in Cairo, a procession of students awaited their arrival. The students marched up and down outside the Semiramas Hotel crying to heaven to bring down a curse on the heads of the Churchills. The students were about again when Clementine and Winston set out for the Abdin Palace to call on King Fuad of Egypt.

As the car reached the palace gates, crowds screamed hatred. Then the mob broke loose. Students engulfed the car, clambering on the running boards. Two of the guards in the car hit out at shrieking attackers, and palace officials rushed out to give added protection. The car eventually managed to pass through the gateway. For their departure, they took a different route back to the hotel, and even then only just escaped violent mobs.

The Churchills decided to go to the Holy City accompanied by Colonel Lawrence and Sir Herbert Samuel, who was then British High Commissioner for Palestine.

Sir Herbert Samuel had come to Cairo to warn the Churchills of a plot to murder them with a bomb or shoot them somewhere along the route from Cairo to Jerusalem.

As Clementine packed for the trip to Jerusalem, Winston received a message from London. An Italian general named Badoglio was preparing a troop movement into Libya for his chief—dictator Mussolini. The Italians were moving into Africa. Winston stood alone for a moment on the balcony of their suite and looked across the wilderness of North Africa. He stepped back into the room and said to Clementine, "If Badoglio is on his way, we'll have to come back here some day."

On the way to the Holy Land, the train stopped at Gaza, and they took the opportunity to tour the city and to visit various local institutions, including a pottery factory. As the party emerged from one building, they found it impossible to pass through the enormous crowd outside, which, by now, was obviously unfriendly. Straining to force a passage, mounted police rode their horses straight at the crowd, but people just seized the horses' bridles and pushed them back. The mob moved forward and was about to swamp the party when Colonel Lawrence held up his hand. His voice rang out. He spoke only a few words, and miraculously, the great crowd parted like the Red Sea allowing the party to return to the train.

Clementine had become accustomed to living with danger. She never showed fear, nor did she ever try to blatantly stop Winston from taking risks. Instead, quietly, she would see that every possible precaution was taken for his safety and would constantly try to introduce additional safeguards with the aid of members of their staff. She was fully conscious of the innumerable attempts on his life, and that these attempts also frequently endangered her life. On their return from the East, they continued to live with danger, for soon afterward came a new threat this time from the Sinn Feiners—the Irish underground organization then engaged in a campaign of murder and outrage.

Winston was in the House of Commons when the news came of the assassination of Sir Henry Wilson by Irish gunmen. If Sir Henry had been shot, Clementine realized only too well that Winston, as Secretary of State for the Colonies, and therefore the man responsible for the conduct of Irish affairs, could be the next target. They were living at the time in Sussex Square, Paddington, London. During the weeks following Sir Henry Wilson's murder, their home was guarded like a fortress, and Clementine was aware that the danger was not only to him, but also to herself and her children, for the stop-at-nothing Sinn Feiners might decide to use the kidnapping of one of them as a weapon against Winston. She daily watched her home searched from top to bottom for bomb plants. A Rolls Royce car completely armored with half-inch steel plates and weighing some two-and-a-half-tons, was placed at their disposal, and two Special Branch men—expert shots—were detailed to shadow the Rolls in a motorcycle and sidecar. Each night, before going to bed, she saw detectives check their house, room by room—they were taking no chances of a gunman slipping through their guard. The Rolls took Winston to Whitehall by a different route every day, as a precaution against possible ambush.

Clementine learned the necesssity of the safeguards when Winston arrived home one evening to tell her of a "near miss." That morning, the armored Rolls had been driving through Hyde Park by way of the Bayswater Road, when he had spotted two men standing back, almost in some bushes, by the side of the road. One of them appeared to signal to another man standing by a tree about one hundred yards or so ahead. Traffic had slowed the car and Winston and his detective guard were both on the alert. "You saw them—if they want to have a go, let's have a go at them." The detective wouldn't let him have his way, and ordered the chauffeur: "No stopping—get your foot down and get going!" The driver steered the car into the middle of the road where it could be screened by other vehicles.

Another safety touch in their home was the addition of a steel plate fitted into the back of Winston's favorite bedroom chair. Clementine added a feminine touch by decoratively covering the plate with attractive tapestry cloth. Every night, Winston would place a fully loaded .45 Colt on this chair. "If they come, Clemmie," he said, "they will receive a warm welcome, and not obtain a walkover."

But even as Sinn Feiners threatened the safety of his wife, children, and self, he worked on for peace for Ireland, and, with typical strategy, arranged a secret meeting between Sir James Craig, then leader of Unionist Northern Ireland, and Michael Collins, leader of the Sinn Feiners, upon whose head the British Government had placed a "dead-or-alive" price.

Even before their marriage, Clementine had heard that Winston not only lived with danger, but invited it.

"Winston told me that his first escape from death or serious injury occurred when he was a child of four," she once said. "He was in Ireland at the time, and one day he was out with his nurse riding a pet donkey when a procession approached. The donkey took fright and started kicking, flinging Winston off and giving him concussion of the brain. He described the incident as his first introduction to Irish politics.

"He also was only eighteen when, while on holiday with his aunt Lady Wimborne at Bournemouth, and playing a game with his younger brother and cousin, he jumped from a bridge crossing the chine, crashed thirty feet to the ground, and regained consciousness three days later. It was three months before he could crawl from his bed."

It was never a shock for Clementine to hear of his miraculous escapes. She grew accustomed to the "surprises."

In 1912, he received his first flying lesson at Eastchurch. The following day, Winston's instructor and the plane in which they had been flying together, crashed, and the pilot was killed. A few weeks later, Winston insisted on making a flight in a new type of seaplane. He was delighted with the test result—the new machine had behaved perfectly— but when he returned home there was a message waiting for him saying the seaplane had dived into the sea a few hours after he had left, taking three men to their death.

Another plane in which he was taking off suddenly turned a somer-sault, struck the ground, and left him hanging head downward, fastened to his seat by his belt. The plane was smashed, but all he suffered were cuts and bruises.

Clementine never let him know by anything she said, that she was unduly worried over these incidents.

Winston would simply say: "Under sufficient stress—starvation, terror, warlike passion, or even cold intellectual frenzy—the modern man we know so well will do the most terrible deeds, and modern woman will back him up."

Clementine shared his brand of fatalism.

7

Dead or Alive

"WINSTON CHURCHILL will not be permitted to leave the United States alive."

That was the information received by the State Department in Washington when the Churchills arrived in the United States, in February, 1932, on a lecture tour. This was no empty threat. The India Office in London had received confirmation of a plot to assassinate Winston in America. He didn't believe in hiding its seriousness from Clementine, nor could it in any way be hidden from her, for Washington had assigned Secret Service agents to reinforce the police in protecting them throughout their stay. Winston told Clementine that an Indian terrorist society with headquarters at San Francisco, and members in almost every city in the U.S.A., had ordered his assassination because he had bitterly opposed the Indian White Paper, urging that Indians were not, as yet, fit to govern themselves. Washington even circulated descriptions of Indians considered likely to cause trouble and be directly involved in the threat.

New York gave the Churchills a typical big city welcome. Waiting for them on the quayside when their ship docked were several cars and motorcyclist policemen to supply a howling-siren escort through the streets all the way to the Waldorf-Astoria Hotel.

The State Department's Chief Special Agent, Mr. R. C. Bannaman, was one of the first to greet them. He told them, "The repeated threats made on your life are believed to come from Hindus, chiefly those in California associated with the Chard party, which is composed of reckless Indians favoring direct action to obtain Indian independence. The threatening letters we received state that Mr. Churchill has incurred this party's enmity by his speeches on India and his pronounced views on the Indian question."

Secret Service shadowers followed them everywhere, aware the terrorists might switch their attention to Mrs. Churchill as a reprisal for her husband's political stand on India. This possibility also wasn't shielded from her. Special bodyguards were posted at every railway station with instructions that no East Indian be admitted to lecture halls in which the Churchills were to appear. Plainclothes detectives were also positioned among audiences.

The first real sign of trouble from the Indian secret societies came at Detroit. As Winston and Clementine entered a lecture hall, Indian "students" paraded outside wtih placards attacking his policies. But it wasn't until they reached Chicago that a dangerous incident occurred. The lecture had, as always, been an outstanding successs. As they left the platform, they both started to speak to members of the audience crowding around them. A group of admirers stood chatting to them in the forecourt of the building when a well-dressed Indian, walking with one hand in his pocket, came through the glass swing doors and headed straight for the Churchills. One of the watchful detectives spotted him, pulled a gun, and pointed it straight at the Indian. The man stopped, spun on his heels, and went crashing through the swing doors into the arms of more waiting detectives. Seeing his colleague held, another Indian waiting outside started to run down the street chased by two more detectives. While all this was happening, Winston and Clementine continued being sociable with the group of admirers.

Although Indian extremists didn't manage to injure Winston or Clementine during that visit to America, a New York taxicab driver nearly rewrote the Churchill story. It happened on the night of December 13, 1931. They had just finished dinner in their hotel and decided to retire early, when the telephone rang. It was an old friend, Bernard Baruch, who was head of the War Industries Board during the two years that Winston was Minister of Munitions. The acquaintanceship, begun through official cables, developed on a personal basis.

It was about 9:30 P.M. when Bernard Baruch telephoned to invite them round to his home to meet some mutual friends. Clementine decided to make an early night of it, and Winston set out alone.

About 10:45 P.M., the phone rang again in their suite. It was a doctor from New York's Lenox Hill Hospital, calling to inform Clementine that Winston had been knocked down by a cab and been taken to the hospital. With her daughter Diana, she rushed to him. He was in a

73

private room, swathed in bandages. The injuries were obviously extensive. She asked to see Dr. Otto Pickhardt and Dr. Foster Kennedy, who had attended him, to learn the nature of his injuries.

Dr. Pickhardt told her, "After a prolonged X-ray examination to determine the full extent of the internal injuries and especially whether there was any danger of pleural hemorrhage ensuing from injuries to the membranes of the lungs and thorax, he is resting comfortably after sustaining severe shock and concussion without loss of consciousness. There are many large bruises on the right arm, chest, and leg together with wounds to the tissues of the forehead and nose which have been stitched. I am afraid he will be unable to do active work for several weeks."

For some time Clementine sat by the bedside holding Winston's hand and speaking to him reassuringly, but his eyes remained shut. Finally they flickered open and she smiled at him. Behind her stood Bernard Baruch.

Then Winston spoke, "Tell me, Baruch, when all is said and done, what is the number of your house?"

"1055."

"How near was I to it when I was smashed up?"

"Not within ten blocks."

Then Winston explained what had happened. The accident occurred as a result of his having momentarily forgotten the difference between the British and the American rule of the road. On his way from the Waldorf-Astoria to the Baruch home, he realized he'd forgotten the exact number of the house. Peering out of the cab scanning the houses as they sped past, he decided to walk across the road and inquire at a likely looking house.

He said to Clemmie, "In England we frequently cross roads along which fast traffic is moving from both directions. I did not think the task I set myself either difficult or rash. But at this moment habit played me a deadly trick. I got out of the cab somewhere about the middle of the road and told the driver to wait. Then I instinctively turned my eyes to the left. At about 200 yards away were the yellow headlights of a swiftly approaching car. I thought I had just time to cross the road before it arrived, and I started to do so in the prepossession—wholly unwarranted—that my only dangers were from the left. The yellow-lighted car drew near, and I increased my pace toward the pavement, perhaps twenty feet away. Suddenly upon my right, I was aware of something utterly unexpected. I turned my head sharply. Right upon me, scarcely its own length away, was what seemed a long dark car rushing forward at full speed. I thought quickly, I am going to be run down and probably killed. Then came the blow. I felt it on my forehead and across the thighs. But besides the blow there was an impact, a shock, a concussion indescribably violent. I do not understand why I was not broken like an eggshell or squashed like a gooseberry. I certainly must be very tough or very lucky or both. I did not lose consciousness for an instant."

He told Clemmie that his mind had been suddenly in possession of the following conclusion, "I have been knocked over by a motor car in America. All those worries about being late are now swept away. They do not matter any more. Here is a real catastrophe. Perhaps it is the end. I experienced no emotion of regret or fear. I simply registered facts without, except for a general sense of disaster, the power to moralize upon them. I had no knowledge whether I was lying on my back or side or face. How long this period lasted I cannot tell. I suppose I ought to have had some very pious and inspiring reflections. However, all that occurred to me was I shall not be able to give my lecture tomorrow night in Brooklyn. Whatever will my poor agent do about it? Then a constable bent over me and asked my name. 'Winston Churchill,' I replied and I thought it lawful and prudent to add, 'The Right Honorable Winston Churchill from England!' 'What is your age?' asked the officer. 'Fifty-seven,' I replied, and at the same moment the odd thought obtruded itself upon my mind. How very old to be knocked down in the street by a car. I shall have a very poor chance of getting over it. When the constable proceeded to demand particulars of the accident my mind and speech apparatus worked apparently without hitch and I said, 'I am entirely to blame; it is all my own fault.' Another constable came with the question 'Do you make any charge against any person?' To which I replied, 'I exonerate everyone.' "

On arrival at the hospital, Winston asked to be allowed to telephone the Waldorf-Astoria so that he could tell Clemmie himself that whatever had happened he was going to get well. He was informed that she was already on the way.

Clementine spent the night at his bedside. Not until the following evening when the doctors assured her that he was completely out of danger and that there were no complications, did she return to the hotel, cheerful, though exhausted by the long strain.

The news broke in Britain and telephones never stopped ringing with condolences and inquiries. Randolph phoned his mother regularly from

London to ask after his father's progress. Then, the following evening, pleurisy developed as a result of the blow to Winston's chest, and there was serious anxiety over his condition. Once more Clementine remained by his bed. At last, Randolph received a cable, "Doing splendidly." Winston was on the mend again.

Among the cables Clementine opened at the Waldorf-Astoria was one from their friend "The Prof"—Professor Lindemann (later Lord Cherwell), Winston's scientific and economic adviser. Professor Lindemann, putting the accident into mathematical perspective, cabled:

> Just received wire delighted good news stop Collision equivalent falling thirty feet onto pavement equal six thousand foot pounds energy equivalent stopping ten pound brick dropped six hundred feet or two charges buck shot point blank range stop Shock presumably proportional rate energy transferred stop Rate inversely proportional thickness cushion surrounding skeleton and give of frame stop If assume average one inch your body transferred during impact at rate eight thousand horsepower stop Congratulations on preparing suitable cushion and skill in taking bump Greetings to all Lindemann Hotel Continental Nice

Only for one other person did she divert attention from her husband during those anxious days and that was for Mario Constansino, driver of the car that had knocked him down. Each day conscience-stricken Mario called at the hospital asking anxiously after the condition of the patient. Hearing this, Clementine invited Mario to call at her hotel. A nervous Mario was ushered into the suite at the Waldorf-Astoria. Clementine quickly put him at ease and offered him tea.

"I wish to assure you that my husband entirely blames himself for the accident," she told Mario. "I understand that you are unemployed. Did the publicity surrounding the accident hinder your efforts to find work?" she asked.

"It hasn't helped," he replied.

"Would you accept a check from us?" she asked tactfully, but Mario declined. "Well, in that case," she added, "would you like to see my husband?"

Mario was delighted with the suggestion and with her promise to make an appointment for him as soon as it was permissible.

A week later, the doctors told her that the patient's steady recovery made it possible for him to leave although his condition still necessitated complete rest and he would be unable to resume his lecture tour as yet. So, "battered but not shattered," as he described himself, Winston left Lenox Hill accompanied by two nurses, to spend Christmas Day at the hotel quietly with Clementine and Diana, but before he did so, Clementine kept her promise to Mario. He was invited to Winston's hospital room where the Churchills entertained him to tea and reassured him again that he was blameless. For half-an-hour the car driver, the victim, and the victim's wife, chatted.

"I never want to drive a car again," said Mario. Winston and Clementine tried to persuade him not to give up the pleasure of motoring, and then, as he was about to leave, she picked up a book from the bedside cabinet and said, "We thought you might like this as a memento of the occcasion." It was an autographed copy of the latest Churchill book—*The Unknown War*.

Ethel Barrymore came to see him at the hotel as soon as he came out of the hospital, and discussing fate and his lucky escape he said, "You know, Ethel, I have a terrible past." Ethel and Clementine both roared at this.

"I think he was thinking about the time he left the Conservative party and for a few years was a Liberal," commented Miss Barrymore, "he was always chiding himself like that, more or less humorously."

While Winston recuperated in his hotel room, an unexpected offer of a "tonic" arrived one afternoon with a ring at the door of his suite.

Clementine opened the door to a young man who presented a card. The well-spoken, well-dressed man, it seemed, disagreed with the restrictions of Prohibition then in force in the United States, preventing Mr. Churchill from enjoying the pleasure and benefit of a glass of whiskey. He therefore offered to supply any quantity of liquor of whatever quality or vintage required, explaining that regular supplies were "fished out of the sea." Clementine diplomatically and graciously declined the bootlegger's offer at the same time expressing her appreciation of the thought. Nevertheless, the following day a number of "sample" bottles of vintage champagne and genuine Scotch were delivered "With compliments and good wishes." The straw round the champagne bottles was, in fact, sea-water stained.

Two weeks later they left for the Bahamas for a short stay before resuming the lecture tour. On their return from Nassau, they began a marathon tour of America. Night after night, week after week, Winston addressed meetings of from 3,000 to 8,000 people at a time, always with Clementine on the platform. It was a tiring tour and he pressed her to stay in New York. She preferred keeping an eye on him, catching trains, making car connections, arriving at meetings, then on to the next train, the next car, and the next meeting.

The tour was a triumph for the Churchills—husband and wife—but the crowning achievement came at the very end when they were the guests of honor at a fabulous dinner given by some of America's greatest financial magnates in New York. This time Winston not only made an after-dinner speech, he held a debate for an hour-and-a-half and allowed himself to be third-degreed by the financial wizards.

One question put to him at the banquet brought the house down. He was asked, "Would you become an American citizen if we could make you President of the United States? I know our Constitution disqualifies you, but we can amend that."

Winston turned to Clementine, gave her a grin, and amid roars of laughter, replied, "There are various little difficulties in the way. However, I have been treated so splendidly in the United States that I shall be disposed, if you can amend the Constitution, seriously to consider the matter."

8

Nights at the Round Table

At Chartwell, Clementine entertained guests from all over the world. Most didn't just come to enjoy the social pleasures of their home—they were part of Winston's personal intelligence service. With their aid, he created an information service on affairs in other countries as good at least as those of the Foreign Office itself, and often better.

Winston used luncheons and dinners to help widen his general knowledge, to debate subjects of topical controversy, and to sharpen his intellect on the strop of the opinions of others.

After a meal was over, rather than retiring to the drawing room, Winston, as a rule, preferred to remain where he was, continuing to talk, with his elbows on the table.

He uses guests as a sounding board, gathering more actual knowledge from them than he could gain from a file of official reports.

"What do people say?" was the question that most frequently launched after-dinner conversation at Chartwell. Those fortunate enough to be asked to lunch or dine with the Churchills found the experience memorable for many reasons—and not only because of the importance of their host. Their hostess, and her influence on the proceedings, was equally impressive.

Listen to a dinner guest's description of his reception at Chartwell: "There are few more flattering experiences than to be one of Clementine Churchill's guests. This is not because she is Winston's wife, but because she has the quality of being able to get the best out of anyone. On arrival at Chartwell, you pass the beautiful garden setting of the semicircular drive, enter the great door, and are shown into the high-ceilinged drawing room, with its long spacious windows and dominating portrait of Winston. Waiting to greet you is the tall, elegant, silver-haired woman, with a smile that immediately makes you welcome. Her clothes are impeccable. You always remember her elegance, but never the details of what she wears—which is the hallmark of a well-dressed woman.

"Her voice is soft and unaffected, her conversation simple, direct. You are not made to feel gratified at being allowed to 'mingle with the mighty.' Clementine offers you a glass of sherry and you find yourself from the start more relaxed than you ever dreamed you could be. You barely notice that because of the nonappearance of your host, the meal is late—you are too flattered by the genuine interest being shown by your hostess in your nervous small talk."

Guests know her as a felicitous hostess, ever watchful of the husband opposite her at the head of the table, ever prepared to stimulate conversation when he becomes moody. Apparently shy, she is in fact always in control of the situation, and may steer the table talk from holidays abroad to Russian scientific progress, the ambitions of Mao Tse-tung, and back to some new recipe she has been trying.

She has the kind of grace that makes people say, "She seems to get lovelier each year." Tall and slim, she moves easily and lightly. Her large gray eyes shine beneath strongly marked thick eyebrows, which are never plucked into the fashionable line. She has a classic profile, which her daughter Sarah has inherited. In her younger days, she wore her hair parted in the middle, but now she prefers a modern style, with curls high on her forehead. Somehow, even in her seventies, she has youth and beauty. Hers is a gracious, well-ordered family life geared to the comfort and peace of mind of the man she married.

Finally, late as usual, Winston arrives, with his poodle Rufus at his heels. He is happiest at meals when the company includes Rufus on his left and Mickey, the tomcat, on his right.

Immediately all are seated, a maid brings in a small mat and a plate of dog food. The mat is laid beside Winston's chair and the bowl handed to him, Winston gives Rufus his meal, and thereafter, the little dog sits quietly at his master's feet.

At first Winston may take over the conversation, but he is just as apt to fall into sudden, complete silence, devoting all his attention to his plate and becoming apparently unaware of everyone and everything. Instantly, Clementine carries the ball, adroitly keeping the conversation flowing. During the entire meal you are always conscious of your hostess. She is always ready to take control of any situation that seems to be getting out of hand. The years have made her expert at handling the entire range of Churchillian temperament from rage, despair, and tears, to gaiety, tenderness, and love. Through the long course of her marriage she has acted as hostess to the world's most eminent men and women, and no guest who has ever sat at her table can ever remember anything going wrong. There have been times, however, when Clementine has had to change the conversation very swiftly to avert disaster.

Mrs. Leo Amery, wife of the ex-Secretary of State for India, was at dinner with Winston when Sir Stafford Cripps, his colleague in the Government of the day, was sitting opposite to him. Cripps was a strict vegetarian. Winston, thoroughly enjoying himself, tucking into turkey and asparagus with hot butter sauce, suddenly leaned over to Mrs. Amery, glanced mischievously at Cripps, who had refused every savory dish, and said, "I am glad I am not a herbivore. I eat what I like, I drink what I like, I do what I like...." Then, after one of his emphatic pauses, he concluded: "...and *he's* the one to have a red nose!"

At another dinner when a well-known personage, a man of the highest rectitude and towering stature, was a guest, his moral sentiments and general air of gloom had made a marked impression.

When he had gone, Winston glowered at Clementine and the other survivors, and demanded, "Who will relieve me of this Wuthering Height?"

Although in dealing with women, Winston is courteous and gentle, and although even with the passing years he retains the boyish charm, which many find so endearing, he is, to put it mildly, a handful and certainly not an easy man to be married to.

Winston's moods are unpredictable. Clementine, on the other hand, is always the diplomat. No matter what happens in her home, she is so self-disciplined that she seldom loses her dignified composure. She appreciates that when her husband "comes home from the office" he may be bringing with him the problems of the future of civilization, and that sometimes when he is late for dinner it is because he is trying to combat the evil ambitions of dictators. So, serenely, she makes sure that he has a good meal. Because he is notoriously unpunctual, she is always on time. He is known for the informality of his attire. She is always dressed perfectly. Above all, she understands her husband's moods and temperament better than anyone else, a fact to which the late Lord Riddell paid tribute when he said, "She is a queen among wives, and manages Winston very well."

To achieve her superb meals, she spends half an hour every morning with the cook, discussing the day's menus. Usually they comprise hors d'œuvres, soup, fresh trout or sole, roast sirloin of beef or plump pheasants, fruit, sweets and cheese, and sometimes one of the new recipes she has copied experimentally from some publication.

She loves flowers, particularly roses, and floral decorations are a feature of her dining room. The centerpiece of the dining table is always arranged at low level, so that guests are not hidden from each other and conversation impeded.

Every morning, after her interview with the cook, she personally supervises the seating plans for luncheon and dinner. Her skill at placing neighbors at table is unerring, though it is no mean feat to juggle with Cabinet Ministers, Service chiefs, top-ranking civil servants, trade union leaders, and perhaps, visiting foreign potentates. To facilitate the trick, she prefers whenever possible to seat the company at a round table.

The routine for their days and nights at the round table varies at their different places of residence. At No. 10, dinners at which Cabinet business was discussed, were usually strictly formal affairs. The guests were all male, and though Clementine organized the meals she seldom took part in them. Having received the guests, and perhaps taken a cocktail with them, she would usually retire to her own room.

To be a Churchill luncheon or dinner guest is, very understandably, a much coveted honor. One famous American who can claim to have achieved this distinction is Mr. Irving Berlin. How he did it is a story worthy of one of his own musical comedies.

It happened that in the British Embassy in Washington worked a Mr. I. Berlin, whose regular appraisals of the American scene, sent to the Foreign Office and subsequently passed to the Prime Minister, were much admired by Winston. He conceived the greatest respect for Mr. Berlin's wit and political shrewdness. One morning, in the course of his routine reading of all the newspapers, he noticed that a Mr. Irving Berlin had arrived in Britain from the United States. Having instructed a secretary to make the necessary contact, he informed Clementine, "We shall be having a Mr. Berlin to lunch today." He was too occupied with weightier matters to explain why.

Irving Berlin arrived, to be greeted by Clementine, and even more warmly by Winston. "You have written some wonderful things," said the Prime Minister. "As you know, I have admired them greatly. Now what, of all that you wrote, do you consider was the best?"

"Well, Mr. Prime Minister," said Irving, "I hardly know, but I guess I would say 'My Heart Stood Still.'"

Winston laughed appreciatively at this apparent piece of wit.

"What's going to happen in the Presidential election?" he inquired.

"Well, sir," said Irving, "a lot of people think that Roosevelt will lose."

"Do they?" said Winston.

"But on the other hand," Irving continued, "a lot of people think Roosevelt will win."

Winston stared at his guest long and hard. Then, suddenly excusing himself, he left the room. "Will you tell me," he asked a secretary, "whom I am lunching with?"

"Yes, sir. Irving Berlin, the famous American song writer."

Clementine looked at Winston as he reentered the room, trying to fathom his table conversation and his general behavior. There was no more talk of politics when Winston resumed his seat at the head of the table. He conversed graciously about nothing in particular.

He insisted on joining Clementine in seeing their guest to the door when it was time for him to leave, and expressed the hope that he would come again. Not until the door closed did he explain the comedy of errors to his puzzled wife.

It was in 1935, while still in the political "wilderness" because of Winston's unrelenting anti-Nazism, that Clementine became hostess for two weeks to two other representatives of show business. Director Anthony Asquith and script writer Lajos Biro had come to teach her husband to write, or to be precise, to teach a form of writing he had never previously attempted—screenwriting.

Producer Alexander Korda had already bought the film rights of Winston's book, *Marlborough,* for £10,000, and now he had engaged him to write the script for a project to be entitled *Twenty-five Years of the Reign of George V*. But the tutors who had come to Chartwell found their pupil had little to learn. As they enjoyed their lunch on the first day of their visit, Winston expounded his ideas.

"We must have a map of Europe with a skeleton hand tearing through it to symbolize the beginning of the Great War," he said. Then, grinning at Clementine, "We must have a Suffragette in the film, fair and frail—physically, not morally frail—with a delicate integument hiding an indomitable spirit!"

Unfortunately, because Korda found production problems insurmountable, the picture was eventually abandoned.

It is a tragedy that there has never been a latter-day Boswell to record in full the fascinating and often dramatic exchanges across the Churchill table, for it is often at luncheon and dinner that Winston is most self-revealing, and Clementine her most skillful. Every Churchill day is a day of surprises. Almost hourly crises arise, which require the most delicate handling by Clementine. A swarm of Cabinet Ministers may arrive unexpectedly for a lunchtime conference, a visiting statesman invited to dinner may have special dietary requirements. She deals with such problems coolly, efficiently, without fuss.

Ten years before the Second World War, at Chartwell, she arranged a small, intimate luncheon party of young people at which the table talk became almost a duel between a youth of nineteen and Winston, with an elder guest interjecting an occasional word. It began when the elder man said, "Your memories, Mr. Churchill, are a romance of adventure and achievement which modern young people will feel they cannot afford to miss. Now, if you had your life to live over again, with all the experience and knowledge of the years you now possess, would you do the same things?"

Winston: "Probably, but I should try to waste less time than I did in my early days. I wasted time until I was twenty-two. It was only then that I got the desire for learning."

Youth: "Would you go in for politics."

Winston: "Politics are greatly changed. They are no longer so interesting. There are not the same prizes. Our politicians are not the brilliantly dominating men they were. They are not given the same position by the public. The world is not the same . . . yet if I lived again, I suppose I should do as I did before; but I should make a different set of mistakes and miss a different set of chances."

Youth: "What *were* your mistakes and missed chances?"

Winston: "I did not acquire a love of learning until I was twenty-two. My effective education was almost entirely technical. Afterwards I wished I had gone to Oxford."

Elder guest: "Oxford might have so leveled your audacious spirit that you might have got learning at the expense of the adventure which is the keynote of your life. Besides, your 'marching pen,' which brought successful authorship, owes something to the influence of those early Army days."

Winston (to the youth): "I hear you are going to Oxford. It is no use going there without a genuine love of learning, otherwise you are wasting time expensively. I tried to make up for lost time when I was

84

twenty-two. I started by reading Gibbon's *Decline and Fall of the Roman Empire*. I read it right through three times. Every young man ought to read it."

Youth: "Why?"

Winston: "It gives you the scale and grandeur of human life and tragedy in the finest English."

Youth: "Would you *care* to live your life again?"

Winston: "Not from the beginning, anyhow. I would like to start at twenty. Thence to twenty-five are the best years. The whole world is then before you. I would not like to have my school days over again. I never enjoyed school. No doubt it was my fault. I was not good either at work or play. I did not like routine."

Youth: "And you wish you had been at a university?"

Winston: "Yes; but I think a boy in the main must choose his own path."

Elder guest: "Should not the parent have some say in the matter?"

Clementine: "In these days it often makes no difference if they try. Modern young people will do as they like. The only time parents really control children is before they are born. After that their nature unfolds remorselessly, petal by petal."

Youth (to Winston): "Have you enjoyed your life?"

Winston: "Yes, indeed, since my school days. I have mostly done what I most wanted.

Youth: "That's all very well. We can't all do that. You had advantages."

Winston (throwing some salt over his left shoulder): "I had a name, I had a little money and no possessions. I had to find my own opportunities."

Elder guest: "You had qualities of push and go which are not given to all young men, you know."

Winston: "Except for my name, all the rest I had to work for, to fight for. When I was twenty-two, with my small Army pay not covering expenses, I realized that I was handicapped and unable to live my life as I wanted to. I wanted learning, and I wanted freedom.

"I realized that there was no freedom without a little money. I had to earn money to get independence. So I set to work. I wrote. I studied. I lectured. I won my freedom. I can hardly remember a day when I have found nothing interesting to do. I am always employed on something."

Youth: "What about the light side of life? Tell me, for instance, do you ever play bridge?"

Winston: "Hardly ever."

Youth: "Funny that so few men of brains do. Now what about politics?"

Winston: "I was troubled about the state of things in this country. The people have the power; they are responsible. Are they paying enough attention to the job they have demanded and undertaken? Are things thrashed out as they ought to be and as they used to be?"

Youth: "You would not advise young men to go in for politics, then?"

Winston: "I did not say that; but the attraction and glamor of Parliament are much less than they used to be. Everywhere democracies and their leaders are shirking facts; hoping to solve problems and pay off perils with well-meant platitudes."

Youth: "Do you ever regret that you didn't give your life to literature?"

Winston: "Why should I regret that?"

Youth: "Do you not think a great pen might do a greater lifework than an eloquent voice and a political genius?"

Winston: "That's an old subject of debate. Perhaps what you say is true, though I am not prepared to admit that I have either the one faculty or the other in any high degree. If I were to pronounce one way or the other, I should say I was much more at home with a pen than on the platform. To speak in public takes a great deal out of me. I never excelled as a platform speaker."

But Clementine also had to learn to contend with a man who frequently at dinner parties will pretend to be deaf so that he can concentrate on his food. She sees that he gets his favorite foods; he prefers meat to fish. His breakfasts must be plain and simple. He likes bacon and eggs, kidney and sometimes some chicken. And always coffee. He has a weakness for liver, cut thick and very lightly done. Whenever they go to a restaurant, he always says exactly how he wants his food cooked, and heaven help them if they don't follow his instructions. Winston always likes clear soup. One evening, in error, he was served with thick soup, and their guests with clear soup.

"What is this white creamy looking stuff?" he growled, and the offending plate was hastily removed.

Clementine's thrifty, strict upbringing was the ideal grounding in housekeeping for one who likes his meals solidly Victorian while proclaiming that, domestically at least, "I very much enjoy the luxury of indecision." The food served at the Churchill tables is always excellent, not because Clementine spends a great deal of money on it but because she takes great pains to see that it is infinitely varied and always of the very best quality.

She is quite unsparing of herself where her duty as a housewife is concerned. Even if she is not well enough to attend to guests personally, she never fails to ensure their comfort. Once, though running a high temperature, she got out of a sickbed an hour before important guests arrived for lunch, to make sure that her every instruction had been carried out.

However much he underestimates his own talents on the platform, Winston has often expressed at the table his strong views on how a speech should be made. Said General Eisenhower, "At dinner one evening, he jumped on me and gave me unshirted hell for speaking from memory and not following the text of a prepared speech. It was at a ceremony and I had been given a speech of 125 words, which I memorized.

" 'Never trust your memory in anything like that, with people following every word you say,' warned Winston."

It was Clementine who passed on to "Ike" at dinner the counsel of the greatest orator of our times. She said, "Winston is a great believer in the use of spectacles. You should wear spectacles—big, round ones, which you can take off and shake in their faces. And if you have notes, don't try to hide them. Shake those in their faces, too."

Winston gave similar advice to Lord Halifax, British Ambassador to the United States during the war years.

"Do you speak from notes?" he asked.

Lord Halifax said that he did.

"That's quite all right," said Winston, "but never try to pretend to your audience that you are not using them. If you do that, you get into a sort of competitive game of hide-and-seek in which you're bound to lose. If you are perfectly open about it, you can keep them waiting as long as you like while you find your place in your notes, and put on your glasses to read them, and they won't mind at all."

Winston's slight difficulty with the letter "s," far from marring his conversation, seems to add a special kind of emphasis from time to time. His Parliamentary and broadcast utterances are deliberately spoken. His table talk, though generally faster, is nevertheless unhurried and broken from time to time with telling effect. Often his vehemence will practically exhaust his guests by its overwhelming power, and it is left to Clementine to bring calm back to the conversation. One day at table, somebody remarked that nothing was worse than war. Winston, almost rising out of his chair, thundered, "Dishonor is worse than war! Slavery is worse than war!"

Field Marshal Montgomery sparked him off another way. They were lunching just before the end of the war when Monty remarked, "Now that it's nearly all over I suppose you will be spending the evening of your days quietly."

"*Evening?*" roared Winston. Then, more softly, "And you, I suppose, will be getting into uniform."

Clementine's warm smile gives a hint of humor. A witty and charming conversationalist, she has the knack of seeming to take you into her confidence with her smile, just as Winston enjoys jolting you into activity with his words. Her knowledge of affairs, political and domestic, is tremendous.

Reminiscences have always been a feature of his table talk, and Clementine, a perfect listener, never ceases to enjoy his retelling of some vivid incident in his career. Even though she may have heard the story in some form before, such is his magic and mastery of words that she ever shows her obvious pleasure. And indeed, to listen to him relating one of his countless exploits, as he pares an apple at the dining table, is an unforgettable experience.

To some luncheon guests he told the story of the destroyer which had dropped a depth charge, but instead of finding a submarine they saw bits of an old wreck come to the surface. "And would you believe it?" he concluded. "There was a door bobbing around with my initials on it!"

Clementine's luncheon and dinner parties have many times proved the turning points of men's careers. Instead of summoning ministers and possible ministers to No. 10, Winston preferred whenever possible to invite those involved in Government shuffles to Chequers or Chartwell. That is how a new stage in the political career of Mr. Harold Macmillan was reached when he and his wife were invited for the weekend to Chequers.

Canada's Mr. Diefenbaker went with some trepidation to dinner with the Churchills. He is a total abstainer. "Sure enough," he said afterward, "when I refused wine and asked her for a soft drink with my meal, Winston began muttering and grumbling about prohibitionists being the curse of North America.

"I protested that I was not a prohibitionist but merely a teetotaller.

" 'Ah!' said Sir Winston. 'That's not so bad. You believe only in doing harm to yourself.' "

Dinner with the Churchills could prove an uncomfortable meal for the most distinguished of guests if, in some way, they had incurred disapproval. On one occasion when Clementine turned the table talk to a discussion on minor vices, Winston said of drinking, "All I can say is that I have taken more out of alcohol than alcohol has taken out of me. But we all despise a man who gets drunk." On smoking, "Some people say I smoke too much. I don't know. If I had not smoked so much, I might have been bad-tempered at the wrong time."

And then, in a reminiscent mood he declared:

"But consider! How can I tell that the soothing influence of tobacco upon my nervous system may not have enabled me to comport myself with calm and courtesy in some awkward personal encounter and negotiation or carried me securely through some critical hours of waiting? How can I tell that my temper would have been as sweet or my companionship as agreeable if I had abjured from my youth the goddess Nicotine? Now I think of it, if I had not turned back to get the matchbox which I had left behind in my dugout in Flanders, might I not have just walked into the shell which pitched so harmlessly one hundred yards ahead?"

Clementine is as much a diplomat when she is a guest of others as when she is hostess in her own home. At a private dinner party which she attended with Winston, the guests included a foreign gentleman of considerable eminence. When dinner was over, the hostess confided to Clementine with some embarrassment that the distinguished foreigner had been seen purloining an exquisite little silver salver. It was one of an antique set and quite irreplaceable. What was she to do? Clementine thought for a few moments, and then spoke quietly to Winston. She told him what had happened, and suggested a plan to retrieve the salver. With an impish smile, he readily agreed to cooperate. Under cover of his table napkin he, also, appropriated a salver. Then, sidling up to the potentate and slyly revealing the piece of silver sticking out of his pocket, he whispered, "I've got one, as well as you; but we'll have to put them back, you know. We've been rumbled!" He duly replaced the salver, and the potentate followed his example.

Anthony Eden has always been one of the Churchills' favorite guests. Clementine and Winston love him like one of the family, and nothing pleased them more when, in 1952, he actually became one of the family by marrying Winston's niece Clarissa.

Lord Beaverbrook is another frequent visitor to Chartwell and Hyde Park Gate. Clementine loves to listen as Winston and "the Beaver" spar verbally—often appearing to be in opposite camps, though in fact they are devoted friends.

The Churchills' guests and friends came from all walks of life: from the world of literature, authors like C. S. Forester; from the theater, friends like Sir Laurence Olivier and Vivien Leigh; from the sporting world, colorful characters like Freddie Mills, the boxer. They were both fans of Charlie Chaplin, so Clementine invited him to lunch one day, and Chaplin did something few people could do—he silenced Winston. Charlie let fly with a long soliloquy on pacifism and peace at almost any price. He obviously meant every word sincerely and for the best, but Winston, shaken by the outburst, looked straight through him and didn't utter one comment. The unbearable atmosphere that followed was blessedly broken by Clementine talking about nothing in particular in the nicest possible way.

Sir John Rothenstein, director of the Tate Gallery, was invited to Chartwell to lunch and to inspect Winston's latest painting. "We fortified ourselves with an excellent lunch, washed down with the contents of certain receptacles which Sir Winston had immortalized in a series of paintings he called his 'bottlescapes,' " Sir John said. "Afterward Sir Winston offered me a cigar. I put it firmly aside, declaring that every man should have at least one virtue, and mine was not smoking. He looked me sternly in the eye and replied, 'There is no such thing as a negative virtue. If I have been of service to my fellow man, it has never been by self-repression, but always by self-expression.' "

Concerning birth he said, at another dinner party, "My mother intended that I should be born in London, but I elected otherwise. I arrived more than a month before my time, while she was staying at Blenheim."

Clementine added smilingly, "Winston is half American and all English."

He nodded. "I am directly descended, through my mother, from an officer who served in Washington's army. I have my pedigree supported by affidavits at every stage if it is challenged."

One of the most notable features of Winston's table talk through the years has been his almost uncanny gift of prophecy. Prompted by a remark of Clementine's concerning scientific development, at a luncheon given years before the Second World War, he said, "May there not be methods of using explosive energy incomparably more intense than anything heretofore discovered? Might not a bomb no bigger than an orange be found to possess a secret power to destroy a whole block of buildings—nay, to concentrate the force of a thousand tons of cordite and blast a township at a stroke?"

Introduction of international affairs into the Churchill table conversation can be relied upon to evoke a response from the host. During a discussion of the situation in Greece, someone remarked that the Greek political leader, Archbishop Damaskinos, was in the habit of securing himself from interruption by hanging a notice on his door: "His Beatitude is at prayer."

"I'd like to try that at Downing Street," said Winston, "but I'm afraid no one would believe it."

Clementine delights in giving parties for children as well as for their parents and is expert at keeping all ages entertained. At an after-Christmas party, all the Churchill children and grandchildren were present; the Macmillans were there with their three grandchildren; Lord De L'Isle and Dudley, former Secretary of State for Air, came with his wife and two daughters; and still more children came with their friends to make up a gathering of twenty-six. Clementine organized games and a conjuring entertainment, Winston gave a film show, and everyone, as always, had a wonderful time.

They both show great sympathy for the problems of young people beginning life in this uncertain modern world. Said Winston, when the topic was raised, "We are ceaselessly disturbed or amused, or at any rate occupied, by fleeting superficial sensations. Old books are unread or undigested. The churches are empty. And the younger generation ask us, 'What are we to do?' Still, there are some very simple things which can be said. Do not be frightened. Do not despair. Keep your head. The trees do not grow up to the sky. Strength will be given as it is needed, and guidance will be given to nations which deserve it. Do the right and simple thing according to your conscience and honor in your own sphere. We know quite well what that is. Search diligently but resolutely for practical solutions. Conquer or go down fighting. No one can do more.

"We ought not to be afraid of running risks. Since when have we learned that we are entitled to security in this transitory world of chance and illusion? The only way to avoid risks is never to have lived at all. Choosing a career is a risk. Marrying is a risk. Childbirth is a risk. All around the most careful man—every breath he draws, every step he takes, every mouthful he eats—are hazards that may be mortal...."

His most scathing utterances have always been reserved for dictators and dictatorship. Three years before the outbreak of war, when, against the general political stream, he was vehemently advocating rearmament, he said, "We live in a country where the people own the government, and not in a country where the government owns the people.... You see these dictators on their pedestals, surrounded by the bayonets of their soldiers and the truncheons of their police ... while in their hearts there is unspoken fear. The little mouse of thought appears in the room and even the mightiest potentates are thrown into panic...."

With such trenchant, uncompromising pronouncements in mind, it is easy to understand why Clementine was delighted by and treasures a catalogue of fruit trees she received from a Hampshire nurseryman. It lists among its offerings: "Winston Dessert (March–May): This new introduction was originally called Winter King, but it transpired that the name was already borne by another variety, so it was appropriately renamed Winston because it will weather storm. Very thick skin. Remains firm until the end of its season. Slightly bitter. Juicy. Prolific. Upright. Fruit hangs tightly to tree after leaf-fall. Late bloomer. Wonderful keeper."

On the subject of dinner with the Churchills, their dear friend, Bernard Baruch had this to say. "The world should be a guest at your dinner table and enjoy the treat of hearing you talk, with a bottle of wine always at hand, of military tactics in the American Civil War, of your early adventures in South Africa, of Gibbon and Macaulay, of the knaves and fools you have known. The spirit with which you could denounce them!

"There is also a quiet side to your life of which the world should know, and which is perhaps best symbolized in your gracious and beautiful wife.

"No one but you knows how enormous has been Clemmie's influence and contribution to your own career. I have sensed your respect and devotion to her in how quickly you would heed her gentle admonition, 'Winston, I wouldn't say that!'"

9

Alone—Together

THROUGH ups and downs, almost unprecedented even in British political life, she walked with him loyally. During his ten years "down," before the Second World War, she fought ceaselessly to soften the bitterness of political exile. In the jungle of politics, a politician—and his wife—are often ruthlessly clawed by their opponents if they lose the slightest foothold. Winston bore the hostility, the snubs, the sneers, that would have destroyed another man, with a fortitude strengthened by her absolute faith in his future. Clementine knew only too well that Winston lived for the day when he could once more assume power and authority. He hated to be out of office.

They made a strange, yet perfectly matched team. Winston, the showman, from the tip of his cigar to the top of one of his many hats, playing to the gallery with his uncanny sense of theater, bathing in the waves of affection rolling towards him from cheering crowds, loving to inspect guards of honor, and reveling in the trappings of high office. And, as Winston added the human, humorous touch in public, Clementine balanced the picture with her charm and strong sense of dignity, as if to remind us all that the showman beside her was also a man of great importance.

During the mid-1930s it seemed he had "missed the bus." He was a lone wolf, champion of lost causes and forgotten loyalties. There was nothing of which political prophets were surer than that he would never be Prime Minister. He had made too many enemies, was still making enemies. His constant warnings of the menace of Hitlerism were dismissed by a public which preferred comfortable words. "Let him write history," they said. "It is too dangerous to allow him to make it."

Clementine heard again the cries of people ignorant of the tragedy about to overwhelm them, calling him "warmonger" during years when he was one of the few to see what was happening; when he was the lone voice in the desert.

She was with him when he went to the Central Hall, in Peckham, London, in 1931. The catcalls against him created an uproar. All over the hall there were fist fights as members of the audience fought to reach the platform while he was speaking. There were running fights in the gallery; men, knocked out by the dozen, were carried outside the hall to recover. During the singing of the National Anthem, many refused to remove their hats, so others proceeded to make them take them off by force. Through it all Clementine listened to Winston, her attention riveted on him as he recalled, "As a young man, I remember the great days of Queen Victoria. I was brought up in that reign and I was present at her Diamond Jubilee. As a young man I saw her carriage surrounded by scores of kings and princes. We were a great nation then and headed the world. We were the world's ironmasters, its cotton spinners, shippers, and bankers. We had the sovereignty of the seas and of the land. We were envied and honored by all. We were rich and peaceful, dwelling in our own habitation. I would like to see some of those glories return. I would like to see this native land of ours resume its rightful place among the nations of the world. Today is Trafalgar Day. I would remind you what Pitt said, 'England has saved herself by her exertions and she will save the world by her example!'"

Through the years Winston and Clementine faced the wrath of those who labeled his policies as "personal glorification and ambition," or those who, when he stopped attacking, accused him of "soft pedaling criticism to win a Cabinet job by his silence."

Her friend, Margot Asquith, Countess of Oxford and Asquith—long an admirer of Winston—said she considered he would be well advised to give up politics entirely. "He is the greatest political historian that we have had since Macaulay, and it is regrettable that he should waste a moment of his time on politics, as his lack of conviction will always prevent him from being either a good leader or a good follower. There are some that you cannot change; you must either swallow them whole, or leave them alone. It is no use your saying you could wish this or that were different, so as to counteract certain deficiencies ... you must make up your mind to take them or leave them. You can do something with talent, but nothing with genius, and Winston Churchill has a touch of— what we all recognize but never can define—Genius."

Clementine refused to agree with well-meaning Margot Asquith's assessment of Winston as an unsuitable leader, or as a politician without a future.

Whichever line he chose, it seemed he could do no right. Two years before the last war when the Government stood firm against rearmament, he attacked it on that issue. When Britain finally rearmed, he was abused for no longer criticizing the Government.

One Sunday morning in 1937, Clementine read in a newspaper and marked for Winston's attention, the following passage. It said: "Will Mr. Churchill be in the new Cabinet? He should be."

Winston persisted in drawing attention to the smell under people's noses even if they preferred to consider that it wasn't there. Ignoring popular feeling, he continued to cry "Danger!"

"I urge the Government to tell the British people exactly what is going on. Let them know the truth...."

When news of Hitler's "blood purge" was telephoned to them one afternoon at Chartwell, he said to her, "The Dark Ages have come again. Germany has gone back to barbarism."

Bernard Baruch was one of the few permitted to share with Clementine the Winston he kept well hidden in those days from the public. "The years between the wars were bleak ones for him," recalls Mr. Baruch, who, whenever he visited their home during that period, was recruited as an ally by Clementine to help boost Winston's morale. "Once, as we walked through his garden, he unburdened himself to me," said Mr. Baruch. "His public career seemed at an end, and he wondered whether he ought not to enter some business. I tried to hearten him by pointing out that, although he might be denied political leadership for a time, he could achieve greatness with his pen. And I told him that I was sure England could not and would not go on ignoring him. Fortunately for her and the world, England did not when the great trial began."

Sometimes they managed to ease the tension by inviting friends, completely unconnected with politics, to stay with them. Noticing in the newspapers that Winston's bachelor days' "flame," Ethel Barrymore, had come to London to appear in a play, Clementine couldn't resist inviting her down to Chartwell. She liked Ethel—and, of course, knew Winston did too—and they had enjoyed her company at lunch the previous time she had been in London.

"I motored down to see the Churchills at Chartwell and spent the night," said Miss Barrymore. "Winston and Clementine showed me about the place, and I remember him waving his hand at the grounds and the house and saying, 'Ethel, all this is out of my pen!' He was out of power then, a voice crying unheeded, and phophesying with what was proved to be uncanny accuracy, the consequence of giving way before Hitler's increasing belligerency."

The social ostracism they bore during those years hurt, but, wherever she went, Clementine walked, head high, certain that her husband was right and everyone else was wrong. Her courage was equal to his. She had shown great courage in marrying him at all, as he was, even when they met, classed as an "unpredictable, egotistical buccaneer of Edwardian politics and a traitor to his class."

At meetings, when his enemies threw bricks, rotten eggs, or even spat at him, she faced them fearlessly with him. Through the years when his hopes and aspirations floundered, she cherished and fostered them; and when he was desolate, cast aside, she comforted him. Whatever his mood or fortune, Winston felt secure and strengthened in the knowledge that his Clementine would remain steadfast.

He was restless with a restlessness inflamed by his sense of imminent catastrophe. Neville Chamberlain was nervous of this restlessness. They were advised that because Mr. Chamberlain had such a high opinion of Winston's ability, it was his intention to offer him a Cabinet post as soon as he had found his feet at Leader of the Party. The call never came.

Discussing why the Cabinet avoided recruiting Winston to its ranks, Sir Archibald Sinclair, one of their closest friends, told Clementine, "He's too big for them and they cannot contain him. You cannot stop a soft tooth with a gold filling."

As 1938 passed, Clementine and the family lived in the constant shadow of his fears for the security of the country.

Even treasured moments with Clementine in the gardens of Chartwell were somehow unrelaxed. Winston lashed himself, trying to escape the terrible frustration by sounding warnings in weekly contributions to the press, and in his speeches to Parliament. He was obsessed with the danger to his country, to the world, to his wife, and his family. To guests who came to their home, both of them talked of little else, for nothing else mattered. They constantly expressed the fear that England would refuse to show her hand until it was not only too late to avoid war, but too late to win a war. For years he had been stumping in and out of meetings all over the country, warning how alarmingly Britain's armament program lagged behind other nations, and demanding a national effort to close the gap.

Wherever he went to wage his one-man war for peace—to public meetings or to the House of Commons—Clementine accompanied him, listening as he cried out, "I predict that the day will come when at some point or other, on some issue or other, you will have to make a stand, and I pray God that when that day comes you may not find that through an unwise policy we are left to make that stand alone."

And, as she looked down from the gallery of the House on March 24, 1938, two weeks after the German invasion of Austria, she watched him, an almost lonely figure in the packed chamber, say, with his head thrust forward, "For five years I have talked to this House on these matters—not with very great success. I have watched this famous island descending incontinently, fecklessly, the stairway which leads to a dark gulf. It is a fine broad stairway at the beginning, but after a bit the carpet ends. A little farther on there are only flagstones, and a little farther on still these break beneath your feet...."

When he resumed his seat, there was complete silence for a moment, as though they all were wrestling with the fears he had stirred within them, struggling to dismiss the warning words from their thoughts as if they had never heard them. The Chamber came to life again, and many of the members who had crowded the benches took their leave.

At Chartwell, Clementine began to entertain international journalists, travelers for British and commercial and financial houses. All came with information for Winston. They were part of his preparation for the war he now felt was inevitable.

A mile away from Chartwell lived their friend, Desmond Morton, who later became Major Sir Desmond Morton, K.C.B., C.M.G. When Winston was Secretary of State for War and Air, he had appointed Desmond Morton to a key position in the Intelligence. Winston obtained permission from the Prime Minister for Morton to talk freely to him and help keep him well informed. Ralph Wigram, whose star was rising in the Foreign Office, was another who regularly came to keep Winston in close touch with world affairs, and Mr. and Mrs. Wigram often stayed at Chartwell.

Informants came to them and talked without reserve. Even when Herr Henlein, leader of the Czech Nazis, arrived in London to test general British opinion of affairs in Czechoslovakia, he came to their apartment at Morpeth Mansions.

Clementine handled the new pattern of visitors with her customary charm and diplomacy. Winston relied on her to create the right atmosphere for all the informal but vital discussions which took place week after week at Chartwell.

"It was of great value to me, and it may be thought also to the country, that I should have the means of conducting searching and precise discussions for so many years in this very small circle," said Winston. "On my side, however, I gathered and contributed a great deal of information from foreign sources."

But the world wanted to listen even less to Winston's words when, delirious with relief, it welcomed the black-coated umbrella-in-hand figure of Neville Chamberlain back from Munich with his "Peace in our time" paper promise from Hitler. Winston cried: "One pound was demanded at the pistol point. When it was given two pounds was demanded; finally the dictators consented to take one pound seventeen and sixpence and the rest in promise of goodwill for the future."

Late on the night of February 20, 1938 a telephone message had reached them at Chartwell. It brought news of the sequel to Chamberlain's gesture of appeasement toward Hitler, and his offering of the hand of friendship to Mussolini. The appeasement gesture had compelled the resignation of their great personal friend, Anthony Eden. Winston was overwhelmed with despair. Here was he, an outcast, an outsider without the power of office. Anthony Eden was their one ally on the inside, thinking and feeling much as they did. Now he was gone.

Clementine, suppressing her own fearful depression at the news, tried, in some measure, to console Winston.

"My heart sank," he declared, "and for a while the dark waters of despair overwhelmed me. In a long life I have had many ups and downs. During all the war soon to come and in its darkest times I never had any trouble in sleeping. In the crisis of 1940, when so much responsibility lay upon me, and also at many very anxious, awkward moments in the following five years, I could always flop into bed and go to sleep after the day's work was done—subject of course to any emergency call. I slept sound and awoke refreshed, and had no feelings except appetite to grapple with whatever the morning's boxes might bring. But now on this night of February 20, 1938, and on this occasion only, sleep deserted me. From midnight till dawn I lay in my bed consumed by emotions of sorrow and fear. There seemed one strong young figure standing up against long, dismal, drawling tides of drift and surrender, of wrong measurements and feeble impulses. My conduct of affairs would have been different from his in various ways; but he seemed to me at this moment to embody the life-hope of the British nation, the grand old British race that had done so much for men, and had yet some more to give. Now he was gone. I watched the daylight slowly creep in through the windows and saw before me in mental gaze the vision of Death."

And then Hitler's marching armies goose-stepped into Czechoslovakia, ripping off the blinkers from the eyes of the freedom-loving peoples of the world. They turned to the only voice that had been unafraid to say in the past what the future would be. Jeers turned to cheers. It was plain for Clementine, and everyone else, to see how, in the House of Commons, his arrival was marked more closely than anyone else—and that included the Prime Minister.

Clementine read letter after letter vindicating Winston as, with almost every post, people wrote to Chartwell asking, "How much longer is Parliament and the country going to allow your energy to operate in a vacuum?"—"Your undoubted gifts and proper grasp of the situation in Europe today make it imperative, for the safety of this country and all that it stands for, that you be given an important post in the Cabinet without delay, preferably that of Minister of Defence, with full control over the defence forces of the nation," declared another letter writer.

The gathering storm had brought the increasing realization that Winston had been right. To reinforce the balance of power, he sought alliance with Russia—". . . but how improvidently foolish we should be when dangers are so great, to put needless barriers in the way of the general associations of the great Russian mass with resistance to an act of Nazi aggression."

A group of the younger Tories were already in almost open revolt, denouncing Chamberlain's weakness towards Germany, and looking to Winston as their leader. "It's all very well for those young fellows," he said to his wife, "but it's Chamberlain who has to press the button. It is a terrible thing at a time like this when you are the one man who has to decide whether to press the button or not."

In the second week of August, the French invited him to visit the "impregnable Maginot Line." On returning home he admitted to Clementine that he had been compelled to cancel the visit he had intended to make to the Duke of Windsor in the south of France, because of a warning from a leading French statesman that his life was in danger. "The Germans believe I am one of their formidable enemies. They will not stop short of assassination."

He believed in her being aware of danger if she was expected to face it. As he looked through the windows of their home at the beautiful and peaceful gardens beyond, he sat wrapped in thought, then said slowly, and sorrowfully, "Before the harvest is gathered in—we shall be at war."

They moved constantly between Chartwell and their London flat in Morpeth Mansions, near Westminster Abbey. M.P.s said they had chosen the Morpeth Mansions apartment because it was so near Parliament which meant that if he heard the division bells ring he could cover the distance to the division lobby in time to record his vote.

Clementine joined ambassadors and peers in the Distinguished Strangers' Gallery of the House on the evening of Friday, September 1. Germany had attacked Poland at dawn that morning. The mobilization of all forces had been ordered.

Few had listened to Churchill during his years in the political wilderness. All listened when the moment came. More than anyone, Clementine knew his whole life had been a preparation for that moment. All eyes were on Winston, sitting in his accustomed seat, his face clearly lined with grief. The debate was brief. He said nothing; not even to members who crowded around him as he left.

The following day was even worse. It was the first time in years that the House had sat on a Saturday. The atmosphere was almost unbearable. Clementine smiled at no one, not even the familiar faces of dear friends. She had come from Parliament Square where she had stood among the strained tense faces of people in the streets, watching the almost endless stream of buses loaded with excited, happy, shouting children heading for the distant open countryside. Children were leaving the city. Evacuation had begun.

Seated in the gallery of the Commons that day, Clementine's eyes were for the silent figure in the corner of the Front Bench below the gangway. For years he had usually had something to say, but most of those around him had been unwilling to listen. Now they waited for his words, but there were none. Clementine watched him as he sat brooding, overcome by the disaster he had foreseen for so long, until he stood up, and walked out slowly and silently.

Later that afternoon Winston returned to Morpeth Mansions and told her that he had just come from No. 10 Downing Street. The Prime Minister had sent for him. He told her Chamberlain, seeing no hope of averting war with Germany, intended to form a small War Cabinet of Ministers without departments, to conduct it, and had invited him to become a member of the War Cabinet. He had agreed to the proposal without comment, and had discussed men and measures at length with the Prime Minister.

After midnight he sat down at his desk and wrote to Mr. Chamberlain: "Aren't we a very old team? I make out that the six you mentioned to me yesterday aggregate 386 years or an average of over 64! Only one year short of the old age pension! If however you added Sinclair (49) and Eden (42) the average comes down to 57½."

After commenting on the Labor party having indicated their unwillingness to share in a National Coalition Cabinet, and his expectation that an announcement would be made of a joint declaration of war by Britain and France that afternoon he ended the note with, "I remain here at your disposal."

But no reply came the next day from Mr. Chamberlain. Last-minute efforts were being made to preserve peace.

Clementine received an unusual group of callers at their flat opposite Westminster Abbey. They were men of prominence from all parties. United in the face of tragedy, they had come to the home of the husband and wife many of them had scorned as outcasts for years, to express their deep anxiety lest Britain should fail in its obligations to invaded Poland.

At nine o'clock that Sunday morning of September 3, 1939, Hitler had been presented with the ultimatum that, unless his army was withdrawn from Poland forthwith, a state of war would exist between Britain and Germany, as from eleven o'clock that morning. Winston and Clementine listened together to the voice of brokenhearted Neville Chamberlain informing the nation in that momentous broadcast that Britain was at war with Germany. Their friend, Brendan Bracken, who later became Minister of Information, was with them.

Winston had interrupted dressing to listen to the broadcast. As soon as it ended, he resumed dressing. Minutes later, the first air-raid warning of the war sounded. Winston paused, collar half on, then, turning to Brendan Bracken, dryly and grudgingly commented, "You know, Brendan, you've *got* to hand it to Hitler. The war's been on only a few minutes and here's an air raid already!" Clementine walked into the room and also remarked on the German's promptitude and precision.

Winston stalked to the entrance of the flats and stood outside in the street staring up into the sky. Clementine hurried after him to persuade him to go to an air-raid shelter. He refused. She reminded him that it was his place to set an example to others. Back he went into the flat, and, grabbing a bottle of brandy, set off with her and members of their staff, down the street to a basement shelter which had been prepared for such an emergency. Clementine talked to him, others talked, but Winston moved around the shelter like a caged animal, hearing no one. Immediately the "All Clear" sounded he was back down the street and up to the roof at Morpeth Mansions where he stood scanning the cloudless sky for aircraft. Clementine stood beside him, saying nothing.

As they gazed over the roofs and spires of London, above them were thirty or forty antiaircraft barrage balloons. Both gave the Government a good mark for this evident sign of preparation.

Winston described the scene in the shelter that day, "Our shelter was one hundred yards down the street and consisted merely of an open basement, not even sand-bagged, in which the tenants of half-a-dozen flats were already assembled. Everyone was cheerful and jocular, as is the English manner when about to encounter the unknown. As I gazed from the doorway along the empty street and at the crowded room below, my imagination drew pictures of ruin and carnage and vast explosions shaking the ground; of buildings clattering down in dust and rubble, of fire brigades and ambulances scurrying through the smoke, beneath the drone of hostile aeroplanes. For had we not all been taught how terrible air raids would be?

"After about ten minutes had passed, the wailings broke out again. I was myself not sure that this was not a reiteration of the previous warning, but a man came running along the street shouting 'All clear,' and we dispersed to our dwellings and went about our business."

Winston's "business" was to hurry to the House of Commons which met at noon. The Prime Minister spoke, Winston spoke, but it was no "I told you so" speech.

It was the first Sunday Parliamentary sitting of the decade. In the streets outside, men were queueing at recruiting offices; lorry-loads of soldiers and arms were speeding by; people were already looking at each other with that "all in it together" feeling which was to become a national spirit.

Clementine listened in the Commons' Chamber to Chamberlain's formal announcement of the commencement of war, then watched Winston rise to pay tribute, without bitterness and with typical generosity, to those who had fought for peace. "In this solemn hour," he said, "it is a consolation to recall and to dwell upon our repeated efforts for peace. All have been ill-starred, but all have been faithful and sincere ... outside, the storms of war may blow and the land may be lashed with the fury of the gales, but in our hearts, this Sunday morning, there is peace. Our hands may be active, but our consciences are at rest...."

Afterwards they joined Sarah and their son-in-law Vic Oliver for lunch at the Olivers' apartment in Westminster. Diana and Duncan Sandys and Randolph Churchill were also there. At the end of the meal they opened a bottle of champagne. Winston stood up, raised his glass, and proposed a toast: "Victory," he said. "No one would listen to my warnings, but now that war is here, we shall have to forget the past. Britain shall never yield to her enemies." Everyone present then signed their names on a sheet of paper dated September 3, 1939.

"I shall join my regiment," said Randolph. Duncan Sandys announced he would be doing the same. Diana and Sarah discussed what war contributions they could make.

Then the phone rang. Winston was wanted on the phone. "I'll take it in the bedroom," he said. There was something in the way he said it, as if he felt this was a moment to be alone.

Clementine and the family remained seated and silent round the dining table. All instinctively felt that this was no ordinary telephone call. Each moment of Winston's absence increased the tension, then the door opened. He stood there with the fingers of both hands spread on his waistcoat looking at his family with tears in his eyes.

No one spoke until Clementine said quietly, "Tell me."

Looking straight at her, and no one else, he said, "They have given me a job again—I am First Lord of the Admiralty."

Everyone excitedly congratulated him—everyone but Clementine. She just sat looking at him.

He spoke again, "It's a wonderful feeling to know that the country needs you. I don't care any more what they said about me—now I can show them what I can do."

"What will you do?" asked Sarah.

"What am I going to do? I'm going to sleep," he answered. It was time for his regular afternoon nap, and nothing and no one would prevent him having it. He retired to the bedroom, leaving the family to discuss the war and the future.

An hour-and-a-half later he was back, refreshed. "Well, good-bye," he said.

"Where are you going?" asked Diana.

"To the Admiralty," he replied. "The *Bremen* is on the high seas, and we're going to get her." And, with that, Winston kissed Clementine and went to war.

10

Rooms in Whitehall

SHE didn't see him again until almost lunchtime the following day.

The night had brought memories to both of them of a quarter of a century before when he had walked out of the Admiralty after being removed from his post as First Lord. They had shared so much since then—triumphs, tragedies, and political oblivion.

As they lunched alone, Winston told her how, when he had walked back into the Admiralty office he had quit in pain and sorrow so long ago, he had observed that the selfsame wooden map-case he had fixed to the wall behind his chair in 1911 was still there. It was a staff officer's duty to daily mark the movements and disposition of the German fleet on the wall chart, and it was Winston's rule to check the chart as soon as he entered the room each morning. "To inculcate in myself and those working with me a sense of ever present danger," he explained.

But, apart from memories that had crowded back, he brought Clementine other news. The night war was declared the Germans had torpedoed and sunk without warning the liner *Athenia,* two hundred miles west of the Hebrides. There were one thousand four hundred passengers on board. Miraculously most of them and the crew had been saved.

After lunch he was due to resume his place on the Treasury bench, and Clementine rode with him once more to the House. He was not, as yet, Prime Minister, but was unquestionably the man to whom everyone turned as he entered the Chamber. He rose to speak, looked up, as always, at Clementine in the gallery, and was given an ovation the like of which had rarely been heard before.

He announced the news of the sinking of the *Athenia.*

This first great naval disaster of the war developed an unusual twist when the Germans, on learning that there had been 311 American citizens aboard, immediately broadcast to the world that the sinking was the work of Winston Churchill!

The telephone rang in the Churchill's apartment as they were finishing dinner that evening, and Winston was asked to take the call. When he came back into the room, he said, "Do you know who that was? The President of the United States. It is remarkable to think of being rung up in this little flat in Victoria Street by the President himself in the midst of a great war." The President had wanted a question answered concerning the *Athenia* incident. Excusing himself to their two guests, Winston added, "This is very important and I must go and see the Prime Minister at once."

Within two days Winston had reintroduced the convoy system to protect Britain's merchant fleets and supplies. By then, Clementine and Mary had moved some of their personal possessions into the small apartment at the top of the great Admiralty building in Whitehall— into rooms originally designed to house the servants of the First Lord.

Knowing Winston would live with his job twenty-four hours a day, there was only one way for her to take care of him—she had to live with the Admiralty, too. Even their apartment in Morpeth Mansions—only at the other end of Whitehall—was too far away for him.

Clementine furnished the small rooms as best she could, bringing in some of the furniture from their London flat and from Chartwell. Converting the small Admiralty apartment into some kind of home was no easy achievement with Winston cramming all the telephones and gadgets in creation into the rooms.

There was no peace in the world, and certainly no peace for anyone in that tiny apartment, with Winston's standing order that in the event of anything important happening, day or night, he was to be told whatever the hour.

His gaudy dressing gown, striped pajamas, slippers, and cigar in mouth, became a familiar awe-inspiring sight in the Admiralty corridors.

As soon as he walked through the door of the Admiralty, he wanted to see the kind of Navy he had been given, and immediately began unannounced visits to all the largest naval bases, beginning with Chatham docks. Clementine accompanied him throughout the tour.

They traveled to Thursoe in Scotland, and on arrival there embarked on a destroyer for Scapa Flow, the Navy's main base. While making for Scapa, a radio signal came through—the great warship *Courageous* had been lost with six hundred dead.

Winston, furious with the lack of defenses at Scapa Flow, ordered the immediate reorganization of the base. Before it could be done, the battleship *Royal Oak* was sunk by a U-boat which penetrated Scapa's defenses.

Winston reeled. To Clementine and to his staff he muttered, "If only they had taken notice of me a few years ago, this would not have happened." His resolve even more determined, they continued the tours as he sought information, trying to repair the neglect of years. Once again, accompanied by Clementine, he set out to see still more for himself, as well as let others see him. He wanted to know what was being done in the shipyards, in the factories, on the aerodromes, in the Army camps, and wanted everyone to see he cared. Popularity was a new thing for him, it was also a novelty for Clementine. She was always there, just beyond the glare of the spotlight in which he now walked. He inspired courage with his bulldog determination and cheerfulness in adversity, and she modestly contributed her share too. The serenity with which she shared responsibilities with him made women feel that she truly understood their fears and anxieties for their husbands, sons, and brothers.

Wherever the already famous square hat, walking stick, and cigar went, confidence and a smile followed. The jutting jaw and hunched shoulders were here, there, and everywhere, and, most of the time, two steps behind him, walked the tall erect woman with the laughing eyes, sincerely enjoying meeting people and obviously proud of her husband's new-found popularity. They were a team, a husband and wife working together for victory.

Every week or so she managed to persuade him to spend a weekend at Chartwell, but soon weekends became as arduous as the weeks. He wouldn't let up a moment and worked a 120-hour week, struggling to remedy deficiencies in naval strength.

He was able to announce that in the first two weeks of the war a tenth of Germany's submarines had been destroyed. They sowed magnetic mines; Britain found the answer. They intensified the U-boat war, hunted them day and night. "I will not say without mercy, because God forbid that we should ever part company with that, at any rate with zeal and not altogether without relish!" said Winston.

After the B.B.C.'s nine o'clock news broadcast on Sunday, October 1, 1939, Winston went to the microphone. Clementine and Mary listened in one of the little rooms above the Admiralty. It was the first of the broadcasts which were to become Britain's greatest "secret weapon"—infusing the entire nation with the will to win, with the spirit of victory.

Hitler, said Winston, had decided when the war was to begin—"It began when *he* wanted it, and it will end only when *we* are convinced that he has had enough!"

Clementine had discussed the first draft of the speech with him, and they had both agreed that this was no time for long words requiring exploration into dictionaries. They felt instinctively that for a man to be a true leader of the people, he must speak with the voice of the people, and must make his appeal in plain, direct language.

"This was their finest hour" rang through the world and into history as "their noblest occasion" could never have done. From that time on, as far as Winston was concerned, dictionaries were for others. Simple words were all he needed for his broadcasts.

The peoples of the free world are still free because, when words were all we had to fight with, Winston chose the right ones. The good humor, the fighting spirit of the people, found their expression in him. Men and women were proud to be sharing part of a lifetime with this man—this score of human beings in one—who will rank in history books with Alexander the Great, with Julius Caesar, Napoleon, Cromwell, Nelson, and Lincoln. They put their trust and lives in the hands of a man who, his friends said, "did his honest and cheerful best to kill himself in the public service."

The drafts of all his speeches were shown to Clementine for comment —comments that were often noted when he revised and polished the scripts until they shone with the literary perfection he demands of himself. Clementine's practical sense enabled her to be the perfect counselor, seeing aspects in a speech that he had sometimes overlooked in his enthusiasm. She had learned much of the politician's art from him, but understood more than he had taught her. She could often sway him on points of detail, or where personalities were concerned. Her shrewdness, her authority, and deep understanding of him, helped fashion many of his words as well as the architecture of his life.

A soldier in a hospital she visited during the war remarked, "She looks like a grand dame without speaking like one." Both she and Winston could speak from the heart, speak with the voice and words of the people.

Many of his greatest speeches were dictated from his bed. Because of his complete absorption when he worked, Clementine was compelled to introduce her own fire-safety measures. Winston had the unfortunate habit of sometimes forgetfully throwing a lighted cigar into the waste-paper basket beside the bed instead of into his basket-style ash tray. As a result, she issued a standing order for a syphon of soda water to be kept handy in the bedroom to deal with the occasional fires he started.

Six weeks after his first great wartime broadcast, he went to the microphone again. While not underrating the dangers, his voice injected confidence into the millions listening. Hitler was "that evil man over there," and Ribbentrop "that prodigious contortionist." Listeners laughed as Winston had meant them to laugh, and the laughter he provoked brought hope.

The range and depth of his knowledge, his almost magical sensitivity to the mood of the man in the street, astonished admirers and opponents alike. Part of the secret was an eagerness to hear the opinions of ordinary people with whom either he or Clementine came into contact. Enveloped as he was in his work, he mainly relied on her to keep a close watch for him on the pulse and temperature of public trends and opinions. She was his liaison with the domestic scene.

During the winter of that year the Churchills became friendly with the Chamberlains, and Mr. and Mrs. Neville Chamberlain came to dine with them in their crammed apartment above Admiralty House. There were just the four of them present. It was quite an event, because it was really the only friendly social conversation they had ever shared with the Chamberlains in all the twenty years they had known them, and it was to become an outstanding occasion in other ways too.

During dinner the war went on and things happened. With the soup an officer came up from the War Room below to report that a U-boat had been sunk. With the dessert he came again and reported that a second U-boat had been sunk; and just before the ladies left the dining room he came a third time to report that yet another U-boat had been sunk. Nothing like this had ever happened before in a single day, and it was more than a year before such a record was repeated.

As the ladies left them, Mrs. Chamberlain, with a naïve and charming glance, said to Winston, "Did you arrange all this on purpose?"

Reported Winston, "I assured her that if she would come again we would produce a similar result."

There were few rays of hope that winter. Winston rarely left his office so it was fortunate that they had set up their little home in the Admiralty itself, otherwise he would not have snatched any moments of relaxation. Clementine tried to introduce as much comfort as possible to ease his endless hours of strain. She devoted particular attention to the room in which he had to spend most of his time—his office. Two arm-chairs were drawn up side by side in front of the cheerful coal fire burning in the grate. Winston would read his papers sitting in one of them. Clementine had all the chairs in the room upholstered in red leather, except the one at his desk which was very plain, with no up-holstery whatever, and a wooden curved back like half a barrel. It looked strangely small for such a big man.

She arranged his desk not square and straight in the room, but side-ways, thereby making it impossible for him to overlook the deceptively distracting peaceful scene in the park below. Constantly, on a table at the side of the desk, stood glasses on a tray, a syphon of soda water, and a metal box looking like a gas-mask container, but actually a tin of biscuits.

The only personal possession introduced into the office was the chart presented to him when he was Minister of Munitions in the First World War. The chart is a graph of gun production, and along the top of it is a row of black lions in silhouette. The first lion is lying down, the next, as the graph rises, sits on its haunches, and as the graph reaches its greatest heights, the lion stands on its legs.

Churchill's only brief relaxation each day was the time spent with Clementine at luncheon or dinner. Every night the ritual was the same. Before going to bed, he would walk into the Operations Room to take final account of the day's information. It was in this Operations Room that he sat tensely through the hours as the *Exeter, Achilles,* and *Ajax* hunted the German pocket battleship, the *Graf Spee,* and it was in this same room twenty-five years before that he had sat as Von Spee, the famous German naval commander, was gunned to death in the battle of the Falkland Islands.

Suddenly, news that lifted everyone's heart reached the room. Un-able to contain his excitement, he rushed upstairs to tell Clementine. The "little ships"—*Exeter, Achilles,* and *Ajax*—had located the *Graf Spee,* which had been roaming the North and South Atlantic, sinking merchant ships on a terrifying scale. Engaging the *Spee,* the three little cruisers hurt her, slowed her up, and chased her into Montevideo har-bor. The British warships were badly knocked about too, but stayed right outside the harbor, waiting for the chance to finish off the *Spee.* The rest is history—the *Spee* was scuttled and the world echoed with the victory.

Soon afterwards, H.M.S. *Cossack* attacked the German prison ship

Altmark in Norwegian waters, freeing 299 British prisoners. Winston, master psychologist as well as master strategist, seized the opportunity to give the nation the tonic it needed.

He saw that these two great victories at sea could be turned into victories for home-front morale, and ordered a welcome-home luncheon to be given at London's ancient Guildhall at which the city would honor the men of the *Ajax* and *Exeter* on their return.

Weeks later the little ships arrived home to a fantastic reception. Clementine and Winston were among the thousands standing on the quayside at Plymouth when the ships sailed into port to a deafening greeting from ships' sirens and cheering crowds. London's turn to honor the crews of the *Exeter* and *Ajax* followed. They came to the city and marched from Waterloo Station to the Horseguard's Parade, where His Majesty King George VI, Winston, the entire Cabinet, and a host of other dignitaries awaited them.

Clementine watched the proceedings from the window of Winston's room in the Admiralty in the company of her personal guest for the occasion—Her Majesty the Queen.

The crews of the two little warships lined up, and Winston presented them to His Majesty, who decorated a number of them. The watching, boisterous thousands hushed as the widow of Marine Wilfrid A. Russell, of the *Exeter,* walked up to His Majesty to receive her husband's posthumous award of the Medal for Conspicuous Gallantry. Immediately following the ceremony, the Queen and Clementine joined the King and Winston on the saluting base to honor the crews' march-past.

When the march-past had ended, the four left the saluting base and moved to a quiet corner of the parade ground where relatives of those who had lost their lives in the Battle of the River Plate action were waiting. The King and Queen and Winston and Clementine spoke to each of them.

This special enclosure on the Horseguard's Parade, which had been exclusively reserved for those who had lost sons or husbands in the battle, was Clementine's personal idea. She never forgot the little things that mattered so much, nor the right things to do, so she arranged for all the bereaved relatives to be comfortably seated to witness the great ceremony from a vantage point close to Admiralty House, and also arranged for coffee and other refreshments to be served to them.

Winston and Celmentine drove to the Guildhall for the great luncheon of honor. Winston was in form. The end of the *Graf Spee,* he said, "has warmed the cockles of our hearts." And the cry of the *Cossack*'s boarding party—"The Navy's here!"—when its crew boarded the *Altmark* to free the prisoners battened down below the hatches, Winston put in the same historic proud place as Nelson's signal at the Battle of Trafalgar.

After the luncheon Winston and Clementine had to wait a few moments outside for their car. They were suddenly surrounded by hundreds of sailors who poured out of the Guildhall. Some shook him by the hand, others slapped him on the back, and some of the too-hearty slaps made Winston wince once or twice. They were moved by the warmth of their greeting, and as he and Clementine entered the car, he was near to tears.

As the appetite of the fighting services for men and munitions grew, it was to Clementine that he turned for expert advice. His years as the special target of the Suffragette movement had made him a little cautious when it came to the role of women in war. He had his own natural prejudices to overcome. To him, the idea of women entering the the line of battle, and fighting in war, was revolting. "The whole civilization of the Western world is based upon the traditions of chivalry which have come down from medieval times and still exert a potent force," he maintained. "It has become a matter of instinct among the most valiant races that women and children should be spared. If the ship is sinking, they must be the first to be placed in the lifeboats. If the house is on fire, they are the first to be rescued. The deepest conceptions of the highest races are based upon the privilege and protection of women from brutal violence, and upon the sacred duty of their menfolk to die in their defense, or sacrifice their lives for their safety. It is this great body of conviction which is outraged by the idea of women standing side by side with men in the bloody trench, and slaughtering human beings with whatever weapons are available. Such a spectacle seems to us unnatural, subhuman, odious, and shameful in the last degree."

Although later in the war his own daughters were to enter the Forces, the chivalrous cavalier in him made him shirk from advocating extensive use of women in war, although he admitted that the immunity of women from violence was taken so much for granted that few appreciated to what extent the protective cloak around them had already been discarded. Women's own demand for equal status had been partially responsible for this, and their place in life had also changed in Hitler's Germany, Mussolini's Italy, and in Soviet Russia. "Thus we see progressive and reactionary forces luring women nearer to danger, and exposing them to the retaliation of the enemy," he declared.

Although admitting that the prejudice against women fighting goes further than the roots of our civilization, extending to the earliest beginnings of mankind, he added, "Everyone will applaud a woman who defended her children against wolves; and when human beings fall to the level of wolves in their pitiless ferocity, the distinction between the sexes perishes with all other human traits."

Clementine recalled the words of Lady Jellicoe in the previous world war, when she had said, "The truth is, this is not a 'man's war,' as wars have been hitherto, but one in which both sexes must share the burden and responsibilities."

"Aerial bombs do not discriminate between the sexes. There is no politeness about gas," said Winston.

Clementine was certain that if the picture were put clearly before them, the women of Britain would flock to reinforce fighting units by taking over administrative duties; helping to operate antiaircraft batteries; and staffing armaments factories despite the knowledge that these factories were certain targets for the *Luftwaffe*. There were many things that women could do, apart from killing, that could add to the fighting power of the Army, Navy, and Air Force, and Clementine assured Winston that if the call were made, the women of Britain would answer it.

Winston sat down and wrote a speech—for women only. When he had completed the draft, Clementine read it through and suggested several alterations. He followed her advice. It was one subject on which she was the undoubted expert in the family.

She was with him on January 27, 1940, in Manchester's great Free Trade Hall when he stood up and walked to the front of the platform to address the packed gathering. The audience was almost entirely women. He spoke to them sympathetically, directly. He had come to the center of industrial Britain to ask for a million women workers to help the war effort. It was a startling beginning. It was, in fact, the opening of something much more—it was also the beginning of a radical social change in a way of life.

The only reserve of female labor in the country was among wives of men already in the Services or the war factories. They would have to create a new pattern for living, to free themselves as much as possible from the ties of family and homes, and devote these hours of freedom to the war. With passion and fire he called, "Come then, let us to the task, to the battle, to the toil—each to our art; each to our station. Fill the armies, rule the air, pour out the munitions, strangle the U-boats, sweep the mines, plough the land, build the ships, guard the streets, succor the wounded, uplift the downcast, honor the brave. Let us go forward together in all parts of the Empire, in all parts of the island. There is not a week, nor a day, nor an hour to lose."

For the first time in his life, Winston—a man's man—managed to appeal to the women, and win them to his side as a powerful ally. The historic speech inspired by his wife's "woman's sense" brought him the million women workers he asked for—and millions more to the Services and factories.

The United States Ambassador, Mr. John G. Winant, considered there was no greater evidence of Britain's unity of purpose than the response of the women. He recalled hearing Winston complain that the R.A.F. required seventy men on the ground to keep a plane in the air. This conversation took place at the Churchills' dinner table. "I was present when the Prime Minister, while talking of the antiaircraft services, criticized the number of soldiers assigned per gun."

Winston appreciated that each pair of hands assigned to a gun was necessary for its intricate manipulation, but other branches of the Army were dangerously short of manpower, so he sent for General Sir Frederick Pile, the chief of the Antiaircraft Command.

Sir Frederick recalled the luncheon meeting that followed. "The Prime Minister, Mrs. Churchill, one or two others concerned with the direction of the war, and myself, were present, when Mr. Churchill looked at me and said, 'General, I have grave news for you.' I said I was very sorry to hear that. 'You are just getting your new weapons and new equipment, and now I want a lot of men from you,' said Winston.

" 'Well, sir, that's all right,' I said.

" 'You're very cheerful about it,' he replied.

" 'I'll replace them with women,' I answered.

" 'If you can do that it's as good as a first-class victory—to gain forty thousand men,' he said. 'If you can get these women as replacements, I'll get Mary to join you as one of them.'

"Mrs. Churchill said, 'That is an excellent suggestion.' Mary wasn't with us at the time, but both her parents were thrilled with the thought, and Mary, who started out as a Private, turned out to be one of my biggest assets. She's a good girl.

"Some doubted whether women would make efficient substitutes for men on the gun sites. Everyone present at this meeting was shattered with the idea, and I remember one Minister remarking, 'This is a most revolutionary proposal and I cannot believe anybody in England will accept it.'

" 'I don't see why not,' said Mrs. Churchill. 'If women can do all that they are doing in fire-fighting and everything else, I don't see why they shouldn't man guns.'

"I pointed out that we would be only asking them, at the moment, to man technical equipment.

" 'They will probably do it a great deal better than men because they are so much more light-fingered and your equipment needs a deft but delicate touch,' Mrs. Churchill added.

"In point of fact, it turned out to be so, and the best batteries in the flying-bomb blitz were those operated by women—they shot down, on the average, far more than the men. The whole thing depended on the delicate balance of the instruments, and men were more heavy-handed than women at this particular job.

"Winston completely agreed with his wife that using women on the antiaircraft guns was a magnificent idea. She was always behind him, and had a tremendous influence on him. For example, when he was difficult with us at times—and that was often—she would say, 'Now, Winston, that's all right, the subject can be let rest for the moment. We are going to have luncheon.' He used to get worked up and stamp round the room, but this didn't deter her one little bit. She bossed him—but in the most delightful way—with great affection and with the deepest understanding of his nature. I was always amazed that this great man could be led along like a sheep by her whenever she thought it necessary. This was partially because of his great admiration for her, and also because he had such a justifiably high regard for her intellect and judgment. She has a first-class brain. Everything she did was, above all, for his good."

Winston continued to push himself beyond all normal limits, and Clementine became increasingly concerned as to how long he could maintain the frightening pace. Her attempts to make him take greater care of his health suddenly received support from an unexpected quarter. A letter arrived from Buckingham Palace. It was a personal message for Winston. After congratulating him on his direction of the Navy, His Majesty added, "I also beg of you to take care of yourself and get as much rest as you possibly can in these critical days."

While disillusioned peacemaker Neville Chamberlain made his war progress pronouncements in tones that sank the hearts of men and women, Winston's words of hope and defiance said what everyone wanted said and raised them up again.

It was a very happy day when Winston could tell Clementine that yet another ship had been launched. With each fresh addition to naval strength, his personal strength and spirit seemed renewed. In spring of 1940, at Barrow-in-Furness, he gave her the honor of launching an aircraft carrier.

On their return from the launching, he handed a news bulletin to her. It stated that Ley, leader of the Nazi Labor Front, in a broadcast from Rotterdam, had announced that he was planning cruises for German workers to spend their holidays at the most popular seaside resorts on the south coast of England! The cruises were scheduled for the late summer of that year—an indication of the confidence of Hitler and his generals in their plan to invade Britain during the summer of 1940. "Do you think the Nazis can get aboard this island?" she asked.

"No," he answered. "But they'll make a mighty try. At least I would if I were Hitler." Then, opening his coat and revealing his revolver in its holster, he added, "If they do try, I'll get a few before they take me," and they both laughed.

The following month he brought her further news—this time of a change in his Cabinet job. Chamberlain had appointed him chief of a committee of Service Ministers whose duty it was to guide the War Cabinet in the general conduct of the war.

From then on not a moment of their lives was lived apart from war and thoughts of war. Winston was completely loyal to Neville Chamberlain, but Chamberlain was unable to give the people the inspired leadership they needed.

Suddenly, Hitler invaded Norway and Denmark. Winston ordered the Fleet into action and a British expeditionary force was sent to help the Norwegians. Without adequate air cover, it had no chance.

Allegations that the Norway campaign had been mishandled were followed by demands for a debate in the House of Commons. M.P.s were bitter and angry. The full force of their wrath came down on Mr. Chamberlain. When, on the second day of the debate, Winston attempted to accept responsibility, his effort was waved aside. Winston wound up the debate for the Government fighting for Chamberlain and denouncing Socialists who had also rejected rearmament. As the hands of the clock moved to ten, when the vote would be taken, neither

Clementine nor anyone else could hear him above the angry shouts from the Socialists' benches.

As Neville Chamberlain left Parliament that night, knowing his Premiership was virtually at an end, a new crisis arose across the Channel in Holland. Chamberlain strove vainly to save his régime by inviting the Socialists to join his Cabinet. In the middle of the negotiations, Hitler began the invasion of Holland, Belgium, and Luxembourg, and the British Expeditionary Force in France faced its Dunkirk.

"I would have answered that we would be lucky if we safely got away twenty or thirty thousand," Churchill told Clementine. "It is now ninety thousand, and more landing every hour." In four momentous days of Dunkirk, the 215,000 British and 120,000 French were rescued.

On the afternoon of May 10, 1940, in the ninth month of the war he had foreseen and striven to forestall, Winston received a message at the Admiralty. It had come from Buckingham Palace. He went straight upstairs to Clementine in the rooms above his office to tell her the King had sent for him.

They had shared many crises in their years together, and even before, in his youth, he had narrowly escaped death, and had said, "These hazards swoop on me out of a cloudless sky, and that I have hitherto come unscathed through them, while it fills my heart with thankfulness to God for His mercies, makes me wonder why I must so often thrust to the brink and then withdraw."

It was in that same little room in which he now broke the momentous news to her, that he had declared to her, and to his friend Lord Riddell, on his dismissal from the Admiralty in the First World War, "I am finished." Lord Riddell had replied, "Not finished at forty, with your remarkable powers!"

"Yes," said Winston, "finished in respect of all I care for. . . ."

Now he was about to achieve his life's ambition. He was the one man all parties—and the people—were ready to follow. He left Clementine and the Admiralty building, looking tense and strained. His hour had come, but what an hour!

As he stepped from the car on returning to the Admiralty, one of his staff, congratulating him, said, "I only wish that the position had come your way in better times for you have taken on an enormous task."

Winston replied gravely, "God alone knows how great it is. All I hope is that it is not too late. I am very much afraid it is. We can only do our best."

With that, he climbed the stairs to his private apartment, and to his wife—Prime Minister of Great Britain.

The night of May 10, 1940, was also her hour. After seeing his advice neglected for so long, he had at last been called upon to try and save his country from the consequences which neglect of his warnings had entailed. His call to office coincided with one of the worst military disasters in modern history, and she realized that had it not been for this catastrophe he might never have reached the Premiership.

On the night he became Prime Minister, he wrote, "As I went to bed at 3 A.M., I was conscious of a profound sense of relief. At last I had the authority to give directions over the whole scene. I felt as if I were walking with Destiny and that all my past life had been but a preparation for this hour and for this trial."

To the Parliament that had unanimously chosen him as its leader, Winston, in his inaugural address, spoke his undying, "I have nothing to offer but blood, toil, tears, and sweat."

Then, in words every man and woman would understand, he cried, "You ask, what is our policy? I will say it is to wage war, by sea, land, and air, with all our might and with all the strength that God can give us. You ask, what is our aim? I can answer in one word: victory—victory at all costs, victory in spite of all terror, victory, however long and hard the road may be; for without victory, there is no survival." The words rang through the Chamber, reflecting the spirit within the people, and turning it into a verbal flag he waved for all to see.

In a congratulatory speech their lifelong personal friend, Liberal leader Sir Archibald Sinclair, declared that everyone was delighted he had replaced Mr. Chamberlain. Although what Winston murmured was an aside made as he remained in his seat, Clementine and many M.P.s present clearly heard him say, "He's a finer man than I could ever be."

Winston was sixty-six. He had waited for supreme Ministerial power through years of drift, dishonor, and disaster. Now he had achieved this power at a critical hour, but knowing his nature, she felt it was, perhaps, fortunate that the hour was critical. He excelled in moments of crisis; he would use the imminence of danger to close the ranks which had begun to gape. Clementine knew power came to him not as a load but as a release. The terrible burden he was about to bear on his broad shoulders was to be her burden too.

11

Blitz

WINSTON was flying back and forth across the Channel for emergency meetings, desperately trying to save what he could from disaster, striving to breathe strength into gasping France. He arranged to go there for yet another conference. Flying weather was bad, and the Air Staff, concerned at the danger, pressed him to abandon the flight. He refused.

"They came to me to see if I could help," said General Lord Ismay, Winston's Chief of Staff at the Ministry of Defence. "They said, 'The Prime Minister's going to France—have you heard?' and I said, 'Yes, I'm going with him.' They warned me that flying conditions were very bad, but I replied that they were pretty rough, but not as bad as all that. They insisted that it was too risky for the Prime Minister to go, but I disagreed and said I thought he ought to go, so off they went to Clemmie to tell her that Winston shouldn't go to France, and to ask her to persuade him not to risk the weather. She listened, and then asked, 'Are the Air Force flying today?' They answered, 'Oh, yes, of course—on operations.' She replied, 'Well, isn't Winston going on an operation?' And that was that."

During one of these cross-Channel visits he went into a little French restaurant for a meal. A woman—later identified as a French duchess—stood waiting for him in the courtyard. As he emerged, she jumped at him, with a knife—determined to kill the Englishman whom she considered responsible for the downfall of France! Winston's bodyguard caught her with a rugby tackle. Clementine was informed of the murder attempt, but, on his return, Winston talked only of the evacuation of Forces.

And when the blitz of 1940 began in all its fury, there was no holding him—he just couldn't help it. The drone of enemy planes overhead, the screaming and crashing of bombs, and the answering thunder and flashing of antiaircraft defenses were an irresistible smell of danger to him. Londoners were taking it, and Winston was determined to take it with them.

He stood with Clementine in a doorway close to No. 10 Downing Street, watching the searchlights tear away the cover of darkness and the antiaircraft barrage turn the sky into a hell. There was an ominous whistling. "Something is coming this way!" someone shouted. A shattering explosion followed almost directly opposite the doorway in which they were standing, and flying shrapnel hit one of their party.

Winston's Cabinet colleagues tried their utmost to persuade him not to take undue risks; not to go off into the night, walking stick in one hand and electric torch in the other, "to see for himself." Many hopelessly tried to stop him taking deliberate risks. It was Clementine who succeeded, and she achieved victory by outmaneuvering him. But then, she knew her Winston. She used a secret weapon—herself. Living with Winston had taught her the value of carefully timed counterattack. She waited.

At first, his jaw and cigar jutting defiantly forward, he was everywhere. No sooner had the "All Clear" sounded after the first heavy attack on London's docks than he was off personally to inspect the devastation. Fires were still raging, but when Winston stepped out of his car hundreds, who had been battered mercilessly, mobbed him, shouting, "Good old Winnie! We thought you'd come and see us."

When he heard this, and caught sight of the tiny paper Union Jacks planted on top of great mounds of death and desolation, he couldn't restrain his emotions, nor his tears. "You see, he really cares; he's crying," said one woman.

Winston, who disliked exercise, walked miles among the rubble and still-smoking skeletons of buildings. As darkness began to creep up on the day, dock authorities became anxious for Winston to leave for home. Recalls Lord Ismay, who accompanied him on that first blitz inspection tour, "He was in one of his most obstinate moods and insisted that he wanted to see everything. Consequently, we were still with him at the brightly lit target when the *Luftwaffe* arrived on the scene and the fireworks started. It was difficult to get a large car out of the area, owing to many of the streets being completely blocked by fallen houses. As we were trying to turn in a very narrow space, a shower of incendiary bombs fell just in front of us. Churchill, feigning innocence, asked what they were. I replied that they were incendiaries, and that we were evidently in the middle of the bull's-eye! It was very late by the time we got back to No. 10 Downing Street, and Cabinet Ministers, secretaries, policemen, and orderlies were waiting in the long passage in great anxiety. Churchill strode through them, without a word, leaving me to be rebuked by all and sundry for having allowed the Prime Minister to take such risks. Fatigue and fright are not conducive to patience, and I am alleged to have told the assembled company, in the language of the barracks room, that anybody who imagined they could control him on jaunts of this kind was welcome to try his hand on the next occasion."

Clementine's "Save-Winston-from-himself" campaign began the next day.

"When he went on yet another tour she went along with him. This time, concerned for *her* safety, he returned home before nightfall," said Lord Ismay. "I was very much aware that this was her technique. Her presence made him cautious for her."

Day after day Winston and Clementine walked together over rubble that was once homes, talking to the homeless, listening to their needs. He became the idol of the people, and the people were lucky in their idol—they could trust him with a tyrant's power because they knew he would not use it like a tyrant. He humbly accepted the confidence they willingly reposed in him. Cheered by families in streets in the East End of London that had been bombed to dust the previous night, he turned a tearstained face to his wife and said, "They greet me like a conquering hero. God knows why. They are a great people." They knew he was doing his best, and that his best was the best that could be done.

He strengthened them with his brand of bombing arithmetic, "It would take ten years," he said, "at the present rate, for half the houses of London to be demolished. After that, of course, progress would be much slower...."

Clementine tramped with him through mud and slush to visit gun sites; joined him as he drove in a jeep through the shattered streets giving his V-sign acknowledgment to the cheering people. She knew he undertook these journeys not only to instill encouragement into the people by his appearance among them, but also because their continued spirit in turn strengthened him.

They went down to the South Coast to inspect invasion defenses. From Rottingdean to Shoreham, one brigade of some three thousand men was stretched in a thin line along ten miles of densely populated coastline. These few troops would have stood little chance against well-organized invasion, even so this was then probably one of the most strongly defended parts of Britain, and few realized how thin was the shield protecting them against Hitler's armies across the Channel. In command of these defenses was Lieutenant General Sir Brian Horrocks.

Sir Brian met Winston and Clementine when they came to see the defenses and watch the Royal Ulster Rifles carry out a small exercise. Said General Brian Horrocks, "Though no one knew of his visit, he was quickly spotted and a large enthusiastic crowd soon gathered. The complete confidence shown in him was most touching, and rather frightening to us who knew that, to all intents and purposes, the military cupboard was bare. During one of these spontaneous demonstrations of affection, I found myself standing at the back behind Mrs. Churchill. There were tears in her eyes, and I heard her murmur, 'Pray God, we don't let them down.'"

When he stubbornly went out at night while bombs were falling, Clementine insisted on going too. She never made any fuss about it, never said, "Look here, Winston, I don't want you to go." She knew it would have been a terrible thing for both of them, for he would have probably done as she asked, but, for the first time, he would have been caged in, and it could have broken him.

Said Lord Ismay, "She knew him completely, knew precisely how to handle him. She might instigate a brake on him, but any actual *decision* to brake would be his. She would work behind the scenes, talk to Cabinet colleagues, and members of their personal staff to enlist help in protecting him in every possible way—in spite of himself. But I have never known her to oppose him directly in such matters. She would tell the staff the line to take—we'd get the 'party' line from her to take with the Boss."

She operated her own "espionage" service on his movements to discover when and where there was likely to be any element of risk, and would then try to engineer herself on such visits. To Winston, it was one thing to be outmaneuvered, another to be denied freedom of decision, even if it was the decision to endanger his own life. Clementine therefore concentrated on demagnetizing, as far as possible, his attraction to danger. She tried to divert his course.

"She persuaded him to use an air-raid shelter *as an example to others,*" added Lord Ismay. "Reluctantly, he agreed, and the disused underground station at nearby Storey's Gate was equipped as a special shelter for the regular occupants and visitors to No. 10." This was the shelter that became known as the "Annex." Winston still preferred working above ground, and sometimes asserted his defiance. And Clementine herself did regular fire-watching duty near Downing Street.

From September 7, 1940, to November 3, an average of two hundred German bombers attacked London every night. Time after time, Winston—and Clementine—remained at Downing Street until well after the alert had sounded and bombs were dropping. He would then step out and walk round St. James's Park before going into the Downing Street Annex. One night they entered the Annex only minutes before a thousand-pound bomb dropped onto the pavement at the end of the street along which they had just walked. Frequently, they would watch the bombing from the flat roof of the Annex and, if he saw a building ablaze close by, he would often say, "We will go over there," and off they went.

Millions of Londoners slept in their beds and took their chances. Others took refuge in the rapidly multiplying brick, concrete, and metal shelters, while thousands more made their way, night after night, to underground railway stations to snatch what little sleep they could on the bare concrete platforms of the tubes.

Suddenly, it was decreed that underground stations should not be used for shelters. Thousands of nightly tube-squatters considered the decision "rubbish," and displayed their opinion by continuing to use the stations as air-raid cover.

One night, without Winston's knowledge, Clementine journeyed into a blitz to "see for herself," and tour tube stations. She saw, and decided. She hurried back to Downing Street in time for dinner with Winston. She had something to tell him. As they ate alone, she explained where she had been and what she had seen. "Something must be done for these people—and quickly," she emphasized, although emphasis was no longer necessary—Winston had heard enough.

"You work something out, Clemmie," he said.

She began immediately, and recruited Lord Beaverbrook as her ally, appreciating that the problem required dynamic speed and organization. Hearing Clementine's report, Lord Beaverbrook visited tube stations, walked among the men, women, and children huddled on the platforms without comfort yet full of spirit. Lord Beaverbrook's report to Winston confirmed everything Clementine had said. Winston questioned the Cabinet on why the tubes couldn't be used stressing that he favored widespread utilization of both the underground stations and tube railway tracks themselves.

Clementine suggested it was important for fixed places to be assigned by ticket in the tube shelters, to avoid overcrowding, unfairness, and to ensure orderliness. She also proposed the installation of bunks in which the shelter-goers could sleep.

Lord Beaverbrook, with customary speed, put Clementine's and his own ideas into effect. Two million bunks were ordered and the tube stations became London's great air-raid dormitories.

It was decided that No. 10 Downing Street was a deathtrap, and would never survive a direct hit. Two bombs brought home the point. One hit the Treasury, at the back of No. 10, splitting its walls on one side and shattering furniture with the blast. The second bomb came closer.

Clementine had completed all the arrangements for a Downing Street dinner that evening. Three Ministers were guests. The night blitz began. Mrs. Landemare, the cook, and the kitchen maid, continued working in the kitchen beside the twenty-five-foot-high plate-glass window. Winston, acting on a premonition, went into the kitchen and, telling the butler to put the dinner on the hotplate in the dining room, ordered everyone there into shelter. He then returned to his dinner and his guests. Within three minutes the bomb hit the house and a blast devastated the kitchen. After the incident, Clementine's insistence that he take stricter raid precautions met with success for the first time.

Before the war, the railway authorities had constructed extensive underground offices below Piccadilly. They were seventy feet below the surface, and covered with strong, high buildings. From the middle of October until the end of that year, Winston and Clementine used this when the night raids began. There, in safety, he was able to transact his conduct of the war, and sleep undisturbed. "One felt a natural compunction at having much more safety than most other people; but so many pressed me that I let them have their way," said Winston.

Eventually, the Annex adjoining No. 10 Downing Street was strengthened, and they moved back. "Here during the rest of the war my wife and I lived comfortably," said Winston years later. "We felt confident in this solid stone building, and only on very rare occasions went down below the armor. My wife even hung up our few pictures in the sittingroom, which I thought it better to keep bare. Her view prevailed and was justified by the splendid view of London on clear nights. They made a place for me with light overhead-cover from splinters, and one could walk in the moonlight and watch the fireworks.

In 1941 I used to take some of my American visitors up there from time to time after dinner. They were always most interested."

When they entertained guests for dinner at Downing Street on blitz nights, they would always see their visitors to their cars, frequently stepping out into the street with them as the searchlights swept the sky, guns boomed, and bombs dropped. And sometimes Clementine arranged for guests to be taken home in armored cars.

During the autumn and winter of that year, Winston took to making frequent night tours of antiaircraft gun sites in action. His disregard of danger was frightening. Clementine requested an armored car to be put at his disposal. "Mr. Churchill won't ride in it," said his chauffeur.

"He will," answered Clementine, "there won't be any other car waiting for him when he goes out."

That night, Winston stepped out of No. 10, saw the new car, and said, "What's this for?"

"Well, sir," answered his bodyguard, detective Thompson, "you're going round the gun sites, the bombs are coming down, and what with all the firing and shrapnel, we've got to keep you reasonably safe from bits of metal in the air."

"I won't ride in it," answered Winston determinedly. "I'll ride in the police car."

"I'm sorry, it's not available," he was informed. Clementine had taken the precaution of making certain no alternative transport would be available. Winston was furious. Without a word, he got into the armored car and was driven off. As they traveled on, shrapnel peppered the car and smashed the hood; bombs rained down narrowly missing the car, which eventually reached Richmond Park.

"Winston watched the gun crews in action," said General Sir Frederick Pile, "and as he was about to leave he strode up to one of my staff-car drivers and asked, "Is this car armored?"

" 'No sir,' came the reply.

" 'Sure?' queried Winston.

" 'Yes sir,' answered the driver.

"Winston immediately commandeered one of my ordinary staff cars, and left his armored car behind. He said the armored car was 'very uncomfortable' and he didn't want it. He didn't see why he should travel around in an 'iron box.' He was furious."

As he was about to enter the car, a strange thing occurred. The nearside door of the car was opened for him—he always sat on the near-side. For no apparent reason, he stopped, turned, opened the door on the other side of the car himself, got in, and sat there instead. He had never done this before. The car moved off, and proceeded to travel along the Kingston bypass at about sixty miles per hour. The raid on London was still on. Suddenly a bomb fell close to the car. The explosion lifted it onto two weels, and as it was about to somersault over, it righted itself again and the car sped on.

"That was a near one," joked Winston, "it must have been my beef on this side that pulled it down."

If he had been sitting on the near-side, the car would have unquestionably turned over as the full force of the explosion lifted up the off-side. Obviously only Winston's extra weight had prevented disaster.

Although he didn't mention this escape to Clementine, she heard about it anyway and decided on a new course of action. Questioning him on the incident, she asked, "Why did you get in on that side?"

"I don't know, I don't know," Winston answered at first. Then he said, "Of course I know. Something said to me 'Stop!' before I reached the car door held open for me. It then appeared to me that I was told I was meant to open the door on the other side and get in and sit there— and that's what I did."

Clementine's renewed counteroffensive worked. She again used his fear for her safety as a weapon. As he was about to leave on his next gun-site tour, she appeared in coat and headscarf, dressed to join him. He protested. Ignoring his protests, she simply got into the car with him.

"Let's go and see Mary," she said, and off the car went to the anti-aircraft unit of which their daughter Mary was a member of the battery crew.

"She was always visiting antiaircraft batteries by day and night, and she went to the searchlight units too," said General Sir Frederick Pile. "Her visits were worth a guinea a minute to me as a morale booster— she was fabulous. She would shake hands with almost everyone, and especially all the girls. Her tours of batteries were not limited to the London area—she went all over the country, including isolated sites in remote places.

"At each site she always inquired about the girls' comfort, would go into their huts, inspect their beds, their equipment, the kitchens and their food, to make sure that they were all that they should be. She was very hot on this kind of thing.

"She traveled down to the South Coast antiaircraft batteries, and would go there with Winston not only to see the batteries in action, but also to be sure of getting him home early, otherwise the man would have stayed there till all hours.

"When she went to bombed areas, she had a remarkable effect on people—she managed to transfer to them a feeling of calmness and confidence.

"I was at Downing Street the morning after one of their blitz-area visits, when Clementine brought in a little posy of flowers for Winston. She said, 'These have just come from one of the women we saw yesterday in the East End to thank you for your visit.' He slumped down on to the table, buried his face in his hands, and wept.

"She would often say to me, 'We've got to look after the Prime Minister. He's being rather naughty about something or other; see that he wraps up; see that he goes in the right car'—in other words the armored car. I frequently switched cars on him when he went into bad territory, and he always grumbled. He used to take a lot from me. He used to say, 'I won't do that!' and then after about five minutes he'd do it.

"Returning from one trip he said, 'I'm very cold—my feet are cold.' I said, 'There's only one thing to do, you must take your shoes off and wrap your feet in a rug.' He refused. I said, 'I've done this many times, and it's a good way of getting your feet warm. Wrap 'em up—take your shoes off.' So he reluctantly said 'All right,' then after a few minutes added, 'You were right, my feet are warm.'

"The rugs were always in our cars—provided by Clementine. She always made certain he had all the comfort and protection that could be provided, and it was up to us to see that he used it. She maneuvered him into the safest car; made sure he had a warm coat, scarf, and anything else that might be necessary.

"She and Winston's assistant, Tommy Thompson, were a strong team. Between the two of them, they endeavored to achieve the best possible job of looking after him. Tommy didn't necessarily go on the various journeys—as a rule, she accompanied him most of the time, but he was a terrible man for ringing up at ten o'clock at night and saying, 'I'm coming!—bombs are dropping on the West End and I'm going down to have a look.' I used to say, 'Alright, sir, if you want to.' I went to meet him right away, and Clementine was usually with him, although he sometimes managed to slip off by himself unexpectedly. He couldn't resist danger and she knew this, which is why she used his fear for her safety as a weapon."

Clementine made many blitz tours without Winston—and often

without his knowledge. "She came with me on innumerable occasions round the First Aid Posts," said Lady Limerick of the British Red Cross Society. "Particularly at a time when the raids were bad, it was a tremendous boost to people's morale that the Prime Minister's wife should turn up informally and unannounced. One night when we were due to make a tour, I went to dinner first at Downing Street. A raid was on, and the Prime Minister wasn't at all pleased that she was going out in the middle of it, but, of course, nothing would daunt her. He wouldn't go so far as to ask her not to go, but he asked her—'Promise you will be careful, and go in the shrapnel-proof car.' She laughed because he scorned the use of this car for himself. I said to him, 'We shall do our best to look after her, needless to say, and not keep her up too late,' but of course, by the time we got back it was the early hours of the morning. He was in the Cabinet Room when we returned, and didn't even know what time we came in.

"He was so preoccupied with all his responsibilities, that he really was unaware of the incredible extent of the work she was doing. She was clever because she always managed to be there when he wanted her. There were the occasions when he knew she was going out, and that was that, but normally he would go to his room, she would go about her varied jobs, but be there to give him dinner at the right time, and being completely absorbed in his own affairs, he probably thought she was almost always there.

"By operating her own intelligence service, and being a very efficient woman, she organized her life in such a way that she was available when he wanted her, and was still able to carry out the many duties she had undertaken. She obtained estimates from the various members of his staff of how long he might be engaged on individual matters during a day, and would then plan her timetable accordingly to give the impression that she was a wife-at-home most of the time.

"We went down to the East End, to Abbey Wood, and as far afield as Chislehurst, in Kent. We covered the Home Counties. The tours were made late at night and during the night. We would usually start out about half-past-eight or nine, when the raids were full on, and not return until the early hours of the morning, visiting several depots each evening.

"She would talk to everyone. We would also go to the rest centers, Red Cross posts in the tubes, and other public shelters."

There were always steel helmets in their car, but Winston refused to wear one, so she refused too. He began to take less chances—he was looking after, protecting his Clemmie. She knew he had to go out, had to be where there was danger, had to share the blitz bombings with the people, and the Service men and women fighting back, and she accepted this position.

Like him, she was completely without fear, but her concern for him was not only because he was her husband, but because she, like him, was convinced that destiny had chosen him to lead his country through the war. Visiting Battle of Britain Fighter Command airfields with her, or antiaircraft batteries, he took every precaution for her safety thereby, in turn, achieving her purpose of making him look increasingly after himself. Nevertheless, on occasions, he still managed to get his own way in some directions.

One night during a heavy bombing she informed his personal guard, "Inspector, I have asked Mr. Churchill to come downstairs to bed in the shelter. He has promised to come down—will you see that he does?" The guard replied, "I will do my best, Madam."

At about 2:30 A.M. Winston walked along the corridor and announced he was going downstairs to bed. There was a grin on his face. Soon afterward, the bell in his guard's room jangled, summoning him to the Prime Minister's room. Winston was standing beside his bed in his dressing gown. Smiling, he said, "Pick up my clothes, I have kept my promise. I have been down here to bed; now I'm going upstairs to sleep."

Winston found it hard to resist going up into St. James's Park in the middle of the night to watch air raids. Clementine, assisted by members of the staff, persisted with all kinds of tactics to make these dangerous outings more difficult for him. One short-lived strategy she instituted was the "boots maneuver."

She instructed Winston's valet, Ives, to hide the Prime Minister's boots at night. In the middle of a raid, Ives was summoned. He found Winston sitting on the edge of his bed in his bare feet. "My boots!" he demanded.

Remembering his instruction, Ives said the boots were being repaired. Winston stood up, looked at Ives long, hard, and silently, for a moment, then stretching out his hand demanded again—"My boots!" And he added, "I will have you know, that as a child, my nursemaid could never prevent me from taking a walk in the park when I wanted to do so. And, as a man, Adolf Hitler certainly won't." Ives had no alternative—he brought the boots.

It was from the Annex, with the bombs crashing down outside as he spoke, that Winston made one of his most memorable broadcasts on October 21, 1940. It was spoken in French, and echoed hope throughout France.

That Winston managed to make this broadcast so great, in a language he speaks notoriously badly, was due in no small measure, to the coaching Clementine gave him in pronunciation of the speech, before the broadcast. To this day, many Frenchmen can recite the last words of that moving message.

"Goodnight then: sleep to gather strength for the morning. For the morning will come. Brightly will it shine on the brave and true, kindly upon all who suffer for the cause, glorious upon the tombs of heroes. Thus will shine the dawn. Vive la France! Long live also the forward march of the common people in all the lands towards their just and true inheritance, and towards the broader and fuller age."

And then the blitz moved to the Provinces—to Glasgow, Coventry, Birmingham, Bristol, Southampton, Liverpool, Plymouth, Devonport, Sheffield, Manchester, Leeds. Winston, with Clementine by his side, went where the bombs went, touring more than sixty different towns, and aerodromes hit by the enemy. Wherever they traveled, they spoke to everyone they could.

During the blitz days of 1941, President Roosevelt, anxious for a first-hand report on the effects of bombing, requested his newly appointed Ambassador in London, Mr. John G. Winant, to tour some of the worst-hit areas. Winston offered a personally conducted tour. In April of that year, Mr. Winant, accompanied by the President's special emissary, Mr. Averell Harriman, joined Winston and Clementine. They left London by train for Swansea. There, they talked to dock workers in the bomb-torn districts; journeyed on by car to a secret weapons establishment, and from there, to Bristol by train.

The train was halted just outside Bristol. The worst raid the city had ever suffered was on. Wave after wave of *Luftwaffe* bombers droned over, guns were firing, and bombs splattering down.

"I was with them on that journey," recalled Lord Ismay, "and our train wasn't allowed to enter the city because of the raid. We were moved into a siding and stayed there. Winston wasn't pleased about this, but there was no alternative, so we remained in the railway siding all night.

"When we finally arrived at Bristol station in the early hours, and were guided to our hotel by the city's Chief Constable, the first thing both Winston and Clementine wanted was a bath."

Winston hates to miss his bath. A surprising number of his world-shaking decisions have been made in his bath. Even when traveling by air he would insist on a bath, and a section of the plane would be screened off for him to splash away in the special canvas bath Clementine always included in his luggage. His love of relaxing in a bath dates back to his days at the front during the First World War when part of his indispensable kit was a tin bathtub shaped like a giant soap dish, in which he would regularly wallow while a gramophone screeched out sugary popular soldier songs of the times. Winston would soak in the tub reading a pocket edition of Shakespeare, or singing along with the phonograph at the top of his voice. Only if the shelling became intensely severe, would he interrupt his bath—to put on his steel helmet before continuing to wallow some more.

After spending that night in the train outside Bristol, Winston and Clementine felt in need of morning bath relaxation, but bombs had interrupted the hotel's hot water supply. Undaunted, the hotel manager was determined to give service to his distinguished guests. "I'll see what I can do," he announced optimistically, and disappeared.

There followed an amazing sight. The entire hotel staff, and they numbered very few as most were away in the Services, joined with all the guests at the hotel to form a human plumbing system. They had heard of the request for a bath and were going to see that they got one. Kettle after kettle of hot water was boiled, and jug after jug of the water relayed by hand upstairs from the basement to the second floor bath which had been prepared. Every link in the human plumbing chain was laughing and so were the recipients of the water at the other end. Always the considerate huband, Winston shared half the bath water with Clementine.

Refreshed, they began their tour of the blitz city. In the early hours of the morning, few people were about. The devastation was terrible and widespread. The city was still on fire and delayed-action bombs kept going off at intervals. Damaged water mains had flooded many streets but, in spite of it all, in half-demolished houses, people were cooking breakfast wherever a stove still functioned.

As Clementine and Winston stood on a pile of rubble that, until the previous night, had been someone's home, an elderly woman came toward them. The Chief Constable introduced her, and they started asking about the bombing. She began to answer, then suddenly said, "Oh, I can't spend any more time talking, I've got to go and clear up my house." Her home had been smashed. Off she went, and Clementine and Winston followed her. The house was in a terrible mess, and before she left the city, Clementine personally arranged for clothing and other help to be sent to the old woman.

"I saw the most amazing thing that morning, that I have ever seen in my life," said Lord Ismay. "We went to one of the rest centers where they were taking people who had been bombed out, and there was an old woman who was the picture of misery and dejection. She'd been bombed, had lost everything, and was sitting down pouring her soul into her handkerchief. Suddenly she looked up, saw Winston, and her whole face lit up. She waved her handkerchief and cried—'Hooray! Hooray! Hooray!'—and the way she looked at him was the nearest thing to blasphemy that I have ever witnessed—that one man could have such an effect. It was the most moving thing I'd ever seen.

"It affected both him and Clementine terribly. Tears were pouring down his face. He was fortunate that he could release emotion. If he hadn't been able to do so; if tears had been so difficult for him as they are for some men, he would have been in agony. But it was incredible the way in which this old woman's hopelessness turned into ecstasy— as if she had seen a vision. Clemmie was as shaken as I was by this incident and the look on that woman's face made me think of the Bible—it was like—to touch the hem of His garment.... I felt, some-how, translated into another world.

"Both Winston and Clemmie were remarkable on these blitz tours. They had a word for everyone. There's no doubt that people regarded her as an angel of mercy. She has this almost magical gift—this great calming effect on others."

During that visit, acting as Chancellor of Bristol University, Winston conferred the honorary degree of Doctor of Laws on Ambassador Winant, on Doctor J. B. Conant, President of Harvard University, in his absence, and on Mr. Menzies, the Prime Minister of Australia. Many of the buildings of the University were still smoldering.

When the tour reached Coventry, Winston needed all of Clementine's consolation and strength. They walked through the havoc, amid the torn walls of the great cathedral, and the smashed ruins of the giant factories, and the homes of the people of the city.

Harry Hopkins, Roosevelt's special emissary, who had also seen some of the devastation elsewhere, visited them at Downing Street, and they could never recall without visible emotion the words he uttered in Glasgow before his departure, when he said, "I suppose you wish to know what I am going to say to President Roosevelt on my return.

Well, I'm going to quote you one verse from that Book of Books in the truth of which my own Scottish mother was brought up: 'Whither thou goest, I will go, and where thou lodgest, I will lodge; thy people shall be my people, and thy God my God.'" And then he added softly, "Even to the end."

Every day hundreds of pitying letters poured into Downing Street from the United States and other countries. While appreciating their well-intentioned sympathy, Clementine asked, "Why are they sorry for us?"

She went alone on an official visit to the city of Nottingham. There she voiced what was in the heart of every woman when she said, "As the war grows in intensity and horror, we women more and more look back to the simple, happy joys of the past—family life now sadly broken up, absent friends, and the limitations of leisure. But we also project our eyes to the future, when, by the fortitude and courage of our people, those blessings of peace will be ours once more."

Her favorite true blitz story was the incident related to her by Lady Reading, founder and head of the Women's Voluntary Service.

Clementine considered Stella Reading—"One British woman who would be qualified to serve in the Cabinet."

Lady Reading's blitz story was of the woman in the city of Bath, who was brought into a rest center after a raid. She had a black eye, was bruised and shaken, though not seriously hurt. Writing up the details of her injuries for official files, a rest center assistant, in the course of asking the usual questions said, "Are you married?"

"Yes," answered the woman.

"Where is your husband?"

"In Libya, the bloody coward!"

On the morning of May 11, 1941, Clementine stood with Winston in the ruins of the House of Commons, which the *Luftwaffe* had bombed to dust during the night.

Winston gripped his walking stick tight as he looked round the shattered Chamber that for years had been the center of his life.

No one in the Prime Minister's party spoke a word. The pain of the moment was too much for him.

He looked at the splintered remnants of the historic members' benches, then stared up at the gallery where Clementine had so often watched him, encouraged him, as he had delivered his speeches during the years in the political wilderness, and in his years as leader. Then, turning to her, he said, "This Chamber must be rebuilt—just as it was! Meanwhile, we shall not miss a single day's debate through this."

After their blitz-cities' tour together, Ambassador Winant sent his report to President Roosevelt. It included a special tribute to Clementine. Mr. Winant wrote:

"I was deeply impressed by the response of the women, who might be described as the homemakers, although many of them also do outside work.

"The Prime Minister's methods of conducting a campaign on what one might call a morale front is unique. He arrives at a town unannounced, is taken to the most seriously bombed area, leaves his automobile and starts walking through the streets without guards. The news of his presence spreads rapidly by word of mouth and before he has gone far crowds flock about him, people call out to him, 'Hello Winnie!' 'Good old Winnie!' 'You will never let us down.' 'That's a man.' I was interested to note that his 'Cheerio' in our earlier visits changed to 'God Bless You' when we reached Bristol where people were still shaken by the bombing. The whole town was back on its feet again and cheering within two hours of his arrival, although no one had got any sleep during the night.

"On these trips the most marked determination and enthusiasm were among the middleaged women who showed great appreciation of Mrs. Churchill's coming. If the future breeds historians of understanding, the service to Great Britain by the Queen and Mrs. Churchill will be given the full measure they deserve.

"Mrs. Churchill is a wonderful person and the look that flashed between her and these mothers of England was something far deeper and more significant than the casual newspaper accounts of social interchange. I often thought of Mrs. Roosevelt.

"It is very difficult for a man to interpret these emotions. However interested a man may be I had a feeling that in this task he was about as useful as a husband at childbirth."

12

The Lady from Washington

IT was Christmas Day, 1941, and Winston for the first time in years was not spending it at home. Clementine switched on the radio and with her family, was reunited with her husband thousands of miles away, at the annual ceremony of the lighting of the White House Christmas tree.

The focal point of Christmas in the United States is the lighting by the President at the White House of the great Christmas tree set up at the far end of the grounds. Touching a switch, the President floods it with multicolored electric lights. This time, it was an extra special occasion for the Christmas-tree tradition, for the White House was entertaining a very distinguished guest. More than 40,000 people had come to watch the tree ceremony and millions on both sides of the Atlantic were listening by their radios, but none more intently than Clementine and her family.

The great gun at Fort Meyer boomed as President and Prime Minister walked out on to the south portico of the White House and stood side by side. Then Mr. Roosevelt pressed the button that switched on the lights all over the great tree.

Introducing his "associate and old friend," the President, speaking briefly, said Mr. Churchill and the British people had "pointed the way in courage and sacrifice for the sake of little children." Then Winston started to deliver the message he had written in his bedroom that morning with thoughts of his wife, children, and grandchildren, 3,000 miles away, uppermost in his mind.

"I spend this anniversary and festival far from my country, far from my family, yet I cannot truthfully say that I feel far from home," he said.

"Whether it be the ties of blood on my mother's side, or the friendships I have developed here over many years of active life, or the commanding sentiment of comradeship in the common cause of great peoples who speak the same language, who kneel at the altars and, to a very large extent, pursue the same ideals, I cannot feel myself a stranger here in the center and at the summit of the United States. I feel a sense of unity and fraternal association which added to the kindliness of your welcome, convinces me that I have a right to sit at your fireside and share your Christmas joys.

"It is a strange Christmas Eve. Almost the whole world is locked in deadly struggle and, with the most terrible weapons that science can devise, the nations advance upon each other. Ill would it be for us at the Christmastide if we were not sure that no greed for the land or wealth of any other people, no vulgar ambition, no morbid lust for material gain at the expense of others, had led us to the field. Here, in the midst of war, raging and roaring over all the lands and seas, creeping nearer to our hearths and homes, here, amid all the tumult, we have tonight the peace of the Spirit in each cottage home and in every generous heart. Therefore we may cast aside for this night at least the cares and dangers which beset us, and make for the children an evening of happiness in a world of storms. Here, then, for one night only, each home throughout the English-speaking world should be a brightly lighted island of happiness and peace.

"Let the children have their night of fun and laughter. Let the gifts of Father Christmas delight their play. Let us grownups share to the full in their unstinted pleasures before we turn again to the stern task and the formidable years that lie before us, resolved that, by our sacrifice and daring, these same children shall not be robbed of their inheritance or denied their right to live in a free and decent world.

"And so, in God's mercy, a Happy Christmas to you all."

As the simple straight-from-the-heart message ended, a marine band led the crowd in carol singing, and a voice, so familiar to the Churchill household, could be heard joining in lustily above the voices of the crowd. Clementine and her family smiled at each other.

"God Save the King" and "The Star-Spangled Banner" ended the gathering. The White House gates were unlocked, and the thousands who had witnessed the great ceremony streamed out. They had celebrated, on the most fitting day, the birth of unity between two branches

135

of the English-speaking race, and had listened to the voice of a friend, speaking for countless men and women the hopes of the whole democratic world.

The following day, the telephone rang at Chequers. It was Winston calling from the White House to wish his wife and family a Merry Christmas, and to tell her that he had been to church with the President and found peace in the simple service and in the enjoyment of singing the hymns. He had listened to Mr. Roosevelt reading Dickens' *Christmas Carol* to his family, and shared their turkey and plum pudding dinner. Each member of the Churchill family in turn went to the telephone to wish their father a "Merry Christmas."

Clementine opened a cablegram from the White House on December 25. It read:

> To Mrs. Churchill:
> Our very warm Christmas Greetings. It is a joy to have Winston with us. He seems very well and I want you to know how grateful I am to you for letting him come.
> Franklin D. Roosevelt.

Winston and President Roosevelt were forever chiding each other and swapping nonsense rhymes—it made a break, now and again, from more serious affairs. The President loved to tease Winston but a wideeyed, innocent Winston got one back on him at lunch one day at the White House, when Mrs. Roosevelt asked what Clementine was doing in the war. Winston acted as if he had never heard of the fantastically active public life Eleanor Roosevelt led with her constant travels away from Washington, her visits to depressed areas, her public speaking, and her activities on behalf of the underprivileged everywhere. In answer to her question about his wife's war work, Winston spoke of Clementine and the wives of his Ministers, praising to the skies the fact that—as he claimed—none of them engaged in any public activities or appearances. "They just stay at home," he said. His unstinted vocal admiration for wives who never undertook any public duties or social work shook everyone present, although no one made any comment at the time. What is more, he had them believing everything he had said on the subject, and it was talked about, by those present, for months.

"That Christmas was the first time Mr. Churchill had been to the White House," recalled Mrs. Eleanor Roosevelt. His wife took the precaution of advising us in advance—through the British Embassy—of his various likes and dislikes. The information was most useful.

"My husband and Mr. Churchill got on extremely well because they liked so many of the same things. They both had a love for the navy, both liked certain kinds of literature, and, aside from work they had to do together, in which they were very sympathetic to each other, they really had a great many things in common.

"Their actual daily routines were completely different. My husband's was conditioned by the way his office had to work and the way other people had to work with him. Mr. Churchill, on the other hand, could plan his day the way he wanted to plan it and because he was a guest. He didn't have an office that had to be visited and kept running.

"That was something we had to get accustomed to. Mr. Churchill's hours and my husband's hours were a little different, to say the least, and by the time Mr. Churchill left, my husband was usually exhausted. Mr. Churchill was always ready, having had a good long afternoon nap, to work until all hours of the night, while my husband never had periods of freedom in the afternoon."

Except for a brief trip to Canada, Winston remained with the Roosevelts until January 14. The grand strategy of the war was designed during that visit; far-reaching military and production programs developed, and the Declaration of the United Nations drafted and signed.

Winston hated to be away from home at Christmas. Later in the war, he was compelled to make the sacrifice again, when, as his family were enjoying their Christmas tree—a present from President Roosevelt— he decided the situation in Athens urgently required his personal presence. Within an hour an airplane was standing by at Northolt Airport and, after being gently reproached by Clementine for deserting the family gathering, he drove to Northolt and left in a Skymaster.

One evening, before dining at the British Embassy in Athens, he sat down at the desk in his bedroom and wrote to Clementine. In his own diary of the visit, Winston noted that night:

"I sent the following telegram to my wife, toward whom I felt penitent because of my desertion on Christmas Eve:

Prime Minister to Mrs. Churchill. December 26, 1944.

"We have had a fruitful day, and so far there is no need to give up hope of some important results. H.M.S. *Ajax* is very comfortable, and one can get a view of the fighting in North Piraeus at quite short range.

We have had to move a mile farther away, as we're getting too many of their trench mortar bombs in our neighborhood. I went into the Embassy up that long road from Piraeus to Athens in an armored car with strong escort, and I addressed all the plucky women on Embassy staff, who have been in continued danger and discomfort for so many weeks, but are in gaiest of moods. . . .

"You will have read about the plot to blow up H.Q. in the Hotel Grand-Bretagne. I do not think it was for my benefit. Still, a ton of dynamite was put in sewers by extremely skilled hands, and with German mechanism, between the time my arrival was known and daylight. I have made friends with the Archbishop, and think it has been very clever to work with him as we have done, leaving the constitutional questions for further treatment later.

"The conference at Greek Foreign Office was intensely dramatic. All those haggard Greek faces round the table, and the Archbishop with his enormous hat, making him, I should think seven feet high, whom we got to preside. The American, Russian, and French Ambassadors were all very glad to be invited. You will hear speeches on radio no doubt, or see them printed in Wednesday's papers. E.L.A.S. arrived late, three in all. Thanks were proposed, with many compliments to us for coming, by the Greek Government, and supported by E.L.A.S. representative, who added reference to Great Britain, 'our great Ally'—all this with guns firing at each other not so far away.

"After some consideration I shook E.L.A.S. delegate's hand, and it was clear from their response that they were gratified. They are the very top ones. We have now left them together, as it was a Greek show. It may break up at any moment. We shall wait for a day or two if necessary to see. At least we have done our best. . . ."

Wherever either of them traveled, and whatever the pressures of duty, there was always a moment for a thought, or a note for each other. In the middle of a dinner party during the Teheran Conference at which Stalin chain-smoked and drank an estimated quart of spirits, a telegram arrived from London for Winston. It was birthday greetings from Clementine. For his Yalta Conference stay, he was housed in a villa that was an incredible mixture of Scottish castle and Moorish palace, with enormous log fires in most of the rooms, and describing it to Clementine, he said, "We could not have found a worse place in the world . . . it is good for typhus and deadly on lice, which thrive in those parts. . . ."

* * *

Clementine had the opportunity of returning Eleanor Roosevelt's hospitality to Winston when the First Lady arrived from Washington for her first look at Blitz Britain.

"When Mr. Churchill came to the White House, he spoke of the time when my husband would visit Britain," recalled Mrs. Roosevelt, "but one felt that he had in mind a visit to celebrate a victory. I do not think it occurred to him that there was any reason why I should go during the war. He assumed, I think, that I would go in my proper capacity as wife when my husband went.

"It was Queen Elizabeth [present Queen Mother] who thought of the idea of inviting me to see the work women were doing in the war, as well as using the opportunity to say 'hello' to some of the United States' Servicemen and Servicewomen stationed in England.

"It was felt that as the President could not come himself, I could be his 'eyes,' and, with my coast-to-coast syndicated newspaper column, also be the 'eyes' of the American people."

From the White House on October 19, 1942, came the following cable:

F.D.R. to Winston S. Churchill
Dear Winston:
I confide my Missus to the care of you and Mrs. Churchill. I know our better halves will hit it off beautifully....

As ever.

Queen Elizabeth, Clementine, and Lady Reading—head of the Women's Voluntary Services—played hostess in turn to Mrs. Roosevelt.

With her secretary, Malvina Thompson, she stayed at Buckingham Palace, and, on the night of her arrival, Winston and Clementine joined General Smuts and his son Captain Jacobus Smuts, Sir Piers Leigh, Lord and Lady Mountbatten, America's Ambassador, John Winant, Mrs. Roosevelt's son Elliott, and Countess Spencer, at a welcome dinner at the Palace. In the morning, Mrs. Roosevelt, who had traveled under the code name of "Rover," started out—anxious to see everything possible, and Clementine, herself a great one for getting about, became Mrs. Roosevelt's self-appointed guide.

"The trip to Britain seemed to offer me the chance of doing something useful, and Mrs. Churchill very kindly elected herself my personal guide during a large part of the visit," continued Mrs. Roosevelt.

"On our first journey we visited a maternity hospital as well as branches of the women's military services, including training establishments. We were touring a munitions factory when the air-raid warning sounded. I looked at Mrs. Churchill wondering what would happen. But the factory girls went right on working, doing what they were doing, and paying no attention whatsoever to the planes overhead.

"We talked to the girls in the antiaircraft gun crews, helping to load the guns; we talked to the air transport auxiliary women pilots who were ferrying new planes to R.A.F. stations or shot-up aircraft to repair shops, and we visited factories in which women did every kind of war work."

With the King and Queen she had her first real look at the devastation. Their first stop was St. Paul's Cathedral, partly because their Majestys wanted to give the fire watchers, who had saved the Cathedral, the satisfaction of a visit from them, and partly to enable Mrs. Roosevelt to stand on the steps of the Cathedral and see what warfare could do to the heart of a city. Clementine took her down to the bomb-torn East End of London and thousands cheered.

"I wanted to see as many blitzed areas as possible, and go among the people, and Mrs. Churchill helped me do just that," said Mrs. Roosevelt. "We talked with people like the old couple, who still slept nightly in an underground shelter in London, though they could easily have been evacuated to a country area. They told us they had lived so long in the shelter that, while they liked to go out in the daytime and sit in their old home—even though there was not enough of it left so that they could sleep there—they preferred to return to the shelter at night rather than move away. We visited Red Cross clubs of all kinds and went to American and British Service camps.

"During my first weekend in England, I got to know Mrs. Churchill more closely when I stayed with them at Chequers, where I watched Mr. Churchill playing on the floor with his grandson."

Mrs. Roosevelt's shrewd comment on her hostess was, "One felt that, being in public life, she had to assume a role and that the role had become a part of her. One wondered what she was like underneath."

Clementine arranged for Winston's special train to be put at Mrs. Roosevelt's disposal for a general tour of the country. "One day, with Mrs. Churchill, we started out early in the morning in the Prime Minister's special train," said Mrs. Roosevelt. "Our first stop was Canterbury. The Dean of the Cathedral met us and took us through the Cathedral, which had not been hit by bombs, though, as everyone knows, the city as a whole was badly damaged. At a women's institute where we stopped later, the pig club was having an exhibition; one young active pig had been named 'Franklin' and a rabbit 'Eleanor.'

"Together with Lady Reading, we also visited nurseries for evacuated or wounded children and saw the way the Women's Voluntary Services organized and performed their vast duties—the way they moved into a town which had just been bombed, with everything from food to laundry services, and looked after workers who had been made homeless and had to be rehoused.

"Our days usually began at eight o'clock and ended at midnight, but I was so interested that, at the time, I did not even realize how weary I was gradually becoming. We lunched with some of the women who were daily feeding the dock workers and saw women from many different backgrounds working side by side just as their men were fighting side by side. We saw how distinctions and values were fast changing.

"One woman told us 'the hardest thing is to keep at your job when you know the bombs are falling near your home and you don't know whether you will find your home and family still there at the end of your day's or night's work!'

"My schedule included, among other things, inspecting twenty-six camps in nineteen days. I had been warned that we would never make it, but we did. I particularly remember going to Dover with Mrs. Churchill and one of the Women's Institutes on the way. She was really very wonderful."

In front-line Dover, which had endured constant shellings from the German long-range guns at Calais, they went everywhere—there were no half measures with Mrs. Roosevelt, she was determined not to miss a thing. Clementine, herself a dynamo of vitality, found it rough going, keeping up with the tall, long-striding Eleanor. She found herself forever running after her. Whirlwind Eleanor achieved what no one had ever managed to do before—left Clementine breathless—so breathless in fact, that finally, from the strenuous effort of trying to keep up with her guest, an exhausted Clementine helplessly and hopelessly suddenly sat down on the street pavement to take a brief desperate rest! Mrs. Roosevelt, until then apparently unconscious of her own strength and incredible walking pace, turned and looked with amazement at her hostess. Then they both burst out laughing.

"I didn't realize I walked so fast," said Mrs. Roosevelt, "nor did I realize I had exhausted her to that extent. I am sure she wasn't as strong as I was in those days, so I think she probably was very exhausted." Eleanor apologized for running Clementine off her feet, but, after a short rest, the Churchill "never-give-in" spirit reasserted itself, and the tour continued.

"I vividly remember the things we saw at Dover," recalled Mrs. Roosevelt. "There had been a bombing at the W.R.N.'s headquarters and we went to see what the damage had been, and also went to see the ships that they took care of. We visited the places where people took refuge in the cliffs. It was a revealing tour because I had come from America where we knew none of this. It was very enlightening."

It was a three-week, almost nonstop whirl of service camps, war factories, and bombed homes.

Back in London, Mrs. Roosevelt went to dinner at Downing Street. It was a small party. The guests were Brendan Bracken, the Minister of Information; Lady Denman, Head of the Women's Land Army; Lady Limerick, of the British Red Cross; Dame Rachel Crowdy, whom Eleanor Roosevelt had met in the United States; General Sir Alan Brooke, Chief of Staff, later Field Marshal the Viscount Alanbrooke; Henry Morgenthau, Jr., Secretary of the United States Treasury; and Mrs. Roosevelt's companion-secretary, Miss Thompson. It was during this dinner that Eleanor learned still more of Clementine's personality. "She had great tact, as I discovered that night," said Mrs. Roosevelt. "We were discussing Loyalist Spain and this subject resulted in a difference of opinion between Mr. Churchill and myself. He had asked Henry Morgenthau whether the United States were sending enough to Spain and whether it was reaching there safely. When Mr. Morgenthau replied that he hoped that sufficient supplies were getting through I said that I thought it a little too late, and that we should have done something to help the Loyalists during their Civil War.

" 'I was for the Franco Government until Germany and Italy went into Spain to help Franco,' said Winston.

" 'I cannot see why the Loyalist Government could not have been helped,' I said, to which the Prime Minister replied, 'You and I would have been the first to lose our heads if the Loyalists had won—the feeling against people like us would have spread.'

" 'Losing my head is unimportant,' I said.

" 'I don't want you to lose your head and neither do I want to lose mine,' Winston answered bitingly.

"Clementine had listened silently to the argument until that point, and then, leaning across the table towards Winston she said quietly, but firmly, 'I think perhaps Mrs. Roosevelt is right.'

"Winston was obviously furious. 'I have held certain beliefs for sixty years and I'm not going to change now,' he replied angrily.

"Things were getting quite difficult, so Mrs. Churchill simply decided that it had better come to an end. Fortunately we had nearly finished dinner, she got up, and just said to her husband, 'I think that the time has come for us to leave you'—and we left. She had decided diplomatically that dinner had better be well and truly over. She was wonderful and a great tactician. I saw then, for the first time, how extremely well she handles him in conversations. She can give and take."

In those brief moments, Clementine clearly revealed to Mrs. Roosevelt that she was not prepared to be a rubber stamp of her husband's opinions if she disagreed with them. Winston's anger, and the electric atmosphere were soon dispelled as Clementine, almost effortlessly, charmed talk back to more comfortable ground.

When Eleanor arrived home on November 17, a cable immediately went off to Downing Street:

F.D.R. to Winston S. Churchill.
Former Naval Person:
Mrs. Roosevelt arrived safely this morning and I met her at airport and found her well and thrilled by every moment of her visit. My thanks to you and Mrs. Churchill for taking such good care of her.

Roosevelt.

Clementine became self-appointed peacemaker between Eleanor and Winston on other occasions when they got into long arguments on how to reorganize the world. At another luncheon discussion, Eleanor insisted, with deep conviction, "The best way to maintain peace is to improve the living conditions of the people in all countries."

Winston countered, "The best means of achieving a durable peace is an agreement between England and the United States to prevent international war by combining their forces. Of course, we might take Russia in, too," he added.

Neither would budge. Clementine changed the subject, and the argument ended in stalemate.

On so many occasions, when Winston has ruffled people for some reason, it is Clementine who smooths feathers again. On one occasion he was at the B.B.C. for a discussion regarding a broadcast. Clementine had gone along, too. The course of conversation was not at all to his liking, and an annoyed Winston startled everyone present by suddenly walking out without a word of explanation. After he had left the room, Clementine stood up, said "Good-bye" charmingly to each person present and removed the shock from the electric atmosphere Winston had left behind.

On January 4, 1944, a letter arrived from the White House that had nothing to do with the war, but everything to do with the ever-increasing affection and warmth between the Churchill and Roosevelt families. The letter read:

> F.D.R. to Mr. and Mrs. Winston S. Churchill, in London.
> Dear Clemmie and Winston:
> I find the enclosed clipping on my return home. Evidently, from one of the paragraphs, the Desert News of Salt Lake City claims there is a direct link between Clemmie and the Mormons.
> And the last sentence shows that Winston is a sixth cousin, twice removed.
> All of this presents to me a most interesting study in heredity. Hitherto I had not observed any outstanding Mormon characteristics in either of you—but I shall be looking for them from now on!
> I have a very high opinion of the Mormons—for they are excellent citizens. However, I shall never forget a stop which my Father and Mother made in Salt Lake City when I was a very small boy. They were walking up and down the station platform and saw two young ladies each wheeling a baby carriage with youngsters in them, each about one year old. My Father asked them if they were waiting for somebody and they replied 'Yes, we are waiting for our husband. He is the engineer of this train.' Perhaps this was the origin of the Good Neighbor policy!
>
> As ever yours,

One quiet evening during a visit by Clementine and Winston to the Roosevelt's Hyde Park home, the four of them sat enjoying each other's companionship, taking things easy awhile as old friends. Eleanor sat knitting, and both she and Clementine burst out laughing when the President leaned over and, taking Winston's arm, remarked, "My dear Winston, the British Empire doesn't exist any longer. It's just a figment of your imagination."

Winston rose slowly, a puckish expression on his face, and pretending to carry a heavy load in his arms, dropped it suddenly on the President's lap. "Do you want India!" he said. "Here it is."

The Churchills and the Roosevelts might have their disagreements, but they made a great combination, and, after Eleanor's blitz visit to Britain, Winston wrote to her, "Your visit has given great pleasure and comfort throughout this island and your presence and speeches have been an inspiration to the many places you have visited in your indefatigable tour. You have certainly left golden footprints behind you." She also left a very tired Clementine.

13

Miracle at Marrakech

We are told that those who hold the reins of Government carry burdens almost too heavy for human strength, and that the strains and stresses of the Premiership, if continued over a period of years, may have the gravest consequences to health.

"It is a convenient doctrine, so long as no one suggests retirement as the obvious remedy. It mutes the voice of criticism and dulls the edge of controversies. No one cares to attack a sick man, especially one who has spent himself in his country's service and whose present plight is due entirely to that fact.

"But is it true that politics must be reckoned among the dangerous occupations? Is Downing Street, in fact, only a shortcut to the grave?"

That was Winston's comment some years ago on the strain of high office. Considering the overwhelming responsibilities he has borne, and the fact that that he has done nearly all the things our mothers told us not to do, it is incredible that he is alive at all, let alone an agile-minded genius in his eighties. Yet Downing Street would have certainly been a shortcut to the grave for him but for the constant loving care of his wife.

Winston is not exactly the easiest of patients, but Clementine has nursed him through appendicitis, paratyphoid, three bouts of pneumonia, and a varied assortment of other illnessses, apart from patching him up after innumerable accidents all over the world. To all of which Winston says, "Live dangerously. Take things as they come. Dread naught. All will be well."

During the war years, Clementine fought her own Battle of Britain —the battle of her husband's health. She had long given up attempting to persuade Winston to tune up his physical condition with regular exercises. His attitude toward overstrenuous exertion was summarized in his comment to her while watching a boat race on television. "Many a fine healthy young man has strained his heart doing that," he remarked.

One winter, hoping to persuade him to try a little body bending, Clementine typed out a list headed "Exercises," and stuck it on the mirror of his dressing table. Sticking notes on his dressing-table mirror was her method of getting him to remember anything she particularly wanted him to do. Unfortunately, the valet altered the heading to read "Pre-natal Exercises." The following morning, while tying his bow tie, Winston carefully studied Clementine's keep-fit suggestions. Then, calling the valet over, he inquired, "Do I look pregnant?"

Clementine, who could be as persistant and determined as her husband, gave up trying to push home any ideas she had nursed of getting Winston to join a physical fitness brigade. He just wasn't having any.

In February, 1943, the people of Britain were shocked to learn that he had contracted pneumonia. He was immediately given the new wonder drug M. & B. 693, but his life was also in danger—from himself. At first, he refused to take his condition seriously and insisted on continuing all his duties in spite of the serious deterioration in his breathing. There was only one person who could handle Winston—"the world's most difficult patient" as his friends called him—and that was his wife. The doctors ordered him to stop all work and remain in bed, but this he refused to do. To all protests he replied simply but firmly, "I *must* do it. There is so much to be done."

Clementine was the only one who could persuade him to take to his bed and stay there. She did this by making the only diplomatic deal possible in the circumstances. She persuaded him to continue the direction of the war from his bed. Ministers, officials, secretaries, attended his bedside in a constant stream for discussions and instructions.

In spite of a rising temperature he carried on, calling for all the State papers he would normally deal with, and dealing with them. He missed nothing. He refused to have anything shelved. Clementine even convinced his medical advisers to be philosophical about his determination not to stop work.

"If he could not employ his phenomenally active brain, he would fret, be extremely restive, and this would not help his recovery," she explained. And, of course, she was right. But a worse crisis was to come the same year.

"The Prime Minister has been in bed for some days with a cold. A touch of pneumonia has now developed in the left lung. His general condition is as satisfactory as can be expected.—Signed: Moran; D. Evan Bedford (Brig.); and R. J. V. Pulvertaft (Lt. Col.), dated December 15."

This, the first announcement of Winston's illness in 1943, was made in the House of Commons by Mr. Clement Attlee, the Deputy Prime Minister.

Winston, who had celebrated his sixty-ninth birthday at Teheran on November 30, had been taken ill while still engaged in the Middle East on winding up business following the conferences with President Roosevelt, Marshal Stalin, and Marshal Chiang Kai-shek. His son Randolph, and daughter Sarah, then a section officer in the W.A.A.F., who had accompanied her father as his A.D.C., were with him. The weather during that fateful winter of 1943 had been treacherous in Egypt, but nevertheless, when he visited Cairo, Winston wore only a light summer suit. Now pneumonia had struck him down for the third time in his life. Mr. Anthony Eden went to see the King at Buckingham Palace to report on the Prime Minister's health. Mr. Eden explained to His Majesty that the Middle Eastern conferences had unquestionably imposed a severe strain upon Winston. He was often at work until 3 A.M. or 4 A.M., yet always was up early and even had foregone the afternoon sleep he normally insisted on at home or wherever he went.

Doctors had advised against the Prime Minister making the journey to the Middle East by air because of the strain involved, but nevertheless the final trip from Cairo to Teheran had to be made by plane, involving the fatigue of flying at high altitudes. The Persian capital is 5,000 feet above sea level.

For Winston, this had been the most strenuous year of the war. His visit to the Middle East was the eighth major mission he had undertaken abroad during the first three years of hostilities. In the course of those missions he was estimated to have traveled approximately 60,000 miles, more than 24,000 miles of which were notched up in that fateful 1943 alone. By the end of December, he would have been absent from the country on his war journeys since the beginning of the year for about twenty weeks. The series of conferences in 1943, which led to the historic meeting of the Prime Minister, Marshal Stalin, and President Roosevelt at Teheran began with the Casablanca Conference in January. Before returning from Casablanca, Winston continued his journey by air to Turkey, Egypt, and Cyprus, and met the Eighth Army again in Sicily on their way to Tunisia.

In May—having recovered from his first attack of pneumonia—he went to Washington for a further conference with President Roosevelt and for the second time had the honor of being invited to address Congress. He visited North Africa again on the way back, and he was then able to congratulate British and American troops in that theater on their final victory. In August, he again crossed the Atlantic to attend the Quebec Conference and from Quebec went to Washington for further discussions with President Roosevelt. In November, he set out for the Teheran and Cairo conferences.

By making these exacting journeys, Winston had played a conspicuous part in coordinating the war plans of the Allies and permanently strengthening the bonds that united them, but he also physically exhausted himself and brought his resistance to illness dangerously low. After the Cairo and Teheran conferences, he had planned a one-night stay in Tunis as the guest of General Eisenhower, after which he intended visiting the troops in Italy. But when he reached Tunis to be greeted by General Eisenhower, he looked ill. On arrival at the White House in Tunis, where he was to stay, he went to bed at once and slept for hours. Then it was discovered he had a temperature and was developing pneumonia.

Lord Moran, Winston's lifelong friend and personal physician, once told an audience of doctors, "The time may come when you may have illness and may not be able to get a nurse. That happened to me at a place called Carthage during the war with a patient of seventy with pneumonia [Mr. Churchill], without a nurse, without a chemist's shop, without another doctor to consult. That first night, the detective and I shared the nurse's duties. Somehow we managed to keep awake.

"Meanwhile, I received a number of telegrams from members of the Cabinet advising me what I should do and what I should not do. One of them went so far as to ask me: 'Do you realize what will happen in England if you come back without your patient?'

"The lesson of that experience is that if you have good nurses the rest does not matter."

On the instructions of Lord Moran, Inspector Thompson, Winston's detective, spent the first night listening to the tempo of the Prime Minister's breathing. He sat outside the bedroom door, tense and anxious. At about 3 A.M., the heavy, fast breathing suddenly stopped. Thompson crept into the room, went to the bedside, and leaned over the pillow.

Mercifully, there was an almost inaudible but regular inhaling and exhaling of breath. It was a terrifying moment for Thompson. He hurried to inform Lord Moran.

A little later, in his fever, Winston said, "I am tired out, body, soul, and spirit." He lay back a moment, then added, "Yes, I am worn out, but all is planned and ready." Suddenly he asked, "Where am I?"

"Tunis, sir—with General Eisenhower," answered Thompson.

"Tunis? Carthage!" exclaimed Winston. "In what better place could I die than here—in the ruins of Carthage?"

"Don't say that, sir!" pleaded Thompson. "The world needs you."

Winston sighed deeply, sank back into the pillows, and fell asleep.

Brigadier Bedford, a noted chest specialist, flew in from Cairo with three nursing sisters to assist Lord Moran. But the finest nurse of all for Winston, the one who seemed to bring about the miracle of recovery, flew into Tunis after being summoned by General Eisenhower. Back in London, came an announcement from No. 10 Downing Street, "Mrs. Churchill regrets that she will not be able to keep any engagements in the immediate future, as she has left the country in order to be with the Prime Minister during his illness and convalescence."

"And then a wonderful thing happened," recallls Inspector Walter H. "Tommy" Thompson—Churchill's bodyguard. "Mrs. Churchill arrived. Her sudden appearance at his bedside gave the Prime Minister tremendous comfort and new strength. From that moment on, he started to come back to us."

When she first arrived by plane, Winston was much too ill even to be told. Then, when he was sufficiently conscious, the doctors permitted her to go to the bedside. She sat quietly beside him without saying a word, and held his hand. Suddenly, his eyes opened. Husband and wife smiled at each other.

"The miracle of that moment is almost impossible to describe," said one of the Prime Minister's staff. "The M. & B. drugs were playing their part in the fight, but Mrs. Churchill's coming there made an almost unbelievable difference to him. It was as if by holding his hand she was giving him a transfusion of her own spirit and strength."

During the first couple of days she was there, he was still only semiconscious, but she stayed by his bed for hours so that whenever he opened his eyes he could see she was with him when he needed her most. The very fact of her being close, of his knowing she was there, was everything to him. Gradually, the temperature began to subside and the pneumonia resolve, although an irregularity of the pulse indicated that the illness had thrown some strain on his heart. Sarah also worked tirelessly at the villa, helping her mother and helping General Eisenhower's staff in every possible way. After two anxious weeks, Winston began to recover strength so rapidly that he was able to tackle work again.

Recalling the illness in his own record of the war years, Winston said, "I became conscious of being very tired. For instance, I noticed that I no longer dried myself after my bath, but lay on the bed wrapped in my towel till I dried naturally ... as I sat on my official boxes near the machines I certainly did feel completely worn out ... I said 'I am afraid I shall have to stay with you longer than I had planned. I am completely at the end of my tether....' So here I was at this pregnant moment on the broad of my back amid the ruins of ancient Carthage...."

On returning from a Christmas Day service conducted by a British Army chaplain, Clementine told Winston a strange story. A white dove, she said, had flown into the hut in which the service was being held, and had alighted on the altar just as the Blessing was being pronounced. "An ecclesiastical hoax!" said Winston.

Christmas Day that year was especially wonderful, for they were also able to celebrate the blessing of his recovery. Clementine and Sarah personally supervised the Christmas-dinner arrangements at the villa, and Winston, tired but happy, thoroughly enjoyed it.

On Christmas morning, a small patrol vessel which had been guarding the Bay, ran up a flag signal spelling out "Happy Christmas!" to the Prime Minister. This pleased Winston enormously, and he was very unhappy when the ship was ordered to haul down the flag to conform to security regulations. The generals flew in and out, and Winston still held the reins.

As he began to progress, Sarah sometimes took it in turns with her mother to sit beside his bed reading him *Pride and Prejudice,* for Winston always enjoyed Jane Austen. Clementine and Lord Moran insisted on a thorough convalescence in a warm climate, and Clementine suggested that Winston's beloved Marrakech would be ideal. Winston had first fallen in love with the rose-red nine-hundred-year-old city, scented with orange and lemon groves, in 1936, when he went there with a small family party and found Lloyd George had had the same idea.

Before beginning his convalescence, the Prime Minister decided to issue a personal message from No. 10 Downing Street to reassure the people that he was progressing well. The statement said: "Now that I am leaving the place where I have been staying for an 'unknown destination' after more than a fortnight's illness, I wish to express my deep gratitude to all who have sent me kind messages or otherwise helped me. I had planned to visit the Italian front as soon as the conference were over, but on December 11, I felt so tired out that I had to ask General Eisenhower for a few days' rest before proceeding. This was accorded me in a most generous manner.

"The next day came the fever, and the day after, when the photographs showed that there was a shadow on one of my lungs, I found that everything had been foreseen by Lord Moran.

"Excellent nurses and the highest medical authorities in the Mediterranean arrived from all quarters as if by magic. This admirable M. & B., from which I did not suffer any inconvenience, was used at the earliest possible moment, and after a week's fever the intruders were repulsed.

"I hope all our battles will be equally well conducted. I feel a good deal better than at any time since leaving England, though of course a few weeks in the sunshine are needed to restore my physical strength.

"The M. & B.—which I may also call Moran and Bedford—did the work most effectively.

"I have not at any time had to relinquish my part in the direction of affairs, and there has not been the slightest delay in giving the decisions that were required from me.

"I am now able to transact business fully. I have a highly efficient nuclear staff, and I am in full daily correspondence with London, though I shall be resting for a few weeks, provided, of course, that we do not have any setbacks.

"I thought that some of those who have been so kind as to inquire or express themselves in friendly terms about me would like to have this personal note from me which they will please take as conveying my sincere thanks."

Actually, although on the mend, the Prime Minister was still far from well, and Clementine was determined he should be fully recovered before returning to Whitehalll. Before leaving Tunis for Marrakech special arrangements were made for the flight, including strict limits on the altitude and the inclusion of an R.A.F. doctor, equipped with oxygen apparatus, in the party. The plane flew at about 7,000 feet and was deliberately making a detour to avoid the Atlas Mountains. Winston behaving momentarily like his old self, insisted on cutting out the detour and taking the more direct route over the mountains. The doctors were against the idea, but an insistent Winston was always difficult to oppose, and he had his way. Slowly the plane climbed, and at every additional 1,000 feet Winston permitted the doctors to check his pulse and breathing. On being told he was responding well, he cried with delight, "Of course I'm all right!"

The one person in that plane who did not try to dissuade him from having his way was Clementine. She would not attempt to dissuade him in such matters. She knew him too well. She knew that even *she* should not stop him. She understood better than anyone else that Winston *had* to defy danger for his own satisfaction. In certain things, she would never openly oppose him. She knew that to do so would be to strangle the very spirit of adventure that had made the man what he was. On arrival at Marrakech, Winston was exhausted but happy. When ordered to go straight to bed by Clementine he went like a good boy and remained there for several days.

When she had flown out to Tunis, Clementine, in preparation for her husband's convalescence, had brought him something she knew he would want—his easel, canvases, and paints. Now, amid the splendor of Marrakech, in the shadow of the beautiful blue mountains, he could relax and enjoy his beloved hobby. When Winston heard that a wonderful view could be had from the top of a high tower, which formed part of the house in which they were staying, he insisted on being carried up to the top of it. A chair was improvised with jutting poles, and two of the staff maneuvered him up the winding stairs to the tower. He stayed only for a few minutes, and was heard to say, "I am too weak to paint, but I am still strong enough to wage war."

However, it was not long before he was busy with his brushes. Clementine left him to paint alone for hours, knowing how engrossed he became. Sometimes she would take the opportunity, while he was happily engaged in his tower, to slip into Marrakech and wander around the quaint stalls of the bazaar. On her return, Winston would be waiting to show her his painting. She was not slow to criticize, often saying, "Look, Winston, don't you think it ought to be...." He would usually agree with her. With each day, and the rest and the sun and his Clemmie, he became more his old self. Lord Beaverbrook had flown out to be with him during his convalescence, and the presence of his old friend was an added tonic.

When General Eisenhower came to see him at Marrakech, doctors were continually taking Winston's temperature, "and," said Ike, "whenever they approached him to remove the thermometer from his mouth, Mr. Churchill had got there first and announced his own temperature."

"I always do that," said Winston. "I believe these doctors are trying to keep me in bed."

Some times Clementine amused Winston after dinner by playing bezique with him, but more often a fairly fierce game of poker would start.

"Usually," said General Sir Leslie Hollis, who was one of Winston's closest wartime aides, "I managed to avoid being drawn into these poker games by pressure of work, but one night Beaverbrook pressed me to join. With great misgivings I did so. I drew the most terrible hands and lost what was, for me, a very considerable sum of money—something like a month's pay. To the others, of course, such a sum was nothing at all. In due course Winston totted up the score and, before I had time to calculate, myself, exactly how much I was down, he said, 'You needn't worry, Hollis. It's all divided by 240!' I am sure that Churchill did this division sum purely for my benefit, and one of the nicest features of his kindliness was the casual way in which he did it."

The days were warm and sunny, the nights cool, clear, and bright with brilliant stars. Together, Winston and Clementine shared again the breathtaking beauty of Marrakech, which they had loved so much before the war. The Moroccan-styled villa in which they were staying belonged to a wealthy American woman and had every modern convenience and luxury. The furnishings of red, green, and gold particularly appealed to Winston's taste for flamboyant colors. He loved it there. As he grew stronger, Clemmie and he would take walks together, enjoying the glorious views of the Moroccan countryside and the snow-capped Atlas Mountains.

To this exotic setting came General Montgomery and General Bedell, President Benes of Czechoslovakia, General Georges, General Sir Henry Maitland-Wilson, General Alexander, Lady Diana and Mr. Duff Cooper, and Mr. Harold Macmillan. General Montgomery came on the evening of December 31, to see Winston and be given his first sight of Overlord—the code name of the invasion plan for Normandy. As it was New Year's Eve, Clementine had arranged a dinner for the Prime Minister, his guests, and his staff.

Monty had first got to know Winston and Clementine in the summer of 1940 at his divisional headquarters on the south coast, near Brighton. Monty had taken them to Lancing College, occupied at the time by the Royal Ulster Rifles, and showed a counterattack on a small airfield which was assumed to have been captured by the Germans. They then worked their way along the coast, finishing up in Brighton in the evening when Winston suggested that Monty have dinner with them at the Royal Albion Hotel. It was at this meal that, on being asked by

Winston what he would drink, Monty replied—"Water," adding that he neither drank nor smoked yet was 100 per cent fit. To which Winston said in a flash that he drank and smoked and was 200 per cent fit.

But it was at Marrakech that Monty's deep friendship with both Winston and Clementine really began. On New Year's Day, 1944, Clementine invited him to join one of her famous picnic lunches. As they drove along in the car Winston and Monty continued to discuss Overlord. Said Lord Montgomery, "We had a quiet refreshing day in the sunshine and the warmth of the Moroccan countryside in winter, and much stimulating conversation. I got to know the Prime Minister and Mrs. Churchill well during that short visit to Marrakech, and it was the beginning of a friendship which developed into my becoming a close friend of them both."

Repeatedly, when discussing the Overlord plan, Winston would say to Clementine and to his generals, "We must take care that the tides do not run red with the blood of American and British youth, or the beaches be choked with their bodies." He expressed this fear many times, and it was unlike Winston to repeat himself so much. Clementine appreciated that the reasons uppermost in his mind were his painful memories of the tragic Gallipoli campaign of the First World War of which he had been the principal exponent. Winston had never changed his views on the Mediterranean of being the "soft underbelly" of Europe. He had also frequently made it plain to Clementine that the second consideration dominating his thoughts on invasion across the English Channel was his concern for the political future of the Balkans and the threat to them from Moscow.

The villa was well organized. Clemmie saw to that. Apart from domestic staff, there were six cipher girls, a map room with a naval officer always on duty, and an army of secretaries. Every two days, Clementine organized a picnic to one of the countless beauty spots in the district; and almost everybody would go and relax—surrounded by a protective guard of military police. Clemmie delighted in finding a new and delectable spot for each picnic. Good surroundings, good food, good company, were the best medicines for Winston. There was, of course, ample food for everyone, but on one occasion her plans went wrong—for the best of reasons. They were enjoying cold chicken when an Alsatian dog, lean and starved beyond description, hovered watchfully and hungrily nearby. Half crawling, the dog advanced and then withdrew, always gaining a little but ever cautious. The sight of the dog distracted everyone from the food. Winston threw the dog a leg of chicken, which was

155

devoured ravenously. Winston stopped eating, his whole attention concentrated on the dog. He threw more and more chicken to the starving dog until the well-laden basket was suddenly empty. There was no more chicken left for the host or the guests. But at least the dog was happier. Gaining confidence, he at last came nearer and nearer and finally nestled in Winston's arms.

Solemnly he addressed the Alsatian, "Dog," he said, "little did you think when you awoke this morning that you would meet a man called Winston Churchill and enjoy the best meal of your life."

In January, 1944, Winston invited General De Gaulle to visit him at Marrakech. Mr. Harold Macmillan, who was then Resident Minister with the Allied Headquarters in North West Africa, and Mr. Duff Cooper (later Viscount Norwich), who was British Representative to the French Committee of Liberation, were seriously concerned about the invitation because of the Prime Minister's open hostility to De Gaulle and great suspicion of him.

Eventually Duff Cooper arrived in preparation for the visit, and after discussion with Winston he was even more troubled about the reception De Gaulle might receive. He confided his fears to Clemmie. The following day Duff Cooper and his wife joined Winston and Clemmie on one of their picnics. Lady Diana, the first Viscountess Norwich, who as Lady Diana Manners was famous as the ravishingly beautiful Madonna in Max Reinhardt's play *The Miracle,* has her own recollection of that day.

"Lady Churchill, Sarah, and I were sent off earlier—willing pioneers —to find a site which must have a vale and rock and gushing stream," she recalled. "These we found in a lessser Grand Canyon, where, far below our olive-treed pitch, the water rushed over high, round boulders.

"The day was charming. Natives passed Biblically with their donkeys. Motors rolled up with the guests and staff. Winston, flanked by two massive detectives, was wearing the same costume in which we had left him sitting in the Persian Garden—a ten-gallon hat on his head (as a protection from the snow-chilled Atlean breezes) and, over his boiler suit, a dilapidated Chinese dragon dressing gown, its loose gold thread hardly holding the escaping cotton padding. Army trucks followed, loaded with food, wine, cushions, and cooks.

"A Moroccan leather chair—the only chair—was brought for Winston and a hard leather cushion put on his lap to balance his tray. The rest of us sat on the spring-green grass, crushing the flowers without a name, as we grabbed for the pigeon, olive-stuffed pastilla, nectar from

156

the Hoggah and brandy for heroes—listening spellbound to the 'Life and Soul' as his conversation bounded from fancy to fancy, from polished prose to soldiers' slang.

"He ate like a healthy young man and drank like one, with 'Lord Moran orders me another glass of brandy' (no come-back from Lord Moran!).

"The picnic was dispersing happily and I was pursuing fly-away paper for the usual aesthetic reasons when, always apprehensive, I saw to my horror that Winston was determined to follow the young and energetic adventuring down the steep trail that zigzagged down the canyon.

"I swallowed my cry of 'Lord Moran, how can you allow your patient... after such a meal and that glut of brandy! Oh, wife! Oh, daughter! Stop him!' They knew better than to try.

"Clemmie said nothing, but watched him with me like a lenient mother who does not wish to spoil her child's fun nor yet his daring.

"Nothing to do then but watch breathlesssly from the brink. The path was single-file narrow. The detectives followed meekly. Down safely, he ordered the detectives to pull him up on to one of the great boulders. Again he survived the effort. How was he ever to climb up again?

"I abated the agony of watching by devising a safe return. It would have to be in the nature of an inverted parachute. The army trucks yielded no rope or hope. Nothing to be found but the long, long strip of picnic tablecloth—too white, too dirty-linen-in-public, but it was better than a straw, and I stumbled down the trail and was rewarded by Winston's immediate welcome of my device.

"He leaned back against his vast unwound cummerbund as the detectives, one at each end, dragged him slowly upwards while he discoursed on the tenderness of women, their flair for improvisation, and the value of linen."

Returning from the picnic Duff Cooper rode with Clemmie, and his wife rode with Winston. Clementine's quiet, generally unrecognized influence over Winston is revealed by Duff Cooper's own personal record.

"During that return drive," he said, "Clemmie told me she had given Winston a lecture that morning on the importance of not quarreling with De Gaulle. He had grumbled at the time, but she thought it would bear fruit."

It almost did not bear fruit, for De Gaulle at first said he would not come, and Winston exploded. He was furious again about De Gaulle, and all Clementine's work appeared to be undone. Winston suggested sending De Gaulle a note saying he was sorry but he would not be able to see him after all, even if he were able to come. Duff Cooper persuaded him from this course and Winston compromised by saying he would agree to receive De Gaulle only on a purely personal basis to "talk about the weather, and the beauty of the place, and then say goodbye." De Gaulle finally came. And Clementine repeated her "don't quarrel" warning to Winston.

Winston, nevertheless, was in a bad mood when the French leader arrived and was not very welcoming. At lunch Clemmie sat next to the General and excelled herself in steering the table conversation in an amusing way. Winston, under her barrage of charm, gradually thawed and, by the time the luncheon was over, had invited De Gaulle to sit next to him. The following day he took the salute with De Gaulle at a review of troops. They stood together, acknowledging the cries of "Vive Churchill!" and "Vive De Gaulle!" Afterward, Clemmie invited everyone to join in another of her wonderful picnics. It was a great success. Winston was smiling, De Gaulle was smiling, and Clementine wore the biggest smile of all.

On the evening of the momentous picnic, just before dinner, Lady Diana and Clementine were talking and thinking of postwar days. Lady Diana said that instead of a grateful country building Winston another Blenheim Palace, they should give him an endowed manor house, with acres for a farm and gardens to build and paint in.

Very quietly Clementine said, "I never think of after the war. You see, I think Winston will die when it is over."

It was a curiously calm and sad conversation. She seemed quite certain and quite resigned to his not surviving long into peace.

"You see, he is seventy and I am sixty and we're putting all we have into this war, and it will take all we have," she said. It was one of those rare moments when Clementine opened up her heart and shared her deepest thoughts—thoughts that she probably would not have shared even with her husband.

At last came the day when Clementine and Lord Moran considered Winston sufficiently fit to return home. The weeks of patient care had brought their reward. After a brief flight to Gibraltar the remainder of the journey was completed by sea in the battleship *King George V*. Winston took over the Admiral's cabin on the bridge and, with Clementine, walked each day about the bridge and deck. But their most cherished memory of this voyage was Winston's tours of the great ship. The Prime Minister ascending the narrow steep gangways, with a sergeant of the Royal Marines using his shoulder to heave the great man's backside up the ladders, made an unforgettable sight. Clementine's peals of laughter were only drowned by Winston's own roars of amusement at this regular occurrence.

At Paddington Station all members of the War Cabinet and other Ministers plus three Chiefs of Staff were there to welcome them home. Winston's arrival had been kept secret, but a crowd soon gathered about the platform and the station approaches, and the cheers were tremendous and heartwarming.

There were cheers again when, within a few hours, Winston entered the House of Commons, completely recovered, for all to see. A beaming Winston looked up at his wife seated in the gallery. The eyes of hundreds of M.P.s joined his own to gaze at the slender, smiling woman above them. And from those thankful M.P.s came a new roar of cheering—a grateful tribute to the lady of No. 10 who had brought their leader back to them.

During the months before D-Day, Winston was again struggling to overcome the aftereffects of pneumonia. Field Marshal Alan Brooke noted in his diary, "I began to feel that the stupendous burden that he had been carrying so valiantly throughout the war was gradually crushing him. I am afraid he is losing ground rapidly, he seems quite incapable for a few minutes on end, and keeps wandering continuously ... he has probably done more for this country than any other human being has ever done; his reputation has reached its climax. It would be a tragedy to blemish such a past during an inevitable decline which has set in. I am filled with apprehension as to where he may lead us."

Field Marshal Smuts, also fearful of Winston's health, warned Clementine that he considered Winston worked too hard and exhausted himself, and that if he maintained his terrible pace, he was doubtful whether he would stay the course. Lord Moran, Winston's personal physician, also sounded a warning, particularly against his expressed intention of journeying to Bermuda for a combined Chiefs of Staff meeting. Lord Moran informed Clementine that he was even putting the warning in writing to the Prime Minister, telling him there were three good reasons why he should not go:

1. That he might become a permanent invalid if he did.
2. Owing to his very recent bout of pneumonia he was quite likely

to get another if he exposed himself to the hardships and fatigues of a journey.

3. The strain of the long journey was liable to bring on a heart attack.

Clementine, with Lord Moran's support, managed to persuade Winston to postpone the trip.

Years later—on February 16, 1950—mysteriously, as if reacting to some bush telegraph message, the world's press began to telephone its condolences. The news had apparently leaked out that the greatest statesman of the century had died that morning. A statement was issued immediately from Chartwell. It said: "I am informed from many quarters that a rumor has been put about that I died this morning. It is quite untrue. It is, however, a good example of the whispering campaign that has been set on foot. It would have been more artistic to keep this one for polling day." The signature was, of course, "Winston S. Churchill."

But the story of the morning of Wednesday, June 24, 1953, was no rumor. It was only a few weeks since the Coronation, and the Cabinet was in session at 10 Downing Street. For three months the Prime Minister had been doubling the job of the Foreign Secretary, Sir Anthony Eden, who was recovering from a serious operation. As always, the pressures of office were heavy, and, in addition, Winston had carried much of the burden of the Coronation preparations, as well as sharing the meetings of the Commonwealth Premiers in London. The Cabinet meeting that June morning was almost at an end when Winston, who had been speaking, suddenly stopped. Ministers were horrified to see him, seated at the head of the Cabinet table, slump apparently unconscious in his chair. But he was not, in fact, unconscious. He was paralyzed. A stroke had attacked his left side and the left side of his face. His left arm and leg were completely paralyzed. His doctor, Lord Moran, was immediately sent for, and so was Clementine.

Winston's eyes were only for his wife as soon as she entered the room. They followed her all the time. There was no panic, no hysteria, on her part; just a calm, efficient and affectionate attention to his comfort and well-being. As at Marrakech, her very presence and air of confidence that everything would be all right were contagious, and reassuring. "Downing Street is no place to be ill," said Clementine. "We must get him home as quickly as possible." She realized that his best hope of recovery lay in his home and his own surroundings at Chartwell. With the care of his Clemmie and Lord Moran, Winston regained sufficient strength to leave Downing Street only forty-eight hours later for Chartwell.

Three days after the stroke an announcement was made that "the Prime Minister has had no respite for a long time from his arduous duties and is in need of a complete rest. He has therefore been advised to abandon his journey to Bermuda and to lighten his duties for at least a month." The news that the Prime Minister's complaint was a stroke remained a State secret.

President Eisenhower spoke for the world when, in a message to his old comrade in arms, he cabled:

Dear Winston,

I am deeply distressed to learn that your physician has advised you to lessen your duties at this time and that consequently you will be unable to come to Bermuda for our talk.

I look upon this only as a temporary deferment of our meeting. Your health is of great concern to all the world, and you must, therefore, bow to the advice of your physician.

Clementine ordered that notices hung on the high brick walls, giving dates when the grounds of Chartwell would be open to the public, be taken down; and she announced: "Owing to Sir Winston Churchill's need at this time for complete rest I have, with great regret, decided that it will not be possible to open the grounds of Chartwell next Wednesday, July 1.

"I offer my sincere apologies to the people representing local charities who were to benefit from the event and to many members of the public who will be disappointed."

But nothing was going to stop Winston carrying on at the head of world affairs as long as there was a chance to bring about a peaceful international understanding. Nothing but an irretrievable breakdown in his health could sidetrack him from that resolve. The curative powers of his wife, his family, and his home worked wonders. His progress was astonishing. Within days, the use of his leg and arm gradually returned. Clementine helped him to exercise and move them. And slowly, walking around the gardens hand in hand, arm in arm, with his wife, the limp with which the stroke had left him also disappeared.

Whenever the weather was fine, he would spend some of the afternoon sitting with Clementine beneath his favorite big yew tree overlooking the lake in which his black swans (a present from Australia) swam serenely in the sun.

The news that he had fallen ill in his seventy-ninth year had startled the world. So vital a part of the present age was he, so triumphantly had he emerged through so many hazards, that everyone seemed to take it for granted that he would go on and on and on.

Only a few months previously, Winston had told President Eisenhower that he did not think of retiring because "the opportunity for the greatest service to my country still lies ahead." His inspired intervention in world affairs had borne out his prediction. To people everywhere this greatest of living statesmen was also the chief repository of humanity's hope for peace.

But, in spite of the encouraging news from Chartwell, many politicians declared that the House of Commons had seen Winston for the last time as Prime Minister, and that he would soon retire from the Premiership. Mr. Emmanuel Shinwell stood up in the House of Commons and asked Mr. R. A. Butler, "Will you tell us what is wrong with the Prime Minister? If you inform the House he is getting along very well, can you tell us what is wrong?"

To which Mr. Butler replied, "There is no mystery about the matter. There has been a statement made that the Prime Minister had to take at least a month's rest. The rest is doing the Prime Minister a great deal of good."

The exact nature of his illness was still being kept an official secret.

A month later, showing no visible signs of his stroke, he reappeared with Clementine in public and drove from Chartwell to Chequers for a fortnight's stay. The journey to Chequers was unnecessary. It was a deliberate gesture, an excuse for Winston to say to the world, "Here I am, still alive and kicking, and back in business again." Here he was, indeed—wearing a light gray suit with a homburg to match, looking a cool, summery, almost debonair figure with his cigar and cane.

When the grapevine which always warns sightseers of excitements to be relished brought out the cheering crowds to welcome him back, he grinned, made the V sign, doffed his hat, waved his cigar, and, as with each familiar gesture the cheers redoubled, turned and beamed at his wife beside him.

In October of that year, he faced his most important ordeal since his absence—speaking to 3,000 delegates to the great Conservative Conference at Margate.

"How's Winnie?" was the one question in everyone's mind and the one answer they were all waiting for. "He's here!" cried Mrs. John Warde, the chairman, peering excitedly into the wings of the platform. The suspense was almost past bearing. And then Winston and his Clemmie were before them. A Winston a little slower perhaps on foot, but agile as ever in the mind. The wrath, the firmness, all the old mannerisms, and the wit, were there.

Only indirectly did he refer to illness, when, taking stock of election prospects, he declared, "It is not a good thing always to be feeling your pulse and taking your temperature. You have to do it sometimes"— and he stuck out his tongue to show his familiarity with the process— "but you don't want to make a habit of it."

His fifty-minute speech, that day, was yet another triumph for him, and for his proud, smiling wife seated behind him on the platform. It was not until almost two years later that the truth of his 1953 illness was finally officially revealed.

In February, 1958, while staying with his publisher, Mr. Emery Reeves at Roquebrune-Cap-Martin, he developed pneumonia and pleurisy again. Clementine picked flowers from the grounds of the Villa La Pausa, which stands on one of the foothills that run down from the Maritime Alps to Cap-Martin, about three miles west of Monte Carlo. As soon as she took the flowers into his suite which consisted of a bedroom, a sitting room, and a bathroom at the east, or Italian, side of the villa, as ill as he was, his first reaction was, "I want to paint them."

Cautioned Clementine, "Not yet."

"You'll see," he said. "I'll be out with the brushes before any of you think I will."

Clementine read to him some of the thousands of "Get well soon" telegrams that had arrived from all over the world. Characteristically, within a few days, he was asking to be propped up in bed so that, with spectacles perched on the end of his nose, he could dictate a number of business letters as well as enjoy the view of the sun-splashed Mediterranean from his window.

When Winston had arrived at the villa in January for a painting holiday, Clementine had not at first been with him. Out of her watchful sight, Winston, muffled in a greatcoat, was seen around sampling grilled lobster and enjoying coffee in restaurants along the coast. He was also heard ordering a liqueur to go with the coffee in his distinctive French that results in Cognac sounding as though it were a piece of machinery (Cog-nack). And now he was ill.

When his physician, Lord Moran, arrived from London, he said, "My dear Winston, they tell me you have been overdoing it again."

"What?" Winston exploded. *"Painting flowers?"*

With the arrival of Clementine, the only person in the world who could really "manage" him, the picture rapidly changed. With a "Now-no-nonsense" air, she would bring him the medicine he had flatly refused to take. And, of course, he took it. Within a few days, "for being a good boy," she permitted him, as a treat, to sit in the window seat of his bedroom and gaze out over the sunlit sea. With his ham and salad meal in bed, she allowed him a small glass of champagne, and afterward a brandy and a cigar. It might not be an ideal choice for any ordinary convalescent, but then this was Winston Churchill. For after dinner she had arranged a further surprise. A record player was moved into his bedroom and together they listened to an hour of Brahms and Mozart.

Three weeks later, he was able, for the first time, to walk in the grounds of the villa. As they strolled slowly, enjoying the sunshine, he took an occasional rest on a little folding stool she had thoughtfully decided to carry with her. A few days later, diners at a hill-top restaurant saw him eating in public for the first time since his illness. In the warm, sun-glossed terrace restaurant, Winston dealt with hors d'oeuvre and asparagus, roast saddle of lamb, stuffed with Provençal herbs and served with an Alsatian white wine, then ice cream, brandy—and a big cigar.

Diners, waiters—everyone beamed, Clementine included. Winston was himself again.

It was, appropriately, St. George's Day, glorious with sunshine, when little more than a month later Winston drove from Chartwell to his second home, the House of Commons. It was more than four months since he was last there, and Clementine joined him for the occasion. She was in her customary seat in the gallery when a fringe of Members on the floor of the Chamber parted to reveal their returning leader. Winston, slowly, as though struggling with the infirmity of his legs, made his way to his corner seat below the Treasury bench. The packed House let itself go with great and joyful cheers. From all sides he was warmed by nods and smiles. All eyes were upon him as he settled down. He looked paler and thinner, but he was back where he belonged.

For years life at Westminster had come to depend on his health. *"Winston has a cold!"* The collective heart of the House of Commons missed a beat whenever that news was announced. And when he returned, fit and well, Parliament breathed again. Even the hearing aid, which Clementine and his old friend Bernard Baruch had persuaded Winston to use in the House, was never regarded by M.P.s as a sign of infirmity. He used the instrument—a tiny amplifier mounted at the end of a pencil-like stick—with similar diplomatic effect to that which society ladies of bygone years achieved with their lorgnettes, flattering by very pointedly applying the instrument to his ear as if not to miss a single word being uttered. Or, on occasion, lowering it deliberately.

A division was called. That meant a march to the lobbies—but Winston marched, even though a little shakily. Another division followed, and Winston was off again, making the circuit to the division lobby and back to his seat. On leaving the Chamber at the end of the debate, he turned at the Bar and bowed to the Speaker, making the customary solemn obeisance to the Chair. Then, with a slight pause, hand on chest, he glanced beneficently around the House, taking it all in and ending his survey at the point in the gallery where his wife sat. From that day he has never left the Chamber without this last ritual, as if harvesting yet another memory of the place to which he has given so many memories and in which he has lived his memorable lifetime.

On Winston's remarkable ability to be the victor so often over illness, his doctor, Lord Moran, has commented, "It's fifty per cent me, fifty per cent Nature, fifty per cent Sir Winston, and fifty per cent Lady Churchill." That adds up to two hundred per cent, but then, Sir Winston is more than just one person.

14

"Let's Go Home"

"LET's go home!"

When Winston and Clementine Churchill say that, they mean only one thing—the place which has brought them their greatest years of happiness, which has been their own special refuge during the good and the bad times; the place which, in their hearts, is the one and only home—Chartwell Manor, near Westerham in Kent.

The drive from Westerham railway station takes you past gardens filled with hawthorn, larkspur, and gigantic rhododendrons, and woods damp and earthy with ancient elms, beeches, and oaks. There is a peaceful air of remoteness about this English countryside. From Westerham the road climbs steadily upward, overlooking the beautiful Weald of Kent. You drive up a winding country lane, make a sharp turn, and suddenly, seemingly out of nowhere, appears the Churchill home.

Its gray stone, its ivy, its apparent timelessness, make it as much a part of the landscape as the trees around it. Nothing mars its beauty. Nothing about it seems out of place. Even the flagstones before the main entrance declare their right to live in the Manor by continuing into the vestibule and on into the main hall.

The Churchills have lived in many houses, but they have had only one real home. Clementine breathed the homeliness, the comfort, and the efficiency into Chartwell, and Chartwell breathes new life into Winston Churchill. Wherever they have lived, Clementine has always seen to it that the house was run completely to Winston's satisfaction.

That, of course, is what is expected of any dutiful housewife, but no housewife in the world has a husband quite like Winston or a home life quite like that of the Churchills.

Clementine has a tremendous sense of normality, and it is this gift that has given the whirlwind that is Winston its anchorage.

It is on Chartwell Manor that she has concentrated the greatest loving care and attention, because she knows that there, above all places in the world, her husband can find some measure of true contentment.

An estate agent would probably describe Chartwell Manor in some such terms as these:

> Desirable Estate of 250 acres. House, standing approximately 500 ft. above sea level, stone built, with tiled roof, and partly covered with wisteria and lemon-scented magnolia. Spacious hall, fine reception rooms, 19 bed and dressing rooms, 8 bathrooms, electric light, Company's water, central heating throughout. Stabling, 3 garages, 3 cottages, a large studio, ideal for painting, swimming pool with floodlight built by owner.

The Manor was originally 80 acres; but after the last war Winston added to the property Chartwell Home Farm, covering about 170 acres, to develop dairy farming and extend his agricultural activities.

"I find farming a very interesting occupation," he once declared. "I think that if I had heard about it when I was young, I probably never should have gone into politics at all."

Winston's literary work and a legacy from Lord Herbert Vane-Tempest, his Irish cousin, made possible the purchase of Chartwell Manor.

Lord Vane-Tempest was killed in a Welsh railway disaster on January 26, 1921. He was unmarried, and his valuable estate known as Garron Tower and the surrounding lands in County Antrim passed to Winston, his first cousin once removed, who was then Secretary of State for War. Included in the estate were fourteen houses in the village of Carnlough. When Winston and Clementine learned that some of the fishermen tenants were hard up, and several of them unemployed, they immediately made each a present of his house, free of all rents. Since the four-roomed dwellings were all in excellent repair and had gardens attached, it was a wonderful and unexpected Christmas gift for the hard-pressed fisher folk.

Winston and Clemmie were more excited about the purchase of

Chartwell Manor than anything else they had ever bought. Already they knew in their hearts that this was to be their real home. Together they walked through the grounds, planning hedges, flower beds, lawns. They would not move in with the family until the comprehensive alterations they had in mind had been completed. Winston personally supervised the structural alterations to the house, while Clementine concentrated on the interior and on the layout of the gardens.

At Chartwell, Winston threw off political care and became like a schoolboy on holiday. He loved playing handyman around the house and grounds, digging and building the bathing pool Clementine wanted, a goldfish pond, and even a tree-top house. The heated swimming pool's boiler-house chimney was cunningly concealed in the trunk of an old oak, and giant rhubarb leaves camouflaged the filtering equipment; a fishery was established with a special spawning section, and lorries brought colossal chunks of mountainside from Wales to add decorative new touches to the landscape.

Clementine was delighted, but her pleasure was somewhat dimmed when, as so often happened, he arrived back in the house from pools and waterfalls, dripping wet. As he walked through the corridors she scurried ahead, spreading newspapers protectively on the floors.

Of the years before the Second World War, he said, "I lived mainly at Chartwell, where I had much to amuse me. I built with my own hands a large part of two cottages and extensive garden walls, and made all kinds of rockeries and waterworks and a large swimming pool which was filtered to limpidity and could be heated to supplement our fickle sunshine.

"Thus I never had a dull or idle moment from morning to midnight, and with my happy family around, dwelt at peace within my habitation."

"As soon as you go into Chartwell Manor, you know she is mistress of the house; you are aware she rules the home, and that you are in an Englishwoman's castle," says Sir Tom O'Brien. "Her influence on the atmosphere is unmistakable, and you feel the same thing in their Hyde Park Gate home.

"Winston in his own home—in spite of the fact that he did so much of his work at home—was never the same brash, driving personality that he was in Downing Street or in the House of Commons. Oh, he was still the same fantastic force, but his wife would make it plain—you are not in Downing Street, not at a Cabinet meeting, not in Parliament —you're at home. This home discipline of hers was a good, essential thing, because without this discipline he would have burned himself out long ago; he wouldn't have lived all these years. Mind you, she is the only person in the world from whom he takes discipline.

"It is wonderful to watch the motherly care she gives him, as well as the wifely care."

Walk through the double-leaved oak front doors of the manor house into the austere yet friendly hall with its walls and staircase of light oak. A small reception room is furnished with the chintz-covered pieces so characteristic of English country houses. There are paintings everywhere. French windows opening onto a stone piazza take up almost one entire side of the room, and through them can be seen a broad expanse of rolling farmlands. The sitting room, used by the family and friends on informal occasions, is quietly furnished in pastel shades with blue predominating.

Clementine's bedroom is surprisingly sparsely furnished; a large bed, an equally large wardrobe, a glass-topped dressing table with stool, and little else. She likes plenty of space about her and spends much time walking about the room, carrying on a conversation or dictating letters. The neutral-shaded fitted carpet in the bedroom blends to perfection with furnishings in soft pastel colors to give a general impression of size and coolness. The neutral background accentuates Clementine's own vivid personality. She loves floral-patterned curtains for her bedroom—her favorite is a water-lily design. There is a big satin-covered bed back, and windows lead onto a little terrace with a wonderful view of the gardens she tends. There is also a dressing room and bathroom adjoining the bedroom. There are no photographs on the walls of her bedroom—she prefers to decorate them with paintings.

Living rooms and sleeping rooms alike are littered with scribbling pads, on which she makes copious notes (which she is frequently unable to decipher afterwards) as ideas occur to her. There are always a pencil and pad beside her bed, and in the morning a collection has to be made of the notes she has written and then scattered about the room. That is probably the only lapse into untidiness to be discovered in her well-ordered personal life.

Her bed linen is generally white, and she likes her pillow slip renewed first thing every morning and again during the day if she goes to bed for a rest. Her dressing table always displays an array of jars and bottles of cosmetics, and her bathroom offers a wide variety of bath essences; yet, though she takes great care in cleansing and preserving her skin, she uses little makeup. She usually washes her own silvery-white hair, never tinted or dyed, and visits a hairdresser only when it needs special styling.

Said a friend recently, "When they were at Admiralty House, once a week she used to go off to her hairdresser's in Dover Street, but nine times out of ten she hadn't been back in the house an hour before she decided she didn't like what they had done to her hair; so she would take it down, brush it out like mad, roll it up in her little curlers, and do it again her own way."

She pays great attention to her hands, and her nails are manicured professionally—short, with no points, and a natural or very pale polish.

Self-discipline plays a large part in the preservation of her youthful beauty and athletic grace. She is very fond of rich French dishes, and whenever she feels she may be putting on a little excess weight she subjects herself to a strict diet: no salt, no fruit, no alcohol, little starch, and only four cups of liquid a day. During dieting days she refrains, whenever possible, from accepting outside invitations. "It is so difficult to resist eating," she says.

A trait in her nature is a preoccupation with cleanliness. When she retires to rest in the afternoon she undresses completely, puts on a nightdress, and slips into bed. When she rises to dress for the evening, she puts on fresh underwear and a fresh nightdress is laid out. She will never wear a garment twice without laundering. Because of her fastidiousness, at one time, when she used to go shopping, she would put any coins she received in change into a separate purse in her handbag. As soon as she arrived home, the coins were washed. She dislikes anything that isn't clean.

Near her bedroom, on the left of the hall, is Winston's magnificent studio. Through the wide double doors half-finished paintings can be seen resting against the walls. Palette and paints lie on a table, ready for use. The boarded floor is bare, for this is the functional, much-lived-in room of a hard-working artist, not a dilettante. Past the studio, along a short passage, are the general office and a smaller office for Clementine's secretary. Walk up the polished oak staircase, turn right, and you are in the famous Churchill study. An ancient room, once the minstrels' gallery, it retains the original, high-arched ceiling extending up to the very roof of the house. This and the room next door are all that remain of the old Attwell Manor, which was begun in the days of Edward III. From the rafters hang wrought-iron lights, and there are decorative iron standard lamps at strategic points around the room. A few pictures hang in the spaces on the walls not entirely concealed by bookshelves. Valuable rugs give color and warmth to the floor of the long, narrow room. Through the rug in the center runs the clear-cut track of Winston's feet. While dictating, he paces the length of the room like a caged lion.

"It's no use getting another rug," said Clementine in despair one day. "If we do, he'll only wear that out, too."

History lives all around you. Above the wide, open fireplace hangs the Union Jack the Allies flew in Italy when they invaded in 1943. (In summer it is quite usual for Winston himself to light the fire at midnight if the air has turned chilly.) In one section of the bookcase is a large diorama of the beach at Arromanches with its Mulberry Harbor. The frame carries the simple title: "D plus 100." On the shelf below stands a small figurine of a snarling bulldog.

Books abound. A long lecternlike stand always carries open works of reference relating to whatever subject happens to be engaging Winston's pen. In fact, reference books are scattered everywhere. The desk, very large and usually very tidy, stands near a window. Behind it is Winston's favorite chair, a tall, carved dark-oak piece with green tapestry seat and arms. Around the fireplace are comfortable tub chairs upholstered in a white material broadly striped in red and blue.

An archway leading from the study takes you into Winston's bedroom, which is directly above that of his wife. Like the latter's, Winston's bedroom is sparsely furnished. There is little on his dressing table but a brush and comb and a bottle of the eau-de-Cologne, which he loves to use daily on his handkerchiefs.

The bedroom, at the very top of the house, is right in the roof itself, and the great bare roof beams are the ceiling. His bedroom is typical—it is full of gadgets. The dressing table in front of the window looks down on the magnificent Chartwell gardens. Winston wants nothing to hinder this view, so his dressing table appears to have no mirror until you pull a cord beside it, and a mirror rises up. Pull the cord again, and down goes the mirror.

Again there are no vivid colors. The dark furniture contrasts with pale cream walls almost covered with Winston's "pin-ups"—dozens of family photographs—most of them in Edwardian clothes. There is a cartoon of Lord Randolph Churchill, a contemporary print of the great Duke of Marlborough, and a portrait of Winston's nurse, Mrs. Everest. There are a desk and four-poster bed, over which hangs the famous charcoal sketch that Sargent made of Winston's beautiful mother, Jennie Jerome. Of this picture, which has been reproduced many times and in many countries, Winston has said, "There is more color in it than there is in any number of paintings I have seen. Is there anyone except Sargent who would dare to put that heavy outline against the light side of the face? And yet how perfectly it models."

His bed is now alongside the wall, and fixed to the wall above the bed is a flap table, which, when opened, spreads in front of him almost the length of the bed. On this rough wooden table, made by a local carpenter, he spreads his newspapers for his morning reading-the-papers routine. Winston has his own special pillow on the four-poster bed. "Once," a member of the household staff said, "we swopped it for another, just to see if we could get away with it—but he knew. He felt the difference immediately." Through double doors in the room he steps down into one of his greatest personal delights—his sunken bathroom.

On the first floor are the dining room with its huge dark-oak beams and rafters, a kitchen, and a large drawing room used on more formal occasions. The drawing room, with carpet, furnishings, and porcelain all in blue, is directly over the studio. In both wings of the first floor there are rooms reserved for guests staying at Chartwell overnight. Staff bedrooms occupy the second floor.

Below ground level, shielded by the low box hedge, is the Churchills' private cinema, a large room, which can seat perhaps a hundred people comfortably.

The cinema is Winston's greatest relaxation. He has little respect for the sacred institution of the English weekend and is seldom unoccupied for a minute. Therefore the responsibility of entertaining guests is mainly left to Clementine. But every weekend at least one film is shown and everybody at Chartwell, staff included, is invited. Film companies send advance copies of their latest productions.

Winston enjoys their private cinema, and on the rare occasions when Clementine visits a public cinema she has to go without him. However, she is never short of escorts. When she attended one charity performance, Lord Montgomery accompanied her. "They asked me to bring somebody nice, so naturally I thought of Lord Montgomery," she said. "He's a very old friend of ours. My husband will stay at home. We have our own cinema and he prefers that."

One Sunday evening at Chartwell, the chosen film was Sir Laurence Olivier's production of *Hamlet*. Throughout most of the performance two voices could be heard declaiming the immortal lines—Olivier's from the screen and Winston's from the audience. Immediately the film had ended, Winston hurried upstairs for a copy of the play.

Throughout dinner he continued to declaim passages, but he did not need the book to prompt him. His memory is phenomenal, as Olivier discovered on another occasion.

Sir Laurence had invited the Churchills to his performance of *Richard III* at the Old Vic. And from the rise of the curtain to the final scene, Winston recited Shakespeare's words, almost putting the actors off. Afterward, they joined the Oliviers for supper, and to Sir Laurence's immense surprise Clementine said that Winston also knew by heart the whole of *Henry IV* and *Henry V*. Almost incredulously, Sir Laurence consulted Winston on his approach to certain speeches in the plays and was instantly given an interpretation.

Clementine loves the theater, which she visits whenever she can. Sometimes Winston may be too busy to accompany her, but when she finds a play which she is certain he will enjoy, she goes again to see it with him. She delights in taking him to plays with titles such as *The Happy Marriage* or *A Woman of No Importance*. Despite his encyclopedic knowledge of Shakespeare, he is no highbrow.

Some years ago a political friend advised them to see Richard Burton playing Coriolanus at the Old Vic. He told Winston, "Shakespeare foresaw you. It is really the story of your life."

Winston and Clementine took his advice and saw the play. A few days later they met their friends again, and Winston said coldly, "I cannot see any parallel between the life of Coriolanus and myself."

"But Coriolanus saved Rome, just as you saved Britain," the friend argued, "and when the war was over the Romans threw out Coriolanus just as the British voters rejected you."

"Yes," said Clementine, "but Winston did not cross over and join the enemy."

Between the walled rose garden of the house and an ornate shelter called the Marlborough pavilion is a vine-covered way. The pavilion is decorated with a frieze carved from slate and painted by their famous artist nephew John Spencer Churchill. It portrays the Battle of Blenheim, at which the family's great hero, the Duke of Marlborough, was the victor. Inside the pavilion are busts of the Duke and Duchess, Prince Eugene of Savoy, and Queen Anne.

During the war years, Chartwell was officially closed, but many times Winston and Clementine longed for a sight of their beloved though deserted house, and they would make a sudden trip with some of their staff to taste—if only for one night—the joys of their home. On one occasion when the news was bad Clementine, sensing that the moment was right, said, "Let's go home this evening," and Winston snatched gratefully at the momentary escape. Together, that night, they walked in their dressing gowns through the rooms of Chartwell. The rhododendrons were blooming and the magnolias brave with the largest, whitest blossoms. The paths were overgrown with weeds and grass; but when, next morning, they strolled arm in arm through the scented gardens, war seemed a long way from that haven of peace. They returned later that day to Downing Street, strengthened and refreshed by the brief hours in the old gray manor house.

Chartwell is close enough to London for guests to motor down for lunch and dinner, and at weekends there is a constant stream of people coming and going. The favorite relaxation of the Churchills is good talk, and Clementine is in sole charge of the social life of the Manor and arranges all invitations.

Recalling a luncheon at Chartwell, Major General Sir Edward Spears said, "There is never a dull moment in the Churchill household, where wit and intelligent discussions of people and affairs combine with a background of peculiar charm into an expression of the best that English civilization in our time can produce. The host was happy and relaxed as he always is with his family, in spite of having just lost an argument with Mrs. Churchill on the propriety of water glasses being filled before the meal was served. Winston had held not, but I observed nevertheless that there was water in the glasses. The meal was gay; remarks, comments, sometimes caustic, never unkind or inconsiderate."

The interest she takes in their beloved Chartwell means a great deal to him. Organizing its daily routine and its special comforts is something only she could do so well.

The staff at the Manor includes a cook, two housemaids, a kitchen maid, Clementine's personal maid, and Winston's valet, and there are never less than two secretaries in attendance.

In no Churchill household has it ever been a case of the staff running the show. There is no disputing who is in command. Clementine runs everything. Every morning she goes down to see the cook and check the menus for the day, the number of guests to be catered for, and the kitchen supplies. After that she visits the secretaries and gives them their instructions, though she would never dream of interfering with any secretarial duties required by her husband. It is never a case of "I told you what to do," and leaving it at that. She follows every job right through to make sure it is done properly.

Their nephew, John Spencer Churchill, says, "At Chartwell it never ceases to amaze me how my aunt copes with the running of the place. Her role is that of an A.D.C. Extraordinary and Super Quartermaster to the greatest of Captains-General. For Chartwell, and indeed any other house my uncle occupies, is not only a kind of military head-quarters but a large factory filled with high-powered executives. To see that this factory runs smoothly with meals at odd hours for visiting experts and the relays of secretaries working through the night calls for tremendously detailed organization.

"In addition to bringing up a large family she has been present to act as gracious hostess to every conceivable sort of guest. Even when she is not feeling well, she never allows anyone to know it.

"The hospitality my uncle and aunt offer at table is quite out of this world. It was always a pleasure to arrive at about 12:30 P.M., in time to accompany my aunt on the short walk round the garden, which she liked before lunch."

A secretary who spent some years in the Churchills' service explained, "There are two Clementines. One is the great lady—a strict disciplinarian with a very real sense of her importance in the scheme of things; the other is very human. Clementine can be very strict one moment and wonderfully charming the next. She was at her most attractive when she was able to drop the responsibilities of being 'the Prime Minister's Lady' and discuss things on a level with you, just like another ordinary woman talking to you."

Though life is comfortable, there is no extravagance at Chartwell. During their early married life, when children had to be clothed and educated and appearances had to be kept up on a limited income, Clementine learned to appreciate the truth of the old adage about "a penny saved." And she still dearly loves a bargain.

One of her wartime secretaries recalls, "She could not be called ungenerous, but she would never pay more than she thought necessary. I remember an instance of that in the very first summer I was with them. She had seen a linen frock of a popular make advertised in the local paper. She pointed it out to me, saying, 'Look! That costs two guineas in town, but here it costs two pounds. It's a very cheap frock, and I'm going to get it.' She was delighted at the thought of being able to save two shillings. I remember that frock. It was of pale blue linen, and when she came back in it, it looked lovely. She used to wear it in the garden, and on her it looked like a Paris model."

Although at Chartwell they occupy separate bedrooms, Winston and

Clementine invariably share the first routine of the day. The sleeping arrangements are essential, for Winston's bedroom is, as is well known, also a kind of an office in which he spends hours looking at correspondence and even dictating his books. Since he sleeps little and customarily does not retire until the small hours, the privacy of separate bedrooms was the obvious solution.

Clementine usually rises at about seven o'clock in the morning. She believes that every woman should take great care of her appearance, and her own success in this direction is patent. Even in her late seventies, she is still a beautiful woman, looking much younger than her years. Every morning her first task is to put on white gloves, clean her face, and set her hair. After that comes breakfast, taken in bed.

At about 8:30, in the room above, Winston is, also awake and having breakfast. Wearing a dressing gown he sits propped against pillows, with his elbows resting on two large sponges. If the sponges are not in position, he eats his breakfast from a bed-table.

Husband and wife seldom meet until lunchtime. Winston has said, "My wife and I have tried two or three times in the past years to have breakfast together but we had to stop, otherwise our marriage would have been wrecked."

Concerning his daily routine, he once remarked, "When one wakes up after daylight one should breakfast; five hours after that, luncheon. Six hours after luncheon, dinner. Thus one becomes independent of the sun, which otherwise meddles too much in one's affairs and upsets the routine of work."

At about 9 A.M. both husband and wife have finished eating and then comes the first joint duty of the day, the ceremony of reading the newspapers. Winston goes through them first, marking items—some, of special interest, with a different colored ink—for Clementine's attention, and she does the same for him.

As he finishes each newspaper, it is taken downstairs to Clementine. The reading of the morning's press usually occupies about four and a half hours, and they draw each other's attention to items of interest in newspapers and magazines.

At 9 A.M. the secretary reports for duty and Clementine deals with correspondence and household affairs from her bedroom, stopping every now and then to read marked newspaper items sent to her room from upstairs.

Occasionally she goes out in the morning to keep an appointment, but usually she works at home, answering her letters and dealing with the management problems of the Churchill houses at Chartwell and in London.

Winston remains in bed until lunchtime, relaxing his body while never ceasing to exercise his brain. Beside his bed are three telephones, and they are seldom silent for more than half an hour.

At about noon comes the Order of the Bath—Winston's bath. He enjoys that pleasure as a crown to his morning's work and loves to wallow in the steaming water, turning the taps on and off with his toes. Sometimes he gets out of the bath to make an important telephone call and then steps back into the water again.

Clementine, with the aid of members of the staff, is forever thinking up new methods of keeping Winston on time. His unpunctuality is one of the terrors of the household. No matter what time guests are due for luncheon, he is invariably late and, but for the ruses adopted by his wife, would be later still.

Sometimes she will send word to him in the bathroom that the guests have already arrived, though they are still on their way. She alters the time of the luncheon. She even instructs the staff to tell Winston that the clocks are slow or that the time is later than it really is.

Winston himself has said, "Unpunctuality is a vile habit," but it is one of his worst faults.

As a young subaltern, he once kept the Prince of Wales (later Edward VII) waiting for almost an hour. When, at last, he arrived the Prince asked, "Do you have an excuse, young man?"

"Indeed I have, sir," said Winston. "I started too late."

Asked why he missed so many trains and airplanes, he explained, "I am a sporting man. I always give them a fair chance to get away."

When he went to Washington, Clementine had to reproach him for being late for President Roosevelt. The President was at the railway station, waiting to greet him, but Winston wasn't ready. The President drove Clementine to the White House and then went back to the station to wait for Winston to emerge from the train.

Being late is really a quirk in Winston's character, for he is always well aware of the time. He seems to derive some kind of pleasure from seeing how worried everybody is getting. However, from time to time, Clementine has given him a sharp lesson. A member of their staff remembers one such occasion early in the Second World War, when Winston was First Lord of the Admiralty.

"The Churchill bedrooms were next door to each other on the top floor of Admiralty House," she says. "I was working in Winston's bed-

177

room. He was resting in bed. Clementine was in the next room, preparing to go out for the evening. She kept popping her head in and saying, 'Are you getting dressed yet, Winston? Are you getting dressed? Look at the time.' Each time, he would reply, 'I'll be all right.' He said it took him thirteen minutes to bathe and dress, and he knew he could do it. She kept on until he finally said to me, 'Fill my bath.'

"Clementine called me into her bedroom. 'Has he gone to bathe?' she asked. I said that he had, and she replied: 'Good! Let me know when he is fully dressed.'

"In due course I reported that Winston was ready. 'Excellent!' she said. 'Now, lock my door.' Mystified, I did so. 'Now,' said Clementine, 'he can wait for me.'

"She was completely dressed, and she proceeded to take off every stitch. Then she said 'Now he can wait until I have put all my clothes on.' And deliberately, leisurely, she proceeded to do just that."

Whenever a train had to be caught, Clementine invariably told Winston three times that it was time to start for the station. One day they got to Euston just in time to see the last carriage leaving the platform. Winston turned to his wife and said indignantly, "The train's pulling out."

"Yes," she said. "I know. You were late again." His face suffused with righteous injury. "But, Clemmie," he protested, *"you only told me twice!"*

Winston's resentment of any attempt at discipline in the home is something which would try the patience of any wife. Once, and only once, Clementine managed to persuade him to go on a diet, only to be told seven hours later, "Well, that's the end of *that!*"

If she had made a record, warning "Don't drop your ash on the carpet, dear," it would have saved the repetition of that injunction to her husband many thousands of times.

Winston likes to pad through the rooms of Chartwell in his sky-blue siren suit and shod with soft black slippers bearing his initials worked in gold. Even more, after lunch, he loves to take a walk around the beautiful grounds ablaze with flowers. Nothing pleases him more than when Clementine is able to share the stroll with him.

Sometimes, while Clementine, wearing slacks, blouse, and gloves, works in the rose garden, Winston potters about the grounds, often getting smothered in mud. In only one aspect of their mutual love of the countryside do husband and wife differ. Winston hates to see a tree damaged or destroyed. Clementine is fascinated to see one fall. Whenever a tree has to be felled, Clementine will stand watching until the job is done.

Winston loves trees; loves to see their reflection in the water; loves to see them silhouetted bare against gray winter skies; loves to paint them in all their moods. But when the afternoon's enjoyment of the grounds is over, it is time for the most rigid discipline of the day—sleep.

He returns to his bedroom, undresses, and sleeps for two hours. He will never miss that rest no matter where he is. On an election tour, a large bed would have to be provided in one of the coaches. If required to attend the House of Commons during the afternoon at question time or for an important debate, a room and bed must be prepared for him within the precincts of the House. Even while visiting the Royal Family—if the visit overlaps Winston's rest period—Clementine will request a bedroom to be put at his disposal and the Queen always sees this is done.

At Chartwell, when no guests are expected, he works in bed until 6 P.M., and Clementine makes sure that, for his rest period, he has his "blinkers"—black eye-pads to shut out the light.

Clementine, too, takes as much rest as possible during the afternoon. Although physically tough, she conserves her strength carefully. If there is to be a dinner party she will frequently stay in bed all day, saying, "I must be fit for tonight." She believes implicitly that ample rest and relaxation conserve and preserve youth and vitality. No one could mistake her insistence on rest for laziness. Even as a woman of fifty she played tennis brilliantly, moving across the court at lightning speed. She has always been quick-thinking, quick-speaking, and quick-moving.

Clementine is an enthusiastic croquet player, with a keen eye and a steady hand. Winston does not share her enthusiasm, but summertime guests at Chartwell usually find themselves playing a game before lunch and another after dinner.

Asked to become an Associate of the Croquet Association, Clementine accepted with delight; but it was then discovered that the new Associate's croquet did not conform to the recognized rules. For years, it seemed, she had been playing on a lawn of the wrong dimensions. On learning this, she immediately ordered the addition of a further five yards of turfing to the Chartwell lawn in readiness for the next croquet season.

Field Marshal Montgomery, a frequent and welcome visitor to Chartwell, had as fellow-guests one weekend Mr. and Mrs. Clement Attlee. All three were keen croquet players, but none could equal the skill of Clementine, who had achieved near-championship standard. Though Winston is also good at the game, he does not approach his wife's class. At that time Winston was Prime Minister and Attlee (later Lord Attlee) leader of the Opposition. Montgomery had still to attain his Viscountcy.

Clementine had frequently opposed Monty at croquet and beaten him soundly; but this time he was her ally against Winston and Attlee, and the two statesmen suffered a total political defeat. Throughout the match Winston and Monty tried to undermine each other with the methods of psychological warfare. There were constant volleys of banter, Winston's thrusts being largely aimed at Monty's abstinence from tobacco and alcohol. They availed nothing. Monty and Clementine completely out-generaled their foes.

She regularly organized tennis tournaments at Chartwell, but Winston seldom watched her play. His brain somehow would not allow him to do so. He might have done it if it were a question of winning anything, but most of the time he had so much else to do. Working is his idea of relaxation.

One of Clementine's methods of self-expression, it must be admitted, has met with somewhat qualified enthusiasm. As a motorist she does not excel. Shortly after the end of the First World War she acquired a little two-seater in which she would drive down to Chartwell. Said one of their staff, "She once got me to go with her because the chauffeur was engaged with the other car. I was scared stiff. When something appeared suddenly in front of us, she'd put up her arms and yell!"

After one or two minor mishaps, Clementine abandoned motoring as a hobby; then, at the age of seventy-two, she decided to take a refresher course to familiarize herself with a new car that had been purchased. Warned by earlier experiences, Winston insisted at first that she should not venture out unless accompanied by a skilled driver. Clementine countered by buying her own car, which she insisted on driving personally, though she had been, to all intent, "off the road" for almost twenty years.

Winston himself is not an easy man to drive, according to those in a position to know. He does not object to speed, but the car must proceed at an even pace. The chauffeur unlucky enough to achieve a bumpy stop or start is liable to receive a "rocket" in true Churchillian style.

Neither Winston nor Clementine likes cars particularly, and prefer to hire them rather than own them. Winston clung to an ancient Austin 10, which he used to carry him around the Chartwell estate. Clementine hated the dilapidated crock, as she hated everything untidy. She arranged to sell it to a local dealer for £40, and bought a new Hillman Minx to replace it.

For once Winston opposed her, insisting, "I want the old car back." It cost £80 to retrieve it, for the dealer had already sold it to another customer for that sum.

Such little excitements apart, Chartwell Manor is a place of quiet contentment. Within its bounds Clementine has tried to bring a little of normality into Winston's abnormal life. His overwhelming personality never at any time overwhelms the gracious, equable woman who is his wife. Her vivacity, her gaiety, her spirit, were ever a complete match for him.

15

A Weekend at Chequers

RELUCTANTLY, during the war, Winston and Clementine had virtually to abandon their beloved Chartwell Manor for Chequers, the official country retreat of the Prime Ministers of Britain. Chartwell, prominently sited on a hill, was a landmark too easily located by bombers.

Chequers Court, a large Tudor country house, stands in a sheltered hollow nearly six hundred feet above sea level, between Great Missenden and Aylesbury in Buckinghamshire. The estate, just forty miles from London, comprises 1,500 acres of mixed farmland, park, and Chiltern beechwoods.

For almost a thousand years, Chequers Court was in private hands, but in January, 1921, its owner, Lord Lee of Fareham, bequeathed the estate to the Premier of the day and his successors in perpetuity. The days had passed, he said, when Ministers of the Crown were always gentlemen of means, but it was desirable that the Crown's chief Minister should possess a country house where he could relax and entertain distinguished visitors.

Over the entrance to Chequers are the words "Pro Patria Omnia"— freely translated by General Eisenhower as "All for the Fatherland," while over a gate leading to part of the gardens are the words, "All care abandon ye who enter here."

Mr. David Lloyd George, who accepted Chequers on behalf of the nation, was delighted with the gift, but not all his successors have been equally fond of their inheritance. Indeed, many who stayed there criticized the house as a cold and drafty edifice, half museum and half architectural fake, filled with heavy furniture of greater historical than artistic interest.

Winston was not particularly fond of Chequers, quite naturally preferring his own beloved Chartwell, where, in any case, most of his books and papers were stored. Nevertheless, since this was plainly to be their principal wartime home, Clementine determinedly set out to make the best of it and soon contrived to add her own touches to the gloomy, uninviting place.

Chequers was coldly magnificent. With its enormous hall, its cavernous fireplaces, its paintings by Rubens, Van Dyck, Turner, Constable, its historic relics—the slippers of Oliver Cromwell, the ruby ring once worn by Elizabeth I, the historic silver and plate, the four-poster beds—it was all very impressive, but never home to the Churchills. Clementine had to bend her tastes and her wishes to its traditions, but she didn't like it one little bit.

Each of the paintings in the hall is described in a catalogue reposing on the big central desk. On this desk there is also a reproduction in red, white, and blue of the Longfellow verse sent to Winston by President Roosevelt. It reads:

> Sail on, O Ship of State!
> Sail on, O Union, strong and great!
> Humanity with all its fears,
> With all the hopes of future years
> Is hanging breathless on thy fate.

The Friday night exit from No. 10 Downing Street became a weekly ritual, with a procession of cars carrying secretaries, telephone operators, detectives—and the Churchills—down to rural Buckinghamshire; but it was never a "get away from it all" weekend, for there was a ceaseless shuttle service of couriers bearing Government dispatch boxes between Whitehall and Chequers, and an almost endless stream of distinguished personages arriving not only as guests for dinner but as V.I.P.s to be consulted on matters of national and international importance.

During those allegedly "quiet" weekends at Chequers, Clementine played hostess to Cabinet Ministers, Service chiefs, and a multitude of home and overseas visitors concerned with the conduct of the war. General Eisenhower, Mr. Mackenzie King, General De Gaulle, General

Smuts, Mr. Harry Hopkins, and Mr. Averell Harriman were among those who came.

Here is a typical weekend guest list, prepared for Clementine by Elizabeth Nel, one of Winston's secretaries:

"The Prime Minister, Mrs. Churchill, Mr. Harry Hopkins, General Marshall, Mr. Brown [private secretary], Commander Thompson—arrive Friday evening to stay weekend.

"Admiral Pound, General Brooke, Air Marshal Portal, General Ismay —to dine and sleep Friday.

"Lord Leathers, Lord Cherwell—to lunch and dine Saturday.

"Air Marshal Douglas—to dine Saturday.

"General Ney, Admiral Mountbatten, Admiral Cunningham—to dine and sleep Saturday.

"Mr. Oliver Lyttleton—to lunch and dine Sunday.

"Air Marshal Harris, General Eaker (U.S.A.)—to dine Sunday.

"Mr. Harriman, General Paget, Mr. A. V. Alexander—to dine and sleep Sunday."

As well as acting as hostess, Clementine, list in hand, would get to work supervising bedroom arrangements, the menus for each meal, and general entertainment requirements.

At the beginning of 1941, Harry Hopkins, President Roosevelt's personal representative, came to England to see for himself (and the President) how the fight was going. He stayed for almost three weeks, and the Churchills took immediately to the frail man who proved himself such a great fighter for freedom. He went everywhere with Winston and spent much time at Chequers, where Clementine, realizing he was a very sick man, mothered him almost as much as she mothered her husband. She persuaded him to rest in bed during the hours when Winston was working in bed; she took special care of his diet, and made sure that he was always dressed warmly against the biting winter cold.

Chequers is an abnormally difficult house to heat, has no central heating, and architects have despaired of installing modern heating because of the fear of injuring the exquisite paneling, some of which is four or five hundred years old.

Hopkins found those weekends at Chequers to be the worst hardship he had to endure in wartime Britain. "It is the coldest house I have ever visited," he told her.

"Harry hates Chequers more than the devil hates holy water," General Eisenhower would say.

Hopkins invariably arrived there with plenty of long woolen underwear, and Clementine made sure there was always a blazing fire in his room, but, even so, he seldom removed his overcoat. His favorite haunt was the ground-floor lavatory, which, he said, was the only room with "central heating." He went there to read his newspapers and dispatches; but even in that room he kept his overcoat wrapped about him.

Bernard Baruch visited Chequers several times. He said, "It was a great treat to sit at the table with Winston and to hear him hold forth —with his inimitable verve and eloquence—on a host of subjects, great and small. In one discussion the subject of German war crimes and punishment came up. There were some original and unique suggestions on what ought to be done with Hitler if he fell into our hands alive. But Winston, I recall, thought it would be much simpler if he were to perish with the evil he had created."

Winston's constant concern for Clementine showed itself one weekend when Admiral of the Fleet Fraser of North Cape, and Sir Charles Portal of Bomber Command were at Chequers. Said Admiral Fraser, "It was dark when I arrived. Mrs. Churchill had gone out visiting hospitals in the neighborhood. This was the period when the air raids were in full swing, and when by 8 P.M. his wife had still not returned, the Prime Minister was becoming more and more anxious.

" 'What a stupid thing to do, to be out late like this and no one knows where she is,' he said, striding up and down the room in his zip siren suit. Rather a case of the pot calling the kettle black, I thought!

"However, she arrived a few minutes later, and as a minor explosion seemed about to occur we deemed it best to retire, although everyone appeared at dinner in the best of spirits. I suppose there are few more devoted couples in the world than Sir Winston and Lady Churchill and it was easy to appreciate his anxiety.

"After dinner, photographs of Chequers and its surroundings, just taken from the air for identification purposes, were put on the screen. To our amazement, in one of them was a large semicircle of ploughed land about five miles away, with a broad arrow in the center pointing straight at Chequers!

"The Prime Minister chuckled, 'Look how well I am looked after! But we had better make inquiries in the morning.'

"On investigation, the strange markings were found to be quite fortuitous; owing to the nature of the ground and obstructing trees, the farmer had to plough his land in this fashion."

One guest at Chequers proved unusually demanding. Winston himself recorded the occasion in his inimitable style, "The inveterate suspicion with which the Russians regarded foreigners was shown by some remarkable incidents during Molotov's stay at Chequers," he wrote.

"On arrival they had asked at once for keys to all the bedrooms. These were provided with some difficulty and thereafter our guests always kept their doors locked. When the staff of Chequers succeeded in getting in to make the beds, they were disturbed to find pistols under the pillows. The three chief members of the mission were attended not only by their own police officers, but by two women who looked after their clothes and tidied their rooms. When the Soviet envoys were absent in London these women kept constant guard over their masters' rooms, only coming down one at a time for their meals.

"Extraordinary precautions were taken for Molotov's personal safety. His room had been thoroughly searched by his police officers, every cupboard and piece of furniture and the walls and floors being meticulously examined by practiced eyes. The bed was the object of particular attention; the mattresses were all prodded in case of infernal machines, and the sheets and blankets were rearranged by the Russians so as to leave an opening in the middle of the bed out of which the occupant could spring at a moment's notice, instead of being tucked in. At night a revolver was laid out beside his dressing gown and his dispatch case. It is always right especially in time of war to take precautions against danger, but every effort should be made to measure its reality. The simplest test is to ask oneself whether the other side have any interest in killing the person concerned. For myself, when I visited Moscow I put complete trust in Russian hospitality.

"Let there be sunshine on both sides of the Iron Curtain; and if ever the sunshine should be equal on both sides, the Curtain will be no more."

"I used to be at Chequers two weekends out of three," said General Sir Frederick Pile, "and it was really a most domestic place in spite of its constant war atmosphere. Clementine somehow still managed to make it a home. When it was time for dinner, she wouldn't have any nonsense.

"She would say to Winston's personal assistant, Tommy Thompson, 'Tommy, collect the Prime Minister. He's upstairs and he'll go on working unless you collect him.' Winston would sometimes come down and say he had a bit more work to do, and she would reply, 'No, we're going in to dinner, and you can talk as long as you like afterwards.' That was her attitude all the time. She made him appreciate that he had got to live to the rules of ordinary domestic life for his health's sake in particular, although he still often managed to duck the rules.

"If there wasn't roast beef for Sunday lunch, then, as far as Winston was concerned, it was a bad lunch. He would say, 'What are we having for lunch?' Once when Clementine told him, he demanded, 'Why haven't we got roast beef?' And she answered, 'I suppose you haven't heard there's a war on and you're rationed like the rest?'

"It was the only time I was there that we didn't have roast beef. She didn't mince words. He loves his food and adores roast beef, which must be underdone. If it's done too much there's hell to pay."

Lord Ismay said, "To keep house—to keep an establishment—over the head of a man like Winston Churchill must have been extraordinarily difficult. Great though the honor must be to serve him—to have no fixed hours at all—to serve a man who may sit down to dinner at half-past eight, or may sit down to dinner at half-past ten was very rough. She used to get very angry with him at times when he tried to get away with it. He would need some excellent excuse, which he often had. I have known us not to leave the table until past midnight.

"You may think I am suggesting he is inconsiderate. Well of course he was inconsiderate—to all of us—but he was far more inconsiderate to himself. The only thing he thought of was the war. Whether anyone was made uncomfortable, or whether he was made extremely uncomfortable, didn't matter a damn—all that mattered was to win the war.

"The fact that he's so very particular about what he eats didn't make things any easier. You couldn't just give him eggs every day or anything like that. Nevertheless she managed to bring some kind of sense and order into his life. Without this he would have been chaotic."

General Sir Frederick Pile continued "... To most people, a meal is a meal, but to the Churchills it is something far more important—it's a holiday combined with talk about the affairs of the world. Clemmie talks with him about every conceivable subject and often greatly influences his ideas, as she did at a time when we were not getting on so well with President Roosevelt.

"There were many difficulties at that period, but one of the trouble spots was our having to buy the old destroyers from the United States, and it broke Winston's heart—he thought they were third-rate, and said so. Nor did he like buying them with our vital currency-earning overseas investments, nor being forced to lease America a part of the Commonwealth as a base because of the destroyer deal. He felt we were being driven into a hard unfair bargain.

"The discussion at lunch ranged round the Roosevelt problem. She said simply, out of the blue, 'Why don't you get Mr. Smuts to talk to Roosevelt about this?'

"Winston jumped up at once and said, 'I will!'

"He put a call through immediately to Smuts in South Africa and asked him—we were still in the room at lunch—if he would talk to Roosevelt about the various points of disagreement between us. He did, and things improved.

"Although Mrs. Churchill was terribly close to so many of the various conduct-of-war problems, she was the one person sufficiently detached to see sometimes the whole picture from a quite different angle. It was genius, because Roosevelt was a man of world importance and who could talk to Roosevelt? But General Smuts was just the right stature and he was also a tremendous friend of both of them—they both admired his statesmanship.

"Discussion of the war was never silenced because she happened to be at the table with us, or anywhere else. She knew everything that was going on. There were no secrets from her. Everything didn't stop for lunch, tea, or dinner—the war was all that mattered the whole time, and if there was business on everyone's mind, it was discussed irrespective of her presence.

"She kept Chequers running, she was ringmaster and hostess, and after a meal, we were all sent off with Winston to his library, and often didn't see her again until the following day. She never came down to breakfast. She would walk in the garden with guests, and often had her own guests staying there—as a rule, they were people such as the wives of Ministers and those connected with the extensive war services in which she was so heavily involved.

"She is a bubbling person—the sort of woman you would like to take out to dinner. If she hadn't been the Prime Minister's wife I might have asked her. Yet although she was always so full of life, at Chequers she had this curious placid effect—she calmed everything down. It was an incredible feat of discipline on her part."

"She was also a very good judge of persons," said Lord Ismay. "She had a keenly discerning idea of who were Winston's real friends, who were his flatterers, and who were the people on whom he could really rely. I don't think that, in many respects, he was nearly as good a judge as she was. She was a very sound and astute assessor of character.

"And in regard to the point Sir Frederick Pile makes about the business and secrets of war continuing in her presence, I can assure you

188

that Winston was very meticulous about letting her into any big items of news, directly he knew it himself.

"After the war, before he became Prime Minister again, she was staying at my home for a week, and he rang one night to tell her that the pound was going to be devalued the next day. He had been told by Attlee, and thought that Clemmie should know at once. No official announcement on the matter had been made as yet.

"Keeping her informed like this on important affairs was habit with him, and throughout the war he did exactly the same. There were no secrets from her. It was an eye-opener to me that he was so meticulous about informing her of official matters like that.

"I think the reason he always did this was because he felt they were so close to each other. It is typical of their marriage. It is such an ideal marriage, I suppose one of the most ideal there has ever been. Winston's attitude was always—'Clemmie will be interested—I must tell her!'"

There were few visitors to Chequers who were not connected in some way with official business, but from time to time Clementine would invite an unexpected guest to help Winston relax a little.

At Chequers, Clementine liked to change from more formal dress into blouse and slacks, while always, after dinner, Winston would don one of the fabulous, almost exotic dressing gowns in which he delighted, and invite their guests to see a film show. Clementine chose the films, and everyone, staff incuded, was asked to the shows, which took place in the long gallery on the first floor.

Often, after a film show, they would go to a small table and play a game of bagatelle. At times, when Winston's attention appeared to be concentrated on the game, he would jump up from the bagatelle board and go to his study or call an immediate meeting of Ministers and chiefs of staff.

Clementine could sense when he was doing one thing while, in reality, concentrating on another. It was the same with his well-known curious habit of marching to music in the great hall when he would put on records of popular songs or military bands then, turning the radiogram's volume full up, march up and down the hall, with head thrust forward, hands in pockets, humming or singing the tune being played.

One weekend, Winston recruited a distinguished partner for one of these dancing sessions. In August, 1941, Canada's Prime Minister, Mackenzie King, came to Chequers. Vividly describing the visit, he said, "At dinner, conversation was very free altogether from any restraint. He was quite clearly enjoying his relaxation from his work and entering completely into the spirit of the occasion with a real buoyancy. He really is a big boy at heart, untiring in energy and interst. . . .

"What appeals to me most is his innate love of truth and right and justice, and his tremendous courage in asserting their claims. Also his great tenderness and lovableness in his own home with his own family.

"He said, 'I have no ambition beyond getting us through this mess. There is nothing that anyone could give me or that I could wish for. They cannot take away what I have done.'

"I said there was a destiny about his life. He had been meant for these times. Speaking of it in a modest way, he said, 'It looks like it, in a way, as though it were meant.'"

Dinner wasn't until nine o'clock on the Sunday evening as Winston was broadcasting at 8:30. The guests joined Clementine to listen to the broadcast.

"There was a profound silence throughout the whole of the speech," recalled Mr. Mackenzie King. "When Mr. Churchill coughed, as he did two or three times, one felt there was a little concern. When the speech was over, no one said a word for some little time. We waited for Mrs. Churchill to speak. There seemed to be unanimity of feeling that it was the best broadcast he had made.

"At the table, both he and Mrs. Churchill said he would receive numerous letters tomorrow in regard to his cough, sending cures of different kinds. He was very much like a boy out of school when the broadcast was over. A great sense of relief.

"After dinner that evening, he turned on the radio for music and began to walk up and down and perform a sort of dance. He turned and asked me, could I not do the same? whereupon I joined him and two of us took each other by the arm and performed a dance together. All present were almost in hysterics with laughter."

"If Clementine entered the room while one of Winston's record sessions was on, she would never interrupt," said Lord Ismay. "She would simply let him carry on marching and singing with absolute seriousness; then, when the music stopped, if he turned to her and smiled, she knew he had come to the decision he had been trying to reach.

"With his immense powers of concentration, he does not like his train of thought to be broken until he has reached a conclusion, although he is not averse to the presence of someone he knows near him, or someone who can answer a question if need be, or be sent to seek information."

The Hawtrey room, with its lovely antique furniture and beautiful paintings, was the second main room of the house. It was the one room in Chequers that they really loved, and, therefore, the place in which he could work best. It was there that he wrote many of his greatest wartime speeches and broadcasts, and there that he spoke to the world on those memorable Sunday nights immediately before the B.B.C.'s nine o'clock news. As he talked into the microphone, Clementine would listen in an adjoining room.

Winston hated fuss and relished danger; nevertheless, Chequers was guarded night and day by detectives, by soldiers in Bren gun carriers, and by roof spotters always on the alert in case Nazi paratroops decided to launch a direct attack on the Prime Minister's country home. The *Luftwaffe* tried many times to hit the house, and once managed to drop bombs in the grounds close by. The only precaution Winston agreed to take was to arrange for a revolver range to be installed in the grounds. There, regularly, he practiced with his rifle, Colt .45 automatic pistol, and Webley service revolver.

When, in the invasion-threatened days, there was talk by visitors who came there, of circumstances which might possibly warrant the evacuation of the King and the Government to safety in Canada, Winston emphatically refuted any such possibility.

"Every man ought to fight to the death on his own soil," he said, "and if they come to London, I shall take a rifle—I'm not a bad shot—I will put myself in a pillbox at the bottom of Downing Street and shoot till I've no more ammunition, and then they can damned well shoot me."

He never shielded Clementine from harsh truth. He considered she was entitled to know. After Dunkirk he told her, as he had told his Cabinet colleagues, that although he was certain the British could reach some form of peace terms with Hitler, he thought the advantage would be short-lived and, in any case, he did not feel it compatible with his own conscience and honor to do this. "We must fight on even though it would undoubtedly mean that women and children at home would suffer terribly." His own road, he said, was clear.

Only intimate friends realized how deeply he felt the sufferings of the ordinary men and women throughout Europe who pinned their faith so blindly on his leadership.

If Clementine continued to welcome distinguished visitors from overseas, it was not because she or Winston had time for social amenities. Guests were welcome because they could reveal what other countries were thinking.

"Have you seen the people?" he would inquire urgently. "I am nothing. But the people . . . they suffer so, and never whimper. They suffer for this stupid war, this criminal war that never should have happened if we had not been so blind. This war that should have been won before we fought it, and that now must be fought through to the end."

Clementine talked constantly of the people with whom they had spoken on the bombed rubble of London and other blitzed cities. "All their possessions wiped out in one blast!" Clementine exclaimed.

"An Englishman's home is a fine phrase," said Winston. "It was never so fine a reality. No one can govern Britain again who forgets the people. They saved Britain, you know, a year ago, and again after the great blitzes. They deserve to win. They deserve to win gloriously. They shall!"

One Saturday, that great wartime American journalist, Quentin Reynolds, went down to Chequers to work with Harry Hopkins on a speech Hopkins was to broadcast the following day from Winston's personal microphone.

Winston was himself preparing a two-hour speech for Parliament. Mr. John Winant came down for a hurried conference. Averell Harriman and his daughter Kathleen also arrived, and there were a host of other weekend guests who were supposed to provide relaxation for Winston—whose main form of relaxation was work.

Miss Dorothy Thompson, the distinguished American political commentator, recalled that at lunch that day they all discussed the Russian front with pessimism. Winston asked her, "Such a state! Was there ever such a state?

"We are the hope of three-fourths of the people of all the world. The people in the remote Chinese villages, on the Russian steppes, cowering in Poland, in the rabbit warrens of Paris, on the dikes of Holland and fjords of Norway. . . . The disarmed and the helpless, crying silently to the Anglo-Saxon world, 'Rescue us!'

"And the price? Suffering . . . our transitory lives. . . . Not all of us will grow old. Why should people work and toil and never have a full belly or secure roof? Strike an international balance sheet on surplus commodities. Give. Share. Produce. Use . . . !

"Must a Chinese peasant live forever on rice and a scrap of fish? Why should he? Did the Dutch ever do anybody any harm? Did they govern their colonies badly? Did they neglect their people? Did they waste their wealth? Did they trample on other nations?

"There is so much to do when all this is over. A wonderful world— or a shambles and a prison."

Miss Thompson asked him, "How are you going to win the war?"

"First," he replied, "we shall see that we do not lose it."

Harry Hopkins wanted Quentin Reynolds to help him write his speech for the B.B.C. and get it into the kind of language which the British public would understand. That is why he had been invited by Clementine to Chequers.

Reynolds said later, "Harry was dog-tired and had a touch of the grippe; at least, that is what he told Mrs. Churchill. I am sure that it was his old ailment bothering him, but he always sloughed that off by saying casually, 'Got a little cold during the trip over.'

"Mrs. Churchill was very concerned about Harry's health. She knew him so well that she could tell when he was in pain by looking at him, I think. Around eleven o'clock in the evening she would start trying to persuade him to go to bed, saying, 'You have a long day tomorrow, and you can have a nice talk with Winston in the morning. I've fixed your bed and put a hot water bottle in it.' I am sure Harry never got such mothering in his life except, maybe, from Mrs. Roosevelt."

In April, 1942, Harry Hopkins came again to Chequers on a Saturday afternoon. This time, however, he found the weekend lacking its usual gaiety and charm. Clementine was ill with general exhaustion, and Winston himself was less than normally exuberant as a result of the terrible strain of the series of battle disasters and the fighting the Services had endured.

Years later, Hopkins, who never forgot the kindness and thoughtfulness he had been shown at Chequers and at Downing Street, wrote the last letter of his life to his two friends. It was dated January 22, 1946, and the Churchills were holidaying at Miami Beach, Florida. He wrote, "Only being laid up in the hospital prevented me from meeting you in the boat the other day. . . .

"All I can say about myself at the moment is that I am getting excellent care while the doctors are struggling over a very bad case of cirrhosis of the liver—not due, I regret to say, from taking too much alcohol. But I must say that I dislike having the effect of a long life of congenial and useful drinking and neither deserve the reputation nor enjoy its pleasures.

"The newspapers indicate you and Clemmie are having a quiet and delightful time and I hope that you won't let any Congressional committee of ours bore you.

"Do give my love to Clemmie and Sarah, all of whom I shall hope to see before you go back, but I want to have a good talk with you over the state of world affairs, to say nothing of our private lives."

A week later Harry Hopkins was dead. A victim of hemochromatosis, a digestive disease. He had been at death's door for nine years.

Every weekend at Chequers was a weekend of history. On the evening of Friday, June 20, 1941, as they drove down to Buckinghamshire, Winston told Clementine that he was sure Germany would attack Russia within days or even hours.

The guests at Chequers that Saturday and Sunday were the American Ambassador, Mr. John Winant and his wife, Mr. and Mrs. Anthony Eden, Lord Cranborne, Lord Beaverbrook, and Sir Stafford Cripps, British Ambassador to Russia, who had come down to tender his resignation on the grounds of ill health. Winston had agreed to accept his resignation.

At dinner the conversation was solely of the imminent threat to the Soviets. Sir Stafford said the Russians had been warned by British Intelligence that Germany would, in all probability, attack them, but they had largely discredited the warning as "wishful thinking."

Winston had given a standing instruction that he was never to be awakened for anything less than the invasion of England, and so a telephone message, which came through from the Foreign Office on Sunday at 4 A.M. was held until he awoke at 8 A.M. It reported that Hitler had attacked Russia on a 1,500-mile front stretching from Finland to the Black Sea.

"Tell the B.B.C. that I will broadcast at nine tonight," he said.

He asked Sir Stafford to return at once to Russia, and Sir Stafford agreed to do so. Then, leaving Clementine to look after the guests, Winston went to his room to write the now famous speech in which, while still attacking the Communist creed, he promised Russia and the Soviet people Britain's complete support. He devoted the whole day to its preparation, breaking off only to lunch briefly with Clementine, Sir Stafford, and his other guests.

He had decided to range Britain's strength behind Russia in spite of the Soviets' unpopularity with the public, and in the face of his advisers' warning that "the country will not stand for it."

"I *know* I am right, Clemmie!" he said.

Sunday, December 7, 1941, brought another fateful evening to Chequers. Winston had been uneasy all day. When lunch was announced, he would not sit down to table. He was waiting restlessly and impatiently for the arrival of the American Ambassador, Mr. Winant, and Mr. Averell Harriman.

Clementine took her other guests in to lunch, leaving Winston pacing up and down outside the main entrance to the house. The meal had been in progress for twenty minutes when Mr. Winant arrived, to be greeted immediately with a demand to know whether he thought there would be war with Japan.

"Yes," said Mr. Winant.

"If they declare war on you, we shall declare war on them within the hour," Winston declared. Then he asked, "If they declare war on us, will you declare war on them?"

Mr. Winant could not answer the question, claiming that only the Congress had the right to declare war, under the United States Constitution.

Winston recognized only too well that if Japan attacked Siam or British territory in the East, Britain would be forced into an Asiatic war that would leave America out. In that event Britain would be left holding the entire baby, and the result could be complete disaster for the country.

"We're late, you know. Get washed, and we will go in to lunch together," he said, dropping the subject.

The afternoon passed quietly. Clementine walked with Mr. Averell Harriman and his daughter Kathleen in the grounds until, feeling not too well, she decided to go to bed for an hour or two.

As usual, she had arranged an excellent dinner. The party entered the dining room a few minutes before nine o'clock, and as they sat down Winston asked the butler to put on the table the little portable radio set which Harry Hopkins had sent as a gift. He switched it on, there were the usual national anthems, and then the news.

The announcer read several official war bulletins, and made an announcement that seemed to refer to Japanese attacks on British vessels in the Dutch East Indies and on American shipping at Hawaii.

It was all rather vague, but Mr. Winant and Mr. Harriman wanted to know more about the references to the attacks on the American ships. As they were discussing the matter, the butler entered the room and, interrupting, said, "It's quite true. We heard it ourselves, outside. The Japs have attacked the Americans."

For a moment there was silence around the table. Then Winston jumped to his feet and declared, "We shall declare war on Japan." However, appreciating in the same instant that he could hardly declare war on the strength of a radio bulletin, he went into his office and phoned President Roosevelt in Washington.

"They have attacked us at Pearl Harbor," Roosevelt told his old friend. "We are all in the same boat now."

Mr. Winant spoke to the President for a few minutes, and then everybody went back into the hall—as Winston later wrote, "to adjust our thoughts to the supreme world event which had occurred, which was of so startling a nature as to make even those who were near the center gasp."

Often during the winter evenings at Chequers, Winston and Clementine would sit together by one of the enormous coal fires and listen to their son-in-law, Vic Oliver, playing the piano. They would get him to play over and over again all Eddie Cantor's famous songs from the film *Whoopee,* and Winston would sing the words in his hoarse, off-key baritone.

One night in 1941, Winston came down from his study with set face and pained eyes. Clementine watched him as he came into the room and then, without a word, poured a glass of port and handed it to him. It was obvious something serious had happened. Sarah and Vic Oliver were among the company, and thinking to relieve the tension, Clementine asked Vic to play something on the piano. He was about to strike up "Lily of Laguna," but feeling that a popular song might be inappropriate to the seriousness of the moment, he changed his mind and began to play Beethoven's *Appassionata* sonata. He had played only a few bars when Winston rose to his feet and thundered, "Stop! Don't play that!"

It was the first time that he had ever raised his voice to his son-in-law and everybody was shocked.

"What is the matter?" Clementine asked.

"I will not have the Dead March played in my house," answered Winston angrily.

"It's not the Dead March," Vic protested. "It's the *Appassionata*."

"You can say what you like," Winston said. "I know it is the Dead March."

Unwisely, perhaps, Vic tried to make his point by playing a few bars of each melody in turn; but as soon as he struck the first notes of the sonata, Winston roared again, "Stop it! Stop it, I say! I want no Dead March, I tell you."

Sarah rushed to the piano and asked her husband to play a popular song instead, while Clementine went across to Winston to placate him.

The following morning it was announced officially that H.M.S. *Hood* had been sunk with heavy loss of life.

The night General Arnold, Commanding General of the U.S. Army Air Forces, went to Chequers, had been preceded by quite a day. All day, Clementine had had to deal with an irrepressible Winston who just couldn't contain his excitement. The evening was to witness the R.A.F.'s first thousand-bomber raid on Germany, and Clementine couldn't make Winston relax an instant, so she finally gave up trying and concentrated on taking care of the comfort of her other guests—the American Ambassador, Mr. Winant, Air Chief Marshal Portal, General Ismay, Averell Harriman, and Admiral Towers.

"As we sat down to dinner I knew beforehand—even without the Prime Minister's jubilation—that the R.A.F. was taking off on the greatest bombardment operation ever lauched," says General Arnold. "This was the real beginning, in the world's eyes and in Germany's eyes, of the campaign we later came to term officially 'Air Offensive Europe'—the 'round the clock' destruction of Germany from the air. That night all of England was a bomber base."

At dinner, Winston asked some technical questions General Arnold couldn't answer, so he telephoned for his pilot Colonel Beebe. When the Colonel was faced with the question of going home, Winston solved it by saying, "You stay here and spend the night."

"But I didn't bring my pajamas," the Colonel answered.

Winston, six inches shorter than the Colonel, obligingly offered to lend him his. They scarcely covered him, but the Colonel slept in the Prime Minister's pajamas that night.

"After breakfast, Admiral Towers and I both had to go to the 'johnny,' continued General Arnold. "The door was one of those cumbersome affairs with locks dating back to Elizabethan times. I had no trouble, but Admiral Towers couldn't get out. He called to me in great consternation to come and help him. Thirty-odd years before he had contributed to the invention of aviation's first safety belt, but it couldn't aid him now.

"I called the valet. He called the plumbers, the carpenters, and the chambermaids. It was Sunday, and they were all down at the pub in the village.

"A bit later, with Mrs. Churchill, I was walking in the garden when to our surprise, we saw the feet, then the blue uniform trousers, and finally the full uniform of an American Admiral climbing out of the first floor of Chequers.

"Mrs. Churchill said, 'My, what an extraordinary way to leave the house!'"

During a subsequent visit by General Arnold to Chequers, conversation somehow got round to a discussion on honeymoons.

"I told Mrs. Churchill about the ride in an ox cart my wife and I had had from the dock at Guam to the little town of Agana when we landed there on our honeymoon," said General Arnold.

"She said, 'Tell Mrs. Arnold when Winnie and I were on our honeymoon we visited Venice. I wanted to ride in a gondola; he insisted on a motor launch—said it was far more healthy; the fumes killed the germs, and so on. So we rode in a gasoline launch!' Clementine added, 'There is not much romance in Winnie.'"

In spite of momentous news constantly breaking the quiet of Chequers at weekends, Clementine somehow managed to maintain an atmosphere of relaxation about the place. Like any country-house hostess in peacetime she was meticulous about her guest book. A visitor was expected to sign it every time he entered the house.

Journeying to the south coast, General Eisenhower dropped in at Chequers unexpectedly for a few minutes. After talking with the Prime Minister, he hurried out to continue his journey, but as he settled into the seat of his car he became aware of the Churchill butler standing beside the car, waiting to speak to him.

"Sir," said the butler, "you have forgotten something." And with that, he handed Clementine's famous guest book to Ike for his signature.

General Mark Clark—Ike's deputy, and later Commander of the Fifth Army—joined his Chief on a visit to Chequers. "At dinner, the only ladies were Mrs. Churchill and Lady Portal," said General Clark. "Churchill told us not to worry about talking about war plans during dinner because 'my wife and Lady Portal know everything.'"

After one of Clementine's evenings, Major General Sir John Kennedy, then Director of Military Operations at the War Office, said, "I had not been to a party on such a splendid scale for a long time. It was delightful, and the war seemed very remote."

During one of Sir John's discussions with Winston, Clementine came in to say that she was going over to Blenheim Palace for lunch. Winston reached for the big gold watch on the table beside his bed and knocked it to the floor. He treasured that watch, and looked down at it silently. "Mrs. Churchill picked it up, put it to her ear, and reported in a phrase, which took my fancy, 'Its little heart is beating quite strongly,'" Sir John reported.

Judge Samuel Rosenman, one of President Roosevelt's closest associates was one guest who couldn't resist putting his impressions of a Chequers weekend down on paper. Recalled Judge Rosenman, "Perhaps a letter which I wrote home the next day while the visit was still fresh in mind will best describe it:

'Dear Dorothy. Chequers is an old estate with a house started in 1430 and reconstructed and added to through the centuries. Some of the original walls are still there. Shades of temporary housing! It is 40 miles, about, from London, in the most beautiful rural area you have ever seen. I assure you it bears no resemblance to the retreat in the Maryland Mountains except, perhaps, in the paucity of the bathrooms....

'I was asked for dinner last night and to spend the night. As per instructions, I arrived at 7:45. The guests were there in country attire except the P.M. who was, I suppose, sleeping in preparation for the evening. Guests were Mr. Fraser, the P.M. of New Zealand; Mr. Churchill, the P.M.'s brother; Lord Cherwell, the P.M.'s economist and statistician; Mrs. Sarah Oliver, the P.M.'s daughter; and a few others.

'At 8:15 I was told to go up and dress for dinner. For me this meant a clean shirt and a black tie, for I was wearing my blue suit. But for the other men, it meant dinner coats. Mine was a good substitute with a black bow tie. The P.M., however, pulled an F.D.R. In fact he went one better. He came down in one of those air raid zipper overall affairs with his shirt collar unbuttoned—and *no* tie. I must add that I was forced to take a bath before dinner by the valet announcing very firmly that my bath was ready. It was way down the cold and drafty hall.

'The house—every part of it—was freezing unless you hugged the great big fireplaces, in which case it meant you broiled.

'We sat down to dinner at 9 p.m.... Dinner was over at 10. Brandy was over at 10:30. I began to envisage bed because I was tired and was trying to keep up the appearance of drinking. I could have slept.

'But at 10:30 the P.M. turns to Sarah and says, "What is the film for tonight?" I thought I had misheard; but the answer was clear—"A

House of One's Own"—and she added turning to me, "Put on your overcoat, it's cold in the cinema room."

'I put on my overcoat. The P.M. put on a loud bathrobe, and we all trotted to the refrigerator where the movie was shown. There were 30 or 40 soldiers, sailors, maids, butler, etc., seated there—as at the White House. Our procession moved in. The P.M. sat down with a whiskey and soda, and I had one forced into my hand too.

'... We stumbled downstairs at about 12:30. By this time in addition to being sleepy, I was cold and hungry.

'The P.M. really was very entertaining. He held the floor, reciting poetry and talking generally until 2:15 A.M., when he suddenly turned to me and wanted to know what I was putting in my food report, whether I was going to take any British food away from them.

'Thereupon followed serious discussion with which I will not bore you. At 3 A.M. someone (bless his soul) suggested bed. The P.M. displayed surprise at the lateness of the hour, but I knew that he was not surprised.

'I had heard from F.D.R. and from Harry about this performance but this is the first time *I* was the victim.

'Someone carried me to bed, for I was too tired to walk—and a comfortable one it was. It was a good thing I had not tried to keep up with drinking or the word "carried" would have been literal.

'I got up at 8:30. At 9:30 I went in to say goodbye to the P.M. who was having breakfast in bed very chipper and gay.

'We had a talk about war crimes and then I drove into London.

'I'm going to try to catch up with some sleep tonight.

'Goodnight and much love. It was quite an experience at Chequers, but protect me from it as a steady diet. I would not have missed it for the world.

'Devotedly,
'Sam.' "

In the years when the *Luftwaffe* was determined to bomb Winston Churchill off the face of the earth, if that could be done, Clementine managed to instigate a precaution reserved for "bombers' moon," nights when the moon was full and the *Luftwaffe* was in the habit of coming over in force. She arranged for a secret "shadow Chequers" at Dytchley Park, near Woodstock, north of Oxford. One of the loveliest of England's stately homes, built in the seventeenth century, Dytchley was owned by Mr. and Mrs. Ronald Tree, who were old friends of the

Churchills. Ronald Tree was then Parliamentary Secretary to Brendan Bracken, the Minister of Information.

Dytchley Park stood close to Blenheim Palace, where Winston was born. Three of its large ground-floor rooms were reserved as offices for him, and in subsequent years—though Winston and Clementine stayed there only during the worst of the bombing nights—the house was to see its share of war history.

When, during a Dytchley weekend, a guest remarked that Winston had given the people courage, he replied, "*I* never gave them courage. I was able to focus *theirs*."

Winston and Clementine were at Dytchley on Sunday, May 11, 1944. Suddenly the Marx Brothers film they were watching was interrupted by an urgent telephone call. It was their friend, the Duke of Hamilton, with a message that a German, piloting his own aircraft and dressed in the uniform of a *Luftwaffe* flight lieutenant, had bailed out over Scotland. After first giving his name as Horn, the man had said that he was Rudolph Hess, Hitler's deputy Fuehrer. He claimed that he had parachuted into Britain to negotiate a "settlement."

Winston was not amused. He growled, "Will you kindly instruct the Duke of Hamilton to tell that to the Marx Brothers?"

But the Marx Brothers' antics soon took a back seat in Dytchley's cinema room to the even crazier story of Hess's mission personally to "negotiate peace with the King."

Chequers was not entirely reserved for official guests. Miss Mary Shearburn, one of Winston's wartime secretaries, remembers with gratitude one of Clementine's thoughtful little actions.

She told me, "My home had been broken up on the outbreak of war, so that when I developed measles in the spring of 1941 there was nowhere for me to go when I left hospital. When I first fell ill Mrs. Churchill had tried very hard to get me into a nursing home, but as they wouldn't take infectious cases, it had to be the Fulham Fever Hospital. I was taken there in an ambulance—complete with a potted plant given to me by Mrs. Churchill as I left, to cheer me up a little.

"Every single day she personally telephoned the hospital for reports on my progress. As soon as I was out of quarantine, knowing that my family was far away, she simply telephoned me at the hospital and said, 'You are going to Chequers to convalesce.' There was no discussion—she had made all the arrangements—and that is where I went."

Miss Shearburn later married Inspector Walter H. Thompson, who was Winston's personal Scotland Yard bodyguard for many years. Thompson's memories of Chequers during the war period were mainly concerned with the extraordinary security safeguards, but he also had this to say:

"The war, quite naturally, came out ahead in all Mr. Churchill's thoughts. Mrs. Churchill had to be secondary, as must be the wife of any famous public servant. I saw how little time a Prime Minister could have with his wife. Actually Winston and his beloved wife had precious little time together and I did not envy her position. If other women in Britain did, they thought more of the honor than of the price of it.

"She was of course justly proud of his achievements, and her pride in those achievements was satisfied also by witnessing and sharing the rare experience of seeing a great man fulfil his destiny. She saw it happening in their joint presence rather than recorded and engraved at the bases of monuments for the generations ahead.

"This was going on while they were alive, not just something that was guaranteed to preserve his name after he passed, and she with him, into history. She knew this, and such moments and hours as they had together or shared with small groups were the more exquisite to her for that reason.

"A man can take some comfort in the knowledge that his name and work will survive and have meaning and use long after his death. Not so a woman. She wants all of her living to take place while she is herself alive, partaking of the many courses of the banquet table which can be laden in such plenty only once. A woman, the world over, would sooner be loved while living than famous when dead. And that is how it was with Mr. and Mrs. Churchill.

"One had a magnificent sense of the indestructibility of the immediate present whenever those two appeared together, and they felt it most of all."

Shortly after the pilotless flying bomb raids began, Clementine and Winston were at Chequers. On the Sunday morning she told him that she wanted to pay a visit to the Hyde Park antiaircraft battery in which their daughter Mary was serving. For some inexplicable reason she felt she must go that very day.

"I was there when she arrived in Hyde Park," said General Sir Frederick Pile, "and Mary's battery was in action—flying bombs were overhead. One passed over us and demolished a house close by.

"As Clementine, Mary, and I stood together, we saw a bomb dive out of the clouds and fall in the direction of Downing Street. It landed on the Guards' Chapel at Wellington Barracks, where a service was in progress, and killed or injured two hundred worshippers, largely men and women of the armed forces."

When Clementine returned to Chequers that day, Winston was in bed, working.

"Mary's battery has been in action today," she said, "and the Guards' Chapel is destroyed."

Viscount Alanbrooke remembers another Sunday at Chequers. It was almost the eve of D-Day.

"In the morning we went to church with Clemmie and Mary," he noted in his diary. "After lunch did some work and after tea we went for a walk. Dinner was followed by the usual film, after which Winston sat by the fire and drank soup. He looked very old and very tired. He said Roosevelt was not very well and that he was no longer the man he had been; this, he said, also applied to himself. He said he could still always sleep well, eat well, and especially, drink well; but that he no longer jumped out of bed in the way he used to, and felt as if he would be quite content to spend the whole day in bed. I have never yet heard him admit that he was beginning to fail."

It was at moments like these, when a tired, exhausted Winston felt at his lowest, that Clementine lifted him up.

Even though the chilly, austere mansion was never a great favorite with Winston, Clementine thought that they should personally add something to Chequers in memory of the many happy and stirring times they had spent there. She suggested that they should offer a gift of beech trees to be planted in an avenue.

Winston and Clementine submitted the offer to the Chequers Trustees, who are responsible for the administration and upkeep of the house and its grounds, and the gift was accepted.

There was always one other important occupant at Chequers—Nelson —their huge black cat, who padded around as if he owned the place, and allowed people to stroke him—sometimes. "Nelson's the bravest cat you ever saw," said Winston. "Once chased a big dog right out of the Admiralty."

The tradition of the Chequers weekends continued after the war when Winston once more became Premier. Mr. Adlai Stevenson arrived for lunch one Sunday, and Winston, who never missed an opportunity of stressing his family's American connections to any visitor from the United States, declared, "My mother was American, my ancestors were officers in Washington's army; so I am myself an English-Speaking Union."

Then, with a broad smile for Clemmie, who was seated at the other end of the table, he went on, "I also have some ties with Scotland which are to me of great significance, ties precious and lasting. First of all, I decided to be born on St. Andrew's Day. I commanded a Scottish battalion of the famous Twenty-first Regiment for five months in the line in France in the last war. I sat for fifteen years as the representative of 'bonny Dundee,' and I might be sitting for it still if the matter rested entirely with me. And it was to Scotland I went to find my wife."

16

Tenants at the White House

WHEN Winston set off on his travels again, Clementine went too, and so did Mary. Conferences had been arranged with Mr. Roosevelt and Mr. Mackenzie King, the Canadian Prime Minister, to plan the total defeat of the Axis powers.

It was the first great Quebec Conference, and Clementine decided to go, not only to look after Winston's health and comfort, but also to make a return visit to the United States in acknowledgment of Mrs. Roosevelt's tour in Britain.

On the night of August 4, 1943, they left London. By the morning they reached the River Clyde where they embarked in one of the old Calais-Dover steamers to reach the *Queen Mary*. In their party was Mary, Averell Harriman and his daughter, all the Chiefs of Staff, Winston's doctor—Lord Moran—Brigadier Orde Wingate and his wife, and a host of other planners, Intelligence, and Service personnel.

Brigadier Wingate, leader of the "Chindits,"—the Long Range Penetration Groups operating behind the Japanese lines—had been unexpectedly summoned to join the party. Clementine and Mary, returning to Downing Street for dinner after being absent all day organizing an Aid to Russia Fund flag day, found the legendary Wingate an unexpected guest. His experiences and theories about jungle fighting made such an impression on them that Winston said simply, "You must come and tell all this to the President," and that was the first Wingate knew of the scheduled departure that night for Quebec.

Wingate was delighted at the opportunity and honor, then remembered that he had had no chance, as yet, of even telling his wife that he was back in England. He was longing to see her, and she was staying

205

with her parents near Aberdeen. Winston went into action—two policemen woke up Lorna Wingate; told her to pack a suitcase, and took her by car to Edinburgh, where at 5 A.M. her husband, still in his baggy tropical uniform, stepped from the Prime Minister's train to give her a wonderful unexpected homecoming surprise.

Clementine, witnessing their station platform reunion from the window of her train compartment, was so moved by their obvious joy in each other, that she spoke to Winston and suggested that Lorna Wingate's name be added to the *Queen Mary*'s passenger list. Mrs. Wingate was invited to join the journey to Quebec, and, of course, immediately accepted.

Aboard ship, there were conference rooms, information rooms—everything continuing with the same precision as in London—including a counterpart of the Prime Minister's famous map room.

The ship observed radio silence. Outgoing messages were transmitted visually to attendant destroyers, which, after putting sufficient distance between themselves and the *Queen Mary* to avoid disclosing her position, passed the messages to London. Winston insisted on having a machine gun mounted in the lifeboat he and his family had been allotted, determined, as he said, to resist capture in the event of the ship being torpedoed.

Recalled Lord Ismay, Winston's Chief of Staff throughout the war, "We sailed in the *Queen Mary* for Halifax on August 5th...the Prime Minister was accompanied by his wife, and daughter Mary. Mrs. Churchill's presence was a great comfort. If the Prime Minister got ill, or was too naughty, she could look after him and stop him as no one else could.

"Junior Officer Mary Churchill, A.T.S., was worth her weight in gold as her father's aide-de-camp. What other member of his staff could march into the Prime Minister's bedroom and make him get up in time for his appointments?"

Brigadier Wingate's wife had her own individual impression of the voyage, "Clementine was unable to use the bathroom of their suite during the voyage as it was required, from time to time, for strategic purposes," said Mrs. Wingate. "Throughout the voyage to Halifax, the Prime Minister had been studying for the first time the details of Overlord—the plan for the invasion of Europe—and foremost in these plans were the synthetic harbors—the Mulberry Harbor as it was later known, which was to enable our forces to be supplied across open beaches.

"In his bathroom, Winston would be frequently seated on a stool, wearing one of his flamboyant dressing gowns, and surrounded by generals and admirals. The bath would be filled, and an admiral would make waves while a general floated little model Mulberry Harbors to illustrate their ingenious efficiency. No bathroom was ever the scene of the birth of such a stupendous military operation. No wonder Clementine could not get into it."

As the *Queen Mary* approached Halifax, Winston, Clementine, Mary, and others on the staff, went on the bridge to view the harbor and watch the pilot manage the difficult task of bringing the great vessel into port.

Mr. Mackenzie King, the Canadian Prime Minister, was waiting to welcome them at Wolfe's Cove. The main party was quartered in the beautiful Chateau Frontenac, which had been completely commandeered for conference personnel—British, American, and Canadian. Winston and Clementine were housed in the Governor General's summer residence, the Citadel—a lovely picturesque building on a hill overlooking Quebec, surrounded by stone ramparts from which could be seen the St. Lawrence River hundreds of feet below.

Anthony Eden arrived by seaplane to join the conference.

One of Winston's secretaries was a Canadian girl whose mother had taken the opportunity of flying from Vancouver to see her during the conference. Clementine, who, like Winston, always found time to think of others, suggested to him that they personally pay half the mother's fare from Vancouver, and he agreed. It was thoughtfulness such as this that helped inspire devotion of staff.

One afternoon, Mr. Mackenzie King had tea and a "very interesting conversation" alone with Clementine.

"She spoke about how much he relied upon me and spoke of how glad he was to be with me and to share days together," said the Canadian Prime Minister. "She told me many things about Winston. One thing was that his being out of office for a number of years and writing the life of Marlborough had had a real affect upon his character. He had discovered that Marlborough possessed great patience. That patience became the secret of his achievements. . . .

"Winston would ask her whether she thought he would ever be back in government again, and she had told him he might not.

"She then told me that when Neville Chamberlain took over and succeeded Baldwin, and did not invite him into the Cabinet, she said then she did not think he would be in any future government. She told me finally it was only four days before the war actually came on that Chamberlain told him he would like to have him in the Cabinet in the event of war.

"But, she went on to say, if war had not come, he would not have been taken into the Cabinet."

The following day he lunched with Clementine, Winston, and Mary, and the subject of Canadian whiskey supplies for British military canteens came up. Mr. Mackenzie King explained that industrial alcohol for war industries was being distilled instead of whiskey.

"This led to my speaking at the table of my course in regard to temperance," said Mackenzie King. "I said I had made up my mind at the beginning of the war that it would be much better to abstain altogether....I felt I would be better in my own health and judgment by taking a rest instead of stimulants and that I had decided also to take nothing for the period of the war."

"You look remarkably well," said a smiling Clementine.

"It is due, in large part, to having given up stimulants," Mackenzie King replied.

"I have not, but I am feeling well," Winston affirmed.

"Everything depends on habits a man has from youth. Were he to give it up completely, it would probably kill him," their guest answered. Mackenzie King recollected, "I felt no embarrassment in the conversation."

The Canadian Prime Minister gave a dinner, and in proposing a toast to Winston's health, spoke of his bringing Clementine with him to Canada, saying it helped to give Canadians an even greater feeling of being part of a family community in the British Commonwealth. When the conference had ended, Winston broadcast to the world from the Citadel.

It was time to leave, but Clementine insisted that before going on to Washington, Winston should snatch the opportunity of enjoying a few days relaxation fishing in Canada. He didn't have a chance to say "No" —she had already made arrangements with Prime Minister Mackenzie King, and off they went to beautiful Snow Lake, in the heart of the logging country, where they stayed in cabins heated by giant log fires.

Winston, Sir Charles Portal, and Viscount Alanbrooke thoroughly enjoyed the fishing together, and Clementine happily watched Winston benefit from this rest tonic he had so badly needed.

In Washington, the President had to go to his Hyde Park home before Winston had completed his work, and he told Winston and Clementine—"Please treat the White House as your home. Invite any-

The bride-to-be, described
in a 1908 issue of the
society magazine, *The
Bystander,* as having
". . . most delicately aquiline
features, fine gray eyes, and
a delightful poise of
the head . . ."

The Right Honorable Winston Churchill, M. P., and his fiancée,
Miss Clementine Hozier, their engagement photograph.

Golf enthusiast Clementine, competing in the Ladies' Parliamentary Golf Tournament at Ranelagh.

Arriving at St. Margaret's, Westminster, for the memorial service to Mr. Gladstone, in 1915.

Being pushed in a bath chair in the summer of 1912, when she was
suffering from the illness that almost crippled her for life.

In their 1924 election campaign in the Abbey Division of Westminster, when Clementine recruited chorus girls to dispatch leaflets...

BATTLING FOR VOTES

And in 1931, touring the Epping constituency with their daughter Diana.

Gripping the little traditional red dispatch box containing the budget secrets, Chancellor of the Exchequer Winston steps out of No. 11 Downing Street with Clementine, their son Randolph, daughter Diana, and Parliamentary Private Secretary Robert Boothby (later Lord Boothby), to present the budget to Parliament.

The Churchills and Chaplin—Charlie Chaplin joins Winston, Clementine, Diana, and Randolph for an after-lunch souvenir picture at Chartwell.

AT WAR

Clementine's austere little bedroom in the secret underground time headquarters of the War Cabinet and Chiefs of Staff in Marsham Street, Westminster. The headquarters has been preserved for its historic interest.

To Russia with love—wearing the uniform of the British Red Cross, Clementine talks with the defenders of Stalingrad in the square dedicated to the memory of the city's fallen heroes.

Sir Winston and Clementine
sit for official portrait
on occasion of his
85th birthday.

Mother and daughters—
with Mary and Diana at
the wedding of Winston's
nephew Giles Romilly.

Grandchildren: Emma, aged 9, Charlotte, 4, and Rupert Christopher, 1, leaving the Churchills' Hyde Park Gate home with their mother, Mrs. Mary Soames, after wishing grandfather a happy 86th birthday.

Randolph and his daughter Arabella join Winston and Clementine in the shade of the patio of Lord Beaverbrook's Riviera villa at Cap-d'Ail.

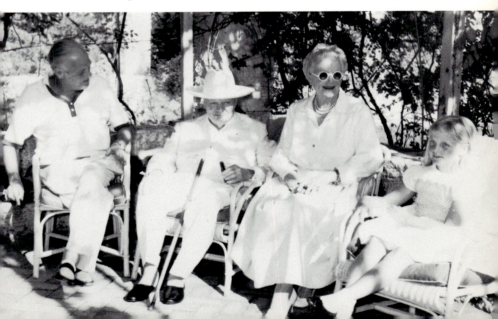

Declares the
candidate for
Woodford: "If I
have to go away . . .

"to meet Marshal
Stalin and President
Truman . . .

"my wife will take
my place during this
campaign.

"Other partnerships
may be temporary . . .

"This coalition . . .

"Goes on for good . . ."

A night out at the theater with Field Marshal Viscount Montgomery of Alamein as her escort.

And a "Welcome to London" for her guests—Marshal Tito and his wife.

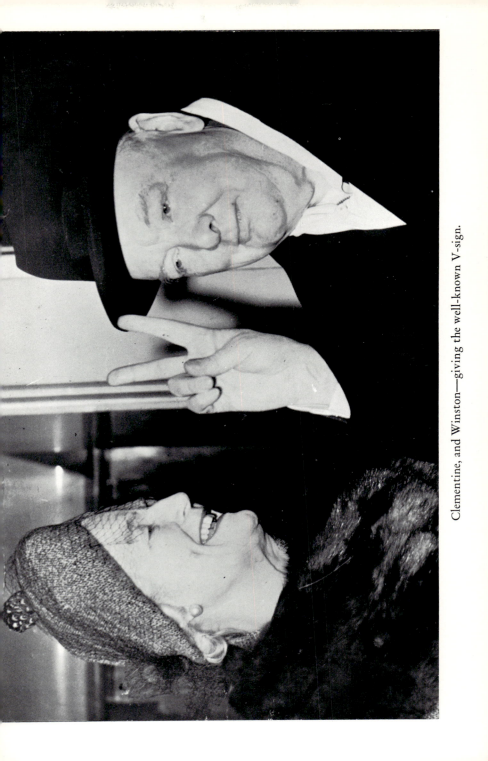

Clementine, and Winston—giving the well-known V-sign.

Two friends get together again—Eleanor Roosevelt and Clementine at a Foyle's literary luncheon held in Mrs. Roosevelt's honor.

Clementine watches from the doorway of No. 10 Downing Street as Winston holds open the car door for the Queen and the Duke of Edinburgh after they had dined with them and other distinguished guests on April 4, 1955—the night before Winston resigned from the Premiership.

Their marriage makes world headlines—a Golden Wedding Day
photograph taken in Lord Beaverbrook's villa at Cap-d'Ail.

one you like to any meals, and do not hesitate to summon any of my advisers with whom you wish to confer at any time. Break your journey to Halifax at Hyde Park and tell me all about it afterwards."

The Churchills accepted his offer and became temporary tenants of the White House. During their Washington stay, Italy was being invaded by the Allied forces and Marshal Badoglio had agreed to sign unconditional surrender terms on September 3. Clementine was with Winston in their suite when an urgent message arrived. Winston read it and his face became very grave. For some reason the agreement with Italy was not being signed. Later that day, the famous Churchill smile returned—a message from General Eisenhower came informing him that the surrender hitch had been overcome.

Also during that visit, Winston received an honorary Doctorate of Law at Harvard University.

When it was time to leave for Halifax they broke their journey at Hyde Park for a farewell get-together with the President and Mrs. Roosevelt to thank them for their hospitality. During the day they spent at Hyde Park—it was also their 35th wedding anniversary—Clementine thoroughly enjoyed a visit to the Roosevelts' museum where she saw how, along with the treasures of the Roosevelt family, gifts from ordinary people all over the country were preserved as well, with the same loving care.

President Roosevelt's comment to Clementine on her husband was, "A great fellow, if you can keep up with him."

They were going home on H.M.S. *Renown*. When the *Renown* left Halifax, they were housed in the Admiral's quarters high above the foredeck, but the voyage was a very uncomfortable one. The roll of the ship made it virtually impossible to sit still, and everything was perpetually sliding about. Winston even found it necessary to light his cigars by candle.

"That was the trip that Mary nearly got washed overboard on the day she was celebrating her twenty-first birthday," said Lord Ismay.

"I had been walking with her along the quarterdeck when we were told not to walk on that part of the ship because the *Renown* was about to execute a zigzag course as an antisubmarine precaution. The quarterdeck was cleared of personnel, and we were zigzagging like mad when I saw Mary out there again escorted by a young naval officer—'Schoolie' —the schoolmaster. He'd started walking with her, obviously delighted to be with this pretty girl. Suddenly the ship swerved violently and a wave came over. We didn't get a chance to shout a warning to them before this enormous wave swept over them and they completely disappeared.

"I was watching it, and I thought I'd have to go. We wouldn't dare face Winston again—we would have to go in after her. God, I was frightened. It was a miracle she wasn't drowned. When the wave receded, she and 'Schoolie' were left clinging to a stanchion. She was carried to safety, battered but not beaten, and after being given a brandy, taken to her cabin to her mother.

"Clemmie brought her round, and both of them later turned up for dinner in the Admiral's cabin. Not a word was said by anyone to Winston about Mary's escape. I don't think that Clemmie, in fact, told him until the end of the voyage."

Mary herself later admitted to her mother that as the wave struck her, she was certain she was about to be washed overboard and drowned.

The following year, the second Quebec Conference was called, and Clementine again made a point of going, particularly because Winston had suffered another minor attack of pneumonia, this time during a trip to Italy.

On Tuesday, September 5, they sailed once more from the Clyde in the *Queen Mary*.

Winston had told Clementine that the time had now come for the liberation of Asia, and he intended that Britain should play its full and equal part in it. He was determined that the United States would never be able to say in later years, "We came to your help in Europe and you left us alone to finish off Japan."

The ship was again a miniature Whitehall, with the Chiefs of Staff meeting the Prime Minister once and sometimes twice a day during the six-day voyage.

"Winston was very ill, tired, and was bad-tempered the whole way and although Clemmie did her utmost to make him comfortable during the voyage, he was irritable and continued to push himself to the limit, and over," said Lord Ismay. "He shouldn't have started that trip."

Viscount Alanbrooke noted in his diary:

"Lunch with Winston and Clemmie. He was not looking at all well and was most desperately flat. A good deal of it may be due to the M. & B. which he has been taking....

"Last night we passed close over a German submarine and intercepted his signals reporting having seen us....

"We had been traveling in the Gulf Stream all day and consequently living in a Turkish bath of hot clamminess. We began with a short C.O.S. meeting and at 12 noon had a meeting lasting until 1:30 P.M. with the P.M. He looked old, unwell, and depressed, evidently found it hard to concentrate and kept holding his head between his hands. . . ."

Also aboard ship, were American troops bound for leave in the United States. To accommodate the Churchill party, sailing time had been delayed several days and, appreciating the situation and the troops' disappointment, Winston personally asked President Roosevelt to make up any time the men had lost through being delayed by him.

While Winston spent most of the voyage working in his stateroom, Clementine occupied the days visiting American wounded on board, talking to each one individually, and bringing them the kind of warmth, conversation, and talk of home that only a mother could give.

Landing at Halifax, the party traveled by train to Quebec. En route, they passed through many small towns, and the news—"The Churchills are coming," had spread in advance—crowds waited to cheer them at every station. At each stop, Winston, Clementine, and Mary, appeared on the platform at the back of the train to wave to the people.

At Quebec, Mr. Mackenzie King was waiting, and so were the President and Mrs. Roosevelt. The Roosevelt train had arrived at 9:40 A.M. and drawn up at a siding.

The Earl of Athlone and Princess Alice—the Governor General and his lady—were there, too. Mr. Roosevelt and his party moved down a wooden ramp and boarded their car. Meanwhile, the Churchill train had drawn into the station about fifty yards from the President's.

Smiling broadly, Winston gave the V sign and shouted to the crowd, "Victory is everywhere."

He walked across with Clementine to shake hands with President and Mrs. Roosevelt in their car. "I'm glad to see you Winston," said the President. "Did you have a nice trip?"

"Well, we had three beautiful days," Winston replied, "but I was frightfully sick at times."

Turning to Clementine the President said, "He has lost a lot of color and I have lost a lot of weight."

The party got into their cars, which took them to the Citadel in procession through streets lined with cheering spectators.

The official cars drove along the narrow sunken roads of the Citadel grounds to the parade ground in front of the residence.

The President remained in the car, but Winston descended and, stick in hand, approached the guard of honor. As President Roosevelt's car left, Winston joined Clementine, who had also left the car, and the two walked together to the Residence. He was obviously delighted to be sharing the occasion with her, and was happy, buoyant, more like his old self.

"On our first night in Quebec, we attended a dinner at the Citadel with Mr. and Mrs. Churchill," said Mrs. Roosevelt. "The dinner was being given by the Governor General, the Earl of Athlone, and his wife, Princess Alice.

"This was the first time I had accompanied my husband to any war conference," said Mrs. Roosevelt. "It came about because when my husband and Mr. Churchill were talking on the telephone making arrangements for the conference, Mr. Churchill had said, 'I am taking Clemmie with me again.'

" 'In that case,' said my husband, 'I'll bring Eleanor.'

"And that is how it happened. My husband thought it would be a nice idea for me to go along too, since Mrs. Churchill was going to be there with the Prime Minister....

"The old Citadel was a very novel experience, and Mrs. Churchill and I enjoyed walking about the Citadel fort, and especially along the ramparts from which we could look down on the St. Lawrence River.

"The Governor General and Princess Alice took us both for a drive in the country one afternoon, and we shared a most enjoyable picnic tea.

"While our husbands were occupied with conferences, we used the time to attend various functions, speak at meetings, and both of us also made French language broadcasts to the Canadian people."

On Sunday, September 17, the Churchills left Quebec by train for another visit to the Roosevelt's Hyde Park home.

"They stayed with us several days," Mrs. Roosevelt continued, "and it was a very busy several days. My husband wanted to fish, I wanted to picnic, and we both got our way."

Afterward, they returned to Halifax and boarded H.M.S. *Renown* for home.

The visit was over, but Clementine's friendship with Eleanor Roosevelt remained, and grew. Whenever, in later years, she traveled to the United States, she never failed to telephone and see Eleanor Roosevelt. Mrs. Roosevelt did the same when she came to Britain, no matter how short her visit. They corresponded, and Clementine regularly kept

Eleanor informed of Winston's health. After his stroke, she wrote Eleanor, "He is getting stronger every day, but it has been an anxious and sad experience."

They were two wives who had a lot in common—they both had unique husbands.

17

The Great Christmas Cake Mystery

In our nursery days we heard with horror how the wicked witch had slain Snow White with a poisoned apple. More cynically, in maturer years, we accepted those hoary devices of the thriller-writer, the doctored cake, the poisoned chocolates and the germ-laden cigarette. But in wartime Downing Street, the clichés of the "penny dreadful" became real and grim reality.

From well-wishers throughout the world came parcels of eggs, fruit, cakes, sweets, butter, sugar, and a hundred scarce delicacies, together with boxes and cabinets of the cigars which Winston loved. He saw none of them. Each consignment as it arrived was subjected to the expert scrutiny of Scotland Yard detectives and usually ended in the furnaces. Most of the gifts were innocent enough, but unless the senders were known personally to Winston and Clementine their offerings were rejected. The risks were too great to be taken.

Sometimes a small hole in the cellophane wrapping of a cigar could reveal where the needle of a hypodermic syringe had been plunged into the tobacco. A minute disarrangement of the top layer in a chocolate box might indicate that the contents had been tampered with by an enemy agent or a maniac. Since the presents were sent anonymously it would have been a waste of time to try to trace the source. It was safer and quicker to burn everything.

Though it was painful to Mrs. Landemare, the cook at No. 10, to see good foodstuffs destroyed, she accepted the situation, and Clementine managed to vary the menus of dinners and lunches with the contents of very welcome food parcels sent to her from New York by Bernard Baruch.

The strict security precautions gave rise to what was to become known as "The Great Christmas Cake Mystery."

Said Winston's detective Thompson, "A beautiful Christmas cake arrived by post at Downing Street. I commandeered it at once. One of the staff must have told Mrs. Churchill about it, for she sent for me and asked me why I had taken the cake. I told her that I was not prepared to take a chance on it.

" 'Perhaps it is alright,' she said hopefully.

" 'How do we know, Madam?' I asked. 'We don't know where it has come from.'

" 'Indeed I do,' she said. 'I have the name and address of the senders.'

"I said, 'Anyone wanting to get rid of Mr. Churchill would not worry about a little thing like giving a false name and address. You might trace the real sender—and again, you might not.'

" 'Well,' she said, still endeavoring to save the cake, 'what are we going to do about it? At least we have a name and address to go on this time.'

" 'We'll check the senders and have the parcel traced. I haven't destroyed the cake yet.'

" 'Oh, good!' she said. 'So long as you haven't destroyed it. It would be so nice to have for our Christmas table.'

"While my investigation was going on the cake was taken down to Chequers, with strict orders from Mrs. Churchill and myself that it was not to be touched.

"In due course we received a report from the security people assigned to the job. Two old ladies had saved their rationed foods all through the year to make that cake for Winston. A local baker had cooked it, and it had been exhibited in his shop before being sent off. The local police told me, 'You can take our word for it that the two old ladies are perfectly genuine—and so is the cake.' Mrs. Churchill was very relieved. She had been banking on that cake. Mrs. Landemare, their cook, had been badgering her, 'Am I to make a Christmas cake or not?' And even the Prime Minister had asked Scotland Yard, 'Please try to get the mystery of the cake solved in time for Christmas.'

"The parcel took quite a while to check really thoroughly, but it was worth while. After Christmas, the two old ladies received a letter of thanks signed personally by Winston Churchill."

A less happy ending attended the arrival of a huge cheese cake, a confection Clementine particularly enjoyed. When it had to be destroyed she was inconsolable.

Said Thompson, "A similar situation arose when we went to America for Mr. Churchill's first meeting with President Roosevelt at the White House. Thousands of cigars were sent to him, but they were all destroyed unless we could verify the source. The signature on every label or accompanying letter had to be checked with the utmost care."

In spite of the misleadingly modest exterior, No. 10 is a very large house. At the rear of the ground floor are the housekeeper's office, the kitchen, and a general office controlling the official and domestic activities and arrangements of the Prime Minister and his wife. On the first floor are the dining room and, adjoining it, a smaller room known as the breakfast room. On this floor, too, is the magnificent drawing room, which Clementine refurnished to her own taste and used for formal occasions and social gatherings.

The bedrooms are directly above the Cabinet room, a long rectangular chamber almost filled by a massive table covered with green felt and surrounded by chairs. Individual blotter pads, paper and pencils are always laid on the table before each chair. Winston would often remain alone in the great Cabinet room, sitting in the Prime Minister's armchair at the head of the table long after his Ministers had gone.

"Clemmie issued express instructions that whenever he remained behind after a Cabinet meeting, he was not to be disturbed or interrupted in any way," said Lord Ismay.

There was no warming fire for Winston's back in his other War Cabinet room in the nearby Annex. Instead, the empty hearth contained a fire bucket, which miraculously caught almost all his cigar butts when he threw them backwards over his shoulder without bothering to watch where they landed.

In the main corridor of "the Hole in the Ground," as the Annex was known, there was a small door bearing a wooden plaque painted: "Prime Minister." In the cubicle behind it, with its walls covered in maps, Winston labored, issued orders, made broadcasts, and generally ran everyone else into the ground. Clementine had another miniature bedroom, in which Mary Churchill would sleep on a camp bed while on leave from the A.T.S. There was no plumbing in the bedrooms. Toilet facilities were limited to a jug of water in a bowl on a table, a china soap dish, and a mirror on a stand.

Below were more bedrooms for the men and women employed on the staff. These were so deep below ground level that pipes for London's sewers and gas and water mains ran through the rooms and enormous rats made them their home.

216

Somehow, in spite of its sprawling immensity, Clementine managed to make No. 10 run smoothly and introduced the maximum comfort possible. The trouble was that official and domestic activities tended to become so inextricably involved that keeping them separated was a continuing nightmare for her and her staff.

There was a connecting passage between No. 10 and the Annex, and on many a morning a visitor being ushered through to the private secretary's office would be confronted by the spectacle of Winston, clad only in a white bath towel, crossing from the bathroom to the bedroom. Unabashed, the Prime Minister, like a senator of ancient Rome, would greet the visitor with a stately, dignified salute which made the situation seem even more grotesque.

Clementine's Aunt Mabell, the Countess of Airlie, came to tea one afternooon, at Storey's Gate. When she arrived, tin-hatted, uniformed guards passed her upstairs to a small lobby where she was ushered through a small door and into a sitting room beautifully furnished, with a Romney over the fireplace, a head of Clementine's mother as a girl, and some modern landscapes on the walls. The soft lighting, the atmosphere of tranquility and elegance seemed far removed from the war, and when her Aunt so remarked, Clementine opened her eyes in surprise.

"Do you know, Aunt Mabell, what this place really is?" she asked. And suddenly her aunt realized that these peaceful rooms were directly above London's great Air Raid Precautions center! As she was about to leave, her aunt said, "Aren't you proud of Winston, Clemmie?"

"Yes, I am," she replied simply—"I always have been."

Months later, Aunt Mabell lunched at Downing Street with Clementine and Winston. The Countess recalled, "When I arrived I found a small party assembled, which included Sir Alan Brooke, Admiral Sir Dudley Pound, and General Ismay. While we were waiting, Clemmie told us that as the Prime Minister did not get up until late she had thought that morning of going into his room to talk to him while he shaved. When she opened the door the room was thick with tobacco smoke and she beheld Winston in bed in his dressing gown, and the whole Cabinet gathered round him. An early Cabinet meeting was being held."

The *Luftwaffe* tried repeatedly to bomb No. 10. "They know very well where our house is, and they keep trying to hit it," said Clementine. "They put one not very far away once. My husband says that when his time has come it will come—but it isn't due yet."

It certainly was not. Three torpedoes were fired by a U-boat at the 35,000-ton battleship *Nelson* west of the Orkneys. All hit the ship, but none exploded. Aboard the *Nelson* at the time, was Winston Churchill.

Admiral Karl Doenitz, Commander in Chief of Hitler's Navy, afterward said bitterly, "The battleship failed to blow up because of faulty torpedoes and because Churchill was aboard."

Clementine was part of the security arrangements surrounding Winston's wartime movements. Hitler would have given almost anything to be able to kill or capture Britain's great leader, and secrecy concerning the Prime Minister's day-to-day whereabouts was imperative; so imperative that when he left the country for his first meeting with President Roosevelt, he posed with Clementine for a photograph, which showed them buying a little charity flag from a smiling woman at the door of No. 10. The photograph was put in "cold storage" for a week before being published on the real flag day. Just another security trick to mislead the enemy.

One day, during the flying bomb period of the war, Clementine told Lady Reading that she was anxious to see the manner in which the Women's Voluntary Services tackled "incidents," during raids.

Recalled Lady Reading, "I went to lunch with them at Downing Street, and my car picked us up afterwards with the latest news of that afternoon's attacks. Too often she went to see people who were expecting her, so she said to me, 'Let's just go like that and let no one know we're coming.' This way she would see things as they really were. It is very seldom given to the great to see a thing as it really is because nearly always a lot of dressing up is done. She wanted to see things without reception committees and all the rest. She wanted to inform herself.

"As we were about to leave, I noticed that she was wearing a lovely new pair of shoes and I said, 'Don't wear those shoes, they'll get ruined, and you had to give your coupons for them.' She answered that they helped her morale and they might help other people's, and she went off looking very nice, as she always does. I have never, never seen her not look as if she's just come out of a bandbox.

"We went first to Paddington, where there had just been a bad bomb incident. It upset her very much. While we were there, a second bomb came down, and as I thought it would be a mistake to get her killed, I suggested that we move on to the Incident Inquiry Point across the river at Battersea. We had hardly been there five minutes when a bomb fell within yards of us, so we said we'd better go down to the East End.

"We reached the East End, and within three minutes a warden yelled,

'Quick!' and nearly pitched her into a brick street shelter as three more flying bombs fell around us in a matter of seconds. I said, 'We'd better go home now—I think it's getting too hot.'

"We jumped into the car, and I had an American driver named Pauline Fenno, who was very careful about always keeping the windows half-cocked. As we drove along toward Westminster, we could hear a bomb overhead. The car in front of us stopped; four men jumped out and lay in the road, and my driver used some bad language, saying that the men were in more danger from being run over by our car than they were from being blown to bits by the bomb. At that moment the buzz bomb fell and shattered the windows of the shops all around us.

"We went on and the traffic lights ahead of us turned red, and my driver automatically stopped. We were the only car in sight. Suddenly my driver said, 'Honestly what a fool I am, just because I work in England, I've stopped for this light which means nothing with a buzz bomb chasing us. What irks me,' she said, 'is that if we get hit, I won't even have a decent obituary. It'll just be, "Lady Reading, Mrs. Churchill, and friend." '

"I must say I was very glad to get Mrs. Churchill back to the Annex on the day the flying bombs chased us. I felt a double responsibility with her because she was a rather precious person to be taken out in the middle of this lot."

Another of Clementine's friends—Lady Hillingdon—deputy chairman of the Women's Voluntary Services, joining her on a journey to Norwich when she went to open an Anglo-American Services Club, recalls, "When we got to Norwich, there was a civic reception with the Lord Mayor, generals, and everything else you can think of. In the middle of lunch, someone whispered in the Lord Mayor's ear, 'The Prime Minister wants to speak to you,' so out went the Lord Mayor. He returned looking rather angry. 'Can you believe it?' he said to me. 'That was the Prime Minister ringing to see whether I would arrange for a sleeping car to be put on the back of the train home you are catching at four o'clock this afternoon. He was afraid Mrs. Churchill would be very tired. How can I get a sleeping car? In any case it's nothing to do with me.'

"But somebody did do something, and when we walked on to the platform, with all the local dignitaries, we were shown to a first-class carriage, the door was flung open, and there were two beds laid out—one each side of the compartment. Mrs. Churchill hissed at me, 'If you don't lie down when we get in this train, I'll murder you! So we both laid down until the train left the station and then went and had tea in the dining car.

"That shows how he used to think about her in the middle of the worst of the war. In the midst of all his problems, he phoned to see that she shouldn't overtire herself on the way back."

Although Winston would sometimes use his influence to obtain for his wife certain extra privileges and comforts that he justifiably felt her work and responsibilities warranted, his personal integrity always prevented him from disclosing official information that might be used accidentally to his family's advantage. Soon after clothes rationing was introduced, Clementine told a dressmaker, as she handed out her clothing coupons for a new dress, "I was caught like all the rest." She added, "The funny thing is that long ago my husband said, 'You had better buy me a handkerchief or two. You never know—they might be rationed.' I never bought those handkerchiefs. I thought he was joking."

Whenever he returned to the Annex from No. 10, she was waiting to welcome him affectionately. Her greeting was not demonstrative, often no more than a comradely hand on his arm, yet the effect on him was plain for all to see. As soon as he walked into the hall he would shout at the top of his voice, "Clemmie, darling! Clemmie, darling!" Sometimes she would hurry to the door to meet him. If she were in her room, he would go to her. The tone of his voice always told her how the day had gone, and if it had gone badly she would comfort him. Just to be charmed by her voice, to hear her say gently, "It will come out all right, you are doing your best," gave him a tremendous spiritual lift. He talked his troubles and his heart out to her.

On the rare occasions when there were no guests, they would either eat together in the dining room or she would have dinner in bed while he had his on a tray beside her. One such evening he returned from No. 10 distressed by some disastrous news, his eyes moist with tears. Clementine sent for a tray of food for him, and he dined in her bedroom.

The fall of Singapore rocked Winston. He felt the blow even more than the loss of France, because, like everybody else, he had always considered the Far Eastern base impregnable. He was despondent, shaken. When friends asked what had happened there, he would shake his head and mutter, "I really don't know."

Clementine and members of his immediate circle did their utmost to break his depression, but nothing seemed to move it. He began to look as if he were at last feeling the strain of office. His sleep, so vital to him, was restless, disturbed. Even the famous afternoon naps no longer fully refreshed him. It was suggested that he should make a trip, the following weekend, to a Service establishment. "You always sleep well after those trips," he was told. "They seem to put new life into you." He was not interested. Clementine realized that a tour of inspection of some kind was the only antidote for his mood. He had to be shaken out of it before he made himself ill. She continued to stress that it was time they were seen together again, among the fighting men and women of the Services. Two weeks later they visited an Army unit, and he seemed to find himself once more. Suddenly turning to her, he said, "We must hold on. All will come right if we have patience."

"When the war started, Winston had to sleep during the day out of necessity, so that he could work far into the night," Clementine said, "but he believes a man should sleep during the day, also, to be at his best during the evening when he joins his wife and friends at dinner. A good meal, with good wine, and then some brandy; that is his great moment of the day."

Clementine had to contend with a husband whom not even his most devoted friends could call considerate, but he was demanding more from himself than from others; and following his own line that all that the human structure required is change, she was forever trying and scheming to achieve some brief mental respite or change for him.

There were seldom more than seven or eight guests to luncheon at Downing Street. Winston usually arrived for a meal dressed in his blue siren suit, and if he were silent and brooding, Clementine would keep the conversation going until some topic ignited a spark which rekindled his attention and eloquence.

The upstairs dining room was used only at the beginning of the war. When they decided it had become too dangerous because of the air raids, Clementine converted the low-ceilinged servants' hall below the ground floor into an alternative dining room, which was used until the completion of the new quarters in the Annex made a new and larger room available there.

Sir Tom O'Brien, M.P. and union leader, was a guest at some of the wartime stag dinners Winston held to discuss Parliamentary business and any other business he wished to pursue.

"On various occasions, several of us on the T.U.C. General Council had to meet the Prime Minister with Ernest Bevin, who was then Minister of Labor," recalled Sir Tom. "We would get together for a conference, and sometimes a meal, at Downing Street, and usually Clementine would look in to see if everything was all right—especially if raids were on.

"She would often come in to indicate that it was getting late, with the watchfulness of a mother, apart from that of a wife. On one occasion she came in after dinner and virtually started to undress Winston in front of us—to undo his tie, loosen his collar, take off his jacket and waistcoat, give him his slippers, and generally make him comfortable.

"This was her way of encouraging him to relax, and it worked like magic. She babied this incredible man, and he loved it. They had complete understanding.

"Mind you, although she was getting him comfortable for the night— it was for the night's work, not for sleep. After people such as ourselves had departed, he would get down to his papers until the early hours.

"Even when we couldn't actually see Clementine around at Downing Street, we felt her presence in the house, and, I think, so did he. He knew there was companionship there all the time, if he needed it. He may have had little time for it in those days, but it was there, and the knowledge of it was of tremendous importance to him.

"I saw how she handled stag parties on an occasion after the war, when, in 1953, Marshal Tito came to London. There was an official dinner given for him at Downing Street. It was a stag, and a distinguished crowd of about fifty guests were present at dinner. I was seated between Lord Moran—Winston's physician—and Field Marshal Alexander. Politicians from all parties were there, as well as Montgomery, admirals, the lot.

"When we adjourned to the lounge, which adjoined the great first-floor dining room, there were several inquiries about Clementine. She was in the house, but not at the party. Anthony Eden came over and said to me, 'Well, this is wonderful, wonderful. Where's Clementine?' He went out to look for her and to see if he could bring her in. We saw her coming along the corridor, past the open door. She had lunched earlier with Tito. As she went by the door, she smiled, waved, and said, 'I'm not coming in.' She knew when to stay away. She was content to smile at all of us, wave to Tito, and laughed when he waved back.

"She wouldn't even come in for coffee because she knew that if she did, it might deflect attention from Tito or from Winston. I have often seen quite the opposite happen with important people, where wives crashed a stag party. But Clementine knew her place even in her own home, and observed the same rules she set Winston.

"To handle a man like Winston required supernatural patience, and

I know he recognized this. Clementine appreciated that, in many respects, Winston had never ceased to be a boy. It was characteristic of him that, years before, when he was Home Secretary, he had absolutely refused to prohibit roller skating on the pavement. He was insistent on the right of little boys to knock down older people in their lust for speed."

The schoolboy traits in him emerge frequently. He is vain about his feet and legs, and sent back a portrait by Bernard Hailstone to have the legs altered to his liking.

A woman from a Mayfair beauty salon used to visit the Annex each week to manicure Clementine's nails. Winston often used to burst into the room, kick off his bedroom slippers, and demand, "What do you think of my feet? *You* haven't got feet like that. Aren't they pretty?"

As a fact, his feet—like his wife's—*are* pretty.

Though the most virile of men, Winston nevertheless likes Clementine to buy eau-de-Cologne for use on his handkerchiefs. He holds the handkerchief by one end and sprays the perfume on to it with an atomizer. When his wife does the spraying for him, he is delighted.

Not all the Downing Street dinners were stag affairs. One evening the chief guest was an emissary from the Vatican. Ambassador Myron Taylor, President Roosevelt's personal representative to the Holy See, had come to London on a mission. He wanted to find a formula to prevent the bombing of Rome.

There were four people at table in the Annex that night: Winston, Clementine, Mr. John Winant, the American Ambassador, and Mr. Taylor.

Himself an Episcopalian of Quaker descent, Myron Taylor sought a compromise between humanity and the needs of war. He argued and Winston argued; yet basically both believed in the same things, despising persecution and oppression and loving freedom.

Winston explained that with Britain fighting for her existence in the Middle East and the Allied invasion of North Africa already planned, any limitation of action might aid the enemy and completely undermine efforts in the Mediterranean.

While recognizing that fact, Mr. Taylor emphasized that the bombing of Rome and the destruction or damaging of the Vatican would offend Catholics throughout the world. He wanted to protect the great spiritual home of millions in its historic setting of priceless antiquity.

Winston understood the point only too well, but stressed his obligation to his forces. If Rome were removed as a possible British target, he urged, Mussolini might be tempted to strike at Alexandria or Cairo, thereby endangering the British armies at Alamein. Neither man would give way.

"It was the most civilized conversation I have ever listened to which involved both spiritual considerations and the use of the destructive tools of war," said John Winant. "It was not a conflict between those two men. It had to do with man's continuing failure to establish peace and freedom through the power of love, and every time that breaks down the only answer must always be an agonizing compromise between the spiritual and the temporal. Similar conflicts arise and pass unnoticed in day-to-day life, but they are forever highlighted by the tragedies of war."

One evening in 1944, when the *Luftwaffe* was making a specialty of incendiary bomb raids, Clementine was presiding at a most important dinner party. Suddenly, the air-raid sirens sounded, and soon after came the "overhead" warning signal. Winston, Clementine, and their guests were compelled to adjourn to the air-raid shelter, where they sat on chairs and stools and waited for the immediate danger to pass. Ranged round the walls of the shelter that evening were King George VI and his entire War Cabinet.

The King, a frequent visitor to No. 10 during the war, continued the dinner-table conversation and swapped jokes with Mr. Clement Attlee, Mr. Ernest Bevin, and Mr. Anthony Eden. Since Clementine saw to it that even the air-raid shelters were provided liberally with refreshments, all enjoyed the interlude.

Every now and then Winston popped his head out of the shelter, just to make sure the house was still in one piece above their heads.

Sometimes voices, that couldn't make themselves heard through official channels, managed to reach Winston's ear via Clementine—provided she considered they had something worthwhile to say. She always had a soft spot for voices crying in the wilderness, what with Winston having done the same for so long.

When Major General Sir Edward Spears consulted Clementine as to the best means of ensuring that a matter important to her husband secured his attention, she advised him, "Put what you have to say in writing. He often does not listen or does not hear if he is thinking of something else. But he will always consider a paper carefully and take in all its implications. He never forgets what he has seen in writing."

Colonel the Hon. F. H. (Fred) Cripps had something important to say about the organization and management of the docks. He felt that the scheme, as it was, was unworkable, so, to ensure that his urgent criticisms didn't get pigeonholed anywhere, he got them to the Prime Minister through the "side" door to No. 10 Downing Street.

"I wrote my own report, after conversation with 'Clemmie' Churchill," related Colonel Cripps, "and she undertook to show it to the Prime Minister."

Clementine seldom intervened in matters of State, but at Downing Street there occurred an exception to the general rule.

The telephone in the Annex jangled one morning, and an overwrought voice at the other end of the line cried, "Listen, Clemmie! Listen to this letter! You know how unlike Duff it is. Oh! Clemmie, what shall we do?"

The caller was Lady Diana Duff Cooper, desperate after reading a letter from her husband, who had gone to Paris on a Government mission. In it, Duff Cooper had confessed to a premonition that he would not return. The letter had been concealed in his wife's passport, obviously in the belief that it would not be discovered for some time. Lady Diana had found it quite by accident and now, frantically anxious, had telephoned the one person who might be able to help. Clementine listened sympathetically, then she said, "How awful! I'll tell Winston at once. He'll send out some Spitfires. Don't worry too much."

Luftwaffe airmen may well have lain in wait to shoot down Britain's important emissary, Duff Cooper, but the escort of Spitfires sent to accompany his aircraft from Paris was sufficient to deter any such attempt. Whatever cards Destiny held in her hands that day, Lady Diana was forevermore convinced that her friend's intervention had trumped them.

There was a night during the later years of the war when Clementine might have been forced to intervene even more dramatically—and publicly—by deputizing for Winston as a broadcaster. Millions in Britain and all over the world listened in stunned silence as, one Sunday evening, the Prime Minister came on the air. The voice was familiar, but where was the incisive phrasing, the bulldog truculence, they had been so eagerly awaiting? The broken, slurred words, emanating from the loudspeaker sounded like those of a tired, bewildered old man. And in camp and saloon bar, parlor, and warden's post, men and women looked at each other, shocked, and declared, "He's drunk!"

But Winston was not drunk. He was ill. It was only by a superhuman effort that he had faced the microphone. Ex-Detective Inspector Thompson was there; and this is what he has to say, "The script, as always, was ready in good time; but even before the broadcast we knew that he was not at all well. Somebody suggested, 'Why not let Mrs. Churchill read it?' but the Prime Minister said, 'No! They expect to hear my voice, and if they don't they'll wonder why.'

"Mrs. Churchill begged him to let her read the speech in his place, but he refused. Several of his colleagues tried to persuade him, with no better success. He insisted on keeping faith with the people he led. When he had finished the speech, we almost carried him from the microphone and put him to bed. Mrs. Churchill sat beside him until he fell asleep."

It is perhaps fortunate that Winston never realized the reception his gallant effort had in some quarters, for drunkenness is a sin he can neither tolerate nor forgive. He has abhorred it since his Sandhurst days. Yet it is a fault of which he has sometimes been accused by people who do not understand his vocal disability.

When he is tired the impediment, which Clementine worked so hard with him to overcome, returns. His speech becomes slurred, and sibilants give him endless trouble.

Said Thompson, "In later years, as he got older, that 's' became more pronounced. When he made that broadcast in 1944, near the end of the war, a lot of people said he was drunk, and there were many arguments about it; but the plain truth was that he was very tired and he had a cold. I can remember an earlier occasion when he was very husky when he spoke. We had all kinds of cough mixture sent to us—people were recommending this one and that one—but it didn't stop the usual 'drunk' yarns."

Though the revelation may destroy a legend, in simple fact Winston neither drinks nor smokes to real excess. He loves good brandy and whiskey, but drinks little of either. He takes a pint of champagne daily —his only health fetish—but may go for days without any other type of alcohol. Though at receptions he is usually seen with a drink in his hand, his glass is seldom replenished. He will make one small whiskey last for several hours, and often his glass contains nothing but iced soda water. Indulgence in spirits, he says, blurs thought, and although he enjoys a drink, he has never been seen drunk.

Inspector Thompson said, "He wakes up in the morning and lights his first cigar. Immediately, his valet or I would take him a glass of ice-cold soda water. He would chew on that cigar, and at lunchtime it would still be only half-smoked. That would be five hours later; and while he's chewing, he's always sipping. He's always got a glass beside him—not whiskey, but ice-cold soda water.

"At lunchtime you put half an inch of whiskey in his tumbler. If you put any more in it, he'll throw it out. He'll taste it, and if it's too strong he'll tell you, 'Take it away. Put more soda in it.' He'll fill the glass up with soda water, and that's drunk at lunchtime. After lunch, if he is going into his office, he will take another drink of about the same strength; but he never takes brandy.

"Very rarely, at eleven o'clock in the morning, if he is going out, he might have a glass of port.

"People think that he smokes no end of cigars; but actually he smokes very few. He makes one last a very long time. It's the same old cigar, hour after hour.

"If he takes a whiskey at lunchtime, there will still be a drop left in the glass at dinnertime.

"At night he has a glass of champagne. He used to say, 'My father told me that if I drank a glass of champagne every night, I'd live a long time.'"

During the bombing in early 1944, General Eisenhower was spending many nights in London. Concerned for his safety, Clementine suggested that he occupy one of the underground shelters in Downing Street. Winston agreed, and she arranged an apartment specially for Ike, complete with kitchen, living room, bedroom, and secret telephone.

Alas! Ike never used nor even saw the place.

Winston's fighting instinct made him ask General Eisenhower for permission to watch the D-Day landings from one of the supporting naval vessels.

Said Ike, "I argued that the chance of his becoming an accidental casualty was too important from the standpoint of the whole war effort, and I refused his request. He replied, with complete accuracy, that while I was in sole command of the operation by virtue of authority delegated to me by both Governments, such authority did not include administrative control over the British organization.

"He said, 'Since this is true, it is not part of your responsibility, my dear General, to determine the exact composition of any ship's company in His Majesty's fleet. This being true," he rather slyly continued, 'by shipping myself as a bona fide member of the ship's complement it would be beyond your authority to prevent my going.'

"All of this I had ruefully to concede, but I forcibly pointed out that he was adding to my personal burdens in this flouting of my instructions. Even, however, while I was acknowledging defeat in the matter, aid came from an unexpected source."

That "unexpected source" was a combination of Clementine, aided and abetted by King George VI and Lord Ismay.

"Winston informed the King himself of his intention to go and watch the D-Day landings," said Lord Ismay. "First of all he got over Admiral Ramsey who was going to command the landings. He was telling him that he wanted to go and see the landings from a destroyer when I caught them at it. When I went into the room, I was obviously very unpopular for coming in at that moment, and Winston said, 'I am just telling the Admiral that I want to watch Overlord go in from a destroyer.' I said I didn't think it was a good idea because he would be right out of touch if important decisions were needed. All I got for that was—'Keep your mouth shut and I'll take you with me.'

"Well, I had no desire to go. He then told Eisenhower and the King, whose immediate reaction was—'That's a good idea—I'll come too.' At that, Winston sat back on his haunches and said, 'I will have to ask the Cabinet.' He put it to the Cabinet and they decided the King couldn't go, and when Winston went back to tell him this, King George said, 'Well, you can't go either.'

"Winston asserted that as Minister of Defence, he had to go—it was part of his job, but the King didn't agree.

"Winston had told Clemmie, of course, but she reserved her fire as, at that moment, she could see it going in her favor and thought his scheme would be killed. When he often told her of some exploit he had in mind, if she knew perfectly well he wouldn't be able to do it, she raised no objection at first. She would bide her time and work behind the scenes to outmaneuver him, if she thought it necessary to stop him for his good, and for the country's good.

"Well, I went with Winston to see the invasion off and we were in a train on a siding at Southampton, about five miles from Ike's headquarters. Clemmie knew he couldn't get aboard a destroyer at Southampton—to do this he would have had to go down to the West Country, so she still held her fire.

"Our concern wasn't because we thought there was danger in his going—I didn't think there was half the risk that Winston took throughout the war flying all over the place as he did. What I was frightened of was that we couldn't tell if all the landings would succeed, and Ike might have been in the position of saying, 'This is a fifty per cent British enterprise and I must have orders from the Combined Chiefs of Staff—am I to push it to the limit, or am I to pull out and have another go later?'

"Well, if we'd have had the most important man on the British side floating about in a destroyer, things would have been very difficult. But I was certain, that if Winston had persisted in going, Clemmie would have stepped in and said, 'Look here, you should be staying behind in case your presence is required for important decisions.'

"I always had the feeling that if I really felt a thing tremendously—as in an incident of this character—and if I couldn't stop him, I would, in the last resort, go and invoke Clemmie's help. She had far greater influence on him than anyone else could possibly have. You see, he had outlived all the great statesmen of his own generation, and there was nobody in the Cabinet, or among the Chiefs of Staff, with comparable experience, brain, or intellect. He was a giant among pygmies. There was no one who really had the right to make him listen—except Clemmie. However strong his advisers might be, I didn't feel that they carried the guns that Clemmie did to handle such a situation.

"The thing that finally killed his D-Day putting-to-sea idea was a letter we organized from the King. The letter reached him at Southampton, and gave Winston no option at all. He is a great Monarchist, and if the King came flat out, as he did, and said he was not to go, he would salute and say, 'Very good, Sir!'

"There was another occasion when Clemmie would have been the only person in the world to handle him, and that was when he flew to Athens after Yalta instead of coming home in the *Franconia,* as had been arranged. He was absolutely worn out. He was seventy years old. He'd had a most disappointing and discouraging conference as we had failed to get decisions on the Polish questions. He'd also had a brute of a cold, and here was the comfortable, beautifully appointed *Franconia,* with the sea most inviting, and the prospect of a voyage to Malta.

"I was very whacked, and said to him when we got on board, 'Isn't it wonderful—we'll have six days rest.' He said, 'I'm flying to Athens.' I said, 'What for? It's all settled.' And he replied, 'I want to make sure.'

"I said, 'You don't want me, do you?' And he replied, 'What for?' So I went back on the boat and never felt such a brute in all my life. Now if Clemmie had been there, I would have gone to her and said, 'You didn't stop him, no one tried to stop him when he ruined his last Christmas to go and save the situation in Athens—that was an urgent and dire necessity. But everything is all right now. Look at him—he must have a rest. We want him—we've got to save him up.'

"If she'd been there, I would have gone to her, and she, and she alone, could have stopped him."

The night of D-Day, Winston hardly left the map room. Clementine joined him a while before retiring. When she kissed him good night, he said to her, "Do you realize that by the time you wake up in the morning twenty thousand men may have been killed?"

Among those recommended for the Victoria Cross, the highest honor Britain can award to any of her fighting men, was a sailor who had been drowned in the performance of the act for which he was cited. When the list reached Winston, Clementine heard that the hero had left a young wife and a posthumous son, just born.

"A decoration alone will be of little value to a mother in such straits," she said.

Winston summoned one of his secretaries, and, dictating a memorandum on the citation, said, "Tell her that the King of England and his Prime Minister will be proud to be the godparents of the son of such a father."

18

To Russia with Love

THE war in Europe was drawing to its close when Clementine received an invitation from the Soviet Government to visit Russia to see for herself the magnificent work achieved by her Red Cross Aid to Russia Fund.

In the summer of 1941, she conceived the idea of a special Red Cross Fund devoted to sending medical supplies to Russia.

She knew the British people earnestly desired to help the Russian people. A variety of different appeals had been launched to raise funds for comforts and other supplies to be sent to the Soviets, but lack of knowledge of needs and conditions threatened to impair the effectiveness of their aim. A national effort was required. With the support of the British Red Cross, Clementine launched the Aid to Russia Fund in October of that year. Within three months, the fund had collected one million pounds. In its first year it reached well over two million, and for four years she made the Aid to Russia Fund her own special "war baby."

The idea originated the evening she asked Winston whether there was any near immediate hope of Britain opening a second military front to relieve the terrible pressure on Russia.

She showed him a petition she had received from Servicemen's wives and mothers calling for the opening of a Second Front, and asked him to read the letter she had sent to housewife Mrs. Phyllis Dobson, of Northenden, Manchester, who had handed the petition to her.

Her reply said, "I am touched by your letter because you tell me that the women who have signed this petition begging for the opening of a Second Front are wives and mothers of men serving in H.M. Forces.

This means that every one of you is prepared to accept the great sacrifice.

"I can assure you that it is a great reinforcement and encouragement to the Government to feel that the women of the country are prepared to give up, if necessary, in the cause of freedom, even the lives of their nearest and dearest.

"We all long to help Russia in her agony. When we feel impatient about a Second Front, do we not think that we should all of us search our hearts and remember the years before the war, when it was impossible to get anybody in the country to advocate or work for rearmament?

"The whole of Europe is now paying for these long years of neglect, but day by day and week by week, we are getting stronger and one day, we hope soon, we shall be able to take powerful and effective action."

Said Winston, "My wife felt very deeply that our inability to give Russia any military help disturbed and distressed the nation increasingly as the months went by and the German armies surged across the Steppes.

"I told her that the Second Front was out of the question and that all that could be done for a long time would be the sending of supplies of all kinds on a large scale.

"Mr. Eden and I encouraged her to explore the possibility of obtaining funds by voluntary subscription for medical aid. This had already been begun by the British Red Cross and St. John's, and my wife was invited by the joint organization to head the appeal for 'Aid to Russia.'"

At the end of October, under Red Cross auspices, Clementine issued her first appeal. It declared, "There is no one in this country whose heart has not been deeply stirred by the appalling drama now going on in Russia. We are amazed at the power of the Russian defense and at the skill with which it is conducted. We have been moved to profound admiration for the valor, the tenacity, and the patriotic self-sacrifice. And, above all, perhaps, we have been shaken with horror and pity at the vast scale of human suffering.

"Among the supplies we have already sent to Russia are 53 emergency operating outfits, 30 blood-transfusion sets, 70,000 surgical needles of various kinds, and 1,000,000 tablets of M. & B. 693. In addition, we have sent half a ton of phenacetin and about 7 tons of absorbent cotton wool. And this is, of course, only a beginning.

"We have declared our aim to be £1,000,000, and we have made a good start. Already the fund totals £370,000 and it is only twelve days old. Our gracious and beloved King and Queen in sending a further

£3,000 to the Red Cross last week, expressed a wish that £1,000 of their joint gift should be allocated to the Aid to Russia Fund. They have set a characteristic example.

"Much depends upon employers, and I would like to say this—wherever the employer provides the facilities to get the fund started the workers come gladly with their weekly pennies. Thus, from the King and Queen to the humblest wage earner and cottage-dweller, we can all take part in this message of goodwill and compassion. Between the cottage and the palace, between those who can spare only pennies and a great imaginative benefactor like Lord Nuffield who can send a check for £50,000, there are millions of people who would like to share in this tribute to the Russian people."

The Executive Committee of the Soviet Red Cross in a letter to Clementine said, "The medical supplies which you are sending to us are being used to assist the sick and wounded of the Red Army as well as the civil population who have suffered so much from the treacherous invasion of the U.S.S.R. by the Hitler hordes."

Lady Limerick, who was Deputy Chairman of the Joint Committee of the Order of St. John and the British Red Cross, said, "Mrs. Churchill did a most outstanding job for the Red Cross. Her dynamic personality overcame all obstacles and difficulties. Eleven months after her Aid to Russia Fund had been opened, it had spent about £1,850,000, and shipped eighteen consignments to the Soviets, including portable X-ray units, motor X-ray units, ambulances, and articles such as 530,000 blankets; 50,000 children's coats; 40,000 children's breechettes, plus pullovers, scarves, mittens, gloves, stockings, balaclava helmets—a fantastic list that the Ministry of Supply officially described as 'almost staggering in its proportions.' All clothing sent was brand new, and was collected and packed by the Women's Voluntary Services.

"Mrs. Churchill's tremendous enthusiasm fires people to help. She won't take 'No' for an answer and charms open many doors. She was like a Queen Bee about the place—full of industry, full of activity. Where she was also so enormously successful was that a great many organizations wanted, for various reasons, to raise money for Russia. Her drive brought cohesion to these different efforts thereby saving the enormous waste of money that would have resulted from the overlapping of work as well as competition for the purchase of goods in short supply.

"Many of these organizations found they were bidding against each other in the open market for supplies, but Mrs. Churchill and her central committee cut out all this waste.

"I had close liaison with her and went frequently to Downing Street, but she regularly came to our headquarters for meetings to discuss details and policies. She was also in frequent contact with Mme Maisky, the wife of the Russian Ambassador, and this involved her in dealing with a slightly embarrassing situation because Mme Maisky used to come forward with long lists of requirements not necessarily related to the official lists from Russia."

Where she obtained her information, nobody knew, but she often said we must have this, that, and the other, and on the lists from Moscow, there was no mention of these things, so Clementine had quite a job handling Mme Maisky, especially as the Soviet Ambassador had said he wanted his wife to deal with all Red Cross matters.

Clementine's shrewd diplomacy with Mme Maisky was planned like a campaign. She wouldn't go to see her unless she had previously anticipated and prepared for possible moves and countermoves that might arise during their discussion.

On occasions she would consult Winston on her Aid to Russia work. At one time she drafted a telegram to send to Anthony Eden, who was in Russia on a mission. She needed an answer on whether a permanent Red Cross representative could be sent there. She showed the draft cable to Winston to make sure it was correctly phrased for diplomatic channels. The following morning, she asked:

"Well, what about that cable? I'd like to have another look at it and redraft it if you agree in principle."

"It was a very good cable," he said. "I've sent it off."

"To that extent, when she was doing official things, she kept him informed," said Lady Limerick, "but as a rule, her line was that he'd got so much on his plate and it wasn't fair to clutter him up with other problems too. She made her own decisions.

"She would walk into committee meetings with a load of ideas, throw them up in the air, and see how they landed. She wasn't unduly disturbed if many of them met with little response, but her ratio of successes was incredibly high. Her ideas were sparking-points. Basically, she worked on the same principle as Winston who also loved chucking hundreds of ideas up into the air to see what happened.

"When she wrote to Sir Stafford Cripps, who was then our Ambassador in Russia, and if she proved to be unsuccessful with a proposal the first time, she would return to the attack, as she did in regard to the question of sending a Red Cross representative there. Sir Stafford Cripps was much against it at the start. Eventually someone was sent and broke the ice, to enable others to go and gather information, for she was insistent that the public in Britain should be told how their Aid to Russia money was being used, otherwise they might not continue to support the fund. She pegged away at getting this information, and eventually she went herself."

Recalled Winston, "For the next four years she devoted herself to this task with enthusiasm and responsibility. In all nearly £8,000,000 were collected by the contributions of rich and poor alike. Many wealthy people made munificent donations, but the bulk of the money came from the weekly subscriptions of the mass of the nation.

"Thus, through the powerful organization of the Red Cross and St. John's, and in spite of heavy losses in the Arctic convoys, medical and surgical supplies and all kinds of comforts and special appliances found their way in an unbroken flow through the icy and deadly seas to the valiant Russian armies and people."

Clementine would go anywhere, do anything, to raise money for her fund. She established her own office at 10 Downing Street, and from there thousands of Thank You letters went out to donors personally signed "Clementine S. Churchill."

Said Winston, "The people were waiting on tiptoe to express what was in their hearts." So when an invitation came from Marshal Stalin to visit Russia, Clementine was delighted and honored, not only with the opportunity it offered to visit a large number of the centers of the war such as Leningrad, Rostov, Stalingrad, Sebastopol, and Odessa, but also because it would enable her personally to arrange for the equipment of two hospitals at Rostov-on-Don, which were to stand as a lasting memorial to her great fund.

Winston was also happy at the Russian eagerness to pay personal tribute to his wife's years of effort.

Said Clementine, "I would so dearly like to see the partnership of the British and Soviet Red Cross continued into the years of peace. Much remains to be done to heal the wounds that the war has inflicted on Russia. Beyond those physical needs, there is a splendid unifying ideal of comradeship in the eternal war against suffering, pain, disease, and death.

"When, in 1941, Germany attacked Russia, I shared the anger we all felt at this new Nazi outrage, and the sorrow that for a long, long time we could send no article of comfort.

"The British Red Cross Aid to Russia Fund provided an outlet for the feelings of admiration, sympathy, and respect which swept the land as the noble struggle of the Russians to defend their country grew in bitterness and strength."

With the feeling of imminent victory everywhere, Clementine felt that at last she could leave Winston for a few weeks. Accompanied by Miss Mabel Johnson, secretary to the Aid to Russia Fund, and Miss Grace Hamblin, her own private secretary, and also Major General J. E. T. Younger of the British Red Cross, she left for Moscow.

When accepting the invitation, she wrote to the Soviet Ambassador, "I look forward to acquainting myself with the work of the Red Cross and the medical institutions of the Soviet Union, also to finding out what more my Aid to Russia Fund can do to help the Soviet Red Cross in their wonderful work."

The instant she had gone, the restraining influence that had miraculously disciplined and kept Winston's phenomenal appetite for work within some kind of bounds disappeared, too. The daily routine, so essential to the maintenance of his physical and mental health and strength, went overboard, and he seldom retired for the night before 4 A.M. His important afternoon rest often began at 8 P.M., and dinner was usually at 9:30, and even 10, after which work continued until the early hours.

But Clementine's visit to Russia had a dual, unpublicized result. Seriously troubled at the deterioration in the relationships between Britain and the Soviet Union, Winston was anxious to know the pulse of the Soviet people and Government. Clementine gathered invaluable impressions on their feelings toward the Soviet's future with her Western allies. At one time he almost postponed her departure because of his concern over the deterioration of Anglo-Soviet relations.

Before leaving, Clementine, at Winston's request, had bought a gold fountain pen, which he asked her to present to Stalin as a souvenir of their meetings during the war. It was similar to his own favorite pen.

"Tell Stalin that with the gift of this pen I express the hope that he will write me many friendly messages with it," added Winston.

They had a rough flight part of the journey, as bad weather forced their aircraft down to a dangerously low altitude over the last hundred miles. On arrival in Moscow, she was met by Mme Molotov, Mme Maisky, and representatives of the People's Commissariat of Public

Health. She was informed that the State guest house had been placed at the disposal of her and her party for the duration of their stay.

After being presented with a bouquet of red and white roses by Mme Molotov, she said, "This is one of the most inspiring and most interesting moments of my life. I have long wished to visit your country, and, during these years with my fellow countrymen and countrywomen, I have followed with admiration and respect, awe and wonder, and affection, the great exploits of your wonderful army and your men and women. I have looked forward with great pleasure to my visit here."

Soon after their arrival, she and Miss Johnson were received at the Kremlin by Stalin. He wanted to thank her personally for her untiring work on behalf of the Aid to Russia Fund.

"I wish on behalf of the Soviet Government to express my gratitude for the medical supplies and equipment which your fund has sent to my country," said Stalin. "We are grateful for it."

Clementine thanked Stalin for the compliment, then took the opportunity of presenting him with her husband's fountain-pen gift and repeating his hope that they would continue to write to each other in friendship. Stalin explained that he always used a blue pencil. "However," said Clementine later, "it all passed off very well."

Mindful of Winston's particular interest in reactions in the Soviet on future Anglo-Russian friendship, Clementine was about to introduce the subject into her conversation with Stalin when he raised the issue himself by asking whether she was aware of "difficulties" between East and West.

"I admitted that I had heard a thing or two before our meeting," said Clementine, and the Marshal remarked, "There are difficulties and there will be difficulties but they will pass and friendship will remain."

Clementine informed Stalin that she wished to travel at leisure and spend as much time as possible with the ordinary people of the places she was to visit. He granted her wish by providing her with a well-equipped train in which to tour the country at a sightseeing speed of 20 m.p.h. to ensure that she saw all she wanted to see.

Smiling, appreciative crowds applauded her everywhere she went, to demonstrate their gratitude for her work.

Accompanied by Mme Kislova of the Society for Cultural Relations with Foreign Countries, plus various other officials, Clementine journeyed first from Moscow to Leningrad. She saw motorways prepared by the Germans in readiness for their occupation of the city—so confident had they been of conquering it. She visited the hospital that called itself "the factory for repairs of the human body." It specialized in severe cases of head wounds, brain operations, shattered limbs, and plastic surgery.

With the help of Mme Kislova, who acted as interpreter, she talked to the men and women of Russia. She found them reluctant to volunteer information about their own sufferings, but "burning with anger against the Germans."

From Leningrad to Stalingrad an appalling scene of destruction met her.

"My first thought was, how like the center of Coventry or the devastation around St. Paul's, except that there havoc and obliteration seem to spread out endlessly," said Clementine. "One building that caught my eye was a wreck that had been ingeniously patched and shored up. I learned that it was the building in whose cellar the Russians had captured von Paulus, the German commander. It was characteristic of them, I thought, to make every effort to preserve this ruin because of its symbolic value. It represented the final overthrow of the enemy after one of the most savage struggles in all human history. Stalingrad was the turning point in the war, and that will be remembered by the Russians for centuries to come.

"In the middle of a big public square in Stalingrad, there was a huge common grave surmounted by an obelisk. This tomb, wherein lie so many of the brave defenders of the city, is called 'The Brothers' Graves,' a name that is moving, simple, and beautiful."

The Germans left 60,000 dead when they were chased out of Stalingrad. The Russians buried them simply by dynamiting a giant valley out of the countryside and burying all the corpses together.

"Were you not afraid of some pestilence breaking out?" she asked officials in Stalingrad.

"We never thought of that until afterwards," the Russians replied.

Determined to see all she could, Clementine always sat in front with the driver whenever they traveled by car. In Stalingrad her charm and sympathy lit up "homes" that were no more than hovels in the ground. In front of one pile of rubble out of which a family had burrowed a shelter, Clementine stopped beside a placard displayed outside which read, "A very fine shop is to open here soon."

"What kind will it be?" Clementine asked the young Russian wife who stood respectfully beside the entrance to her "home" to greet the wife of Winston Churchill.

"A barber's," was the reply.

In the hospital wards, nurses enthusiastically and gratefully applauded her. In the streets, waving and applauding crowds trailed her. She found few Russians curious about British life or affairs, but their gratitude for the Aid to Russia Fund was obvious.

Few would talk of the days and nights of horror they had endured in the nightmare of German occupation. "We do not even want to think about the Germans," they would say.

Clementine confessed that she had never been more deeply moved in her life than by the spectacle of child victims of the seige of Stalingrad being cared for at a children's home. The *Luftwaffe* had marked this hospital on their maps as a special target for their bombers.

As she toured the wards of the children's home, Clementine saw boys who had fought with partisans and who were still suffering from wounds, children injured during the bombing of evacuation trains, children whose both parents were at the front, and children whose parents would never return. She walked into one gymnastic class where the bodies of babies from eight months old were being repaired from the ravages of war, and watched a little boy of eight months perform astonishing physical feats while his woman instructor held him up by the heels. The little body firmly swayed to and fro like a trained gymnast. When Clementine expressed her amazement, the instructor said with a smile, "Oh, any intelligent mother could do that if she chose to learn. If she loves her child, neither he nor she need ever have any fear."

Language was no barrier between her and the children she met. "When I was in a room with a group of them I would sometimes feel a small hand put into mine. I would look down and find a two-year-old with soft brown eyes who would pull me away to show me the bed where she slept or to give me a toy," said Clementine.

Leningrad had a special surprise for her—the entire city, including the Lord Mayor, the Council, stars of stage, ballet, and opera, all turned out to greet her. And the Lord Mayor, Mr. Popkov, gave a great dinner in her honor. "Would you like to dine first or hear a little music first?" he asked.

"I would like to hear the music," she replied. As if by magic, chairs were brought in and the concert, which lasted for more than an hour, began.

But the guest of honor had a return surprise for her hosts. Toward the end of the evening, she joined in the community singing of Russian folk songs. When they began the "Song of the Volga Boatmen," she sang that one too and surprised her hosts with her familiarity with their famous traditional song.

She found the despoiled spa towns of the Caucasus packed with Red Army convalescents. Sebastopol was "a sight to wring one's heart," she said. "Before the Nazis destroyed it in their blind rage, it must have been a dream of beauty, as lovely as a poem, with its many pillared and frescoed houses."

Wherever she traveled, she brought to the people of Russia an understanding of the warm friendship felt by the people of Britain for them. She helped Russians to a better knowledge of their allies—a knowledge for which they had long thirsted. Her strenuous tour was of tremendous service.

In the Crimea she stayed at Vorontzov Palace where her husband had lived during the Crimea Conference. There she relaxed a while from the strain of the tour by visiting such shrines of literature as Chekov's house, where she was received by his sister Marian, then eighty-two years old.

One of the most vivid memories for her of the Russian journey was the visit to the Young Pioneers Camp at Artek in the Crimea. Practically every child in Russia is a Young Pioneer, and Artek is their most famous camp. Every year thousands of children between the ages of seven and fourteen go there for a six weeks' stay. The voices of 600 children sang to her that day the haunting melody of "The Song of Lenin"—a song of tragedy, a song of hope.

Then, in the city of Odessa, liberated after two and a half years of occupation, came two links with home—one happy, one tragic.

On arrival at Odessa she found a large number of British P.O.W.s waiting to be repatriated and asked to be taken to see them immediately. A ship, which was to transport them to Britain and home, was in port. Clementine brought the men their first real touch of home as she moved and talked among them. The next day she went to the dockside to wave them "God Speed" as they sailed.

"It heightened for us the happy sense of liberation that filled the air," she said.

"As war news poured in, it made the pulses beat faster to see our own men going home, free from the miseries of captivity, and knowing that soon they would be with their families again after the long and bitter separation."

Also in Odessa was a camp of 1,000 French civilians deported by the

Germans for forced labor. Most of them carried the tattoo identification marks of the slave laborer. Clementine stopped to speak to one of the women among them and asked her name. The woman stared, faltered, and then murmured, "I think I know it now, but up to a week ago I used to think of myself by my number only," she said, looking at the terrible branded figures on her arm.

Clementine stood on street corners in Odessa watching the groups of marching men and women—freed slave laborers, freed P.O.W.s—of all nationalities. Then came another kind of tragedy. It was Friday, April 13, 1945, when a message brought news to her—President Roosevelt had died.

While the President was having his portrait painted, he complained of a "terrific headache," then collapsed, and died a few hours later without regaining consciousness.

On his return from the Yalta Conference, Winston had shared with Clementine his terrible fear for the President's health. "I noticed that the President was ailing. His captivating smile, his gay and charming manner, had not deserted him, but his face has a transparency, an air of purification, and often there was a faraway look in his eyes," he said. "When I took leave of him in Alexandria harbor, I must confess that I had an indefinable sense of fear that his health and strength were on the ebb."

Clementine was traveling from Leningrad to Moscow, but was only due to stop briefly at Moscow Station, on her way elsewhere. As the train drew in, she saw Molotov and his wife waiting on the platform. They boarded the train, entered her compartment, and Molotov said, "We come with bad news—President Roosevelt is dead." Clementine asked the Molotovs to join her in a two-minute silence in the carriage.

Although Winston had told her how terribly ill the President had looked at the Yalta Conference, the news nevertheless came as a tremendous shock. It was even more shattering because she knew that at such a moment Winston would need her, yet here she was thousands of miles away from him on a mission of mercy she had undertaken. She wanted to fly home but knew she couldn't. Instead she waited for the telephone call she was sure would come.

Clementine knew the shock would, in many ways, be even worse for him than the morning soon after Pearl Harbor when the telephone by his bedside had rung, and a voice said, "Prime Minister, I have to report to you that the *Prince of Wales* and the *Repulse* have both been sunk by the Japanese...."

With the destruction of these two warships, there were no American or British capital ships in the Pacific or Indian oceans, except the American survivors of Pearl Harbor, and the Japanese were supreme over the vast area.

"In all the war I never received a more direct shock," Winston had said. But the President's death hurt deeply, and more personally.

Both she and Winston had been looking forward to welcoming President and Mrs. Roosevelt on a "Thank you" visit to Britain which had been arranged for the month of May. The Roosevelts had already accepted the invitation from the King and Queen.

When Judge Samuel Rosenman had been a guest at Chequers, Winston had asked Judge Rosenman to give the President a message, "Will you tell him for me that he is going to get from the British people the greatest reception ever accorded to any human being since Lord Nelson made his triumphant return to London?

"I want you to tell him that when he sees the reception he is going to get, he should realize that it is not an artificial or stimulated one. It will come genuinely and spontaneously from the hearts of the British people; they all love him for what he has done to save them from destruction by the Huns. They love him also for what he has done for the cause of peace in the world, for what he has done to relieve their fear that the horrors they have been through for five years might come upon them again in increased fury."

At 3 A.M. the night bell in his personal detective's bedroom rang, and Inspector Thompson hurried to discover the reason for the alarm. He found Winston pacing up and down his bedroom, his head sunk low, his eyes fixed on the floor.

"President Roosevelt has passed away," he said, "your friend and mine, Thompson. . . . We have to start all over again, and it is Friday the thirteenth. . . ."

Winston had always told Clementine that without Roosevelt and the Americans behind him, Britain would surely have been lost. Winston and Clementine dearly cherished their friendship with Franklin and Eleanor Roosevelt. It was, as Winston said, "a friendship which was forged in the fire of war."

The telephone rang in Clementine's quarters in Russia. It was London, and Winston.

Together, over the telephone, they shared their loss. His first impulse he told her, had been to fly to the funeral and he had ordered an airplane to stand by, but the pressures of Cabinet and Parliamentary arrangements could make this impossible.

"I have lost a great friend. One of the greatest ever," he said.

Winston sent Eleanor Roosevelt and her family a message of sympathy from Downing Street. Clementine sent her own from Russia.

When the all-too-short telephone call ended, he needed to go on talking, so he talked to members of his staff. "No one realized what that man meant to the country, meant to the world. He was a great friend to us all. He gave us immeasurable help at a time when we most needed it," he told his staff.

"He was loved by millions and hated too, as a wizard who gets things done. I'll be hated. But I'm composed about it. It requires no resignation on my part. I am sure it took none for Franklin.

"But at least he had the peace and satisfaction to know his work was done. To see it done just before the end. His task was completed at Yalta. He died on the eve of victory, but he saw the wings of it. And he heard them."

The following day, Winston cabled a message to Stalin. It said:

"I have been greatly distressed by the death of President Roosevelt, with whom I had in the last five-and-a-half years established very close personal ties of friendship. This sad event makes it all the more valuable that you and I are linked together by many pleasant courtesies and memories, even in the midst of all the perils and difficulties that we have surmounted.

"I must take the occasion to thank you and Molotov for all the kindness with which you have received my wife during her visit to Moscow, and for all the care that is being taken of her on her journey through Russia. We regard it as a great honor that she should receive the Order of the Red Banner of Labor on account of the work she has done to mitigate the terrible sufferings of the wounded soldiers of the heroic Red Army. The amount of money she collected is perhaps not great, but it is a love offering not only of the rich, but mainly of the pennies of the poor, who have been proud to make their small weekly contribution. In the friendship of the masses of our peoples, in the comprehension of their Governments, and in the mutual respect of their armies the future of the world will reside."

A day later Winston received a reply from Stalin which said:

"I have received your message on the occasion of the death of President Roosevelt.

"In President Franklin Roosevelt the Soviet people saw a distinguished statesman and an unswerving champion of close cooperation between the three States.

"The friendly attitude of President Franklin Roosevelt to the U.S.S.R. will always be most highly valued and remembered by the Soviet people. So far as I personally am concerned I feel exceptionally deeply the burden of the loss of this great man, who was our mutual friend."

Winston's tribute in Parliament to the President was printed in full by the Russian newspaper *Pravda,* and the report was translated in Moscow for Clementine.

In spite of her strong personal desire to return home at once, she continued the tour.

She had received a telegram from the Chairman of Kursk Council. The Chairman, Mme Maslennisova, proved to be, said Clementine, one of the most remarkable women she had ever met. Mme Maslennisova had organized thousands of women to help rebuild the shattered city. "I saw them working with a will among the ruins," said Clementine. "I am sorry they had only spades with which to clear away the rubble—I wished they could have had bulldozers."

But it was at the children's hospital at Kursk that she was confronted with one of the most terrible moments of the tour. The director of the hospital went over to a bed where a little girl was lying.

"Allow me to present to you the only living Jew in Kursk," he said, grimly raising the child in her bed for Clementine to see. "All the other Jews have been wiped out." This little girl, the sole survivor, had been saved by hiding under a mattress. On her little arm was the infamous Nazi tattoo of shame.

Clementine became extremely friendly with Mme Molotov, and, on returning to Moscow, she visited the school at which Mme Molotov's daughter Svetlana was a pupil, and watched an English lesson at the school conducted by a Russian woman who had spent only three years studying the English language, but who nevertheless had managed to achieve excellent pronunciation and intonation.

The lesson was conducted by question and answer.

"What color is your tie?"

"The color of my tie is red."

In Moscow, Clementine Churchill received two decorations. One was the Order of the Red Banner of Labor, the other the Distinguished Service Badge of the Russian Red Cross. She and Miss Johnson received their decorations at the Kremlin. Clementine was asked to extend her left hand, and a medallion was placed on the palm, while her services in organizing aid to the Soviet Red Cross and the peoples of the Soviet Union were cited.

Presentation of the Distingushed Service Badge of the Red Cross was made at a meeting of the Praesidium of the Red Cross. The ceremony lasted two hours, and Clementine, in reply, said that she felt there was no happiness before us or the world unless the great Soviet Union and the English-speaking world know each other, understand each other, and remain friends.

Speaking frankly to Mme Molotov, Clementine said, "Unless the friendship that has been established between the Soviet Union and the English-speaking peoples during the war continues, increases, and deepens, there will be very little happiness in the immediate future for the world, and by the immediate future I don't just mean the short span of our lives, but the lives of our children, grandchildren, and great-grandchildren. I hope that, in a small way, my visit will help.

"During my tour of your country I have been struck by the devastation, but still more by the way your people are rebuilding what has been ruined.

"I have noted the intense veneration of this country for science and learning in every form of art, and also the wonderful position achieved by women in such a short time.

"Wherever you go in this country you find tremendous love and care lavished on the children and it is wonderful to see."

It was Clementine's wish as well as that of the Aid to Russia Committee that there should be some permanent memorial to commemorate the link forged between the peoples of the United Kingdom and the U.S.S.R., and at first it was thought it might take the form of erecting a hospital. Instead, the Soviet authorities undertook to provide the hospital buildings and suggested they should be equipped from the Aid to Russia Fund.

At Rostov-on-Don two hospitals—the Central City Hospital and the Clinical Hospital—had been almost destroyed. Clementine and her Committee promised to equip the Central 1,000-bed hospital, and the Scottish Central Council Branch of the British Red Cross undertook to do the same for the 500-bed Clinical Hospital, and equip it they did, down to such items as blotters, inkstands, and pen trays. Plaques acknowledging the gifts were placed on the hospital buildings.

The snowball of victory began to grow, and the war in Europe approached its final phase. From the British Embassy in Moscow, Clementine received her own private news service of momentous events—Mussolini's capture and execution by anti-Fascists; three days later, the news of the death of Hitler; the Italian surrender to Field Marshal Harold Alexander; and then the mass surrender in Germany to Field Marshal Bernard Montgomery.

On May 7, when she learned that Admiral Doenitz had surrendered unconditionally on behalf of Germany, she longed to be with Winston in the hour of triumph, but she had promised to be present at a number of ceremonies in her honor in Moscow and couldn't leave. On that Monday in May, everyone knew the war in Europe was over—though it was not to be officially over until the following day. The excitement of Moscow was electric. Crowds in the streets milled around, impatient for the news they knew would come any second.

Recalled Clementine, "The memory of my last week in Moscow is unforgettable because of the affecting power of the emotions with which it was charged. It was May 8,—VE Day in Britain. In the Embassy I heard my husband's voice broadcasting from London the announcement for which the world had been waiting."

Winston ended the broadcast with—"Advance Britannia! Long live the Cause of Freedom! God save the King!"

"M. Edouard Herriot, the great French statesman, and his wife, who had been recently liberated after many hardships and discomforts from their German captivity, were with us in Moscow," said Clementine.

"After the broadcast, M. Herriot said to me, 'I am afraid you may think it unmanly of me to weep. But I have just heard Mr. Churchill's voice. The last time I heard his voice was on that day in Tours in 1940, when he implored the French Government to hold firm and continue the struggle. His noble words of leadership that day were unavailing. When I heard the French Government's answer, and knew that they meant to give up the fight, tears streamed down Mr. Churchill's face. So you will understand if I weep today.'"

In London, Winston attended a Service of Thanksgiving at St. Margaret's, Westminster, while in Moscow, Clementine attended a similar service in the British Mission building. It was conducted by a Royal Navy Volunteer Reserve Officer who was a Methodist minister, and an address was given by the "Red Dean" of Canterbury, Dr. Hewlett Johnson, who had only arrived in Moscow the night before. "Let's ask him to preach," Clementine had suggested, and Dr. Hewlett Johnson's moving address took as its theme the death of Franklin Roosevelt.

Clementine could not share Winston's historic, glorious day when he left 10 Downing Street to make his Victory in Europe statement to the House of Commons. She could not be there to see the thousands in Parliament Square cheering and shouting "Good old Winnie!" but she heard them over the radio and heard how the Prime Minister's car was almost pushed to Parliament by excited crowds.

It was a holiday in everyone's hearts, and Winston, always with the right words to say, told the happy faces below him, "Why don't you take the day off tomorrow as well!" He began to sing the opening words of "Land of Hope and Glory," and the thousands echoed it as one voice.

These were moments Clementine could not see, but in her heart she shared them just the same.

Then, from Winston to Clementine came the following message, "It would be a good thing if you broadcast to the Russian people tomorrow, Wednesday, provided that were agreeable at the Kremlin. If so, you might give them the following message from me, of which, of course, our Embassy would obtain approval:

"Prime Minister to Marshal Stalin, to the Red Army, and to the Russian people. From the British nation I send you heartfelt greetings on the splendid victories you have won in driving the invader from your soil and laying the Nazi tyrant low. It is my firm belief that on the friendship and understanding between the British and Russian peoples depends the future of mankind. Here in our island home, we are thinking today very often about you all, and we send you from the bottom of our hearts our wishes for your happiness and well-being, and that after all the sacrifices and sufferings of the dark valley through which we have marched together, we may also in loyal comradeship and sympathy walk in the sunshine of victorious peace. I have asked my wife to speak these few words of friendship and admiration to you all.

"Let me know what you will do. Much love, W."

This was Winston's formal VE message to Clementine. His informal one, he passed on to her himself by telephone. Even in the golden moments of victory he was anxious for the future, anxious for the continuation of Anglo-Soviet friendship.

"How are we to work together if an Iron Curtain is to be drawn down between us and only occasionally raised to allow a face, and not a very pleasant face at that, to peer through at us?" he said.

At a luncheon given by the Soviet Government in Clementine's honor two days before she left Moscow, Mme Molotov presented her with a diamond ring.

"We ask you to accept this ring as a token of eternal friendship," said Mme Molotov. "May the relations between our two countries be as bright, as pure, and as lasting as this stone."

Thanking Mme Molotov, Clementine said she would in particular think of the ring as a symbol of Soviet womanhood, whose achievements in the war and in the rebuilding of their country had won undying admiration. She added, "I must also confess I take a very feminine pleasure in the beauty of the stone!"

Her last night in Moscow she spent seeing the *Swan Lake* ballet. At the fall of the curtain, the prima ballerina moved toward Clementine's box, applauding and smiling, and the whole company followed. The great, distinguished audience took up the applause to give a standing ovation to the woman who had done so much for their people.

Said Clementine, "I pray as I turn to take my farewell look at Moscow, 'May difficulties and misunderstandings pass, may friendship remain.'"

On returning to London, the Fund's secretary, Miss Mabel Johnson, presented a report on their Russian journey to the British Red Cross, and Clementine supplemented this report with her own personal impressions of the experience. It is from this diary of the tour that I have taken her memories of the visit, and in this same record she wrote, "It seems to me that the contact we have made is like a lifeline, which in her hour of peril and sorrow the British Red Cross threw to Soviet Russia. If things go well, as pray God they may, this lifeline will be strengthened by other organizations representing the whole field of human intercourse. But if, alas, the relations between our two countries should go through dark hours, let us show that our lifeline, though slender, is strong. What a wonderful thing it would be if the Red Cross were able to hold together a trembling and dissolving Europe!"

Months later, as the first chill of the Cold War began to be felt, she recalled, "On Victory Day I remember being struck with astonishment that the Armistice was signed in Rheims and only it seemed as an afterthought in Berlin. This was rather incomprehensible to the Russians, and I confess that being rather cut off from home news, it was incomprehensible to me.

"I mention this because now that there are widening rifts and cooling feelings and dark suspicions, we must sometimes try to transport ourselves across the continent of Europe and imagine what a Russian would feel, isolated after the 1917 revolution for twenty-five long years, then drawn by terrible necessity into partnership and then, with the Nazi terror laid low, reverting to his loneliness.

"We do not want to be cut off from one another in the human race. However queer the Kremlin may behave, I am sure that the Russian people, if only we can get their human touch, want to be friends. The lifeline which the British Red Cross threw to the Soviet Red Cross still holds fast. If it is to be severed the fault must not lie with us.

"During that memorable visit I learned how different an event seemed when you viewed it in Moscow instead of London or Washington."

On May 14, Winston accompanied by Field Marshal Philip Chetwode, was at the Northolt airfield of the R.A.F. Transport Command waiting for Clementine's return from Russia. When the plane had taxied to a halt, the second the plane door opened, Clementine, wearing the uniform of the British Red Cross, almost burst out, to be greeted warmly by Winston.

They had been parted during historic days. They were to be together during still more momentous ones.

Clementine had much to tell him of her visit, and, in particular, of her conversation with Stalin. "You hear people say, 'You only see the things in Russia that they want you to see.' That is a very foolish argument.

"These tremendous people are halfway through the most terrific experiment ever tried. All these years the Soviet Union has been quite happy to be left alone, but the war has made a tremendous difference.

"They are thrilled and astonished to find that all over the world their courage is acclaimed. We must not come to hasty conclusions until we know all the facts. I am certain that if we persevere now, friendship will increase."

Clementine had one extra little duty to perform in connection with her Russian visit. She had learned that her interpreter, Mme Kislova, was a lover of Jane Austen. As soon as she reached home, Clementine sent for a copy of *Emma,* and posted it with a "Thank you for everything" note to Mme Kislova.

19

A Woman's Work

WINSTON talked repeatedly of Clementine's experiences in Russia. She had given him much to think about on the Soviet role in the future. Long after her return from Moscow, he would recall aspects of her visit—from the Moscow luncheon party for which all the Russian women invited had to be provided with dresses by the State, to the children of the country being instilled with the creed:

"I love Lenin,
Lenin was poor, therefore I love poverty,
Lenin went hungry, therefore I can go hungry.
Lenin was often cold, therefore I shall not ask for warmth."

"Christianity with a tomahawk," commented Winston.

Her personal success in public life is no mere reflected popularity. It is her own. Wherever she goes, whether she is making a speech at a political rally, visiting victims in a flood area, or walking over a pile of rubble, which was a home before being bombed to dust, she is liked for herself, liked for the genuine smile that never degenerates into a fixed grin.

Few are aware of the time and effort she has devoted to causes. Apart from the countless duties, both public and private, she had to perform during the Second World War, she made time for many causes, including getting more comfortable quarters for Service women.

"As the war goes on, women of my age are increasingly concerned about their daughters," she said.

"They are doing splendidly, but we do not want them in the monotony and hardness of their duties to forget the happiness and comforts and duties of home."

Later, thinking of the thousands of girls living in hostels all over the country, girls who Clementine felt should have the chance to develop their own characters before undertaking responsibilities of raising their own families, she set a new target for the Y.W.C.A., an organization that was one of her greatest interests.—"For every girl a room of her own, with a lock on the door—a really cosy bed sit—that is my most ardent desire," she declared.

Clementine raised the banner for each girl to have a place in which she could enjoy freedom to contemplate; to think for herself and be herself.

Addressing a meeting of fellow committee members at the Y.W.C.A., she said, "I do wish dormitories could be abolished. When I first began visiting hostels, I was often told that the girls liked sleeping together, having got used to it in the Forces. But I think that even if this were really so they would soon grow out of it if they had a room of their own.

"This of course does not apply to young girls between sixteen and eighteen, for whom dormitories are suitable and whose salaries are not high enough to pay for a single room.

"But it is necessary—this room of her own—for the girls who have to leave home and their family to earn their own living."

Clementine didn't just talk—she went to see, to plan for herself. Studying the problems of overcrowding in existing hostels, she made frequent unexpected visits to inspect hostels in their "everyday clothes," and not wearing, perhaps, a party dress for her benefit.

After a visit to a hostel housing fifty girls, she said the place was only suitable for thirty-five girls. "But where are the surplus fifteen girls to go to?" she asked. "Some hostels have waiting lists as long as my arm," she added.

"Also, by reducing the numbers, you incur a loss of income, which would have to be made up." Clementine, economic and careful housekeeper, didn't forget that extra comfort must be paid for from somewhere.

Her answer was to compile a new "Hostels Constitution." With her committee she prepared and wrote a hostels handbook to which she devoted great time, thought, and effort.

She told the committee, "It doesn't always follow that girls are necessarily happiest in pale blue and white paint hostels. A residence director who loves and understands her girls is the first essential. Residence directors need to have so many qualities, and I formed a warm regard and admiration for them. They do a difficult and demanding and fatiguing job, and in addition, they have always imperative necessity of making both ends meet.

"All this is a great strain upon their temperament and character and, of course, not every residence director is an angel any more than every nurse is a Florence Nightingale."

Clementine's Y.W.C.A. committee handbook didn't speak dream language—it got down to basic essentials, basic necessities.

"An ablutions block in evey hostel with a ratio of not more than four girls to each washbasin, eight to each lavatory, and ten to each bath," it demanded.

"The ablutions block, if possible, to be situated at the end of each floor. Each washbasin to have a partition round it." That final point was a typically considerate suggestion from a woman who loves and respects privacy.

"A laundry in every hostel, with space to dry clothes and an airing cupboard; one electric iron to every six girls," the handbook continued.

Clementine's lead—unknown to the public and to the mothers of the daughters for whose welfare she was so concerned—was taken up as the new aim of the worldwide Y.W.C.A. organization, with its network of clubs, hostels, and cafeterias for women and girls in sixty-nine countries.

To help make her "every girl her own room" desire a reality, Clementine pulled out all stops to raise funds. She even achieved a miracle in its cause by persuading Winston, the artist, to sell one of his paintings.

It was the only picture he has ever allowed to be publicly auctioned. The picture—the blue drawing room at Trent Park—was sold to a Brazilian collector for 1,250 guineas. The money helped to build more of those Y.W.C.A. rooms.

Clementine was delighted with the result of the sale, but furious a little later when she heard that the Brazilian collector had admitted that he would have bid up to £13,000 for it if necessary.

"Her tremendous wartime work for the Forces—and, in particular, for the girls in the Forces—led to her taking great interest in hostels in later years," said Miss Ruth Walder, National General Secretary of the Y.W.C.A.

Her fund-raising activities are fantastic—nothing is too much trouble for her if it is to help a worthy cause. Her annual or biennial open days at Chartwell usually net about £600 each. She holds little luncheon get-togethers at home for people whose aid she wishes to recruit for raising money for her pet charities. If Winston is around he pops his head in to say hello to her guests, then vanishes to let her get on with the task of finding ways and means of getting cash for new hostel improvements.

"Lady Churchill frequently deflects to us money she is offered," said Miss Walder. "The most memorable example of this occurred in 1949 when an admirer of hers from Canada asked her whether she would accept a gift of a mink coat from him. Apart from owning a great newspaper, the admirer also happened to have interests in a firm of furriers and in mink farms.

"Mrs. Churchill told him that as much as she would love to have the coat, she would prefer its value in cash to give to charity."

The admirer who bred minks was obviously a very generous sport—he sent a check, and Clementine wrote to the Y.W.C.A.:

"This cheque has just reached me from J. W. McConnell, the proprietor of the *Montreal Star*. I made his acquaintance towards the end of the war when I accompanied my husband to the second Quebec Conference. At that time I was President of the Wartime Appeal for the Y.W.C.A., and he very kindly gave me £1,000 for the fund.

"He was in London in October with Mrs. McConnell and they came to see me and offered to give me a mink coat! He is a very generous man and distributes them to his many acquaintances. (Among his many activities he is Chairman of a famous firm of furriers called Holt Renfrew.) I told him I would much rather have some money for the work I was trying to do for the Y.W.C.A. and I talked to him at some length about the hostels. He promised to send me a cheque, but nothing happened, and so I was afraid I had bored him. But now here comes Christmas and this wonderful gift...."

The check in lieu of the mink coat was for £10,000!

Apart from her extensive general work for the Y.W.C.A., she became the President of the War and National Service Fund of the organization from 1941 to 1946; Chairman of the Hostels Committee from 1948 to 1952.

In 1944, she launched the first of a series of special broadcasts to India. She said, "For the first time in history, women are no longer waiting at home for their menfolk. We are no longer called upon to listen for news, good or bad, of our husbands and sons who are fighting for us.

"We are, indeed, the chief target of the enemy. You in India can

253

have no conception of the tyranny that would overtake you if the British were beaten."

In addition to her Aid to Russia movement, and all her other efforts, she also became chairman of a maternity hospital—a duty she took very seriously. Each fresh task she undertook, she investigated thoroughly, studying requirements, planning solutions. She is meticulous in everything. But, although a stickler for etiquette and certain formalities, she knows when and how to be informal.

On a surprise visit to a hostel for girls working in munition factories, she walked into a factory dance. In no time at all she was dancing with one of the factory superintendents, thoroughly enjoying herself. Visiting a W.V.S. canteen, she found trade booming so she went behind the counter to lend a hand pouring tea. During her visit to a canteen for Servicemen, one of the canteen organizers commented, "I watched her greet some of our sailors and airmen, and she approached each one as if he were the one person she had come to meet."

Her perceptive eye and inquiring mind makes a visit from her to any institution an unforgettable experience for everyone else.

Meeting the staff, she would make a point of talking to at least every alternate person, and not just a courtesy word, but asking them questions—questions that always revealed an intimate knowledge of their work and duties.

Anyone presented to her was truly staggered at her knowledge of their personal background. The secret was her insistence on detailed briefing before each visit on everyone she might encounter.

For a Royal Air Force horticultural show at which she was to present the trophies, she arrived half-an-hour before expected, to make a quiet advance examination of exhibits.

Putting on her glasses every few minutes to take a closer look, she turned to one of the officers to say, "I cannot help reflecting all this, and flying too. I have never seen such vegetables in all my life—so beautifully grown and polished."

Says Harold Macmillan, "She is not only the wife of one whose name will be treasured as long as the English language is spoken, but she has also endeared herself to the friends she has made. All through her political life, she has served with her husband."

If she considers anything wrong, she says so whether her opinion is unpopular or not. She was visiting Britain's first day nursery for spastic children when she spotted press photographers taking pictures by flashlight of a five-year-old patient.

Clementine was furious. "Children might easily be put back by that sort of thing," she said angrily. For the rest of the afternoon, pictures were taken without flashlights. And the unfortunate children were left alone. Only when she was satisfied that her wishes were being respected, did she continue the tour of the clinic.

Told that the National Spastic Society had been set up by parents of spastics, she said, "It is an old saying that 'God helps those who help themselves.' Let us vary the phrase and say, 'We will all help these courageous people who have not given up hope and who help themselves and their children.'"

When fifty-three-year-old Francis Stanislaw, founder of the "Eye Will Crusade" wrote to her, she agreed to leave her eyes to an eye bank so that some day a blind boy or girl might see again with the cornea of her eyes. No appeal she can answer is ever refused.

Her work has never been a token effort. For years, she has coped with a large daily postbag. She personally reads every letter and dictates the reply to her secretary, signing all her letters personally.

They can cover all manner of inquiries ranging from an old-age pensioner asking her to intervene to get a rent reduction, to thanking a little girl for offering to make Winston a face cloth for his birthday and suggesting that he might prefer blue to pink edging.

She also turned her attention to helping the millions of refugees throughout the world, and became the spirit behind the World Refugee Year, which set out to raise millions to help the stateless.

Without the urgency of a war or a disaster visible to all, the task on behalf of the refugees was more difficult. Fifty influential people were invited by the Duchess of Marlborough to Londonderry House. The idea was to find an initial £35,000 for the fund. It was a tall opening target, and the chances of achieving it seemed, at first, remote. Clementine walked into the room. She spoke, and her words had the Churchillian ring about them, "Remember there are no British refugees anywhere in the world," she observed simply.

The case was won. The fifty left, and the money was found in record time. But that was only the beginning.

She broadcast, addressed gatherings, talked to people in all walks of life, urging them to help, and spoke words that made sense—words of sincerity. Her speeches were never "ghosted." What she said, she meant, and wrote herself.

She told people, "If we think carefully, we realize how lucky we have been in having the security and comfort of a house, an accepted place within a community—a sense of belonging.

"Since the war, millions of refugees in various parts of the world have lost country, home, possessions, jobs, friends, relations, and sometimes their health. Many have waited ten years and more in camps and shacks for a chance to start a new life. A new generation is now being born in these camps. A new race of stateless camp dwellers. Even the young somehow know they are different."

Like Winston, to propel people into action, she didn't hesitate to make them face unpleasant facts, repeating again and again the story she had heard of a young refugee boy living in a camp in Austria who, with his father, was watching a camp being built in a nearby village.

" 'Daddy,' he asked. 'What sort of people can live in houses?'

"I am glad I did not have to answer that boy's questions," said Clementine.

"Let us face the fearful fact that if we had lost the war we might have been refugees. Some people will say 'Charity begins at home.' It may begin at home, but I believe it doesn't end there.

"We must not neglect those less fortunate than ourselves, however far they may be from us and how very easy it is to overlook them. They are our responsibility—a responsibility laid upon us 2,000 years ago by Our Lord. 'Inasmuch as ye have done it unto one of the least of these my brethren, ye have done it unto me.' "

In later years, she could have justifiably taken things easy, and given up most of her work. But for her, as with Winston, "Living is working."

As the distinguished writer Hannen Swaffer once said of her, "She rose from obscurity to world prominence in which her inward grace shone resplendently beside the glory of her husband's triumphs."

Presenting prizes at Berkhamsted School for Girls of which she is an old pupil, she gave "one or two safe wrinkles gathered by making a great many mistakes myself over a long life."

She said, "If you find yourself in competition with men, never become aggressive in your rivalry. She who forces her point may well lose her advantage. You will gain far more by quietly holding to your convictions.

"But even this must be done with art, and above all with good humor. Never enlarge, except to a tried and trusted confidante, about your difficulties."

256

Greeted by a crowd serenading her with "Oh my darling Clementine!" she laughed and said she was neither "lost," nor "gone forever."

Any woman with the temerity to describe her extraordinary husband as being "too chirpy" and to cope with his chirpiness is a force to be reckoned with. Little wonder that introducing her at a political meeting Lord Cottesloe declared, "How she was able to do so much public work while at the same time looking after her man-eating tiger is one of the miracles of those war years."

But even her "man-eating tiger" of a husband is unaware of the extent of her work—she just doesn't let him know, as Miss Edna Rowe, Hostels Adviser to the Y.W.C.A., witnessed for herself at Downing Street one day.

"We were both studying the plans of a hostel to be built at Cheltenham. The plans were all spread out on a table in her room, when Mr. Churchill marched in.

"Mrs. Churchill whipped round as the door opened, stood with her back to the table, and somehow managed to prevent him spotting the plans. Distracting his attention, she quickly answered the problem he had come to sort out, and practically shooed him out of the room without his even realizing it. She returned smiling, and this wonderful woman to whom so many people owe so much, said, 'I didn't want him to see the plans. He mustn't know—he gets so cross if he thinks I'm doing too much.'"

20

Bitter Victory

"WE are going to Paris!" Winston announced to Clementine. His excitement at the prospect of visiting Paris for the first time since the Liberation was irrepressible.

Everything had been arranged. They were to go on November 10; be present the following morning at a great Armistice Day military parade; and be seen by the largest possible number of people, without any previous announcement being made.

Scotland Yard and the French police were worried. There were still large numbers of Germans in Paris, and there was no doubt that an attempt might be made to assassinate Winston if he appeared in the streets.

Both he and the Cabinet were acquainted with the risk, and several members of the Cabinet pressed him not to go. He felt that he, as a symbol of Britain, should be there on the anniversary of Armistice Day, and that, in any case, there was danger in any large crowd.

He discussed the police warnings with Clementine and explained his reasons for wanting to go. Unlike many of his well-intentioned Cabinet colleagues, she said nothing to dissuade him this time. She appreciated how great was his desire to share this day with millions of Parisians he had helped liberate, and realized how much sharing such a day of triumph meant to him. She started to pack for Winston, Mary, and herself.

In Paris, they found the entire first floor of the Quai D'Orsay at their disposal. But Winston's day was really made when Clementine, with a delighted grin, led him into the bathroom of their suite. What he saw there made him as happy as a schoolboy. It was a golden bath. He was even more deliriously excited on being informed that she had discovered that the bath had been specially installed for Goering's personal use. And he was still more delighted on hearing that Foreign Secretary Anthony Eden's bath was only a silver one.

Next morning, Clementine, Winston, and Mary, joined Mme and General De Gaulle for the drive to the Arc de Triomphe. The welcome was overwhelming. Cheering, waving Parisians were everywhere —on the boulevards, hanging from windows, on every roof. From all sides they cried—"De Gaulle!—Churchill!"

At the Arc de Triomphe, they watched a march-past lasting nearly an hour, then proceeded to the statue of Clemenceau to lay another wreath, and on to the tomb of Marshal Foch.

Following the Victory review seated beside Mme De Gaulle, Clementine watched Winston and the General as they drove, in an open car, to the Arc de Triomphe to lay their wreath, and as together, defying any Nazi assassins who might have been left behind in the city, they walked half-a-mile down the Champs Élysées to rejoin their wives.

After the ceremony, there was lunch at Rue St. Dominic—De Gaulle's headquarters. Once more, Clementine's cautionary warnings to keep on good terms with De Gaulle were heeded by Winston, and they hit it off well. Both were in excellent humor.

At the luncheon, Winston made a short speech in English. When they returned to their suite, Clementine suggested he make the next speech in French. She was sure the audience would love his fractured brand of French. He took her advice the next day, and French, "as she is spoke" by Winston, was a howling success.

Paris was crazy with joy. Winston and Clementine walked at every opportunity, and wherever they went in the city, thousands yelled themselves hoarse, trying to pass on to them some measure of their eternal gratitude.

*　　*　　*

Nazi Germany had been crushed, victory in Europe won, but Clementine knew better than anyone, that, to Winston, the task was far from over. For Winston, there were two victories yet to be achieved— the war with Japan and the reconstruction of Britain. But, with the coming of peace in Europe, he embarked on a nationwide election tour amid a delirium of welcome.

What neither he, nor Clementine, nor any of his entourage realized, was that the nation's new religion—Churchillism—was not reverence for a policy, but worship of a man. The masses were still suspicious of the class he represented.

It is a notorious fact that the leader of a democracy usually suffers a steady decline in popularity during a war, and, as great as he was, Winston was not immune from the changing values of public opinion.

Early in the war, Winston had promised Clementine that he wouldn't commit the same mistake as Lloyd George had made in seeking to retain power once hostilities had ended. They both remembered only too well how, in the months that followed World War I, Lloyd George's popularity and prestige vanished until he was finally dismissed from office.

Although preoccupied with the responsibilities of war, they were well aware of the wind of social change blowing through Britain. However, neither doubted that the architect of victory would also be commissioned by the nation to build the peace. Both were confident that the people would continue to listen to the Churchill voice.

Winston had little time for internal affairs. Throughout the war, it was Clementine who kept him in touch with the masses. She began to caution him of the growing, and almost overwhelming desire of both working and middle classes, for social reform. He accepted her advice but stressed his anxiety to avoid Party politics until the great task of reconstruction was well on its way. He wanted the great all-party Coalition Cabinet to continue cooperation in solving the problems of the peace. "At the very least, Clemmie," he said, "there should be no General Election until after the end of the war with Japan."

Pressure within the Labor Party was too great—the Coalition Government was dissolved, and a Conservative "caretaker" Government formed until such time as elections decided whom the people wished to rule.

Winston hated the idea of an election so soon when there was still so much to be done, in winning the peace. He was impatient with the election, irritated by it, and showed this in many ways. As a result, much of the burden of his personal election arrangements fell on Clementine's shoulders. As always, she was ready to accept more than her share.

She knew that the war years had taken their toll of his strength and that, while in the past he had always treated an election as a good healthy British game, at this stage, he resented devoting precious time and energy to domestic front battles.

Together, they began to campaign in his own constituency of Woodford in Essex, where he was being opposed by a hopeful farmer. In spite of drizzling, miserable rain they had a tremendous welcome, and wherever he stopped to speak, Clementine held an umbrella over his head. At unofficial halts he merely got out of the car, removed his famous square bowler hat, greeted constituents, and stepped back again into the car. In some places as they drove off, crowds sang, "For he's a jolly good fellow!" At Chigwell station they got out of the car and mounted into a gray open tourer from which he addressed the crowd.

It was then that he asked them to support his wife if he had to go away on "international business." "We will sir!" shouted the crowd.

He was in good form that day. "You will all have to be quiet if my voice is to be heard; the young must have consideration for the old."

And, taking off his bowler, he emphasized that his "caretaker" Government consisted of "the best brains he could find," by pointing at his own head. Realizing it might be taken personally, he said, "I am of course, talking in general. I mean gray matter."

Winston and Clementine perched themselves on the folded roof at the back of the car to acknowledge the cheers. At one stop, hat in hand and ignoring rain, he addressed the crowd saying, "At my age, having already passed the allotted span, I might well have claimed relief from the burden which victory has not lightened. I feel, however, that my faculties and energies are as good as they have ever been. Therefore, unless relieved by the nation, I cannot shrink from the tasks which have devolved upon me.

"The war itself is not finished. The causes for which we drew the sword are not yet fully won—are not yet safe. I still hope to take my share in a peace which shall be both worldwide and lasting, out of which will come victories and social progress not less than those in battle for which we are already well spoken of throughout the world."

As he spoke, he ignored the rain, and avoided Clementine's offered umbrella protection until an old lady in the crowd called out, "Please sir, do put on your hat. We don't want you to catch cold."

Then Winston and Clementine began a thousand-mile election tour of the cities and villages of Britain. But before the exhausting drive, they decided to spend a quiet weekend at Chequers. On the way, their car was diverted to Uxbridge, Beaconsfield, and Aylesbury, where whole populations turned out to greet them. At Uxbridge, they were almost torn from the car by overenthusiastic crowds, who had waited more than two hours.

People strained to touch their hands, and at one time, it was nearly impossible to proceed.

"Will you turn back?" Winston was asked.

"No, go on," came the reply. And on the car went.

Standing up, he waved his bowler, while Clementine remained seated, waving and smiling to the crowd.

Suddenly the happy thousands roared and surged forward. Someone even tore the cigar from his fingers. Winston beamed . . . they knew the answer of Uxbridge!

When the car stopped to enable him to speak a moment, he said, "It was not by my desire that this election has come about, but we are bound from time to time to consult the people in this country. Irrespective of party, God bless you all."

On went the car—on to High Wycombe where 15,000 waited outside the Red Lion Hotel—where Disraeli made his first political speech as a candidate for Wycombe in 1832. Winston was puffing away at a new cigar. "Where did Disraeli speak?" he inquired. The spot was indicated to him. He entered the hotel, climbed briskly from a bedroom window, and crossed steps made of beer crates to position himself on the front of the platform beside the head of the large red lion, where Disraeli had stood.

Clementine had cautioned Winston, with her unerring instinct, that with the war's end, the greatest desire of returning servicemen and women, as well as civilians whose dearest possessions had been bombed, would be for homes. Remembering this, he told the crowd at High Wycombe, "We must have the homes. There are half a million young men who want to marry, and half a million young women who want to have half a million young children as a first installment. It will be a terrible thing if the British race ever fell behind in its growth.

"I will do everything in human power, if I am charged with the responsibility for power, to get the maximum number of houses in the shortest possible time.

"And if there are combines, rings, or monopolies, we will march through them and over them as our troops have marched over so many rivers and fortified lines.

"I am going shortly to Berlin to meet Mr. Truman and Marshal Stalin. Because the election was on—and I have no right to say I shall be returned, that I shall have the honor of representing the country—I said to my colleague, Mr. Attlee, 'Come along with me as a friend and counsellor' and he said 'I will.'

"I cannot conceive how we could differ. Now I hear with surprise that he may not be a free agent, that there may be forces behind him to tell him what to do.

"We must have good solid ground for speaking, and whoever speaks must speak in the name of this country."

After the weekend's rest at Chequers, their thousand-mile tour began. It was an informal friendly pilgrimage. Wherever a crowd gathered, Winston and Clementine stopped for a "chat." Sarah also joined them on the tour.

They were already an hour behind their timetable when an eleven-year-old crippled boy hobbled out on crutches almost into the path of the car. Clementine, seeing the child, ordered the car to stop. It came alongside the flushed and excited boy who, with trembling hands thrust a bunch of red roses, poppies, white stocks, and blue pansies into her hands, then shyly asked whether the Prime Minister would give him his autograph. Winston drew his fountain pen from his pocket and the boy, whose name was Roy Clarke, proudly produced a picture of himself in a folded mount. Winston took it on his knee, and on the leaf facing Roy's photograph, inscribed "Winston S. Churchill."

"Have you lost your foot in an accident?" inquired Clementine.

Roy replied that he had been paralyzed from birth.

"That is a great misfortune," replied Clementine. "Is everything possible being done for him? Is he having the best medical attention?" she asked the boy's mother, who now stood beside him.

Clementine smiled at Roy and said, "You heard about President Roosevelt. He suffered from the same affliction as you, yet look how he triumphed over it. Whenever you feel downhearted about your trouble, always think of that great man."

By this time a crowd of neighbors and friends had gathered round the car, but before Winston gave the order to continue, he asked Roy to stand on the running board so they could have a photograph taken together.

The first day of the tour they drove through the Midlands—Rugby, Leamington, Warwick, Coventry, Birmingham—they made about fifteen stops every day and Winston, Clementine, and Sarah spoke to as many people as possible. The following day, they headed for Leeds, Halifax, Bradford, Preston, then on to Glasgow and Edinburgh.

A special train followed them from point to point throughout the tour. They slept in the train and in it Winston continued with official work. The tour imposed a great physical strain on him, for, in addition to the long road journeys and the speech-making each day, he was constantly occupied with Government business until midnight or the early hours.

With each electioneering day that passed, Clementine observed Winston's impatience grow with what he felt to be an ill-timed interruption of the completion of the war. Warned Winston in a message to electors, "We have to put this land of ours on its feet again. On September 3rd, 1939, we began an heroic crusade for right and freedom. Our hard task is not yet finished.

"We have still to beat the Japanese, to work with our Allies, to ensure that victory leads to a durable peace, to put this land of ours on its feet again.

"Believing that these tasks call for continued national unity, I invited the leaders of the Labor and opposition Liberal parties to stay in the Government to help us to finish the job. They refused."

And then, in a radio broadcast, an angry Winston began to make personal attacks on Labor leaders, who had served with him in the Coalition Government. He warned that Socialism would result in a "Gestapo." His tactics began to boomerang; public opinion began to harden against him.

Addressing a number of women's meetings, Clementine sensed this changing opinion and warned Winston. She knew in her heart that these attacks of his were resentment at being forced at this crucial stage, to engage in domestic warfare instead of international warfare. She knew he was fighting the election with little of his customary humor and tolerance.

Only Winston knew how enormous had been Clemmie's influence and contribution to his own career. He normally treasured and respected her advice and would quickly heed a gentle admonition, "Winston, I wouldn't say that." Now almost for the first time, her advice seemed to fall on deaf ears—ears that were only listening for the sound of final and certain victory in war.

People were saying—"Where is the Churchill of yesteryear?" Many said, "We can make allowances for him as the self-appointed hammer of the Socialists, but we remember when he had anti-Socialist virus in as violent a form as this, twenty years ago." People began to wonder what had become of the gay, humorous, grinning Churchill who hitherto could always see the funny side even of higher Statesmanship.

Where was the man who could pause at the end of a great passage about fighting on the beaches, in the fields, to add under his breath in the hearing of his colleagues, who knew Britain's defenselessness, "and we'll hit them on the head with bottles. We have nothing else." Or the man who had announced at so desperate a moment that Britain was all ready for the invader—"and so are the fishes."

There was no glimpse of that Churchill in any of his election speeches. He had become harsh, humorless, without a quip—his campaign one unrelieved blistering of the Socialists. What had happened? What had clouded the happy side of his genius?

More than anyone, Clementine had the answer. She knew how worried he was about future world security. Nevertheless, she was still convinced he would win—even the pessimists were certain he would get a majority of thirty seats. Overwhelming defeat was never seriously considered.

Said Winston, "It is no use people saying you can vote for the Liberals and Labor and 'the Old Man' will be in anyhow. It is no use people thinking I can continue to serve unless I have a great majority when I return to the House."

Clementine made her own eve-of-poll tour of Winston's personal constituency at Woodford, addressing six mass meetings. Speaking in the open air at Wanstead Park, she said, "I would like my husband to have a very great majority, and a great demonstration of your confidence in him. I would like very much for him to know that when you vote for him you do it because you feel he has done a good job of work, and that he will serve the nation well in the future." Then she added, "I deplore the fact that an election is being held before the termination of war with Japan. It is not the doing of my husband. He got on extremely well with all parties."

For years, she had given up platform speaking. She had returned to the platform for her son Randolph to help him fight a by-election, and that had been the first time Randolph had heard his mother speak in public. She faced a stormy meeting and handled hecklers like a veteran.

When she made a political speech, she wasn't just voicing her husband's opinions. The opinions were her own. While Winston in any election busied himself in the main with national issues, she would personally lead the local fight in his own constituency of Woodford. Her speeches didn't echo round the world like Winston's utterances, but they deserved to. So self-effacing has she always been, that when, on occasion, she spoke in public with skill, wit, and understanding, and an obvious gift of oratory, audiences were visibly surprised. It was no case of Winston's oratory rubbing off on her, for had she not, even in the earliest days of their marriage, proven herself a capable, confident, courageous speaker?

She had a reputation for shyness, but it was a deceptive shyness, as electioneering crowds and guests who came to their home soon discovered. When she felt she could be of value, she never hesitated to fight on political platforms for Winston, and for her son Randolph.

However, although a great admirer of women who achieve brilliant careers, her view is that a wife should first further her husband's career rather than let the marriage divide into two separate streams. Now, in this crucial 1945 Parliamentary battle, Winston needed all the help she could give.

As she made her election-eve tour, she spoke from the back of a lorry. She climbed aboard the two-ton lorry and, smiling from beneath an umbrella, as the rain poured down, appealed to constituents to "give my husband a great solid magnificent vote.

"I would like you to put a cross against his name, firstly, to show that you think he and the Government have fought the war manfully and with skill, and secondly, to show you believe that he will be able to bring the resources of his brains, imagination, and driving power to the tasks of peace as he has brought them to the tasks of war."

She paused, and added, with a hint of wistfulness, "It would make me very happy if, at the end of my husband's life, he were to be associated with the great reforms which he proposed in his four-year plan issued two years ago."

Clementine noted the growing public reaction to the bitter campaign he had been waging when he addressed an open-air mass meeting at Walthamstow Stadium. It was Winston's own home ground—his own constituency area—yet hecklers from all sides started to shout him down. The opposition and interruptions were so bad that he could scarcely finish his speech.

Two days later, at Tooting, London, a firework was thrown at them. It hit him in the face, and exploded a few inches away. Miraculously, they were unhurt.

On July 5, the people voted. It was a big day for Winston and Clementine. They spent it together. First at the polling booth in Woodford.

Outside she made him put on his hat because of the biting wind. He looked tired, but she went on smiling. She was still smiling when Winston told his local party workers later, "My dear wife has come to my aid and has taken a definite and recognizable part." Clementine added to the helpers gathered around her, "I am sure you will be prepared to give my husband your prayers and help."

The poll was to remain sealed until the 26th of that month to enable the complete votes of the Forces overseas to be counted.

Meanwhile, Clementine was invited to Oxford University to receive the honorary degree of Doctor of Civil Law. With her that day, receiving honorary Doctorates of Civil Law, were Admiral Lord Louis Mountbatten; Admiral King and Admiral Stark of the U.S. Navy; General Spaatz of the U.S. Air Force; Admiral of the Fleet Andrew Browne Cunningham; Admiral of the Fleet Sir James Somerville; General Crerar of the Canadian Army; Marshal of the R.A.F. Lord Portal of Hungerford; Air Chief Marshal Lord Dowding, Sir Ramaswami Mudaliar, Head of the Indian Delegation to the United Nations; and Lieutenant Colonel Nawab Sir Malik Khizar Hayat Khan Tiwana, Premier of the Punjab.

The Chancellor, Lord Halifax, greeted her, as "The consort of our Jove the unconquerable, and one who watched over and sustained him while he sustained a tottering world."

Winston, who accompanied her to the ceremony, was given a special seat in the Sheldonian Theater so that immediately on receiving her degree, Clementine could obey the injunction of the public orator to: "Let her assume the same silks as her husband and take her customary place—at his side."

At the ceremony, the Public Orator of the University painted a word picture of the "man about the Churchill house...."

"Preoccupied with problems of world government, he forgets there is a time for meals, or he'll look in for a meal unexpectedly, so that his wife must hoard her rations for him ounce by ounce.

"And all of a sudden he's out of the house and off for a conference anywhere and everywhere. What could a wife do? Either she goes with him or she fetches him home from Egypt more dead than alive, or, to get her own back drives off to Moscow herself.

"Besides, he's a perfect volcano, scattering cigar ash all over the house."

She was described as a wife with a difference. When her husband came home from the office, the problem he brought with him was the fate of civilization. When he was late for dinner or dropped ash on the carpet it was, perhaps, because he was preoccupied with the worries of the world.

While he juggled with the world's problems, and with stopping the tide of evil men such as Hitler, she made sure he had a good dinner remembering only too well that an army—and all the soldiers in it— marches on its stomach.

"A home," she once said, "should be happy, gay, and comfortable, where children can be brought up, and where true peace and contentment can be enjoyed."

*　　　*　　　*

The 1945 General Election results were still a question mark, and the Potsdam Conference was due to open in the latter half of July, so the Churchills decided to accept the offer of a brief holiday at a château in France owned by a retired industrialist. It was three miles from the Spanish frontier. With Clementine and Mary, Winston, who had badly needed this break, began to unwind a little, although one day at lunch he remarked, "Soon we shall have to go back to London to see if they've thrown me in the gutter."

When the time came to leave for Potsdam, Clementine needed to get back to London, so she sent Mary to Berlin to look after Winston.

Even Stalin was convinced Winston would be returned as Premier, asserting that all his information from Communist and other sources, confirmed his belief that he would win by a majority of about eighty.

Winston preferred not to prophesy. He wouldn't even forecast the outcome to Clementine, because, he said, he was unsure how the Forces had voted. On July 25, he arrived back at Northolt Airport. He and Clementine dined alone that night.

The Conservative party's Central Office was confident the Party would retain a substantial majority. Winston's famous map room at the Ministry of Defence headquarters had been temporarily requisitioned to deal, this time, with a political battlefield.

In his siren suit, Winston sat in the Prime Minister's chair throughout that evening of Results Night watching election results coming through and being chalked up on a giant scoreboard on the wall. By the time he was ready to retire, the results were still obscure.

Winston kissed Clementine goodnight, and went to bed in the belief that the people would wish him to continue his work. He hoped it would be possible to reconstitute the National Coalition Government in the proportions of the new House of Commons.

Just before dawn, he awoke with a sharp stab of almost physical pain. A hitherto subconscious conviction that he had been beaten, dominated his mind. He was suddenly sure that all the pressure of great events, on and against which he had for so long mentally maintained his "flying speed," was about to cease; that he would fall, and that the power to shape the future would be denied him. The knowledge and experience he had gathered, the authority and goodwill he had earned in so many countries, would vanish. He fell asleep again, and didn't wake until nine o'clock.

Clementine went with Mary to Woodford where a Northhampton-shire farmer named Hancock, with no real political experience and no hope of toppling his opponent, was giving Winston a run in his own constituency.

As the votes were counted, Clementine became increasingly alarmed at the size of the steadily mounting poll in favor of her husband's unknown rival. She was so shaken that she telephoned Winston, to hear equally staggering news of Socialist gains pouring in from all over. She didn't wait for the Woodford result. She had to be with Winston.

One of the staff brought the Woodford figures—his opponent had polled 10,488 votes! Even on his own homeground, people had turned so heavily on him, and politically smacked him in the face, after all his prodigious efforts on their behalf throughout the war years. The votes took his constituency opponent nowhere near winning the seat, but there were, nevertheless, 10,488 hurtful stabs at Winston and Clementine's hearts.

The overall results were clear. By noon defeat was a fact. To the astonishment of the whole world, he had been repudiated by his countrymen.

Winston and Clementine lunched alone. There was little conversation. Looking at Winston she said, "It may well be a blessing in disguise." He replied, "At the moment it seems quite effectively disguised."

He left her to go to his room and telephone the Palace. At four o'clock in the afternoon he had an audience with the King and resigned, advising His Majesty to send for Mr. Attlee.

That night he issued his farewell statement to the nation from 10 Downing Street.

The decision of the British people has been recorded in the votes counted today. I have therefore laid down the charge which was placed upon me in darker times.

I regret I have not been permitted to finish the work against Japan. For this however, all plans and preparations have been made, and the results may come much quicker than we have hitherto been entitled to expect.

Immense responsibilities abroad and at home fall upon the new Government and we must all hope that they will be successful in bearing them.

It only remains for me to express to the British people, for whom I have acted in these perilous years, my profound gratitude for their unflinching, unswerving support which they have given me during my task, and for the many expressions of kindness which they have shown towards their servant.

So confident had they been of victory that Clementine had even arranged a small family dinner party to celebrate the results with a few friends. The dinner was held. Winston was almost silent throughout; stunned by his rejection. She feared the effect of the shock.

As much as he wanted to be present when Japan surrendered unconditionally, Winston's considerations of duty took precedence as always. Constitutionally he could have awaited the meeting of Parliament before taking his dismissal from the House of Commons. This would have enabled him to present, before resignation, Japan's surrender, but the need for Britain to be represented with proper authority at the Potsdam Conference made all delay contrary to the public interest. Moreover, "The verdict of the electors had been so overwhelmingly expressed that I did not wish to remain even for an hour responsible for their affairs," said Winston.

Winston's four-year-old namesake grandson had to have things carefully explained to him when his grandfather was startlingly no longer Prime Minister. He listened to a long explanation from his grandmother of just what change of government means. Finally, asked if he understood he said, "Yes, I see. I've got a new grandpa now."

More than anything else it was the armies of freedom that Winston had led for so long, the young men and women of the Services, who had swung the vote toward Socialism. In their eyes, Winston's stature had been temporarily diminished by his own insistence on the introduction of narrower animosities in the Party fight, thereby allowing greater national issues to slip into the background.

Clementine bore the terrible cruelty of the moment with him. She felt, just as deeply, this harsh snatching away of responsibility at the very climax of the war, with Japan still to be finished off, and the peace yet to be won. But, as a politician's wife, she knew gratitude belongs to history, not politics. Firmly, sympathetically, she emphasized to him that the crushing defeat inflicted upon his Party in no way brought into question his place in history, nor in the affection and gratitude of the people who had followed him, nor in national pride. The universal acclaim with which he had been received throughout their election travels had clearly shown that, she stressed.

Winston knew that in her was a spirit that equaled his own. In triumph she was gracious and proud, with a tinge of humility. In disaster, defeat, and disappointment, never disheartened. Throughout a career full of contrast and frequently punctuated with disasters that would have broken the strongest heart, she never wavered. Nor did her faith in him, or in the future, waver now.

Many of their friends urged him to leave Parliament and devote himself to writing the history of the war. Clementine absolutely disagreed, although she didn't really want him to be Premier again. He had served his country magnificently yet the people's "thanks" had been vicious rejection. Nevertheless, she said, "For Winston to leave Parliament would be unthinkable—he is a child of the House of Commons."

Nor would Winston retire from the leadership of the Opposition, she asserted. "A little later," he said, "it would be easy for me to retire gracefully in an odor of civic freedoms, and the plan crossed my mind frequently. I feel now, however, that the situation is so serious and what may have to come so grave, that I am resolved toward carrying the flag so long as I have the necessary energy."

As for resigning from Party leadership, he declared, "My horse may not be a very good one, but at least it is better than being in the infantry."

Winston and Clementine Churchill moved out of 10 Downing Street. "We shall be coming back, Clemmie," he said, as the door shut behind them.

21

The Order of the Boot

THE big Inquest began. Civilian and Servicemen and women gloried triumphantly in the Socialist victory, but, beneath it all, they were ashamed of what they had done to Winston. They strove to clear their consciences by echoing the Labor Party's declarations that: "He was not the man to correct the social ills of the past."

Conservatives explained his defeat by saying that Britain's anti-capitalists had spent the war years undermining his abilities as a domestic politician with carefully sown propaganda. Others explained it as a desire of the people for a change after six years of war, adding that if Winston had not assumed leadership of the same Party that had been in power at the outbreak of war, he would have been returned as Prime Minister. People told themselves that they hadn't voted against him, but against the Party.

Winston was offered the Royal honor of the Order of the Bath. Declining he said, "How can I accept the Order of the Bath, Clemmie, when the people of England have just given me the order of the boot?"

The day he strode back into the House of Commons, no longer Prime Minister, but leader only of the Opposition, Clementine sat watching from the Distinguished Strangers' Gallery in the House.

As he entered the Chamber, the bitterness of his defeat was made even more bitter, and her strength went out to him as he had to endure "The Red Flag" being sung by some of the victorious Socialist M.P.s in the place which, throughout his life, he had regarded as the temple of his faith. He glared his contempt at the Government benches across the floor of the Chamber, and at this insult to Parliamentary tradition and glory.

In the midst of the war he had worked out a plan for peacetime development of Britain. He had believed he would see it through, with at least two Parliaments—ten years. Now the nation had spurned Winston the politician, although it still adored and respected Winston the man.

In the very moment of victory, Clementine had to witness the worst experience of Winston's political life, as the triumphant and crowded Socialist benches roared with laughter at one of his fiercest attacks on the Attlee Government. The gusts of laughter stung him like a whiplash. He stared incredulously.

When she joined him outside the Chamber, he kept repeating, unbelievingly, "They *laughed* at me . . . they *laughed* at me!"

Astonishment turned to bitterness, and this time Clementine was too terribly wounded by his rejection herself to be able, in any way, to soften the terrible blow for him.

When, with great throngs massed outside Buckingham Palace, the King received Winston at the war's end, he offered him any honor he would care to take—including a dukedom. Winston reportedly replied, "If your Majesty would allow me to decline—I have work to do yet." The King did not press him.

Winston had no intention of being kicked out of Downing Street, and then promoted out of the House of Commons—no matter how well-meant the promotion offered.

At first his resentment goaded him into frequent ill-tempered, almost childish, outbursts in Parliament against his opponents. Before long, even many of their closest friends cautioned Clementine that in his desire to damage the Socialists, Winston was doing and saying things that only damaged his own Party.

For the first time since he had taken the reins of supreme leadership, "the Old Man" was being regarded by many prominent Tories as a liability, and blatant hints were dropped that he should retire from Party leadership.

Winston had other ideas. His favorite retort to those who suggested retirement was, "Gladstone was Premier when he was eighty and *I am a youngster!*"

Then, as if to ram home his point, he stuck out his tongue in a schoolboy gesture of disdain to Socialist Ministers seated on the Front Bench opposite him. His sense of rejection had even begun to swamp his sense of Parliamentary dignity.

It was then that Clementine decided to make him forsake the Parliamentary arena a while and take a well-earned rest and holiday.

"Man has only to conquer his last and worst enemy—himself," her husband had once said. She knew he must either conquer this bitterness, or destroy himself.

"Never give in! Never give in! Never, Never, Never, Never!—in nothing great or small, large or petty—never give in except to convictions of honor and good sense," he had always told her.

She was determined not to let *his* spirit give in. Although in his seventies, he was still so vital, so versatile, so full of the future. For good or ill, he had always looked vigorously ahead.

Then people whom she had never met, whose names she did not know, came to her aid. Winston became the man on the whole world's conscience—thousands of letters in every language and from every land poured into their home, with messages of sympathy at his repudiation after victory; gratitude for his years of leadership, encouragement for the future. Clementine took the letters to him, made him read handfuls, read dozens of them to him herself.

The flow of "thank you for freedom" gifts swelled into a flood. A man in Portugal sent him 116 gallons of old port wine; the Stockowners' Association of Australia sent him a kangaroo; Spain sent the stuffed head of a bull that had been born with a white V on its forehead; Jamaica sent enough cigars to keep him puffing happily for a year; people of New Zealand sent a generous gift of money which Clementine gave to St. Mary's Hospital in London—the hospital at which Sir Alexander Fleming had discovered that great lifesaving secret weapon of war—penicillin; an elderly woman living in London sent her precious Admiral de Ruyter chair, plus a beautiful dessert-service for Clementine. From King Ibn Saud came a jeweled sword and dagger. From Switzerland came a perpetual motion clock, impossible to wind, but guaranteed to run forever. A group of Maoris in New Zealand offered a male or female kiwi. Each day brought a fresh offering of gifts from the great and humble all over the world, to the greatest man of our time. Clementine used them to breathe new fire, new fight, into dispirited Winston.

Invitations came with almost every mail from the United States. "This is just the change you need," said Clementine, so they traveled to the United States, where he accepted honorary degrees from several American colleges.

Finally, at Westminster College, in Fulton, Missouri, her wisdom in persuading him to temporarily leave the British political scene bore fruit —the great warning voice of Winston Churchill—the voice that had shouted to awaken the world of the thirties to the creeping menace of Fascism—startled the world again with a warning of the growing shadow of Communism.

Clementine knew that if Winston so frequently did not see eye to eye with his contemporaries, it was because he so often saw farther ahead. When victory was in our grasp, he looked beyond it and saw that Soviet Russia had become a "mortal danger to the free world," but the same peoples to whom his words had been lifebelts in the turbulence of war did not want to listen any more. As on so many other occasions throughout his career, conveniently deaf ears preferred not to hear his uncomfortable prophecies, while many who did, denounced, derided, or ignored them. People wanted no more talk of war; they wanted to enjoy their newly restored normality. It took immense moral courage at such a time to cry aloud that danger again threatened, that preparedness was still necessary.

Clementine read the first draft of his historic Fulton speech, and realized it was certain to meet with harsh criticism. She was also just as certain that her husband would be, as he had been so many times before, vindicated by events. As she watched him rise to speak before the distinguished audience at Fulton, she could sense the unspoken question on everyone's lips, "Had the great man lost his grip?" She had already heard him rehearse before her in the privacy of their room the tremendous answer he was about to give them.

"Last time I saw it all coming and cried aloud to my own fellow countrymen and to the world, but no one paid any attention. . . . If the Western democracies stand together in strict adherence to the principles of the United Nations Charter their influence for furthering those principles will be immense, and no one is likely to molest them. If, however, they become divided or falter in their duty and if these all-important years are allowed to slip away—then indeed catastrophe may overwhelm us all. . . ."

His call at Fulton gave birth to the awareness of danger that ultimately led to the North Atlantic Treaty Organization; to the Marshall Plan; to the great airlift to Berlin; and other attempts to halt the march of Communism in Western Europe.

Once again his vision lit the way ahead. At the very moment when the Stalin régime still appeared to be our ally, Winston could foresee the Cold War, and fearlessly said so in defiance of current popular belief.

"I have not always been wrong!" he added.

This was no more a dispirited, politically embittered Churchill. Here he was, again in the forefront, fighting for the things he cherished most —freedom, democracy. But Clementine still considered it too soon to return to London and the Parliamentary fray. She insisted on taking him on holiday.

Airport authorities fussed around him to see if they could be of service. Winston replied, "You are very kind. I do not need anything, and you must remember that I am no longer a very important person."

He still received full V.I.P. treatment, with flowers for Clementine and Customs officers apologizing for bothering them. They even changed the aircraft at his request and altered the lunch menus aboard the plane.

They became known as "the Prisoners of the Château" in Switzerland. At Château Choisi, on the shores of Lake Leman, scores of armed police patrolled the grounds, and police speedboats constantly maneuvered within fifty yards of the shore.

Police built a nest in a high tree in the château's grounds from which a look-out man could survey surrounding territory and observe every movement. Miles of territory around the château were marked off as a no-man's land on which neither pedestrian nor car was permitted to loiter.

All this security was just too much for Clementine. She asked the police to relax some of the precautions, "otherwise your overzealousness will spoil the holiday."

She supervised the refurnishing of the château with priceless Louis XV furniture obligingly loaned by local inhabitants. She had a bar built in one room and stocked it with an extensive range of wines, aperitifs, brandies, and champagnes.

An album, among their most treasured possessions, contains a record of this visit as seen through the eyes of school children.

When the schoolmaster of the little village of Emmenbrücke asked his pupils, as a drawing lesson, to illustrate Mr. Churchill's Swiss holiday, the well-known characteristics readily came to their pencils. There were drawings of Winston sunning himself, or striding down the street with his coat tails flapping, or sailing on the lake in a bow tie, shirt-sleeves and braces, or wearing various strange hats. The album containing these drawings was presented to them by the schoolmaster "as a token of affection from the children of Switzerland."

After Switzerland, Clementine took Winston to other beauty spots where he could relax.

Unfortunately, privacy is a luxury they seldom get. On a typically "strictly private" visit to Aix-en-Provence, within hours, the first twelve "See Churchill Excursion" motor coaches arrived, some from two hundred miles away. By the afternoon, their car was halted every few yards by cheering people as they drove round the town. By the evening, hundreds were clamoring to register at the same hotel, and masses of roses and gladioli were being delivered in an almost endless stream to their suite from people who had somehow managed to discover Clementine's favorite flowers.

When, accompanied by Mary and her husband, they arrived to occupy what they thought was a small suite of rooms, they found instead a whole floor of the best hotel reserved for them, with each room containing valuable pictures and furniture lent by the townspeople who had got wind of their coming. And the town council, striving to obligingly ensure for them privacy and freedom of movement, supplied a dozen police on motorcycles to follow them everywhere!

"Holiday rejoicing is necessary to human spirit," says Winston, and Clementine Churchill knows how to care for the holiday spirit in him. She firmly believes in husband and wife holidaying together and has seldom taken a vacation alone. She likes to be around when Winston feels a desire to relax in the sun, for even on holiday he requires everything about him to work with almost clockwork precision. His idea of a holiday is a mixture of work and play. Physically and mentally he is far too active to remain "unemployed" for long in restful idleness.

When they take off on holiday, a staff, including a principal private secretary and masses of documents, also frequently take off with them. So far as Clementine is concerned, preparations for a Churchill holiday virtually entail the organization and launching of a combined operation of which she is the officer-in-charge.

Winston always expects everything necessary for his personal comfort, convenience, and efficiency to be on hand, and Clementine's meticulous nature ensures that almost every possible eventuality is provided for. For one visit, when they and their staff occupied eighteen rooms in a hotel in Syracuse, she sent thirty-two trunks and suitcases ahead by rail.

On holiday she would decline all official invitations and see that he remained undisturbed in his room with every newspaper she could get for him until about 11 A.M., when he usually reappeared in his favorite large yellow straw hat. Afternoons, they usually preferred to take a motorboat or car ride, with easel and paints, to some quiet spot where he could indulge in his favorite pastime.

"Winston likes to eat, sleep, and enjoy the sun, and add to his large collection of paintings," says Clementine. "He says that trying to paint a picture is like trying to fight a battle. It is, if anything, more exciting than fighting it successfully; but the principle is the same. It is the same kind of problem as unfolding a long, sustained, intellectual argument."

When Winston felt the urge to paint he was usually left alone in peace and quiet. Holidays, Winston used to read and revise proofs of his latest literary work, and they also offered the opportunity for considering future strategy. Away from the detailed work of Westminster, he could paint in the political scene with those broad imaginative strokes of which he is the master.

When the Churchills take a holiday nothing is too much trouble for anyone to make it enjoyable. The French air base at Marrakech altered its routine because planes taking off at 7:30 A.M. woke up vacationing Winston. Clementine, informing the French Air Force authorities of the disturbance, said, "I do not know if you can help in any way."

"At your service, Madam," the colonel at the training base replied, and issued the order: "No planes to take off before 9 A.M. while he is here."

The Marrakech Hotel, Mamounia, also pulled out all stops—the hotel's French pastrycook produced a magnificent painting palette with a miniature easel, paintbrush, and a picture of Rabat on the easel. It was entirely made of colored sugar, including the picture on the easel, and for Clementine there were some sugar red roses, of which there were also masses of real specimens in her rooms.

When they arrived at Marrakech on holiday, a crowd of hundreds on the airfield shouted "Vive Churchill!" as their plane came out of the sky; a French Air Force guard of honor was waiting; the British Ambassador motored 200 miles from Rabat to meet them; King Mohammed of Morocco sent a planeload of V.I.P.s to greet them, and the Governor of Marrakech was on hand, too.

They drove to the hotel along the sandy, palm-tree lined road in the Governor's car flanked by uniformed Moroccan outriders. As they walked into the hotel, an American business man on holiday stepped from among the onlookers and pressed a cigar into Winston's hand.

Clementine had also packed something special for him. A case of his favorite champagne.

They had first visited Marrakech in 1936, after Lloyd George had praised its beauty. Clementine and Winston particularly loved to visit the "Square of Death" in Marrakech—an incredible African market-place with the wares spread on the ground or on little stalls. All Africa seems to make for this famous square, which is like a scene from the *Arabian Nights* with its snake charmers, magicians, conjurors, story-tellers, and fire-eaters.

"I must paint it, Clemmie," Winston said, as they walked one after-noon through the packed square. The question was how. The solution came after Clementine had conferred with a commercial-minded shop-keeper in the square, who, appreciating her offered opportunity of making a profit without selling any of his wares, temporarily closed up to let Winston use his shop as a painter's vantage point.

Another of their favorite holiday calls is Lord Beaverbrook's fifteen-room villa, at Cap-d'Ail.

Surrounded by municipal counsellors and wearing his official tricolor sash, M. Leon Gramaglia, Mayor of Cap-d'Ail, always waits for the Churchills—Winston is honorary mayor of Cap-d'Ail.

M. Gramaglia welcomes them in front of the Beaverbrook villa. Lord Beaverbrook usually contrives to be away when they come so that they may enjoy the run of the house to themselves. A small car with only a driving seat and an armchair in the back, which Lord Beaver-brook uses to go down to his private beach, is at their disposal there.

Picnicking and sightseeing together is one of their greatest delights. Clementine never forgets to pack his pet pair of brilliant red bathing trunks and the thermometer he uses to test the Mediterranean Sea's temperature before taking a dip.

As mentioned, Clementine disliked holidaying away from Winston, but at one time, when illness compelled her to take a rest without him, she went to Ceylon. It was suggested that she be away for a couple of months, but she felt three weeks would be long enough apart from him. Arriving in Colombo, she said she was "looking forward to seeing a rogue elephant"—an elephant of savage temper living apart from the herd. "But I will run and climb a tree if he tries to catch me," she laughed.

Little is heard of Clementine's own state of health. The years of in-tense strain exacted one particular kind of toll on her—painful attacks of neuritis, which often compelled her to cancel engagements for weeks.

On the whole her health has always been very good, but from time to time, when she suffers the bouts of neuritis, she prefers to be alone—to go to a nursing home, or to a spa, or suggest that Winston go away for a holiday. She prefers to suffer in silence, away from everyone else—including Winston.

Because of her neuritis she once had to decline an invitation to a Mansion House luncheon given in honor of the Queen, and her sixty-ninth birthday party had to be canceled because of it. Whenever a bout of neuritis prevented her from joining Winston on holiday, he would telephone every evening at 9:30 just to say "Good night, darling."

During one of their holidays together they, and Sarah, made up a party with the Duke and Duchess of Windsor to celebrate New Year's Eve at Monte Carlo's Sporting Club. At midnight everyone rose from the tables, linked hands, and sang "Auld Lang Syne." Suddenly the entire four hundred people present stood up, and, turning toward Clementine and Winston, sang, "For they are jolly good fellows." Winston rose to make his "V" sign while Clementine and Sarah trapped large balloons from among hundreds released, and burst them over his head.

"Taking him away for a long time during that crucial period in his life, following his 1945 election defeat, was a deliberate policy on Clementine's part," said their friend, Sir Tom O'Brien, "and it showed her political and personal judgment at its best. In her wisdom, she took him from the scene of his victory and of his defeat. Had she left him to wander all the time round the House of Commons, God knows what would have happened. Had she let him remain in Parliament during that period, his life would almost certainly have ended in tragedy because he was eating himself up with bitterness. He kept repeating over and over, 'When I was turned out of office, I thought it was a very hard thing, after all I had done.'

"Had he remained much longer in the House of Commons in the state of mind he was in, he might have destroyed his legend because his pain and feeling of ingratitude at being discarded in the election was making him lash out wildly and affecting his sense of statesmanship and diplomacy.

"There was no question that she saved his mind, saved his dignity. He certainly could not have concentrated on his historic books later had she not taken him away and helped him clear his mind and heart of the terrible bitterness that had taken possession of him. Had it not been for the enforced series of holidays she made him take from 1945 on; had he stayed in London, and rumbled through the House, he would undoubtedly have become a corroded force—the iron would have entered his soul, and he wouldn't have been the great postwar statesman he became when he was elected Prime Minister for the second time. In my view, all that is due to his wife. Her wisdom, her assessment of the situation, and her realization that her husband was growing bitterer and bitterer, made her decide and say: 'This has got to stop' —and stopped it was.

"Wherever they traveled, during their first postwar round of holidays, they received the acclaim and blessings of peoples he helped to free from tyranny. The gratitude of these people helped Clementine breathe new life, new fight, back into Winston."

"We often think it would be a good idea to take a holiday abroad and get some rest in the sun," says Clementine. "When one lays down power and responsibility all sorts of other things fall away at the same time. A holiday is very enjoyable, but there is nothing like coming home again."

22

A Man About the House

In October, 1945, the Churchills moved into their new town house, 28 Hyde Park Gate, a quiet cul-de-sac near Kensington Gardens and only about fifteen minutes by car from the Houses of Parliament. Using short cuts, the chauffeur can bring the journey down to seven minutes, which suits Winston very well, especially in the event of sudden calls to a Commons division.

Modest yet spacious, the house has the graceful high ceilings that Clementine and Winston like so much. The rooms were decorated in soft shades of peach and cream. Most of the floors are of polished oak.

Along the entrance hall to the left, and entered by a balcony and a short flight of stairs, is the dining room. Twenty guests could be accommodated comfortably around its beautiful oak table.

From the dining room, French windows open onto a walled garden where trees shade a grass plot surrounded by rockeries and ferns. Though it is fine for the dogs to play in, neither Winston nor Clementine has ever devoted much time to the little garden; it is too cramped for their liking.

Clementine divided the house into eight bedrooms and three reception rooms, including the dining room.

As in every Churchill house there is a large library, and quarters for the secretaries. The main difference between Hyde Park Gate and her other homes is that Clementine has introduced a note of modernity, and there is fitted furniture in many of the rooms.

She transformed an awkward little room in the house into a delightful, intimate room, furnishing it with a long table with fitted seats behind it.

Clementine was having tea with a visitor in this room one afternoon when in burst a jacketless Winston in his shirt-sleeves calling—"Clemmie! Clemmie! Where are you?"

As he came in, Clementine sprang up to introduce Winston, slightly surprised at finding himself semi-dressed among company. "This is my husband," Clementine announced simply, as if anyone could mistake him. Winston gave a courteous little bow, got what he had come for—confirmation of the time of their evening appointment—and departed after another polite little bow.

You can always tell when the Churchills are in residence, for as the front door opens the scent of incense reaches you. Clementine lights the incense burner on the stairs as soon as they come home to Hyde Park Gate. It is a gentle, pleasant fragrance, which seems to offend nobody and which Winston loves, perhaps because it is an unusual perfume for a London house. He loves the unusual. He is a contradiction in himself: a champion of traditions, yet a lover of the unconventional, and not least in the matter of personal attire.

Clementine, meticulous about her own appearance, tried persistently to improve Winston's sartorial standards. She fussed around him, and he reveled in her attentions, but in the end he contrived to get his own way in his style of dress—as in so many other things. Within their own home, she made no protest about his often outrageous attire and the flamboyant dressing gowns for which he has a predilection, but she strove her utmost to make him dress for public appearances in a manner more becoming a great statesman. Frequently she succeeded in modifying his dress, and he, in turn, delighted in modifying her modifications. The result was usually eye-compelling, irresistible.

Clementine could not resist accompanying him to the House of Commons on one of his "better dressed" days to see for herself how the results were received. It was a warm July day. Together they walked into the St. Stephen's entrance of the House, and Clementine took her seat in the gallery to watch his entry into the Chamber.

Winston was a cool symphony in black and white. He wore no vest, and below his bow tie an expanse of white shirt gleamed against the background of a well-cut black jacket. His silver-gray trousers, wide in cut, impeccably creased, were a work of art.

But not for long did he remain cool. Astonished, delighted Members gave him a tremendous welcome. There was a roar of cheers for his sartorial achievement. Winston blushed—and tripped over the walking stick of a near neighbor on the front bench. That minor mishap suddenly revealed, for all to see, Mr. Churchill's *chef-d'œuvre*—black shoes with silver zip fasteners instead of laces. The cheering swelled to even greater volume. Winston now looking very warm, sat down. Then, with a broad grin across his cherubic face, he looked up at Clemmie in the gallery. Her smile was even wider than his.

Often the compromise which Clementine reached with her husband in her efforts to inject sanity into his clothes produced startling results.

One day in 1922, when he was leader of the Coalition Liberals in the House of Commons, Winston succumbed to her persuasion and, for the first time, turned up at Westminster wearing a silk hat. Mr. Austen Chamberlain, then Leader of the House, was the only other Member on the Treasury bench who wore a topper.

At the last moment, Winston decided to dodge his new-found splendor and walked hatless into the Chamber to answer questions; but looking up to the gallery and catching Clementine's cold frown he surrendered, left the Chamber, and returned a moment later to place the new silk hat boldly and jauntily upon the back of his head.

It is an infringement of order for a Member to wear a hat while speaking or moving to or from his place. Sitting, he may please himself, though few Members elect to cover their heads. Mr. Chamberlain arrived a minute or two later, and confronted by a silk-hatted Churchill, could not hide his laughing admiration of his rather self-conscious colleague.

Some months later, society was presented with an even more astonishing spectacle, Winston, as "the noblest Roman of them all," dressed in a red-and-gold toga, sandals, head crowned with laurel wreath, and accompanied by Clementine as the Empress.

They dined in their Roman splendor at the house of the Duchess of Roxburghe before going on to a Leap-Year's Eve ball given by the Duchess of Marlborough in Carlton House Terrace.

The laurel wreath was symptomatic. Hardly a month went by without Winston finding some new sort of covering for his head. A hat was not a hat to him. It was a discovery, a challenge, a fresh expression of his personality.

At the historic battle of Sydney Street, press photographs reveal, detectives and bystanders wore bowlers and caps. Winston alone considered a shiny silk hat *de rigeur* for anarchist-hunting. When he took Stanley Baldwin for a ride in his new car, both men wore trilbys—but Winston wore his back to front. During a general election, when silk hats and smart bowlers were the rule for vote-seeking candidates, Winston, canvassing at Woodford, elected to wear a gray half-topper, a stunted creation, which appeared to be cut off halfway up the crown.

After spring-cleaning Winston's wardrobe, Clementine once listed the following collection: three species of top hat, five kinds of trilby hat, one Sherlock Holmes deerstalker, one cap, one cap with a peak, one "Muller" (a square-topped hat, which derived its name from Franz Muller, a German who in 1880 murdered a bank cashier in a train, threw the body into a tunnel near Bethnal Green, and was captured because his hat, with his name on the lining, fell on to the rails). Clementine's list also included one naval cocked hat, two kinds of bowler, one cocked hat for Court dress, one Irishman's "Paddy" hat (with clay), one "Paddy" hat (without clay), one mortarboard, one St. Andrew's cap, one army pillbox, one Hussars' busby, two kinds of Panama, one artist's beret, one military forage cap, one steel helmet, one railway engine driver's cap, a rakish Mexican sombrero, and a green creation turned up all round, with a jaunty pocket effect on the left, which women might class as a kind of toque of rather uncertain origin.

Clementine's revelation moved that arbiter of British men's fashion *The Tailor and Cutter* to comment upon Winston in the following terms:

"Sartorially he has been a chameleon and suspect among his countrymen. A statesman should be known by one or two features, not for variety. Monocle and orchid were priceless assets to Joseph Chamberlain. Everyone thought of Gladstone in terms of collars. Stanley Baldwin's homely pipe took the popular fancy, suggesting gaiters, muddy boots, and pigs. Anthony Eden's adoption of the Foreign Office hat secured him the Foreign Office. Lloyd George's purple smoking jacket and patriarchal cloak created a diverse character. Neville Chamberlain's umbrella was notorious.

"Let us glance at Winston's wardrobe. What protean changes its hats represent, embracing official and naval cocked hats, army pillbox, Hussar's busby, service cap, steel helmet, sombrero, Oxford degree hat, artist's beret and paper hat worn at a children's party!

"Mr. Churchill was faithful for a time to an astrakhan-trimmed overcoat—the only man to wear one to a hunt with velvet hat and pink coat. And painting from Nature he has worn white overall and broad-brimmed straw headgear, cigar between teeth. During a spot of bricklaying he put on an old suit, soft felt hat, and gloves. Never an elegant dresser, he loved variety because it suited his temperament. A man who plays many parts needs many costumes."

Clementine was highly amused by this commentary on her husband's wardrobe and bought a copy of the journal to give to him.

Long ago, however, Winston himself had revealed the secret of why he became a noted collector of hats, why they interest him just as other men are interested in a collection of sticks or pipes, why he possesses practically every known type of twentieth-century headgear in his wardrobe, and why all have been worn at one time or another.

He said, "One of the most necessary features of the equipment of a public man is some distinctive mark which everyone learns to look for and to recognize. Disraeli's forelock, Mr. Gladstone's collars, Lord Randolph Churchill's moustache, Mr. Chamberlain's eyeglass, Mr. Baldwin's pipes—these 'properties' are of the greatest value.

"I have never indulged in any of them, so, to fill the need, cartoonists have invented the legend of my hats. This arose in the following way.

"I was at Southport during the General Election of 1910. I went for a walk with my wife along the sands. A very tiny felt hat—I do not know where it came from—had been packed with my luggage. It lay on the hall table, and without thinking I put it on. As we came back from our walk, there was the photographer! And he took this picture.

"Ever since the cartoonists and paragraphists have dwelt on my hats; how many there are; how strange and queer; and how I am always changing them, and what importance I attach to them, and so on. It is all rubbish, and it is all founded upon this photograph. Well, if it is a help to these worthy gentlemen in their hard work, why should I complain? Indeed, I think I will convert the legend into a reality by buying myself a new hat on purpose!"

Winston said that in 1931, and he has been buying and collecting new hats, like the famous astrakhan cap he acquired in 1945 at the Crimean Conference, ever since. On one of his trips to America, in the *Berengaria,* his hats inspired a sweepstake. Passengers bet on what he would wear, but none guessed right. He entered the saloon with a red fez perched rakishly on his head, and the sweep money was returned.

Clementine is constantly trying to control her husband's rebellion against formal clothing, but there are times when she sees eye to eye with him. She approved his taste for siren suits during the war and continued to buy them for him. Once she went personally to a famous outfitter's shop in London's Regent Street to purchase several more, all in quiet, tasteful shades.

A few days later Winston sent for the outfitter's man, asking him to bring along a new range of siren-suit patterns.

Without consulting Clementine, he plumped for a dashing saxe blue, made to measure, with four outsize pockets. Vivid, violent, it was just the job for a hard-working artist. It cost eighteen guineas.

The Tailor and Cutter brought its commentary on the Churchill splendor up to date. It said:

"He takes his hats as he has taken the world, and punches them, and dents them, and crams them unyieldingly into position.

"He overcomes a new style for almost every occasion; but like a bronco-busting cowboy, he retains his respect for hats after he has knocked the guts out of them. It is not altogether surprising that Sir Winston Churchill does not look quite at home in an Anthony Eden. The sight of Sir Anthony in a homburg engenders a desire to throw a small wooden ball and try to knock it off. The sight of Sir Winston does not so much engender a rising feeling that you'd like to knock his hat off as an uneasy anxiety that you'd better hang on to your own.

"Sir Winston in a homburg seldom manages to look better than an impish jelly baby that is something in the city."

Clementine added that commentary, too, to her private collection of personal cuttings on her husband.

He prefers the easy comfort of old clothes. Ex-Inspector Thompson relates, "When I first went to him in 1921, he had that mountain of a coat with the astrakhan collar. It was very heavy indeed. Years later, as I was helping him on with it one morning, he said to me, 'You know, Thompson, this is a good old coat. You know, it's really new. It's had a new inside, a new outside, a new astrakhan collar, and it's still a good coat.'"

That Winston often looks comparatively well dressed is due to the efforts of his wife and the watchful eye of his valet. His wardrobe contains few suits, and when he has finally been convinced that he must have new ones it is Clementine who orders them from an old-established firm of tailors in Savile Row, personally choosing the cloth and the quality. It may be true that "there is no substitute for wool"; but Winston has always preferred silk underwear of unchanging style, and Clementine orders twelve sets at a time.

Winston never enters shops. Clementine has said, "He doesn't need any money. He never does any shopping, and somebody else always buys his railway tickets for him."

He is no lover of personal jewelry, and prefers plain cuff links and studs. His gold watch and chain, and the gold signet ring bearing the Marlborough crest, which he wears on the third finger of his right hand, were gifts from his father. The stick which he usually carries is a long, plain cane with an unadorned gold knob. He once had another, of great sentimental value. How he came to part with it is in itself a story.

Both Winston and Clementine cling so fiercely to their personal possessions that they might almost be termed hoarders. They hate to part with any article which has sentimental associations, but when the appeal is to their hearts, they weaken.

One of Winston's greatest loves was a beautiful gold-headed malacca cane. A gift from King Edward VII, it bore on its gold head the inscription: *W.S.C., Turf Club.* He took it with him wherever he traveled.

Then, some years before the last war, he suddenly discovered that he had lost it. The cane he was carrying—identical in every respect except for the inscription—was not his own. He realized at once what had happened. He had picked up the wrong stick when leaving some function or other. But when? And where? It could have been at any of a hundred places on any of as many days.

Clementine organized the search in her efficient fashion. She went methodically through Winston's engagement book, making inquiries at every house, club, and business office that he had visited. Nobody could throw any light on the mystery; and Winston, who hated even to lose worn-out clothes, was in deepest misery.

As a last resort, Clementine inserted an advertisement in the personal column of *The Times.* "LOST, probably on Friday, March 28," it ran, "a gold-headed malacca cane, marked 'W.S.C., Turf Club.' Mr. Churchill has taken by mistake an almost identical cane, but since this has neither the name nor the address upon it he is unable to return it—2 Sussex Square, W.2."

It worked. Just before noon on the day the advertisement appeared, Clementine received a telephone message from the Marlborough Club. It reported that the stick was "safe and well" and in good hands, but—in Germany!

It was now clear what had happened. Winston had been entertained to luncheon at the Marlborough Club by his supporters in his fight for the Abbey division of Westminster. Leaving hurriedly to keep another appointment, he had picked up the stick which so markedly resembled his own, while its owner, coming down later, had taken the other and left immediately for Germany. Now, thanks to his wife's detective work, Winston was happy again.

Years went by. One day they visited the Limbless Ex-Servicemen's Center at Wellhampton. Winston, carrying his beloved cane, stopped to talk to an ex-soldier from Norfolk, who had lost a leg in the First World War and was having an artificial limb fitted.

"You have a special limb and can walk without a stick?" Winston inquired.

"Yes," said the disabled man, "but I should like that stick of yours."

Winston looked at Clementine, then turned to the old soldier and said, "Here are my hand, my heart—and my stick. Look after it. It has been all over the world with me."

There is one department in which he himself has to admit that scope for nonconformity is lacking. Asked by a barber what style of haircut he would like, he smoothed the wisps on his pate and said, "A man of my limited resources cannot presume to have a hair style. Get on and cut it."

Unlike her husband, Clementine is intensely interested in fashion and spends a great deal of time and money in keeping her wardrobe up to date. Mrs. Thompson, the wife of Winston's former bodyguard, who, as Miss Shearburn, was one of the Prime Minister's secretaries, said, "Her dress sense was very, very good. She spent little time in shops; things were sent to her at Chequers or Chartwell or wherever she was staying. Once, during the summer before the war, she wanted a new nightdress. She wrote to the Irish linen place in Regent Street, and they sent six nightdresses for her to choose from. She liked them so much that she bought all six.

"While we were living at Admiralty House, she saw a snow leopard coat somewhere, and decided she would like one. She had two sent from different firms, and finally chose the one she preferred. It was perfectly wonderful, and she was like a child about it, but she said, 'Don't say anything to Winston. I don't want him to know about it yet. He doesn't know it, but it's going to be his Easter egg to me.'

"And someone sent her a huge square of silk. She was delighted. She called me in, and said, 'Look at this. Isn't it lovely? But it's much too big for a scarf. What can I do with it?' We talked about it for half an hour. She was going to turn it into a sun-top, and this, that and the other; but I don't remember that we came to any firm decision.

"At times she would ignore the fact that you were a member of her husband's staff and treat you as an equal. She would say, 'I want a cup of tea. Come in and have one with me.' Then she would give you a cigarette and talk about clothes."

Clementine has lovely feet and she is correspondingly particular about her shoes. They must be beautiful, and of the finest quality. At

Chartwell, dozens of pairs stand in long racks in the corridor outside her bedroom.

Like Winston, she does not care for jewelry and is seldom seen wearing anything more elaborate than a string of pearls and, occasionally, a diamanté brooch.

Her clothes are simple and elegant, and most are designed on flowing classical lines. For casual wear at Chartwell in the summer, she favors slacks and shirt of matching blue or tangerine lined. For visiting, or garden parties, she prefers tailored linen dresses to more elaborate attire. On warm evenings, she may put on one of a number of flowered chiffon dresses, rather full-skirted, with draped bodice, low neckline, and generally sleeveless. For dining in the winter, she usually wears black and invariably carries a large chiffon or silk square in a pastel shade of green, pink, or blue.

It is a peculiarity of her shopping that she usually has to buy her own birthday and Christmas presents (officially designated as "from Winston"). Obsessed with his thoughts on matters of world import, or engrossed in writing a book, he is likely to forget such matters as his wife's birthday gift. It is a strange lapse, since he is so devoted to her that one intimate friend commented, "He treats her like a piece of porcelain. She was, and is, the only woman in his life."

Before meeting Clementine, Winston had shown little interest in women. He had been too busy trying to make himself financially independent and to establish his position in the world. Though he worshiped his mother, the knowledge that it was her money which was supporting him during his Army career never ceased to irk him, and his main objective was to put an end to that situation. Only when he had achieved his aim could he bring himself to think seriously of courtship and marriage. So it is true that the beautiful Clementine was the first and only woman in his life; and she it was who helped him to attain his ambitions.

Intolerant of criticism and opposition from others, he will accept both from her, because she alone knows how to handle him in the right manner. One evening she was with Winston at a reception for about forty people. The gathering included M.P.s and trade union leaders. Winston was discoursing in a light vein on a political topic of the day when Clementine intervened, "Do make it clearer, do make it clearer for your audience," she said. "Let me say it for you." And she did just that, explaining very simply things that Winston, with his relish for phrases, had been, perhaps, wrapping up a little too much.

He shrugged shoulders, spread out his hands helplessly and good-humoredly, and said, "What can I do?"

His audience—and Clementine—roared with laughter. But, in fact, she *did* make the topic clearer to everyone. However, when she stepped into a conversation, she always did it in a way that couldn't possibly embarrass him.

Both Winston and Clementine can fly into sudden anger, but the loss of temper never lasts long; nor do they bear ill will against those who have offended them. No one has ever heard them arguing or quarreling seriously with each other. Occasionally a good-humored outburst has been provoked by Clementine's love of expensive clothes, for though Winston delights in seeing her dressed to perfection, the bills have, at times, given him, like so many husbands, some shocks. "Do you realize how many articles *that* is going to cost me?" he would say with gentle reproof on hearing how much she had spent on a new dress. Clementine, an expert on economies in other directions, would promise to go easier with clothes expenditure in the future, but it was a promise she rarely found the will power to keep.

On one prewar occasion, Winston advanced six pounds for the purchase of a new dress for their daughter Diana, warning that on no account must it cost more. That evening Diana appeared in a dress that had plainly cost much more than the stipulated amount, and waited in some trepidation for the inevitable explosion. Winston made her parade up and down the room, studying her from every angle, and even feeling the quality of the fabric in the new dress. He then pronounced judgment. "I heartily approve," he declared, and there was an audible sigh of relief from mother and daughter.

Winston's kindness is not confined to the women of his family. Mrs. Thompson, who, as his secretary, encountered him in his most difficult moods, testified, "He is a charming man; charming in the way of saying the right thing which makes you respond. One evening down at Chartwell we had been working very late. Goodness! I was tired, and so was he. He said 'Good night' to me as I was leaving, and then he suddenly called, 'Are you tired, Miss Shearburn?'

"I said, 'No,' because of course I could not admit it. There was a little silence; then, not looking at me any more, he shook his head. 'No,' he said. 'You wouldn't be. You are a soldier's daughter.'

"Nothing would have made me admit I was tired. I would have gone on until I dropped. He always said the right thing, and she has a superb way with people too. A friend of the family once described her as a grand and sweet woman who hitched her wagon to a hurricane and has been more often in the driver's seat of this particular hurricane than is supposed. And the friend added that even with a hurricane, her hands are gentle and her sense of direction admirable."

Winston and Clementine have a husband-and-wife understanding. Although they share many interests, others they pursue absolutely alone. She agrees with him that the cultivation of a hobby and of new forms of interest is a policy of first importance to a public man, and she would never selfishly deny him outlets that are so essential to his well-being. Their mutual code for living is, "It is no use doing what you like. You have got to like what you do."

Winston says, "Broadly speaking, human beings may be divided into three classes: Those who are billed to death, those who are worried to death, and those who are bored to death."

Says Clementine, "A man can wear out a particular part of his mind by continually using it and tiring it, just as in the same way he can wear out the elbows of his coat. There is, however, this difference between the living cells of the brain and inanimate articles: one cannot mend the frayed elbows of a coat by rubbing the sleeve or shoulders; but the tired parts of the mind can be rested and strengthened not merely by rest but by using other parts."

She never interrupts or interferes with Winston's hobbies. She recognizes that when he works he is wholly absorbed in what he is doing and hates interruption, whether he is busy with a spade in the garden, a paintbrush in his studio, or a pen in his library. He is a dynamic worker, who, at times, can be so lazy that he will ring the bell for someone to hand him cigars, which are lying just out of his reach.

Clementine and Winston love reading. Although Winston can spare little time for this form of relaxation, he enjoys the Hornblower novels of C. S. Forester. Clementine prefers the classics.

Both can become almost fanatically keen on a pursuit. Clementine maintains that those whose work is their pleasure are those who most need the means of banishing it at intervals from their minds. She has always preferred active sports, whereas Winston never took kindly to athletic exercise. Clementine tried to interest him in golf. He replied that he was a great admirer of the game. He admired it so much that he liked to stand far away to see its finer points and niceties. He admired its influence on the health, character, and temper of those who took part in the game.

He had no doubt, he continued, that men who would face the game of golf were men upon whom the nation could confidently rely. Golf was the sport of kings—and of politicians. It was such a great stimulus to eloquence that some of his finest perorations had been achieved while he had been negotiating with his niblick a recalcitrant ball in a venomous bunker.

But, he concluded, he had never found anything like painting to take one's mind, for a spell, off grave matters. "Golf is no use to me for this purpose," he said. "I find myself thinking of serious business after a time."

Often she will take a picnic tea out to him and stay to talk about the progress of the current masterpiece. She has said, "He is difficult sometimes. Just when I have got his luncheon ready, he suddenly gets a huge plan of putting the world to rights and wanders into the garden to work it out."

She frequently arranges visits to friends for "painting weekends." One Sunday at Lady Paget's house at Kingston Hill, Winston and his friend, Sir John Lavery, were painting together, watched by Clementine, when a hearty voice behind them called, "Hallo! Winston, when did you begin this game?"

Without turning, he replied, "The day you kicked me out of the Admiralty, Lord Charles."

The intruder, Lord Charles Beresford, retorted, "Well, who knows? Perhaps I may have saved a great master."

Clementine loved to arrange special surprises, which she knew would particularly please him. That is how the little, unassuming Swiss paintmaker, Willy Sax, came to Chartwelll.

Winston and Clementine had met him during a visit to Zürich in 1946. Winston had bought from him some special reds and blues, and ever since had been having paints made for him in the small factory founded by the Sax family almost ninety years ago.

Sax, accompanied by two of Switzerland's best-known painters, arrived at Chartwell for lunch at Clementine's secret invitation. The visit gave great happiness to everybody, and to Winston most of all. Willy is one of the few people in the world who owns a Churchill painting. It was a gift to him from his most distinguished customer. An oil painting, depicting a humpback bridge spanning a placid stream in the south of France, it hangs over the piano in the music room of his old-fashioned suburban house.

Winston is so busy turning out paintings by the hundreds that he seldom finds time to title his works. He leaves that to Clementine. The picture she called "The Messenger" (it depicts a man walking through a snow-covered village) became a best-selling Christmas card. Winston paints Clementine's personal Christmas card every year. He leaves the choice of the picture to her, but insists that the message should be simple and sincere, and printed in clear, plain type. In the following year he disposes of the reproduction rights to a firm which manufactures cards for world distribution. More than 20,000 copies of "The Olive Trees"—Clementine's favorite of all her husband's pictures—have been sold. The original hangs in one of the living rooms at Chartwell.

It has been estimated that Winston's collection of his own paintings would be worth something in the region of two and a half million pounds, but he had no intention of selling. His painting output has been fantastic, but he hates parting with his work.

Sir Charles Wheeler, President of the Royal Academy, says that when he was arranging the Churchill Exhibition, he suggested, "Altogether, you must have painted about four hundred pictures."

"More like five hundred," Winston replied.

All collectors would love to own a Churchill painting. El Glaoui, Pasha of Marrakech, one of Winston's and Clementine's oldest friends, told them that he would "pay anything" to get one. In North Africa, it is said, one genuine Churchill painting is valued at six wives.

"When I get to Heaven," Winston said many years ago, "I mean to spend a considerable portion of my first million years in painting, and so get to the bottom of the subject." Meanwhile he is content to work on in his studio at Chartwell, with his unframed pictures of Chartwell, Marrakech, Cairo, Venice, and the Côte d'Azur stacked all around him. And dominating the south wall of the studio is a portrait of the woman who first handed him a paintbox—Clementine, gay-hatted and smiling, painted in a haze of blue.

A cable from Chartwell usually means that top priority action is required for something of the utmost importance. Such a cable was received one day in San Giovanni in Italy. There was no doubt of its urgency. It concerned goldfish. A few hours later, twenty-five *pesci rossi,* the world's most exotic goldfish, were on their way in special heated tanks to Chartwell.

The fish at the Churchill country home had been dying mysteriously, and Clementine, remembering the fish breeders of San Giovanni, who had sent Winston a gift of four rare varieties as "a token of respect and admiration," was sure they would come to the rescue. They did; and, what is more, continued to send by air mail every week small cellophane packets of dried fleas to feed the *pesci rossi*.

Winston loves his fish. Whenever he and Clementine are in residence at Chartwell he never misses his daily visit to the pool to feed them and to squat down and tickle their underbellies. In his study, Winston has four glass tanks containing about 120 tropical fish, including black mollies, zebras, and Siamese fighting fish. "I find contemplation of the fish one of the greatest forms of relaxation I have ever known," he says.

Two of the most important residents of Chartwell are Rufus, the poodle, and Mickey, the cat. Whenever Winston and Clementine go away and Rufus has to be left behind, Clementine gives one of the maids instructions on grooming, exercising, and feeding him. She knows how much Winston would worry if he were not properly cared for. Rufus is, in fact, the second of his name. The original Rufus was run down by a car in Kensington High Street, while out for a walk with one of the maids. The girl ran home, crying, to Clementine, who had to break the news to Winston.

There was only one thing to do, and she wasted no time about it. She bought another poodle, choosing a dog exactly like the one they had lost. Once again Clementine filled a gap in her husband's life.

Clementine's astuteness in the matter of raising funds for charity led to the opening of the Chartwell grounds to the public. On "open days" lines of coaches stretch for one and a half miles, cars are parked for another two miles, and five thousand people at a time turn the Churchills' country home into a replica of Hampstead Heath on a Bank Holiday.

She does not merely throw open the gates of her home for the benefit of charities, she personally acts as hostess to the crowds, appreciating that it is the magic of the Churchill name that attracts the visitors; that for the thousands who come, it is a form of pilgrimage. She chats to as many as possible, pointing out favorite spots and telling everybody to be sure to see her pet black swans with their cygnets. One visitor asked her if Winston would be coming.

"Not today, I'm afraid," she said gently. "He has one or two things on his mind."

Someone else asked how Winston gets about the steep terraces to the lake and his black swans. "He strolls downhill to feed the swans and goldfish, and the car picks him up at the bottom," Clementine replied. On every open day the crowds are amused by the notice in red-penciled letters which is tied to Winston's basket chair near the diving board at the swimming pool It says, simply and effectively: "No diving (not deep enough)—W.S.C."

So far as Clementine was concerned, his worst domestic habit used to be "climbing into the syimming pool at Chartwell, then suddenly remembering something important, getting out, paddling into the house without stopping to dry, and leaving large footprints on my polished floors."

Gifts from people all over the world pour into Chartwell and Hyde Park Gate in an almost continuous flow: champagne and turkeys from France, oysters from Australia, cigars from America and Cuba. Clementine personally sorts the packages and sends a gracious letter of thanks to each sender.

Winston, who likes his cigars long and strong, offered one to Prince George of Denmark after dinner at Hyde Park Gate, and the prince declined. "You don't know what you are missing," said Winston. Prince George allowed himself to be persuaded. He took a cigar, lit it—and within minutes was ill.

When the Churchills visited Balmoral, crowds waiting at Ballater Station to watch the Queen greet her guests, saw Winston light a cigar as he stepped from the train. He had taken only a few puffs when the Queen appeared on the platform. As he walked to meet her, the cigar vanished as if by magic; and as the royal greetings were made, the Queen was heard to ask, "Where is your cigar, Sir Winston?"

Beaming, he replied, "I've parked it, your Majesty."

Later, the stationmaster, Mr. Milne, found the "disappearing Havana" among the plants in one of the ornamental flower beds.

Clementine occasionally smokes a Turkish cigarette while she is having an afternoon cup of tea. Winston doesn't like cigarettes, although he has been known to accept one at a party.

Not until publication of his war books had increased his fortune were Winston and Clementine able to gratify their ambition to own a string of racehorses. It was Mary's husband, Christopher Soames, who suggested they should become racehorse owners. They were delighted with the idea. At a house party in Warwick Castle, Winston had been discussing racing with the Aga Khan when Clementine remarked that he knew far more about racehorses than anybody realized. Winston promptly confirmed her claim by reciting, almost in one breath, the names of the past fifty Derby winners and their sires and dams. It was an extraordinary feat of memory.

The Churchill-Soames team had already walked away with honors as dairy farmers by winning first place in the national milk record competitions with the Chartwell herd of Jersey cows. Now, backed additionally by the expert judgment of Walter Nightingall, the Epsom trainer, they began to buy horses, beginning with a colt which was to become famous as Columnist II. Carrying the chocolate and pink, which had been the racing colors of Winston's father and grandfather, Columnist II, who cost only some £1,500, won thirteen of the twenty-four races in which he was entered and earned more than £22,000 in prize money.

When circumstances prevented Winston and Clementine from seeing their horses run, they never failed to telephone Walter Nightingall to ask what the chances were for the race.

A West Essex Conservative party fête clashed with the appearance at Ascot of the Churchill horse le Prétendant. The race was due to begin at 3:40 P.M., and Winston and Clementine arrived at the fête at 3:35. The Ascot meeting was being televised, so Clementine told the fête organizers, "I think that if no one would mind, we should like to watch the TV first and postpone the speeches until immediately after the race." Into the TV room they went, and as their horse romped home the winner, Winston was bobbing up and down with excitement in an armchair, while his wife—hands clenched in front of her as though gripping reins—appeared to be riding le Prétendant past the post.

The only disadvantage they find in their racing is that any Churchill horse, irrespective of form, is usually backed down to odds-on favorite by the heavy betting of thousands of loyal supporters, who wager from sentiment and superstition alone; but they both love the sport, and often visit the lonely, empty Epsom Downs to watch their horses in trial gallops.

As they were leaving a racetrack after a meeting at which Winston's luck had been in, a young boy pushed his way forward through the crowd. "Oh! Sir Winston," he said, "weren't you thrilled to have a ticket on the winner?"

Clementine smiled as Winston replied in a serious, deliberate tone, "Well, young man, I *have* had bigger moments in my life."

23

The Children

THE redheaded girl bent over the passport application form and began to fill in the questionnaire.

Surname: Churchill.

Christian names: Sarah, Millicent, Hermione.

Father's occupation: Painter.

That is what she wrote, with a smile, and of course it is true—he is a painter—as well. But, behind Sarah's written jest, lies something deeper.

Clementine's children have grown up and lived in the glow of their father's glory. They have also been handicapped by it. They are all rightly proud to be his children, but also recognize how fortunate they are to be Clementine's children.

Their father is devoted to them and always snatched every possible moment he could to share with them, but those moments were few. It was Clementine who kept the family a family. She bore the brunt of troubles caused by a family that inherited its father's independence of character.

They had four daughters and one son. Diana, in 1909, Randolph in 1911, Sarah in 1914, Marigold in 1918, and Mary in 1919.

For years their mother tried to shield them even from the knowledge that their father was a famous public figure. In the same way as she has always tried to keep a sense of normality about her home life, she was anxious to protect her children for as long as possible from the dangers of living in the public eye.

When the Germans started bombing London in the First World

War, she evacuated Diana, Randolph, and Sarah to an old Kentish farmhouse run by a cousin of Winston's. Eight other little Churchills from other branches of the family joined them. Diana and Randolph were almost inseparable, fighting constant battles in the fields. Sarah preferred to climb walls and treees alone, and her adventurousness was rewarded by a crop of scars, many of which she still bears.

Clementine managed to keep the children out of the glare of limelight until Winston, in 1924, was appointed Chancellor of the Exchequer and the family moved to Downing Street, next door to the Prime Minister. She still played down their father's importance, so much so that Sarah and Mary used to be quite overwhelmed when the Prime Minister, Mr. Stanley Baldwin, used to pat their heads.

"When we moved to Downing Street my mother impressed on us that father's importance was not so great as that of the man next door—the Prime Minister, Mr. Baldwin," says Sarah.

The children's first "blooding" in politics had occurred a few years earlier when, on his way to speak for a friend who was fighting a Liverpool by-election, Winston drove with his family in an open car through the city's streets. Supporters of the Opposition party gave the Churchill children a taste of politics. They surrounded the car, shook fists at them, booed them, even threw things at them, and a brick narrowly missed Diana. Clementine calmed them as the car slowly drove on, explaining, "In your father's business such things sometimes happen."

"Election campaigning was tremendously fascinating," recalls Sarah. "Diana and I, dressed alike, would accompany Father and Mother on tours, forming a kind of family platform. We were involved in many free fights. Liverpool was particularly tough, but we became quite used to being booed and hissed and even pelted with bricks that sometimes landed in the car. It was a marvelous training for the stage. Neither boos nor bricks could disturb me now.

"As a little girl, I particularly remember one of my father's friends, who was awfully good at games." [The friend was Mr. Lloyd George.] "We all loved Lloyd George," said Sarah. "He is the earliest friend I can remember, outside the immediate family circle.

"Politics were in the very air we breathed as children," Sarah recalls.

But the most important of Clementine's children was Winston, so she had to have the help of nannies to bring up the others. Miss White, "Moppet," as she was known, was the best of these. Miss White was Clementine's cousin. When she was with the family, Clementine was able to devote as much time and attention as was necessary to Winston.

As the only son, Randolph more than any of them felt the effects of the shadow of his father's image. Clementine strove to give Randolph some of the stability and roots she had given Winston. Winston himself had struggled for years to overcome the handicap of being the son of a famous father, and Clementine well realized how much help Randolph would need to fight the same fight.

Even Randolph's schooling was affected by his father's shadow, for, although they had wanted the boy to attend Harrow School, he finally went to Eton for a rather unusual reason. When Winston went to Harrow to put his son's name down for the school, on stepping out of his cab, he found himself being hissed at by some of the boys—perhaps as a result of some of his unpopular political views. He immediately got in the cab again and drove straight to Eton.

Randolph was only eighteen when he stepped into the political arena. Clementine and Winston went to a little village meeting in Essex to hear their son give his first political speech and help his father in an election battle. She had listened to Randolph rehearse the speech at home, had given him advice on intonation, expression, and on platform speaking in general. Now the moment of trial had come. Dressed in a new suit, his thick mop of hair smartly combed to one side, young Randolph stepped forward to address the meeting after a smile of confident encouragement from his mother—the same smile that Winston has always sought before making so many of his speeches.

In a firm, clear voice Randolph said his piece. It finished to a roar of applause. The obviously proud father moved to his feet and said, "I have not had the pleasure of hearing him before, and from what I have heard I think I can say that after having fought and contested elections now for thirty years—this being my fourteenth—I can see at no great distance a moment when I shall be able to sit at home in comfortable retirement and feel that the torch which falls from my exhausted hands will be carried boldly forward by another. But that is not going to happen immediately. At any rate, not until after this election has been fought."

There were now two politicians in the Churchill family. Clementine left the hall that night with her own two favorite politicians at either side of her.

Three years later came another great night in their family life— Randolph's twenty-first birthday party. Clementine decided to organize a very special kind of party. There would be a dinner at the fashionable Claridge's Hotel, she would receive all the guests, then disappear and leave the celebration to the men. She chose the guest list. It finally totaled more than seventy—all men—many of them, like their host, distinguished fathers accompanying promising sons. Clementine, the only woman present, welcomed her guests to the great Claridge's dining room. Radiantly, she greeted famous fathers and sons.

Viscount Hailsham and his son Mr. Quintin Hogg arrived. Lord Beaverbrook and his son the Hon. Max Aitken; Viscount Rothermere with the Hon. Esmond Harmsworth; Lord Camrose with the Hon. Seymour Berry. From the peerage, politics, and the Services, they came —the Marquis of Reading, the Marquis of Salisbury, Admiral of the Fleet Lord Beatty, Sir Archibald Sinclair, Admiral of the Fleet Sir Roger Keyes. Mr. Bryan Guinness, Sir John Laybury, Mr. Robert Boothby, Major G. Lloyd George, were announced. The night of June 16, 1932, was to be a night that neither Randolph, Winston, nor Clementine would ever forget.

She assembled her guests round the oval dinner table. To the right of Winston, who sat at the center, she placed the Marquis of Salisbury, opposite him, the Duke of Marlborough. Randolph she sat beside Lord Reading. Then, as soon as she was satisfied that all her guests were comfortably and correctly seated, she diplomatically slipped away.

The young Lord Birkenhead stood up, and, leaning forward with the studied nonchalance of his famous father, proposed the health of Randolph. He showed that he was already a master of humorous invective. In cultivated tones and language, he sketched Randolph Churchill's (according to him) rather graceless career at school and indifference to discipline at Oxford. Thereafter, he depicted his rise to fame as a public figure. Amid loud laughter, Lord Birkenhead described his inability to force a way into Winston's office owing to the crowd of retainers and a number of income-tax collectors, who came to take toll of the youngest payer of super tax in the kingdom.

Then Randolph himself got up, and, with grace and modesty, captured everyone. He chided Lord Birkenhead for harping upon youthful indiscretions, and bade him remember how lucky it was for his career that a veil of oblivion was allowed to fall over it. But his final remark brought down the house, when he said he hoped the younger generation would copy their elders and produce sons as competent as the proposer of the toast and himself.

Sir Austen Chamberlain rose next to propose the health of the Younger Generation, and recall the party at which he, his father, and young Winston had been present. He was ten years older than Winston and had come prepared to dislike a political upstart. His father, the famous Joe Chamberlain, on returning from the party, had however, assured him that he wished that some of the elder statesmen there had been half as stimulating as Randolph's son.

It was the turn of the young men to reply in the persons of Mr. Quintin Hogg, Mr. Seymour Berry, and the Duke of Marlborough.

Then came Winston's moment. He spoke of how the generation of fathers to which he belonged had witnessed the extension of an enormous empire, and had made it secure during the war. He could not believe that the younger generation was not equal to the task of consolidation or would prove faithless in patriotic purpose.

Lord Hugh Cecil followed to describe with gusto the idealism of the early Winston, admitting that anyone who came to know Winston succumbed to one common emotion—love and affection.

Lord Beaverbrook, Lord Hailsham, and Mr. Esmond Harmsworth added their words of wisdom and advice to young Randolph, and it was long past midnight when the celebration broke up. Clementine was waiting at home for the two men of her family. She had stayed up to hear whether everything she had planned had gone well, and to give them both a good night kiss on a great day in their lives.

Already, at the age of twenty-one, Randolph was saying, The "sky should be the limit of youth's ambition. My two main ambitions are to make an immense fortune and to be Prime Minister. In twenty years' time, however, when I shall probably have fought four or five unsuccessful elections and have been bankrupt more than once, I do not see then why I should regret my youthful ambition however laughable this may appear in more experienced eyes."

The previous year, when he had been invited to make a lecture tour of the United States, his mother had encouraged him to go. With an engaging cocksureness, he informed the people of America how the British Empire should be run, and criticized the "invertebrates," as he called them, who were then running it.

Audiences were amused. They liked the youth with the Churchill touch, the Churchill rhetoric, and the Churchill manner. There was no mistaking the uncanny resemblance between son and father.

There is a close parallel between Winston's admiration for his mother, and the Churchill children's admiration for Clementine. As soon as Randolph was interested in a girl he used to say, "Why don't you do your hair like my mother does?" or "You know, my mother could really show you how to dress."

From his early twenties, Randolph started hitting the headlines... being washed overboard on a yacht with the fabulous June, Lady Inverclyde... interviewing the Kaiser... dressing up as a woman for a Cecil Beaton party.... For a time his efforts to get into Parliament were frustrated by the independent line he took. Like all the Churchills, he couldn't run easily in Party harness. Fighting colorfully, but unsuccessfully, three by-elections in two years, he went off to Hollywood to appear as an extra in a House of Commons scene in the film *Parnell*.

Not until 1940, when Winston became Prime Minister, did Randolph finally enter Westminster as unopposed Conservative member for the Lancashire constituency of Preston. Winston acted as one of his son's sponsors when he was introduced to the House of Commons and smiled broadly at Clementine seated in the gallery when Randolph, in his maiden speech, appealed for indulgence because of embarrassment caused by "paternal propinquity."

There was no doubt about his brilliance, no doubt of his courage, both moral and physical, but he was nevertheless, a young man with a handicap—his father. But even his enemies couldn't ignore his war record. He appeared on the staff of G.H.Q. Middle East as a military spokesman; disappeared into the western desert on long-range desert Commando raids; arrived in South Africa to consult with General Smuts; and then, in New York, predicted the end of the war in 1943 or 1944. He parachuted into Yugoslavia to meet Tito; joined his father for the Teheran talks with Roosevelt and Stalin; went with him again to Athens during the violent days of the Greek Communist uprising. When German airborne troops raided Marshal Tito's H.Q., Randolph succeeded in escaping to the mountains with the Marshal.

Winston always had the greatest possible affection and regard for Randolph, but it was Clementine who understood Randolph best. Father and son argued frequently, and Randolph, if he thought he was right, seldom budged his opinion an inch, no matter how much his father told him off. Their temperaments, so alike, were usually apt to clash in flaming political arguments. Clementine had to keep the peace between them.

In spite of their frequent arguments, Randolph asserts, "Unquestionably, the man I most admire in the world is my father. My admiration for him is not necessarily due to the belief that he is the greatest and the best man in the world, but I have naturally had more opportunities to cultivate admiration for him than I have for anyone else. Perhaps it is for this reason that so many people admire their fathers more than anyone else.

"I admire him for his courage and for his love of adventure, for his complete sincerity, for his tolerance, and for his immense capacity for hard work and concentration. Curiously enough my admiration for him is in no way diminished by the fact that he has always been extremely kind to me." And the woman Randolph most admires in the world is his mother.

Randolph married in 1939, and had a son called Winston Churchill. The marriage was dissolved in 1945. Three years later he married again.

One Sunday, reading the newspapers in bed, Clementine marked a passage in an article published in the *Observer,* and sent it to Winston's bedroom. The passage read: "No one can set the adrenalin flowing simply by the rumor of his approach, like Randolph Churchill. At the news that he has arrived at a party, at a press conference, at a railway station, hearts pump more madly, temperatures rise, lips tighten, voices sharpen. It is like the day war was declared over again."

Another newspaper clipping she kept for Winston was a defense of Randolph by Malcolm Muggeridge in which he declared, "Hostesses on both sides of the Atlantic may grow pale at the prospect of one of his visitations, but they know that, as a topic of conversation, he is inexhaustibly diverting. As a conversationalist himself he is often as devastating as one of those hurricanes which sweep away whole towns in their train; as a stimulant, in absentia of other conversationalists, he is in the very top class.

"For myself, I would not have him otherwise. Like the sirens in the blitz, his arrival at any social gathering sends everyone scampering for cover; produces that slight shiver and taughtening of the nerves which presages danger and excitement. When the 'all clear' sounds and he departs, there is a corresponding sense of relief, but the intervening experience (as long as one has not been personally involved in the explosion) is exhilarating or at any rate memorable."

Perhaps one of the greatest, yet lesser-known qualities of Clementine and Winston is their love of children. Children instinctively sense someone who truly loves them, and even strange children, meeting Clementine or Winston for the first time, take to them immediately.

As a boy, Winston was starved for fatherly affection. His father, Lord Randolph, was too busy to spare him much time. Winston consequently endeavored never to be "too busy" for his own children, but whatever he was unable to give them, Clementine more than made up for. Together, they completely complement each other in the love and affection they give to their family.

Of all her children, it was Diana with whom Clementine was closest although she never showed favorites among her family. In later years, Mary became very close, mainly because, for so long, she lived on the Chartwell estate, which her husband managed, and because her children were forever making Chartwell Manor their own and running in to kiss grandma and grandpa.

Diana was eldest, and an intelligent, sophisticated young woman with whom her mother could be companionable. As soon as she was in her teens, Clementine treated her as an equal.

When Diana married John Milner Bailey, eldest son of South African millionaire, Sir Abe Bailey, Mary and Sarah were among the six bridesmaids. The ceremony took place at St. Margaret's, Westminster, and, reminiscent of her parents' own wedding, many of the congregation stood on the seats to watch the wedding procession.

Clementine gave a magnificent reception at the Duke of Marlborough's house in Carlton House Terrace. Lucky wedding favors of white heather were distributed to eight hundred guests.

But the lucky wedding favors did not bring good fortune to the bride and groom. Within months of the ceremony, the marriage was virtually over. It ended in divorce.

Like her parents, Diana was an emphatic personality. As a little girl, she went on one occasion to see a theatrical performance with her parents. She was dressed in bright green, which toned perfectly with her red hair and fair complexion. "I am Miss Diana Churchill," she informed someone.

One onlooker, who did not know who the mischievous looking child in green was, whispered to his neighbor, "I've seen that little girl before," he said. "She had a row with one of my kids at the seaside."

"They say that girls inherit their fathers' qualities," remarked someone else.

After her first marriage ended in divorce, Diana wed Duncan Sandys —already at that time a rising politician. Both Clementine and Winston agreed he would go a long way, but Diana and Duncan separated, were later divorced, and she announced that she would revert to the name of Diana Churchill.

In poise, style, and looks it is Sarah who completely takes after her mother. In most other respects, Sarah has her father's character. Whereas Diana is the intellectual dreamer among the Churchill girls, Sarah— who is now Lady Audley—is the complete individualist. Even as a child, she was highly imaginative, and forever busy with her own thoughts. "To a certain extent I lived in a secret life of my own apart from the happy one I shared with my brother and sisters," she says.

Facially, Sarah has her mother's fine bone structure, her serious expression, and her smile. But her red hair is an inheritance from her father.

Clementine's nickname for Sarah is "Mule." Counters Sarah, "Stubbornness can also be called firmness in certain circumstances." But pet names have always been the custom in the Churchills' home.

Winston would often lean across the dining table, affectionately squeeze Clementine's hand, and purr, "Dear cat!" To which she would affectionately reply, "Dear pig."

Mary was known among the family as "Mary the Chimp," and every member of the family has an affectionate noise reserved for him. When they were living at Admiralty House in the early part of the last war, Winston would return to their apartment for a meal and "Meow!" at the door, and an answering "Meow!" would come from Clementine.

It was at Admiralty House that Sarah was born during the First World War, on October 7, 1914. When she was very little, her mother arranged for her to be given roller skating lessons. She was getting on well when suddenly she went down with a wallop. "Well, we've had a great many falls, haven't we?" asked her instructor as the lesson ended.

"I don't know why *you* fell down," answered Sarah, with a very emphatic expression in her green eyes, "but *I* fell down because I wished to." Admission of defeat doesn't come easily to a Churchill—not even a small one.

Understanding Sarah's desire to be alone with her thoughts, Clementine asked Winston to build her a treetop Wendy house at Chartwell. Years later Sarah was to fly to one just like the house that Winston built when she played the role of Peter Pan on the stage.

She was in her teens when artist William Nicholson, visiting Chartwell frequently to paint a conversation piece of Clementine and Winston, suggested Sarah might like to join his granddaughter in having dancing lessons.

306

"I think he noticed this lumbering teenager clumping about the house and sensed I needed something to do," said Sarah. That was the beginning of Sarah's theater ambitions. "Any opposition the family made—and it was only mild—was because of the fact that I was such a clumsy child. My entire early life was punctuated by sudden and noisy tumbles. Once I cut my head open and almost bled to death when I tangled with a barbed-wire fence, while racing across a field with Randolph. I also fell off a fifteen-foot wall.

"Whenever there was a loud crash, the family would look at each other and exclaim, 'That's Sarah!' so the very idea of my wanting to be a dancer when I could scarcely keep my feet at ordinary activities amused them."

But she was stage-struck and had made up her mind to become a dancer and an actress. Winston didn't like the idea. It was Clementine who persuaded him to let her go on with her career. She had long been prepared for Sarah to break out on her own in some way, and when she saw that Sarah had made up her mind to succeed in a career of her own choosing, she backed her ambitions all the way.

Confided Sarah to her mother, "I don't want my parentage to make any difference either to my career or to my friendship with other girls. My parentage has nothing to do with it one way or the other. I want a stage career. I mean to stand or fall on my own merit."

Years later shy, independent Sarah admitted, "I didn't become an actress to find myself. To lose myself was what I wanted."

Her still anxious father said to Sarah, "What about your scars? You can't even keep on your feet when you are *not* dancing." And then added, "It's for you to decide. But if you are going to be an actress take it seriously."

Some weeks later, Clementine and Winston sat in the audience at London's Adelphi Theater, watching the revue *Follow the Sun,* and the third girl from the left in the chorus was a "Miss Smith." "Miss Smith" was Sarah.

Society was shocked, so were many of the Churchills' friends. Clementine simply said: "Bless you Sarah."—and went to see the show five times.

She was proud that Sarah had insisted, "I won't be billed as the daughter of anybody. I stand on my own feet."

Clementine had already been to the out-of-town opening of the show in Manchester on one of the foggiest nights of the year. She saw it three times in Manchester alone, then went again with Winston when it came to London. It was during the run of *Follow the Sun,* that Sarah became friendly with its star comedian from America, Viennese-born Vic Oliver.

One morning Sarah handed a letter to her friend Jenny Nicholson, daughter of Robert Graves, the poet, and said, "Please be sure to give this letter to my mother." With that, she took the boat train for the New York-bound liner *Bremen.* Jenny Nicholson put the letter on a train to Westerham. A few hours later, Clementine opened it at Chartwell. In the letter, Sarah told her mother that she had eloped to marry Vic Oliver. Clementine broke the news to Winston and the rest of the family.

When Sarah's letter arrived at Chartwell, Randolph left immediately for New York. On arrival, he went straight to her hotel to find that she was being chaperoned by Lady Astor. For hours, brother and sister talked. He was not there as an instrument of parental opposition, but as brother and confidant.

When the storm of publicity broke, Sarah and Vic Oliver dined with Bernard Baruch. "Well, children," he said, "tell me the whole story." Sarah explained her concern over what her parents would think of the situation. Mr. Baruch allayed their fears like a guardian uncle. "I'll talk to the family," he promised, and did.

On Christmas Day, 1936, twenty-two-year-old Sarah married thirty-eight-year-old Vic Oliver. Clementine cabled: "Best wishes and a Happy Christmas." The marriage was happy for two years, then rifts appeared.

On September 3, 1941, Sarah joined the Women's Auxiliary Air Force a month after her younger sister Mary had joined the A.T.S. She abandoned her successful stage and radio career to do more direct work for the nation. She also told Vic Oliver that their marriage had been a mistake. With her father completely absorbed in fighting the war, it was to her mother Sarah turned. Clementine advised that work was the best answer, and saw to it that, apart from her duties in the W.A.A.F., Sarah acted as her father's aide on some of his wartime travels.

Sarah became another Churchill at war, and wrote a little poem echoing the hour, which she showed to her parents one weekend at Chequers. It read:

Arise, oh countrymen, arise
And with defiance face the darkening skies.

Turn on the tyrant and say
The black night is yours but we will have the day.
Dreams, hopes, faiths may yet dissolve;
You may break our hearts, but never our resolve.

She became a photographic officer. One of her fellow officers—Constance Babington Smith, who authored the history of photographic intelligence in World War II, said, "Sarah was definitely an asset on the station for, apart from the good job she did, when the station was shared by Americans, she was especially good at getting along with them. Having an American grandmother, I think, helped her to see their point of view."

Miss Babington Smith also remembers one particular forty-eight-hour leave weekend at Chequers. At the time, preparations were in hand for the North African landings known as "Operation Torch."

It was nearly 1 A.M.; Sarah was curled up in a big chair near the fire; and Winston was pacing up and down. The clock struck. "At this very minute," announced Winston with measured gravity, "at this very minute, under cover of darkness, the 643 ships that are carrying our troops on a great enterprise are approaching the shores of Africa."

"644," said Sarah's voice from the armchair.

"What's that?" questioned Winston.

"I've been working on Torch for months!" said Sarah.

"Why didn't you tell me?"

"I was told not to mention it to anyone," she replied.

Winston grinned. "Suppose you thought I didn't know," he added.

In March, 1945, Sarah was divorced from Vic Oliver following a petition presented by him on the grounds of her desertion.

At the end of the year, demobilized from the W.A.A.F., she returned to the stage at a little theater at Henley-on-Thames, and the Churchill family turned up almost in full strength, led by her mother, who was accompanied by Randolph, Mary, son-in-law Duncan Sandys, and the American Ambassador, Mr. John Winant. Winston was busy that night, so Clementine brought him a few nights later.

Then, in the spring of 1948, Sarah brought a guest to "meet the family" at Chartwell. His name was Anthony Beauchamp—a distinguished society photographer, whom Sarah had known for some time. Tony Beauchamp loved to recall that nerve-racking first meeting with the Churchills.

"It was terrifying," he said, "but in the nicest possible way. When we

309

reached Chartwell, Sarah ran up the path ahead of me and vanished
behind a bush. Then I heard a tremendous 'Wow!'—it literally exploded
across the quiet countryside. I later learned that this was the traditional
Churchill family greeting for each other, adopted from the call of Sir
Winston's famous Australian black swans. The 'Wow!' had become
part of the family special vocabulary of expression. Sarah reappeared
from behind the bush with her arm round her father. I was suddenly
scared stiff, aware that no less 'suitable' prospective husband for his
daughter could exist. I was still very nervous when we walked into the
house to meet her mother. Suddenly, I felt more at ease. She had a wonderful knack of making you feel immediately at home and more comfortable. Although I knew I was being inspected, she somehow made
me feel she was as much on my side as on Sarah's. The whole family
was there for lunch, and I was able to enjoy the meal, mainly thanks
to the charm and soothing influence of her mother."

Clementine and Winston made their new prospective son-in-law feel
at home. Some months later, he was invited to join them for a week
when they were staying in Monte Carlo with Sarah. Sarah was very
much in love with Tony, and her mother, more than anyone else, knew
this. She felt that although he was a complete stranger to their world,
this could be a much better match than Sarah's first marriage.

One afternoon, sitting in the Riviera sun alone with Clementine,
Tony discussed gambling. They, in fact, discussed most things—except
Sarah—although this was the subject uppermost in both their minds.

"Winston likes to pay an occasional visit to the Casino," Clementine
remarked. "He likes to try his luck now and again."

Tony mentioned that a friend of his had told him of a roulette system
that always worked the first time. "After that, you can lose a fortune
with it, as I did," added the friend.

"Tell Winston about this system," advised Clementine, "he will be
very interested."

Tony took her advice and, on the last night of his Monte Carlo stay,
joined Winston at the Casino. Tony decided to try out the system—
and won, and won again. Winston watched his run of luck, and started
to place his own bets the same way. Chips began to pile up in front of
him, too, and he beamed with pleasure. It turned out to be the best
night Winston had ever had at roulette. Said Tony, "He began to take
a more benevolent view of me after that evening. Her shrewd advice
to me worked out very well."

When Winston returned to the hotel with his winnings, he happily described Tony to Clementine and Sarah as a "very clever young man indeed."

Sarah accepted a theatrical tour of the United States starring in the Philip Barry play, *Philadelphia Story*. She scored a tremendous hit. Tony was unable to join her for several months because of his own work commitments. Then, as he was about to leave for America, Clementine asked him down to Chartwell. She was a mother concerned over a daughter who had already had one unfortunate marriage.

Beside Winston's beloved fishponds, where he keeps his golden carp, the prospective father-in-law and prospective son-in-law discussed the future. A little later, when Winston had left for a while, Clementine also talked about Sarah and of her concern for her happiness. Clementine was obviously still considering the prospects of a marriage between Sarah and Tony, but of one thing she was sure—she knew her daughter was in love.

On October 7, 1949, at a private house at Sea Island, Georgia, before an improvised altar banked high with masses of chrysanthemums, dahlias, magnolia, and ivy, Sarah and Tony were married. There were no preparations for a formal wedding, they wanted it quiet. It didn't stay quiet for long.

After the ceremony they drove to a secluded honeymoon bungalow on the island. Located on the moonlit ocean side, it was a dream setting for the first night of a marriage. Suddenly, in their secret hideaway, the telephone rang. Sarah answered. It was a call from England. Clementine was speaking from Chartwell. She was upset. "Why didn't you let us know you were getting married?" she asked Sarah. "Our first knowledge of it was through reading the papers."

Sarah explained that she had in fact sent them a cable the day before but had sent it to their London home, which was obviously why they hadn't received it as yet.

Tony and Sarah continued their independent careers—Sarah went to Hollywood to star with Fred Astaire in *Wedding Bells;* Tony concentrated on photography and producing television series.

Clementine saw Sarah and Tony spending almost half of each year apart; rarely being in the same place at the same time. She herself had seldom been apart from Winston, and now she was anxious again for Sarah, appreciating that constant separations make shaky foundations for a sound marriage. As Sarah later admitted, "I lived for years in traveling trunks and hotels and on B.O.A.C. and T.W.A., and never properly unpacked once."

311

Clementine and Winston were proud of her achievements as an actress, but they were concerned about her. The end was tragedy. When they were 6,000 miles apart, Anthony Beauchamp, overworked and ill, was found dead from an overdose of sleeping drugs in his London apartment.

When she returned to England after being a top-salary star for nine years in America, Sarah began all over again on the stage of the tiny Connaught theater in Worthing, Sussex, with a local repertory company in which the average wage of the cast was £6 a week. In the audience, the night of her comeback, sat her mother and father.

"Of what I know of children of famous people, if they have been brought up happily and properly, they are entirely unconscious of their parents' fame," said Sarah. "They expect to compete fairly in the career they have chosen."

During the months that followed, she spent as much time as she could with her mother and father, but especially with her mother. To help her ease tension, Clementine suggested she follow her father's example, and take up painting. "Daddy encouraged me," said Sarah. "He says it is a great way of relaxing—he didn't start until he was forty." The months back with her family were just what Sarah needed.

Then, at Christmas, Clementine organized a fifteen-strong family party to visit the Scala Theater, London. The party included Winston and four of their grandchildren. The occasion was Sarah's debut as Peter Pan. Clementine led eleven of the party down to the front row of the stalls, while Winston sat with his grandchildren and hundreds of other children around him, in the front row of the circle where there were fewer stairs for him to climb.

Sarah, in coffee-colored tights, flew through the air with the greatest of ease. "I made ninety-six scheduled flights a week in this play. I felt like British European Airways," said Sarah afterward.

And, of the daughter who had gone her own way and lived her own life, Winston said at the end of the performance: "I am very proud of her. I think she is wonderful."

"And so do I," added her mother.

PART III.   HOW TO LOOK AFTER FATHER

ONE of Winston's greatest strengths has been the family life Clementine wove around him. In everything, this was the mainspring of his

312

existence. Clementine employed all her resourcefulness to free his mind from personal worries, reassuring him, supporting him with her confident cheerfulness.

And whenever domestic or other duties, or her own health prevented her from joining him on journeys, she made sure all her daughters were well briefed on "How to look after father."

Lloyd George said she had once told him that if she should die she would leave behind written instructions to her successor on how to manage Winston.

"Chief item? His food," said Clementine. "First and most important is to feed him well. You must give him a good dinner. His dinner is a very important item in his daily routine," she stressed.

"Whatever the Good Earth offers, I am willing to take. I am a very simple person," Winston would say. "One slice of ham well presented is better than a steak that weighs three pounds. I hate wading through a long dinner. Give me a few well-cooked dishes that I can really enjoy." He considered English cooking "at its best about as good as anything you can get."

Knowing that, at some time during most of his travels he would feel like indulging in his delight in picnicking, she issued standing instructions to her daughters and members of his staff, on the preparation of his picnic sandwiches. "The sandwiches should be solid and substantial. Get hold of a large loaf and don't cut the slices too thin—or too thick, either. Trim the crusts off the edges and put plenty of butter on the bread. Be sure there's enough beef for him to know it's a beef sandwich. Be sure that the beef comes clear to the edge of the bread. He doesn't like to bite twice into a sandwich before he can tell what's inside it.

"He likes fish. He insists on meat being roasted because in roasting none of the juices and none of the flavor is lost." Winston also enjoys a perfectly done lamb chop, considers soup "a good culinary institution," is a firm believer in salads, and prefers to prepare the dressing himself. His preparation of a dressing is a ritual in itself. He has a special weakness for all kinds of cheese, which he likes to eat with his salad.

In her instructions, Clementine would add, "Don't forget the bowl of fruit in rooms." A well-filled bowl is always kept in his rooms, as he loves to bite into a peach or an apple at odd times of the day or night.

"He likes anything—as long as it's the best." And she would emphasize, "See that he is on time for meals and appointments. See that he wears an overcoat when it is cold." The rest of the things that matter, as far as his welfare was concerned, she would endeavor to attend to personally.

As a mother, Clementine has never allowed herself to become dependent on her children for companionship. She loves her family around her but is not lost without them. Interests the whole family can share are important to her, but the family's greatest interest, of course, has always been Winston. She encouraged her daughters to take over for her, from time to time, even in the undertaking of civic and political duties in their father's constituency, and all the children take a keen interest in the Chartwell estate.

On one journey to Yalta, during the war, it was Sarah's turn to deputize for her mother. Clementine sent her on ahead of the rest of the party particularly to inspect that most important of all rooms in Winston's way of life—the bedroom. Sarah was horrified to find her father's room only contained an ordinary, narrow single bed. "My father is used to sleeping in a large bed," she informed the Russian official in charge of living arrangements. "My father not only sleeps in bed, he works in bed, and it is most important that he be given a double bed."

Ferreting around the quarters, she discovered that President Roosevelt and his Secretary of State, Mr. Stettinius, had each been supplied with a double bed. She suggested that Mr. Stettinius's double bed should be moved into the Churchill suite so that the Big Two, at least, would have a large bed apiece.

"I regret this cannot be done," replied the Soviet commandant, "but I will go into the matter further." The result was that a special train was dispatched to fetch a larger bed. It arrived in time to make Winston's first night at Yalta a good night's rest.

Nothing was too much trouble for the Russians. Sarah casually mentioned one evening that caviar tasted much better with the addition of lemon juice. Three days later a large lemon tree covered with fruit, was planted in the orangery adjoining the dining room, in which Stalin toasted Churchill as "the man who is born once in a hundred years."

Later, Sarah, again deputizing for her mother, acted as hostess at a reception for King Ibn Saud, at the Hotel de Lac, at Fayoum Oasis. Making preparations for the luncheon, she was confronted with an unexpected problem—she was informed that neither smoking nor alcoholic beverages was allowed in the Royal presence. After consulting her father, it was decided the matter should be raised at once. Winston informed the interpreter that if it was the religion of His Majesty to deprive himself of smoking and alcohol, he must point out that his rule of life prescribed as an absolutely sacred rite, the smoking of cigars and the drinking of alcohol before, after, and, if need be, during all meals and in the intervals between them.

King Ibn Saud graciously accepted the position, and his own cup-bearer even offered the Prime Minister a glass of water from the sacred well of Mecca—"the most delicious that I have ever tasted," said Winston.

The King traveled with an entourage of some fifty persons, including two sons, his Prime Minister, and his Astrologer. He also had with him flocks of sheep to be killed according to Moslem rites before being prepared for cooking and eating. He had also brought with him a special royal tribute for all the Churchill womenfolk—an enormous portmanteau. Winston, who had been warned beforehand that an interchange of presents was expected during the course of the meeting, had asked Clementine to do some shopping for him before his departure. She selected a small case of perfumes costing £100. But, in addition to the women's portmanteau, the King distributed diamond-hilted, jeweled swords to everyone, as well as other gifts.

Not to be outdone, Winston, on the spur of the moment, said, "What we bring are but tokens. His Majesty's Government has decided to present you with the finest car in the world, with every comfort for peace and every security against hostile action."

When later, Sarah unpacked the portmanteau, she found it laden with beautiful Arab robes, several vessels of rare and delicious perfume, plus half-a-dozen cardboard boxes, one of which contained a diamond valued at £1,200. There were a number of other gems, and several necklaces of Red Sea pearls. When, on reaching England, Winston and Sarah were met at the airport by Clementine, Sarah excitedly told her mother of the magnificent gift for her from King Ibn Saud. There was only one snag, she couldn't keep it. Winston handed over all the valuables to the Treasury to help pay for the sumptuous car Winston had promised the King.

For the great Potsdam Conference with Stalin and President Truman, it was Mary's turn to deputize for her mother, who was unable to leave her own duties at home.

Mary substituted for her mother on several other journeys. She accompanied her father and General De Gaulle on a hundred-mile drive through blizzards, ice, and snow-covered roads in the Jura mountains, to inspect units of the French Army.

Mary also possessed the Churchill spirit even as a child. Wandering away from her mother for a few moments during an election campaign at Epping, Mary, aged six-and-a-half, did some canvassing of her own. "Well, *are* you going to be Conservative or *aren't* you?" said Mary, holding her pencil poised over a piece of paper, "because if you are not, I shall cross your name off, and whenever I pass you in the street I shall say 'Shame! Shame!' You must not be Liberal," she said with determined emphasis. "I despise them. Nobody ought to vote for Mr. Sharp [her father's Liberal opponent]. Mr. Sharp said that my papa broke his promises, and I said 'Pooh! pooh!' to him. My papa has never broken a promise. You must make up your mind quickly what you are going to be. If you do not decide to be Conservative I shall never come to see you, and I shall take a house twenty miles away from you so that you can't come and see me."

"But I might have a fast car," said one person under fire from little Mary.

"Then I shall go and live in France so as not to see you."

"But I could go and live in Paris," came the reply.

"Then I should go to Australia and have a pet kangaroo and a bush baby and a ring opossum."

When the object of one of her arguments said he wasn't convinced and was going to vote Socialist, Mary, eyes blazing, reared as if about to attack him physically, then, controlling herself, said, "You are *disgusting!*" Then, remembering her mother's discipline on how a lady should behave in public, and with a touch of Churchill diplomacy, she added, as her mother reappeared on the scene, "If you change your mind, let me know. Don't forget."

Clementine was expecting Mary when she went to Westcliff for a seaside holiday with her cousin, Miss White. They stayed at a house called Marylands.

"The baby will surely arrive here, Clemmie," said Miss White, "and you'll have to call it Mary after the name of the house. And it surely did arrive there, and they called it Mary.

At the age of fifteen, Mary still only looked about ten or twelve and would think nothing of walking barefoot into her father's office at night with a dirty old mackintosh over her pajamas. She loved to gossip, and read poetry she'd written to her father, mother, and members of the household staff—and it was very good poetry.

Mary loved her horse and used to do a lot of riding at Chartwell, but she had to leave the horse behind when the family left Chartwell for

Admiralty House at the beginning of the war. She cried for days at being parted from the horse.

But for the war, Mary, the only one of the Churchills to inherit the beautiful dark brows of her grandmother, Lady Randolph Churchill, would have been *the* debutante of 1940. Not just because she was Winston Churchill's youngest child, but because of her own charm and beauty. But the war stopped the Courts, so Mary could not make the traditional curtsy to the King and Queen, and enjoy acclamation as the "Season's loveliest deb." Instead, her mother arranged for her to come out on Leap Year night at a great charity ball held on behalf of Queen Charlotte's Hospital.

Clementine chose a white dress for her to set off her youthful freshness, adding a wreath of white flowers to her hair, and giving her a Victorian posy basket to carry. But there is no picture of Mary Churchill in her coming-out dress—her mother forbade it to be taken. Mary had never posed for a studio portrait in her life, and she just wouldn't be photographed—even at the proud age of seventeen-and-a-half. When photographers asked Mary to pose in her coming-out gown, Clementine answered. "Thank you, it is very kind, but Mary would rather not." Knowing her daughter to be a sweet seventeen who preferred riding, country walks, and looking after the pets at Chartwell, Clementine was determined to protect her as much as she could from the dangers of too much limelight too soon.

It was in 1941, at the age of eighteen, that Mary, who had been working as an assistant librarian in a hospital, stepped out on her own to become Private Mary Churchill, A.T.S. "Mummy and Daddy were delighted that I should keep the army in the family," said Mary. Winston had, of course, served in the previous war with the rank of Lieutenant Colonel.

Of Mary, in the early days of the war, Major General Sir Edward Spears recalled, "The Prime Minister had asked me to dine. Mrs. Churchill and Mary were also there. I had always thought Mary Churchill when a child the most enchanting of little girls. Vigorous, gay, eyes forever sparkling, she was always in movement, always laughing. She was one of the type that gave the eyes that watched her joy, and the heart a respite from sadness. Now she was a child no longer, but a girl in her teens promising beauty. Mrs. Churchill was perfectly composed as usual, making as always the meal over which she presided a very civilized occasion. . . ."

Private Mary Churchill passed her preliminary selection test for anti-aircraft work and was posted to a mixed battery. Her mother introduced only one careful parental note into Mary's choice of wartime career—she arranged for Mary's friend, Judy Montague, daughter of her own cousin, to be in the same unit. Clementine also saw to it that she was treated as just an ordinary girl. Mary slept in a hut with twenty girls, made her own bed, cleaned the hut in her turn, and sometimes served in the officers' mess. And Mary enjoyed herself as an ordinary girl too—even to the point of getting spanked in public by an ordinary soldier.

Mary, by now Sergeant Mary Churchill, was dancing with an American sergeant at a local hop near her unit. The sergeant, all six-foot-one of him, towered over her, and his outsize feet trod all over her. Finally she could take it no longer, and made some remarks about his standard of dancing. He wasn't going to be dressed down by a woman and, without hesitation, laid Mary across his knees and gave her a good spanking in front of everyone. His big hands pumped up and down, dishing out punishment, while Mary yelled the roof off.

When someone told him he had just tanned the behind of Winston Churchill's daughter, he simply said, "Well, whaddaya know!" Mary—brave campaigner that she was—stayed until the last waltz, although she couldn't sit out any more dances for the rest of the evening.

In 1947, Clementine added an eighteenth-century touch to the reception she organized for eight hundred guests at the Dorchester Hotel, London, to celebrate the wedding of Mary to Captain Christopher Soames, at St. Margaret's, Westminster. With her typical flair for showmanship and taste, she arranged for twenty-four candelabra to be used to supplement the hotel's lighting in the ballroom, so that the bride and groom could walk out of the dancing shadows to the platform where they cut the three-tier cake made for them by Mr. Frank Boreham, the baker, who had supplied the Churchill family at Chartwell for twenty-four years.

Mary's husband became Winston and Clementine's new son, taking over Chartwell farm and transforming it into a thriving business. He also supervised Winston's string of racehorses; became an M.P.; his father-in-law's Parliamentary Private Secretary, and a Government Minister.

When he became a Minister, Mary began to take on similar social and political duties that her mother had fulfilled nearly forty years ago, and Clementine taught her to understand and to undertake the kind of responsibilities with which she herself had to contend as a young wife. Mary was to be the one who, more than her other daughters, was to follow her footsteps.

Mary had very special "how-to-look-after-father" guidance from her mother when she deputized for Clementine during part of Winston's convalescence after his stroke in 1953.

Mary, and her husband Christopher Soames, were with the Prime Minister when he went to Lord Beaverbrook's house at Cap-d'Ail, for some recuperation in the French Riviera's sunshine. Learning that Winston's friend, Sir Tom O'Brien, was also holidaying close by, Christopher Soames telephoned to invite him to lunch with his father-in-law.

"I went there for lunch, and it was the first time that anyone from Britain had seen the Prime Minister since his stroke, and few seemed to know how he was really progressing," said Sir Tom. "I fully expected to see him in bed, laid up hard. Instead of that, he was in the lounge reading his newspaper, and got up to greet me as I walked in. We went out into the garden, had a drink there with Mary and Christopher, and it was almost impossible to realize he had just gone through such a serious illness ordeal. Thinking that Clementine was there, I said to Mary, 'Is your mother upstairs?—I would like to see her.'

" 'My mother,' said Mary, 'is a great woman as well as a great wife. My mother feels that the later she comes to see my father, the better it will be for him.'

"I asked what she meant, and she replied, 'Well, he is recovering remarkably, and whatever irritations he has, he's got to have them with himself, so she's keeping well out of the way. My mother is a wise woman.'

"That is a tribute from her child to her mother's knowledge and patience. It was a human family thing. We spent the afternoon talking about every conceivable subject, and although Clementine wasn't there in person, there was the feeling that she was nevertheless present somehow.

"I think Mary is closest, of all the daughters, to her mother's disposition. Sweet, understanding—with that domestic warmth—that love of family that her mother has.

"Lady Churchill has always been a wonderful mother. She has had difficult times with her children, as have millions of other parents, but the children of a public man have their troubles blazoned across the world, they can't be suppressed, can't be hidden. Their mother has

319

acquitted herself with great dignity through various domestic crises in the family. Few women can do that. They would, in some way, betray lack of trust in their children or would publicly indicate some rebuke but not Clementine. Whatever her domestic difficulties, she behaved with that tact and understanding that has made her such a remarkable woman."

Again following in her mother's footsteps, Mary kept some of her work for good causes secret from her father. But she also kept it secret from her mother for a very long time. Mary plays a very active part in the organizing and reorganizing of Church Army hostels. Clementine admitted to a friend, "I only discovered this quite by chance. She didn't even tell me."

The rest of Clementine and Winston's family consists of their grandchildren, Julian, Edwina, and Celia—the children of Mr. and Mrs. Duncan Sandys, and Winston and Arabella—Randolph's son and daughter. Mary gave them five grandchildren, including a Winston Soames, and a Clementine Soames. Mary also gave her mother and father something else—her very birth brought them consolation at a time of great personal tragedy.

The night of August 23, 1921, was a never-to-be-forgotten night in the lives of Clementine and Winston. Marigold Frances Churchill was their fourth child. Marigold had her father's gingery red hair, and her mother's engaging smile. Already, at the age of three, she was a miniature ball of fire, delighting in reciting nursery rhymes to everyone in sight and running races with servants round the dining table. She was a "Mummy's girl" shadowing her mother almost everywhere. Marigold clung much more to her mother than shy Sarah.

During the summer of 1921, Clementine sent Marigold and her nanny, Miss White, away for some sea air at Broadstairs, Kent. Marigold was having a wonderful time on the beach when she was suddenly taken ill. Clementine hurried down. Marigold was too ill to be moved, and doctors were unable to diagnose accurately the nature of the illness.

Winston, Chancellor of the Exchequer at the time, couldn't get down to Broadstairs until the weekend, and then had to return to London on the Sunday night because of urgent Ministry business.

Clementine and Miss White hardly left Marigold's bedside, taking it in turn to watch over her day and night. The instant Winston was able to free himself of his ministerial duties, he hurried down there again to be by his wife and child, but was compelled to return again to Whitehall.

320

One morning at No. 11 Downing Street, a message from Clementine sent him rushing back to Broadstairs. For a time, he sat with Clementine beside Marigold's bed. In the early evening, he went out into the grounds of the house on South Cliff Parade and just walked up and down, tears streaming down his face. He spoke to no one. Clementine remained inside with Marigold. His wife called him, and he hurried in. Within moments, he reappeared in the garden. For the first time in hours, he turned to one of his staff and spoke, "I know you were very fond of her," he said. "I'm sure you'd like to see her."

Winston was like a man lost and could not stop his tears. Clementine joined him, but there were no tears from her. The rigid self-discipline, now so much a part of her makeup, seemed to grip the emotions within her. She didn't cry, nor did she speak. She had just lost her child. Now her one concern was to comfort her husband in his grief.

Clementine's discipline of herself seldom allowed her to lower the barrier she kept permanently in front of her innermost feelings. She steeled herself against personal tragedy in her own way and looked at the other side of death. She treasured the memory of her dead sister with a photograph of her lying in her coffin. She had the photograph taken because her sister had looked so beautiful even in death. When her mother died at Dieppe, Clementine and Winston went across together. Again she restrained her tears.

Only to their friend Professor Lindemann did she, years later, give a revealing insight into her emotions when, in a letter of condolence to the Professor at the death of his mother, she wrote, "The loss of one's mother is a sad milestone in one's life. After that one is nobody's child and it is a lonely feeling."

Joy and laughter she will let everyone see. Sorrow she will share with no one except her husband. Clementine will talk of her mother, talk of her sister, but never of Marigold.

24

The Distinguished Stranger

On June 8, 1946, Winston and Clementine took their places on the great V.I.P. grandstand erected for that day of days—the Victory Parade. There, with the Royal Family, Mr. and Mrs. Clement Attlee, and finally joined by the King, they witnessed the great march- and drive-past of representatives from every branch of the fighting services and of the civilians who had fought equally well in the Home Front line. When the massive parade was over, they all went to Downing Street for lunch, and in the evening, to the House of Commons to watch the victory fireworks display over the Thames. There they found the King, the Queen, Queen Mary, Princess Elizabeth and Princess Margaret, the Duchess of Kent, the Crown Prince of Norway, the Athlones, and the Attlee family. It was a gathering of gatherings, a night of nights, a day and night of emotions for them that no words could possibly capture.

Winston by now was his fighting self again, and Clementine was back in her customary seat in the Distinguished Strangers' Gallery of the House of Commons watching him in action.

One day as he was attacking Socialist expenditure, one of the members on the Labor benches of the House cried, "Why don't you sell your horse?"—a reference to his racehorse Columnist II, which had already run several races and become a popular favorite.

Winston turned to the interrupter. "Well, that at least is a piece of property which has increased its value since it came under my control," he countered. "As a matter of fact, I was strongly tempted to sell the horse; but I am doing my best to fight against a profit motive."

He looked up at Clementine with a boyish, impish grin as he heard her laugh above the roar of amusement on the floor of the House.

It was in 1946 that a group of their friends bought Chartwell Manor for the National Trust, evolving a financial arrangement whereby the Churchills could live at Chartwell tax-free for the rest of their lives, after which it would go to the National Trust as a memorial of Winston's services to the Commonwealth. Some years before the war, their personal finances were hard hit—Winston had never been a rich man —and, at one time, it seemed they would be forced to sell the house they cherished so much. Preliminary plans were even made for its sale. Now, through the offices of their friends, Chartwell Manor was secured for them.

With his wife's moral support, affection, and understanding, Winston recovered from the wounds, which the election defeat had inflicted upon him. He became Leader of the Opposition with a capital "O." He fought the Socialists ferociously, moved votes of censure regularly, battled Herbert Morrison every Thursday over such small things as the business for the following week.

It was a fighting example to the Tory party, bewildered by its downfall after years of power. On world problems he was still the world's greatest statesman, and, time after time, Clementine was there in the Distinguished Strangers' Gallery of the House of Commons, smiling down her encouragement.

Whenever he made an important speech in Parliament, as he rose to speak, he never failed to look to the gallery where Clementine sat, and she would acknowledge his gaze with a little encouraging wave. Then, when he had finished, and before resuming his seat, he would look again to her for the smile of approval. That is the way it had always been, and always will be so long as the M.P. for Woodford serves his country.

In March, 1949, the Churchills—Winston, Clementine, Mary and her husband Captain Christopher Soames—were on their way to America again, this time on the liner *Queen Elizabeth*. Winston was going principally to deliver an address to members of the Massachusetts Institute of Technology at Boston.

Examining the passenger list, Clementine spotted four familiar names —Sir Will Lawther, President of the National Union of Mineworkers, Mr. Arthur Deakin, of the Transport and General Workers, Mr. Jack Tanner, of the Amalgamated Engineering Union, and Mr. Lincoln Evans, of the Iron and Steel Trades.

Appreciating only too well Winston's enjoyment of lively controversial conversation, she arranged to give a party for the Trade-Union leaders. The party in the Churchill suite, with the four distinguished guests, lasted four-and-a-half hours.

Recalled Arthur Deakin, "I remarked that nationalization was a good thing for Britain, and that Labor would win the next General Election. Winston and Clementine, of course, strongly disagreed. Will [Sir Will Lawther] offered them a nine-to-four bet that the Conservatives would lose the Election.

"'Those are very high odds,' Clementine remarked, to which Will replied, 'What do the odds matter, if you are going to win?'"

Winston was in his seventy-fifth year, and his health had never been better. Throughout the voyage he worked two secretaries from early morning until past midnight. At least once a day he visited the bridge with Clementine to speak to the Captain and members of the staff.

It was their first visit to the United States since January, 1946, and so many reporters, broadcasters, and photographers—nearly two hundred —wanted to meet them that a coastguard cutter and two tugs—a record number of craft for such an occasion—had to be provided to take them all to the harbor entrance, where they clambered aboard the liner. Twenty-eight Secret Service men also boarded the liner at the same time, to protect them against demonstrators waiting for them to land.

As the *Queen Elizabeth* slid into the Cunard dock, Winston and Clementine entered the liner's cinema where the press conference was to be held. They were both obviously affected by the spontaneous outburst of applause that greeted their appearance. Winston waved his cigar and said, "Good morning, ladies and gentlemen. I am glad to see so many of you present," and the conference had been informally declared open. He sidestepped a question about the average man's life in Britain with the answer, "It is a topic which might lead into controversy which you know we try to avoid." They grinned, and he added, "except on proper occasions." After the interview, the Churchills posed for photographers on the veranda deck.

Waiting for them on the pier was their friend and host, Mr. Bernard Baruch. As they stepped ashore Secret Service men and a large motorcycle escort surrounded the car in which they left with Mr. Baruch. As the car turned into Twelfth Avenue, pickets representing the National Council of American-Soviet Friendship and other political organizations, were waiting for them to flash protest banners and chant, "Go home Mr. Churchill, we don't want another war." Winston peered from the car and his fingers gave the well-known V salute to the pickets, and Clementine gave them a great big smile. The police escort stayed with them through the heart of the city to the apartment building on Fifth Avenue overlooking Central Park where they were to stay. A special squad of uniformed and plainclothes police had been assigned to guard the building.

The Churchills rarely visited the United States without meeting their friend, financier Baruch, adviser and confidant to presidents, and key figure in American affairs in both world wars. Says Clementine, "I always love to see Winston and Bernard Baruch together—they are two like souls basking in one another's radiance."

Baruch, millionaire, philosopher, philanthropist, and "Elder Statesman," was one of their closest friends. Theirs was one of the most striking and influential Anglo-American friendships. Winston and Clementine both dearly loved this six-foot-four silver-haired statesman, whose favorite office was a park bench. Baruch would find friends for the Churchills all along their lecture tour routes in the United States; would put them up at his apartment, and generally do everything to make their visit as smooth as possible. In return, Clementine and Winston would plan, on their side of the Atlantic, motor tours for him through beautiful country and "highly conservative" constituencies; a visit to Nelson's flag ship *Victory;* or days watching yacht races.

For years, photographs of Winston have occupied places of honor in the Baruch home—one glowers at you from the top of the television set, while for the Douglas Chandor portrait of Winston entitled, "The Old Bulldog," Baruch gave over $25,000—said to be the highest price ever paid for a contemporary portrait in the United States at the time of its purchase. It dominates the apartment's formal drawing room. Pausing in front of the portrait, Baruch would say, "Doesn't he look like a bulldog?" And for the Baruch guest room, Winston selected one of his very best paintings—a landscape.

During one of their trips to New York, the three of them made a nostalgic pilgrimage to Winston's mother's birthplace in Brooklyn. A plaque had been put on the house to commemorate the home of Jenny Jerome who became Lady Randolph Churchill.

They were overwhelmed by their reception in America. "Winston considered it a great compliment that they should make a private person so welcome," Clementine said to Bernard Baruch.

"I think Winston is even more highly regarded over here than in his own country," Mr. Baruch answered. "He defies convention, ignores the rules, loves short cuts, takes breathless chances, and generally conducts himself as a lusty youth, all of which seems to leave the British a little uneasy, while it tickles us enormously. And of course," added Mr. Baruch with a smile, "we never forget that he is half American."

One evening at dinner, he told her his story of the only American who ever beat Winston in a verbal exchange—"It was Harry Hopkins," he said. When Winston first went to the White House during the war, some Royal Marines were sent along to add a bit of color to the guard of honor.

"During the initial ceremonies at the White House, Harry kept jumping up and looking out of the window at the Royal Marines drawn up to attention on the lawn. This eventually irked Winston so much that he turned to Harry and said, "What's the matter with you, Harry? They are Royal Marines, nothing more.'

" 'Yes, sir, I know they are Royal Marines, Mr. Prime Minister,' answered Harry. 'And the last time Royal Marines were in that yard they burned this joint.' "

While staying at the Baruch apartment, the streams of callers made it difficult for Winston to find time to work on the speech he was to deliver in Boston.

Then the day came, and it was another triumph. One of her platform companions remarked to Clementine, "There is no other man alive today who could have made such a speech about the promise and realization of this century. His breadth of vision, his clarity and his warmth and his force of conviction must have clarified and fortified the minds of millions."

The Boston speech was the biggest TV occasion since President Truman's own inauguration. Millions heard it, millions saw him speak in their own homes. It was also the occasion for an unusual twist. Toward the end of the speech, Winston sipped a drink of water from a glass, and this action delayed the end of his speech by a minute. But, rather than cut him off before he had finished, the broadcasting company let him overrun his time, and canceled a commercial program scheduled to follow him. To compensate the advertiser and the cast of the show, they had to pay out over $15,000—which undoubtedly made that glass of water the costliest ever.

When told of this later, his comment to Clementine was, "It's amazing to think that every expression on my face was being viewed by millions. I hope the raw material was as good as the method of distribution."

*   *   *

The wounds had completely healed by the 1950 General Election. Clementine was confident they would be returning to 10 Downing Street.

She was not really keen on his returning to Downing Street, but recognizing that, at that time, the fortunes of the Conservative party vitally needed him to resume the Premiership for at least two years, she did not press him to quit the leadership of the Party.

Without her—his "devoted aide," as he himself calls her—it is doubtful whether he would have come so robustly and so magnificently through life. Winston's eloquent testimony to her is better than anyone else could hope to give.

After General Lord Ismay had proposed a toast to them both at a private party, Winston, in replying, said, "I could never have succeeded without her."

And at Strasbourg, his eyes brimming with tears, he declared, "It would not be possible for any public man to get through what I have gone through without the devoted assistance of what we call in England one's 'better half.' "

It was not the only public tribute he paid to her. He once wrote, "My marriage was much the most fortunate and joyous event which happened to me in the whole of my life, for what can be more glorious than to be united in one's walk through life with a being incapable of an ignoble thought."

"My most brilliant achievement was my ability to be able to persuade my wife to marry me," he once remarked.

Those who know her well are aware she could have made a considerable mark in her own right. Instead, she devoted herself to spoiling, encouraging, and, above all, giving stability to the fantastic genius that is her husband. How different might have been his career, and the history of the world, if she had chosen otherwise for herself?

On polling day, 1950, she was the first member of the Churchill family to vote in London. She drove from their home in Hyde Park Gate early in the morning and gave the V sign to the canvassers.

Winston arrived at the same polling station a little later. As he went

327

in to vote, Winston removed his hat, put on his glasses, and studied the candidates' list. He then entered a booth and stayed for a minute and a half.

"He is thinking it over," someone cracked. Winston emerged, shook hands, and they were greeted all the way down the street by other cars, honking V in Morse code chorus. They drove to Woodford, where hundreds lined the streets for them.

Leaving Woodford Memorial Hall after a meeting in the constituency, they found themselves surrounded by members of the local Labor party League of Youth. Young Socialists offered them handfuls of the Labor party leaflets.

"No," exclaimed Clementine, "I daren't take them. They might convert me."

Election night they spent together at their Hyde Park Gate home. When it was over, Winston beamed at Clementine. "I like the look of this House much better than the old one," he said, although his party had not been returned to power.

On October 31, 1950, 275 Conservative Peers and M.P.s gave a dinner to mark the fiftieth anniversary of Winston's first return to Parliament. This was one great milestone Clementine had to miss. She had promised to attend an important engagement in Edinburgh on the night of the banquet and so missed an occasion granted to few Parliamentarians in any age. Even so, Clementine was still, in certain respects, represented at the dinner. Each course traced his Parliamentary life from election at Oldham in 1900. Sherries, turtle soup, and appetizers were named after two of his constituencies. Fillets of sole were named after the Cinque Ports of Dover, Hastings, Sandwich, New Romney, and Hythe of which he had been Warden since 1941. Mushrooms from his 1941–45 electorate of Epping Forest followed. Partridge on toast with English sauce became "Les perdreaux rôtis sur canapés Clementine," and in this sense Clementine was there. Dinner was topped off with coffee, "hot and strong à la Winston Spencer Churchill."

At the opening of the Festival of Britain, organized to mark the centenary of the Great Exhibition in Hyde Park of 1851, and to display the British contribution to civilization, past, present, and future, in science, the arts, and industrial design, Winston and Clementine were among the many distinguished guests at the royal opening day. The King and Queen, Queen Mary, and all the members of the Royal Family were there, but suddenly Winston was absent. Clementine had to go hunting for him—she found him riding up and down, and down and up, over and over again, on an escalator—he had never been on one before.

*   *   *

The voters were about to go to the polls in the 1951 General Election, and the spirit of victory was in the air once more in their home.

Clementine felt an overwhelming certainty that Winston would be back in Parliament as Prime Minister. She was sure that after fifty-two years of political life, he was about to become Prime Minister of a peacetime Britain, with a strong and workable majority.

She joined him in fighting the election on the high cost of living at home, and the fall in British prestige abroad.

This time the Socialists made the big campaign blunder—they branded him "a warmonger." Furious at this attack, Clementine denounced it as "cruel, ungrateful, and the opposite of the truth. Bursting as he does with the sense of justice and fair play which inspires the British people, Winston is sure these taunts and insults will recoil upon the heads of those that make them."

Once again she gave him her arm, her charm, and her strength on a nationwide electioneering tour. It was a prodigious feat of stamina on both their parts.

No two cities were treated to the same speech; a new speech was composed and typed out an hour or so before it was delivered. Clementine was always there doing her utmost to lessen the fatigue of the journeying, supervising staff, domestic affairs, and innumerable political arrangements, ensuring everything was as Winston liked it to be—the baggage on the trains, the wardrobe, the arsenal of cigars and papers of reference, including the famous dispatch boxes that he had kept from his tenure of various Crown offices.

Always on the cushions of his special railway coach were two or three of these boxes, including those of the Ministry of Munitions from the First World War, and another with the dulled gold lettering of the "Chancellor of the Exchequer." Clementine carried on the important morning routine of carefully scrutinizing all the newspapers, looking for items that might be necessary or valuable ammunition for Winston to consider and use. And she made sure that every afternoon he took his very necessary after-lunch nap and rest after smoking a comforting postluncheon cigar.

Voices continued accusing Winston of being "not interested" in the problems of peace and concerned only with war. While the war was on, that was in fact true, and Clementine had told friends, "Winston says that unless we win the war, we need not plan for the peace, for there will be none!" While the cries of "Warmonger!" grew in volume, Winston dreamed of, and worked for, his now famous Four Year Plan with its visionary schemes for fuller employment and trade, and for social welfare. The mind that had invented labor exchanges to offer men work was very much concerned with the problems of peace.

Only Clementine completely understood his intolerance of the election, his complicated character, his irascibility, and his gentleness, with its deep understanding of the difficulties of others. She went alone to his constituency at Woodford, and five hundred people heard her deliver a full-scale attack on the Government's foreign policy and, in particular, its treatment of the Palestine problem. She condemned what she called "an instance of the most appalling bungling, which committed all the arms being used by the Arabs against the Jews to be provided by Britain, and allowed British officers to command the Arab legions.

"What you have to consider," she said, "is the hopeless inadequacy and incompetence shown by the Government; incompetence in carrying out a program to which their hearts, souls, and minds have been devoted for years. For years it has been their faith that everything should be nationalized in this country. When they are in power and begin to do it, you have Mr. Shinwell saying the reason nationalization so far is not a success, is that the Socialist party was totally unprepared for it. The reason it has not worked well is that they have not yet learned how to do it. Right through you find this incompetence which is very depressing."

At a women's conference at Central Hall, Westminster, she said the right things in the right way when she proclaimed, "In the next election the Conservatives will be returned to power. Then will come their opportunity; they will have to be very brave, very wise, and very patient. It might not be possible to unpick everything the Socialists have done, and they would have to consider very carefully what might be unpicked, what must be rearranged, and what they could do."

At another meeting, she shrewdly aimed at election targets with an accuracy women particularly appreciated. She brought home the housing shortage. "The Labor Government is putting up houses all over the country at the rate of 500 a day. But before the war, the Conservatives turned them out, like shelling peas, at 1,000 a day," she declared.

Then she bowled a bombshell into the shopping baskets by asking and answering, "Why is food so expensive?—Because of the enormous army of food officials. The officials used to cost £4,000,000 a year; now they cost £14,000,000. We believe that by trying to be better housekeepers the country will be put on its legs." She knew how to hit home on domestic issues, and never lost touch with the mass of women.

The last speech of the campaign had been arranged for Plymouth, where their son Randolph was campaigning at nearby Devonport. Before they left for Plymouth, they listened to the radio election address of the then Prime Minister, Clement Attlee. When Attlee finished, Winston said nothing for a moment, then Clementine, with that political shrewdness seldom seen by the public and equal to that of her husband, said, "Winston, I think that is a very good speech—but it is a recessional speech."

"Very well put, Clemmie, that's exactly the right word for it," said Winston, with an appreciative smile.

The air of defeatism in the Attlee broadcast made them even more certain of victory. Accompanied by Sarah, their son-in-law, photographer Anthony Beauchamp, and Randolph's son, young Winston, they left by train to appear before a crowd of 10,000 at Plymouth Argyll football ground.

After attacking the Socialist warmonger charges, Winston added the kind of human note that endeared him to the crowd when he said, "I am always glad to come to the West Country, and here we have the candidates for Totnes, Tavistock, Bodmin, and Sutton, and," he said, glancing at Randolph, "as you will understand, last but not least to me, Devonport."

That night they dined with Lord and Lady Astor at their house on Plymouth Hoe. Thousands who knew they were inside milled around outside, hoping to catch a glimpse of them. "Don't disappoint them, Winston," said Clemmie. "Speak to them," she advised. He took her advice, and from the balcony of the Astor home made an informal speech that was unreported. It was impromptu and straight from the heart.

"Whichever way you vote," he told the crowd, "whether it is for us or for the Socialists, at least you must give us a good working majority. It will be far better to return the Socialists to power once again than to send us back with a majority so small that it would be impossible to govern."

As he said this, there were a few boos from the crowd, to which he replied, "I must say I like to hear some boos. After all, if you have a

331

right to have cheers, you have a right to have boos." Then, speaking slowly and with emphasis, he went on, "I would rather have a Socialist Government for four or five years—" There were cheers and boos.

Turning to the booing section of the crowd, he observed, "Don't do them in the wrong place," and continued, "—than to have a continuance of this present indeterminate miserable situation."

Winston went on, "Don't you think it is time there should be a new eye on the sea, a new hand on the tiller, a new approach to our foreign and our home problems?"

There was an overwhelming "Yes!" Winston, turning to Clementine, remarked, "I think the majority is with me."

Jacob Astor got his Socialist opponent out at Plymouth but Randolph, though succeeding in greatly reducing the Socialist majority at Devonport, failed to win the seat.

Winston and Clementine returned to Hyde Park Gate for election day, and attended the Conservative election party at the Savoy Hotel given by Lord Camrose of the *Daily Telegraph*. By the time they went home, the Socialists and Conservatives seemed to be running level. Winston and Clementine remained confident. In the early hours of the morning, when key constituencies had clearly indicated the result, Clementine crossed the room to Winston and kissed him, he kissed her, and neither spoke a word. For both of them this triumph softened the bitterness of the 1945 defeat.

In the middle of that night, a crowd gathered outside their home, and voices started calling "Winnie!" Exhausted by the strenuous campaign, he little felt like answering their calls—he just wanted to go to bed. Clementine, wearing the two red roses on her black dress he had given her to mark the occasion, had retired to her room, too, but the crowd refused to go. Finally, in their dressing gowns, they appeared at the window to give a happy victory wave. Satisfied, the crowd gave a last cheer and quietly left to give "the Old Man" a well-deserved night's sleep.

"I have the reins of the country in my hands again, Clementine," he said. She kissed him good night and went to her room.

The famous poured into Chartwell to consult with Winston before the formation of the new Government. Life was hectic and exciting, and Clementine had her hands full acting as hostess to the ceaseless stream of notabilities. At seventy-seven, her husband once more held the destiny of his country in his hands. At his age, his statesmanship, his leadership, his vitality, his extraordinary and varied talents, towered above the world.

After the election, Winston said, "My dear wife has come to my aid and has taken a definite and recognizable part." At a Primrose League meeting at the Royal Albert Hall, in London, he announced, "I am sorry my wife was not able to come here today, but she has to spare herself in order to discharge the many tasks and duties which fall upon her, and I thought you would be willing that she should be resting this afternoon." And, on a visit to Manchester, he declared, "I have enjoyed every minute of my visit, but there is one source of great regret—that I have not been able to bring my wife with me."

Clementine had her own postelection comment, "Those who wonder why my husband continued to bear in public affairs a burden that would crush many a younger man, the answer is that Winston thinks things are being managed so badly!"

It was with a new kind of confidence, a confidence founded not on the past, but one based on the future, that they returned to No. 10 Downing Street.

25

That Was No Lady

CLEMENTINE and Winston sailed for America again in December, 1952, and Mary and her husband, Christopher Soames, were with them in mid-Atlantic, when they joined passengers in the main lounge to welcome in the New Year. As they appeared in the lounge, dancing stopped and everyone crowded round. Champagne was poured, and, as midnight struck, bells and hooters sounded throughout the ship. Winston rose, took Clementine's hand on one side, and Mary's on the other, and joined in "Auld Lang Syne." Then he kissed Clementine as they went to their table. On the stage a bearded figure pronounced the death of 1952, followed by a young girl representing 1953. The purser welcomed the New Year, "and our distinguished guests, Mr. and Mrs. Churchill."

"Some of you," Winston said, "may think that I have gone off the stage with the old year."

"Never!" came a deafening shout from everyone.

He smiled. "You have given me a mandate to progress into the future," he declared, and sat down as cheers ran round the ballroom, and guests stood with glasses raised to toast the Churchills.

Fifteen minutes later they were back in their suite—and he was back at work.

Visiting Canada, Winston, in an interview, was asked, "Mr. Churchill, why am I not calling you Sir Winston?"

"Why what?" exclaimed Winston.

"Why are you not knighted?" persisted the interviewer. Winston looked thoughtful, then at Clementine, and they both laughed. Suddenly, he became serious and said, "I don't want to make merry over 'sirs,'" he explained with complete gravity, "but you know, titles are all matters of taste—and I don't believe I've got the taste. My own unadorned name will have to do me, I'm afraid."

Years later, at the Coronation of Queen Elizabeth II, in June, 1953, leading the magnificent procession of Commonwealth Prime Ministers in Westminster Abbey came a resplendent Sir Winston in the plumes and dazzling robes of a Knight of the Garter—the honor he had refused after his political defeat in the 1945 election.

As the procession moved through the Abbey, he paused momentarily to speak to his wife in the pew in front before taking his place in his stall in the choir.

When Winston accepted the Order of the Garter from Queen Elizabeth, Clementine had said, "Now we will have to have our visiting cards changed."

Winston remembered this remark when they were on their way to Windsor Castle for the investiture ceremony of the Garter. As their car drove past a village railway station, Winston, observing the word "Ladies," a sign indicating the whereabouts of the station toilets, pointed to the notice and said to Clementine, "As from tomorrow you will be entitled to go in there!"

Winston had refused an offer of the Garter in 1945, immediately after his defeat in the post-war election. An official announcement said "he begged His Majesty [George VI] that, in the present circumstances, he might be allowed to decline." At that time, recommendations to the Order were made by the Prime Minister of the day—then Mr. Clement Attlee. The procedure was changed, and it became for the Sovereign alone to decide who should be admitted.

So Winston, who throughout his fifty-three years in public life had steadfastly refused a title, assumed one—by personal wish of the Queen.

With Clementine he drove to Windsor from Downing Street, and the ceremony took place before dinner, in one of the drawing rooms.

The seventy-eight-year-old Prime Minister knelt before his young Queen to receive his knighthood. He couldn't quite get accustomed to the title at first, for a few days later, at a Conservative Women's National Conference in Westminster, when he suddenly had to excuse himself to return to the House of Commons, as he regretfully took his leave of the 3,000 women present, he added, "Mrs. Churchill will represent me in my absence."

Clementine had herself been created Dame Grand Cross of the Order

335

of the British Empire for her wartime services, but she always disliked her official title of Dame Clementine Churchill, and used it rarely, preferring to be known as Mrs. Churchill. She was delighted in fact, when, in accordance with custom, she was able to lose the designation of Dame as soon as Winston was created a Knight.

Clementine tackled every task with supreme confidence. Only once was she visibly shaken and really nervous, and that was when she went to accept the Nobel Prize for literature on his behalf

It was December, 1953, and Winston was busy meeting world statesmen across the other side of the Atlantic.

If the Nobel Prize winner is unable to receive the reward in person, it is customary for his country's ambassador to do so, but, acknowledging the tremendous part Clementine had played in her husband's life and career, the Swedes invited her to receive it in his place. The Swedes recognized her as an outstanding personality on her own merit, with amazing qualifications for managing a husband who is at times a volcano and at times a whirlwind.

To one woman who complimented her on being married to such a great man, she replied, with a laugh, "Oh! Do you think it is amusing all the time, every day? If you do, you are very wrong. Not so long ago I said to Winston that if I had to be born a second time and was asked if I would be willing to marry a man of genius, I am not quite sure that I would answer 'Yes'!"

But she *had* married a genius, and here she was, excited and very nervous at the thought of representing him at the great, historic, Nobel Prize ceremony. On many occasions she had stepped in when he had been unable to make a public appearance and then, and only then, had she used his words, his speech.

One evening, when he was suffering from a severe bronchial cold, she had taken his place at a political dinner and read his speech on the Suez Canal crisis. The doctor's advice was that if Winston didn't stay home for a few days, he would be unable to shake off his bronchitis, so Clementine insisted on deputizing for him at that important dinner, and reading his speech for him.

Another time she stood in for him at the launching of the Cunard liner *Saxonia,* on the Clydeside. The ship was the largest to be built to go up the St. Lawrence River to Montreal. But before reading Winston's message at the launching, she added a personal note. She said, "I asked Sir Winston for a message; he spoke very quickly and I had to grab a piece of paper to scribble it down. Then I pinched his arm and said, 'Now pay attention while I read it back.' He did, and here is the message...."

Now here she was going to Stockholm to deliver another kind of message from him. With Mary to support her morale, she crossed to Stockholm to be the guest of King Gustav.

In the privacy of her suite in the royal palace she practiced the speech she was to make at the Nobel Prize banquet. "I must rehearse and make sure that I have it right—the speech isn't very long, but I have never had to read a message from him on such an important occasion before," she said to Mary. And, for the first time, cool, calm, composed Clementine admitted she was having a mild attack of "stomach butter-flies."

"It's not the place, but *The Speech* that is upsetting me. I'm just a tiny bit nervous about reading Winston's speech at the banquet."

Sensing how she would feel, Winston began to bombard her with a series of cables from distant Bermuda.

Said the first, "I will keep my fingers crossed while you read my speech." Said the second, with painful memories of his New York taxi accident, "Be careful in the Stockholm traffic. It still keeps left like ours but may soon change to right." And the third, which arrived on her breakfast tray on the morning of the banquet, said, "Good luck and all my love, Winnie."

"A trip round the world would be a good way to spend the prize-money," [£12,000] commented Clementine. "That is something I've always wished to do, and I might have made the trip if the money had been awarded to me."

She confided to Mary, "As it is a short speech if I talk quickly it will be over in less than five minutes."

Clementine and Mary shook Stockholm by wearing exactly the same shaped hats. Clementine's was a turquoise blue with a veil, and Mary's white, without a veil. King Gustav Adolph and Queen Louise person-ally conducted them on a tour round the Summer Palace at Drotting-holm, then came the great day.

She arrived for the presentation looking every inch, as she is, a queen among women. She had dressed in a steel-gray evening dress with pale blue tulle stole and a diamond tiara and white gloves.

Two thousand people, representing science, art, and fashion, stood as she curtsied to the King in Stockholm's magnificent concert hall.

She had listened in the past to hundreds of speeches, from the great and the lowly, praising Winston, but she had never heard greater tributes to him than were paid that day in Stockholm.

"The Grand Old Man" of Swedish literature, Dr. Sigfried Siwertz, painted a glowing word-picture of the life, personality, and achievements of the first statesman ever to receive the Nobel Prize award. Then Dr. Siwertz bowed low to Clementine sitting with Mary a little to the left of the six members of the Swedish Royal Family. Speaking in English, he said, "The Swedish Academy expresses joy at your presence and asks you to convey our respects to Sir Winston. The Nobel Prize for Literature is meant to give luster to the author. In this case, the author gives luster to the prize."

Clementine walked a few paces to where King Gustav Adolph stood, and curtsied. The King grasped her hand, which he held for almost a minute as he spoke in a low voice to her. Then he handed her the Nobel book and medal while a triumphal fanfare sounded. Applause for her was prolonged and loud, contrasting with the restrained handclapping that normally greeted other prizewinners. But it was still not yet time for Clementine to carry out her speech duty. Her reply was to be reserved for the banquet to be held later in the lakeside Town Hall.

The prize for medicine was shared between Professor Hans Albert Krebs, of Great Britain, and Professor Fritz Albert Lipmann of the United States. Mrs. Krebs and the three Krebs children, a girl of eleven and boys of fourteen and nine, were all seated on the platform. They were only two seats away from the King for nearly two hours. Clementine noticed that the children had sat all this time somewhat awed by the magnificence of the hall and the distinguished great audience. As she left the concert hall she paused by the Krebs family, talked to Mrs. Krebs, and then to all three children, congratulating them on behaving so well. "You deserve your own 'peace prize' for the effort and strain of the occasion," said Clementine.

Immediately after the ceremony, most of the guests scrambled for taxis or walked through the streets to the Town Hall for the banquet. Attended by 950 guests, the banquet was held in a large hall with 1,000 candles burning in candelabra. It was a magnificent setting for a magnificent occasion. The hall was decorated with Byzantine mosaics in tens of thousands of tiny, gilded pieces; Romans staring glassy-eyed, and ancient Swedish heroes wielding swords and battle-axes. Men were in evening dress covered in colorful Swedish orders, and elegant women in elegant dresses.

Clementine stood to read Winston's words—a typical Churchillian

338

speech full of that rolling rhetoric, which, as much as his writings, had gained him the Nobel Prize.

On his behalf in a clear, firm voice, Clementine declared: "The Nobel Prize for Literature is an honor for me, alike unique and unexpected, and I grieve that my duties have not allowed me to receive it myself here in Stockholm from the hands of His Majesty, your beloved and justly respected sovereign. I am grateful that I am allowed to confide this task to my wife.

"The roll on which my name has been inscribed represents much that is outstanding in the world's literature of the twentieth century. I am proud but also must admit awestruck at your decision to include me. I do hope you are right.

"I feel that we are both running a considerable risk that I do not deserve it. But I shall have no misgivings if you have none."

The great banqueting room roared with laughter, and Clementine paused, smiling happily at the reception of her husband's humor.

She continued, "Sir Alfred Nobel died in 1896. We have entered an age of storm and tragedy. The power of man has grown in every sphere except over himself. Never in the field of action have events seemed so harshly to dwarf personalities. Rarely in history have brutal facts so dominated thought, or has such a widespread individual virtue found so dim a collective focus.

"The fearful question confronts us: Have our problems got beyond our control? Undoubtedly we are passing through a phase where this may be so. Well may we humble ourselves and seek for guidance and mercy.

"We in Europe and the Western world who have planned for health and social security, who have marveled at the triumphs of medicine and science, and who have aimed at justice and freedom for all, have nevertheless been witness of famine, misery, cruelty and destruction before which pale the deeds of Attila and Genghis Khan.

"And we who, first in the League of Nations and now in the United Nations, have attempted to give an abiding foundation to the peace of which men have dreamed so long, have lived to see a world marred by cleavages and threatened by discords even greater and more violent than those which convulsed Europe after the fall of the Roman Empire.

"It is upon this dark background that we can appreciate the majesty and hope which inspired the conception of Alfred Nobel. He has left behind him a bright and enduring beam of culture of purpose and inspiration to a generation which stands in sore need. This world-

339

famous institution points a true path for us to follow. Let us therefore confront the clatter and rigidity we see around us with tolerance, variety, and calm.

"The world looks with admiration and, indeed, with comfort to Scandinavia, where three countries, without sacrificing their sovereignty live united in their thought, in their practice, and in their healthy way of life. From such fountains, new and brighter opportunities may come to all mankind.

"These are, I believe, the sentiments which may animate those whom the Nobel foundation elects to honor, in the sure knowledge that they will thus be respecting the ideals and wishes of its illustrious founder."

Clementine sat down to a tremendous ovation. The most frightening minutes of her life were over.

She was wearing the same evening dress she had worn at the prize-giving but with the addition of her sash as a Dame of the Order of the British Empire and her medals.

Following the banquet came the great ball, attended by 550 students, with dancing in the splendid brick-walled lower hall. Clementine and Mary watched the dancers from a balcony overlooking the hall. She was seated beside the King and Queen. Here she was in the place of honor in the gallery of the Town Hall, and below were students and their friends celebrating the event.

Suddenly, some of the students started to sing, and everyone on the floor took up the words and melody of the song. It was "Oh my darling, Oh my darling, Oh my darling, Clementine!"—and they sang it in English. It was a rare, unforgettable moment in more ways than one. Clementine, who seldom reveals her emotions before others, this time could not hide her tears. She stood up, waved, and smiled as the students below clapped and cheered. The Nobel prize she had accepted had been to honor her husband. This demonstration by the great crowd of Swedish students was to honor her.

26

The Shadow M.P.

CLEMENTINE CHURCHILL's main career in life has been to give the greatest statesman of our age the stability without which his finest qualities might never have come to fruition, but, had she wished, she could have been an M.P. in her own right. She has the ability, the experience, and the right sense of leadership for it.

She once defined the duties of an M.P. thus: "First is to do what in his faithful and disinterested judgment he believes right and necessary for the honor and safety of our beloved country. The second duty is to his constituents, of whom he is the representative but not the delegate. It is only in the third place that a man's duty to the party organization or program takes rank. There is no doubt of the order in which they stand in any healthy manifestation of democracy.

"Latitude and tolerance ought to be allowed to members of a party. Leaders should prove their capacity to cope in the House of Commons, and on the platform, with personal opponents, however misguided or ambitious they might happen to be."

Every M.P., she told her election workers at Woodford, must use Parliament as the place where "true statements can be brought before the people." She believes that it is useless to send members to the House of Commons just to say the popular things of the moment, merely endeavoring to give satisfaction to the Government whips by cheering loudly every ministerial platitude, and walking through the lobbies oblivious to the criticisms they hear.

Like Winston, she maintains, "People talk about our parliamentary institutions and parliamentary democracy. If these are to survive, it will not be because the constituencies return tame, docile, subservient members and try to stamp out every form of independent judgment."

"Winston," she says, "considers that in politics, if you have something good to give, give a little at a time, but, if you have something bad to get rid of, give it altogether and brace the recipient to receive it."

When Winston took over at Woodford she was with him, working very hard, constantly beside him when he spoke, and herself often addressing meetings in all parts of the constituency. Winston became Member for Woodford when his old constituency, the Epping division of Essex, was split in 1945 into two divisions.

Said Mr. Rowland Arnison, when he was Chairman of the Woodford Conservative Association, "It is wrong to assume that Sir Winston's eminence as a world statesman makes his Parliamentary election automatic. We never take his victory for granted. That is why his wife's work during election time is a tower of strength to her husband—as at all other times.

"No man knows more about fighting an election than Winston, for there is no man living who has been a candidate more often. Since he first stood for Oldham in a by-election in 1899 and was defeated, he has fought in every general election and in several by-elections.

"His wife is of tremendous importance to him as a candidate. Though as President of the Woodford Conservative Association, she naturally takes a close interest in all constituency matters, her most important role is at election time when she plays a personal part in every phase of the campaign.

"In recent years, Winston has traveled the country to speak in support of other candidates, and during his absence on these tours his wife has held the fort here.

"Many of our divisional meetings end with a call of 'Three cheers for Churchill!' Whereupon he will come forward and, with his broadest smile, call for another three—for his wife."

In any election campaign, Winston is a firm believer in a thorough house-to-house canvass. Once satisfied that the organization is running smoothly, he leaves the details of the subsequent stages of the campaign to Clementine and her efficient team of workers.

After the election, Winston and Clementine personally answer the thousands of letters that they receive during the campaign from well-wishers. Their letters of thanks to the campaign workers are far from mere formal acknowledgments of services rendered.

Winston is, of course, unable to visit Woodford as frequently as he would like. After the war, as Leader of the Opposition and determined to get back into power, he was usually busy with Party affairs in London. When he became Prime Minister he was tied even more closely to Westminster. And since retiring from the Premiership, advancing years have taken their toll, and facing large audiences involves considerable physical strain.

The situation is acccepted sympathetically in the constituency. His constituency agent, Colonel Barlow Wheeler, said, "When he comes down here to meetings, he does a magnificent job; but he is no longer able to rush about and keep one appointment here and another there.

"Even at his advanced age it might be all right for a chap who was not so well known. If I asked a Cabinet Minister to come here and give a talk on current affairs, he would be lucky if more than a hundred people turned up to listen to him. When Sir Winston comes, I have to take the largest hall in the borough. We can squash six hundred into it, together with about ninety reporters of the world's press who always come in case it's the last time; and then, outside, there's another crowd of five or six hundred, according to the weather.

"It's not just a matter of his coming down and talking to his executive council, the officers of the branches, or anything of that sort. As soon as word gets around that he is coming, it becomes a world affair. Every journalist is here in case it proves to be the last time Sir Winston speaks to his constituents.

"With any ordinary M.P.—even as old as Sir Winston—it would be easier. He could fix things up privately over the telephone, come down to talk to the local council, perhaps have a meal and talk to his local party executive for an hour or so, and then be off. Nobody would know and nobody would mind. We should tell the next week's local papers that he had been, and that would be that. Everybody would be quite interested, but the visit wouldn't cause the flutter it does now."

Some Woodford Tories have been heard to refer affectionately to Clementine as "Our Shadow M.P." This implies no lack of loyalty to Winston. It is an acknowledgment of the immense amount of work she puts into the constituency. In order to spare Winston's strength, she has shouldered most of the constituency duties, particularly on the important social side, which would be carried normally by the sitting Member.

There are few dinners or dinner-dances of the branches which she does not attend, either alone or with one of her secretaries. The garden parties, the little summer fêtes, which mean so much to local residents, know her well; and at such affairs as the occasional divisional whist drive, she is usually on hand to present the prizes. Wherever she appears, she always brings a special message from Winston.

When she attends the annual dinner and dance of the Woodford Conservative Association, she invariably announces that she does not intend to make a speech; and invariably is persuaded to "say a few words." Under pressure she finally says, "Well, I'll tell you what we'll do. I will propose a vote of thanks to the principal speaker." That enables her to talk briefly to an audience that knows and always enjoys her, and usually she manages to say something that exactly fits the occasion.

"When she says something she shouldn't, it's just as good fun," reports one admirer. "I remember her coming out with some brilliant stuff about the Conservative party—only to suddenly realize that she was at a Lord Mayor's reception, where politics are strictly taboo."

Her humor, at times, can be more than informal. As guest of honor at a Woodford Conservatives' annual dinner and dance, she said in reply to a toast, "I understand that this dinner was open to anybody who liked to buy a ticket, and if there are any ladies and gentlemen here who belong to the opposite Party, I hope they enjoy themselves just as much as we do.

"I hope that when the next election comes, they will put their cross against the name of you know who, although I should not cadge for votes!"

Clementine takes a real interest in Woodford's civic affairs and frequently deputizes for Winston at such functions as the opening of a hospital wing or an old folks' home. That is an arrangement which suits everybody perfectly.

Colonel Barlow Wheeler explained, "If Sir Winston agreed to come down for some minor event of that sort, it would be embarrassing even for the organizers. A simple little local affair would take on world importance certainly neither sought nor desired by the organization concerned.

"When he does appear at some function, Sir Winston inevitably becomes the central figure, much against his will. He has to be carefully guarded from the kind of people who *must* pester any celebrity, so that, in fact, nobody gets a word with him at all. Lady Churchill, on the other hand, can wander about in the crowd, speaking to everybody, and everyone is delighted. Sir Winston would like to be equally sociable, but he can't. It's impossible. He gets mobbed wherever he goes, if the chance is given. People will almost fight to touch his hand—just to say they have done so."

Clementine has become expert at protecting him from such misplaced enthusiasm. Unobtrusively but very firmly, she manages always to be between Winston and the thrusting well-wisher. Says one who has watched her in action, "She seems to flutter in front of him. You might say she bears the brunt of the attack to see that he isn't surrounded."

Although she has been President of the Woodford Conservative Association since 1945, Clementine appears to have no personal political ambitions. When, in 1952, Winston suffered his first stroke, there was considerable concern in the constituency as to whether he would be able to carry on as its Member.

"It was quite on the cards at that time," Colonel Barlow Wheeler admits, "that Lady Churchill might have been asked to stand in his place, but I don't think she would have done so. She is not a political figure; yet over the years I have noticed that she has vast knowledge and is a biting political speaker.

"She is not merely an echo of her husband. She knows her stuff very well indeed. She has a strong will, and a very strong grasp of situations and of people. Her audiences are conscious that they wouldn't get very far by heckling her. She has a command which is quite superb, and reacts swiftly to attack. In any audience there is always somebody who is a bit of a nuisance, but it is remarkable how she can 'freeze' such people. The heckler suddenly realizes that it is no use going on with the argument he thought he was going to enjoy. She can be positively icy; but more generally, she is known and loved for her warmth and sympathy."

She has for years led a women's advisory committee composed of representatives from ten branches in the constituency. She makes it a regular practice to talk to the committee of her husband's work, of her husband's opinions, and of her own opinions. Giving her "woman's point of view" on nationalization to a meeting of the committee, she said, "We must fight to prevent everything becoming nationalized, for by entirely quashing private enterprise the Government is taking all the fun out of life.

"Nationalization is dull, dreary, and weary, whereas private enterprise is full of hopes, vigor, and fun."

When she visited the first two permanent council houses completed after the war, she said, "Every day we read in the papers how unhappy and desperate people have invaded former army huts and empty temporary buildings and installed themselves there.

"These people are referred to by the very ungraceful term 'squatters,' and I wish the word would not be used about respectable citizens whose only desire is to have a home and to keep their families together, and who are perfectly willing to pay rent, rates, and taxes."

Before going into the constituency to deal with any particular problem, Clementine makes sure she is properly briefed. Her research is methodical, meticulous. When, by telephone, she has acquired all the necessary background, she composes her speech. When she has polished it to her own satisfaction, she is likely to ring up Colonel Barlow Wheeler, read it over to him, and ask, "Now, is there anything in that to offend anybody?" She takes tremendous care.

In most constituencies the sitting Member of Parliament holds weekly or monthly "surgeries" at which people with troubles can explain their problems and enlist his help. Because of Winston's peculiar eminence, this, in Woodford, is impossible. The office would be crowded with celebrity-hunters, whose only desire would be to be able to boast later that they had been in "a private conversation with Churchill."

Nevertheless, the electors of Woodford are served better than most, for Winston employs a staff of secretaries, headed by a lady known as the constituency private secretary, to deal with the letters which come in from constituents. Many letters relate only to routine matters, such as requests for seats in the visitors' gallery of the House of Commons, but others call for more serious attention. A widow may be finding difficulty in obtaining her pension; an invalid father may desperately need his son's release from the Services; a young couple may be involved in a worrying housing dispute. Applicants like these get wonderful service, for their letters are sent direct to the Ministers concerned, accompanied by a note: "Sir Winston would like to know the answer to this one." Two days later Winston knows the answer—initialed personally by the Minister, not by his fourth deputy or a clerk.

The grateful constituent may not know it, but the mainspring of this organization that answers the cry for help so swiftly and so well is Clementine.

At election time, she virtually assumes the role of commander in chief of the campaign. During the crucial election of 1955, she made three tours of the entire constituency, visiting committee rooms, conferring with the Association executives, cheering on the voluntary helpers, making each one feel that it was on him or her alone that success depended. Her unfailing good humor, her apparently inexhaustible energy, her genius for being in the right spot at the right time, inspired

346

her little army much as Monty inspired his Desert Rats. And when Winston came down to address a meeting of his supporters, she would always be at his side on the platform.

On polling days, Winston and Clementine arrive in Woodford in midmorning and drive around the streets in an open car equipped with a loudspeaker. Lunch is usually eaten in the home of a friend, and then Clementine makes sure that Winston sleeps for two or three hours. In the evening, before dinner, they drive around the streets again, this time calling at polling booths and committee rooms to greet and encourage the workers; then, after a light dinner, they go on to the Town Hall for the culminating ceremony of the day—the counting of the votes.

Restless, excited, but always smiling confidently, they walk among the tables where the enumerators are busy, stopping now and then to chat to the officials and other old friends. Then Winston retires to a quieter room where he can smoke and listen to results coming in from other parts of the country over a portable radio set.

Woodford is not a very large constituency, and the counting of votes is usually completed by midnight. At about a quarter to the hour, Winston returns to the big hall to see how the fight is going, and whether he is likely to have a greater or a smaller majority than last time. He is also mentally preparing the speech he will make after the result of the poll has been declared. The purpose of the speech is to thank the returning officer and his assistants for running the election efficiently, and Winston sticks rigidly to that theme. He usually manages to bring in a reference to "this Conservative stronghold," but there is otherwise no political flavor.

As soon as it is plain that he has been reelected, he walks over to his opponent and says, "It appears that I shall have to make the speech of thanks, and you will second it. I propose to say nothing about politics but to thank the returning officer. I hope that is agreeable to you?"

It is all very friendly, very correct. Woodford elections are seldom marred by bitterness or unpleasant incidents. For the unsuccessful candidate it is something of a political honor to have been chosen to do battle against the greatest statesman of our time, and he takes his defeat gracefully.

The moment comes when the two candidates step out onto the balcony to hear the returning officer declare the result to the great crowd assembled in the street. Invariably the electors reserve their loudest cheer for the "Shadow M.P." standing happily at the elbow of the victor.

Eagerly awaited by the Woodford Conservatives are Clementine's invitations to visit Chartwell to see the gardens in their full summer glory. A party is made up—it might be members of the Association's executive committee, the women's advisory committee, or a crowd of the younger supporters—and is driven down to Kent by bus. Clementine personally receives the guests and takes them to see Winston, who thoroughly enjoys these informal afternoons.

Said Mrs. Doris Moss, the present Chairman of the Woodford Conservatives, who has been on several of the excursions, "She is very clever about it. Unobtrusively, she keeps everybody moving so that people are not clustered about him and getting in his way. Before you can say 'nines,' everybody has shaken hands with him and been led smartly away without realizing it to another part of the grounds to see the flowers. So Winston can toddle off and do whatever he likes without worrying about the visitors at all."

Colonel Barlow Wheeler usually accompanies each party and performs the introductions. The procedure, he explains, is simple and effective, "I line them up and take them into the drawing room to meet Lady Churchill. I say, 'This is Mrs. Snooks,' and she says, 'How do you do?' Then she turns round and says, 'This is my husband,' as if nobody had ever heard of him at all. I think it's rather sweet. Some of the people look quite startled, though. I think they expect a fanfare of trumpets and a red-coated toastmaster crying, 'The Rt. Hon. Sir Winston Churchill, K.G., P.C., O.M., C.H., F.R.S., M.P. for Woodford,' or something of that sort. But not a bit of it. It's 'This is my husband,' and everybody looking around, wondering who her husband can be. It always makes me laugh. I don't know what happens when they are entertaining foreign royalty or diplomats, but with ordinary people like us they are just two people enjoying themselves in their own home."

On sunny days, tea is taken on the terrace, but if the day is chilly or wet the party is entertained in the drawing room on the first floor of the house. Normally between sixty and eighty visitors will sit down to tea at a number of small tables. Clementine will preside at one, and secretaries and other members of the Chartwell ménage join the others.

Said the Colonel, "Lady Churchill doesn't go around saying 'How d'you do' until after everybody has had tea. She would consider it bad manners to interrupt your tea; but she takes infinite pains to see that by the time the party is over she has had a friendly little private talk with every one of us. It is quite incredible how she manages it in the time.

"You see, it isn't a matter of saying 'Hello!' and passing quickly to

348

the next guest. She has taken care to get a complete briefing on every-one present. If a man is chairman or secretary of a committee, or particularly interested in a local charity, youth club, or something like that, he is astonished and delighted to be asked for the latest news of his activities. It really makes the afternoon for him. And once she has met a person, she doesn't forget him. Next time he meets her, he is greeted as an old friend. She really is an impeccable hostess."

When tea is held in the first-floor drawing room, Winston is not present. Clementine does not allow him to climb stairs. He sits in the smaller drawing room on the ground floor, and will chat with any visitor who happens to find his way there. This, however, can lead to difficulties, for Winston is not above making tactical use of his imperfect hearing.

Their constituency agent admitted, "I have been very embarrassed on one or two occasions when some fellow infinitely higher than myself in our organization has sat down to tell Sir Winston something or other, and Churchill has turned to me and snapped, 'What's he talking about?' He doesn't hear a word if he doesn't know the chap."

Clementine is expert at relieving situations like that. If she thinks that a guest is becoming a nuisance, she steps in, and before he knows what has happened he has been firmly but tactfully whisked away to inspect the goldfish or admire the paintings in the studio.

For the party at large, the program includes a visit to the ponds to feed the goldfish and watch the black swans; thence to the swimming pool, the kitchen gardens, and the rose walk the Churchill family gave to Winston and Clementine on their golden wedding anniversary, and on to the studio to see the paintings. Youngsters among the visitors invariably find themselves steered onto the croquet court, though they may never have touched a mallet before in their lives. It is Clementine's way of keeping them happily out of mischief.

Colonel Barlow Wheeler has vivid memories of one of his first meetings with the Churchills. He had just been selected as Woodford's Conservative party agent, but his appointment was subject to Winston's personal approval. Accordingly, with the chairman of the Association and a few other local notabilities, he was invited to lunch at No. 10 Downing Street.

Winston was at a Cabinet meeting, so Clementine received her guests in the drawing room. After they had drunk a glass of sherry, she said, "I don't think there's any point in waiting for my husband. I don't know how long he's going to be. It might be another hour or it might be five minutes." And in they went to lunch—about eight people in all, sitting at a round table. Clementine kept the conversation general.

"Then," the Colonel remembers, "Winston came in, looking as black as thunder. I suppose he hadn't made his mind up about some situation or other. He just sort of grunted, 'Good afternoon,' sat down, and got on with his soup. I had been placed on his left.

"After a while, his face cleared. Obviously he had made a decision about his problem and dismissed it from his mind. He began to take an interest in the luncheon party, and said a few words to my companion (he knew them all except me). Then he turned right round—he does not usually bend his neck—and looking straight at me, demanded, 'Who are *you*?' It shook me to the core.

"I said nervously, 'My name is Barlow Wheeler.' "

" 'Well, what are you doing here?' "

"I was terrified. After all, he was the Prime Minister and my potential boss. I thought, 'Oh! My God. This is frightful.'

"Lady Churchill intervened at once. 'Don't be rude, Winston!' she said.

"He looked at her impishly. 'I thought it was a very frank question,' he retorted.

"I summoned enough nerve to explain, and after that everything was all right. He said he was very glad to see me, and by the time we returned to the drawing room I knew I need not worry about my appointment."

The Colonel is inclined to agree that he was asked not only a frank but a fair question.

"You see," he explains, "he hadn't the faintest idea whom he was going to find at his luncheon table on any day of the week. It might have been a Trade Union official or anybody. He had probably said some time before, 'We ought to have Mr. So-and-so to lunch.' He was very good with Trade Union people, and invariably invited at least two of their senior men to every State function.

"Oh, yes—it was a fair question. He looked around the table, saw a chap he didn't know, and wanted to find out who he was. That's all."

Another guest at the luncheon, Sir James Hawkey, then Chairman of the Woodford Conservative Association, like Winston was hard of hearing. He had a hearing aid, but for some reason or other chose not to wear it on this occasion. Clementine, however, remembered and was reminded of another omission. She turned to Winston and asked, "Where is your hearing aid?"

350

He looked up from his soup with a puckish smile.

"I can hear anything I want to hear," he said.

"Well, I want you to hear *me* now," said Clementine. "Get your hearing aid, please." Winston sent for it, but he did not put it in place. During the rest of the luncheon he and his old friend Sir James remained blissfully unconscious of what was being said around them.

There was to be another slightly embarrassing moment for Colonel Barlow Wheeler when he was invited to a cocktail party at No. 10, to meet some newly elected Tory members.

He recalls, "My wife and I were looking at one of the pictures when Churchill came up, shook hands, and said 'Good evening.' He stared, puzzled, and then inquired, 'It's Barlow Wheeler, isn't it?' I said 'Yes,' and he went away. About ten minutes later, walking into another room, he found us looking at another picture. Again he shook hands, stared at me, and said, 'Barlow Wheeler, isn't it?' Once more I agreed.

"A quarter of an hour went by. We were examining a piece of sculpture depicting Winston painting at Marrakech when, behind my back, I heard the familiar, gruff 'Good evening.' I turned, and there he was, with hand outstretched. But just as I was about to take it, he grinned and said, 'Oh, no! You're not going to catch me again.'

"He never made a similar mistake. If he saw me at even the most crowded affair, he would come across the room to chat with me.

"He is delighted to recognize anybody. I think he tends to look at perfect strangers with the uneasy feeling that he *ought* to recognize them. I suppose it happens to most men of his eminence, meeting so many people every day."

Here, again, Clementine is a great help to Winston. At every function she is constantly on the alert. Suddenly she will whisper something to him, and he will turn and beam at a guest he had failed to notice. Nobody has a chance to feel slighted or overlooked while Clementine is around.

Still another memorable evening for his agent came during the 1955 election. There were some accounts that had to be signed, and the Colonel rang Winston to say that he would bring them to London.

"I arrived at Hyde Park Gate at about half-past six," he says, "and told my wife, who had come with me for the drive, 'I'll just nip in and get these things signed; then we'll have a spot of dinner somewhere.' Sir Winston, wearing a red velvet siren suit, received me in the drawing room. 'Have a drink,' he said.

351

" 'I'd like to, very much,' I said, 'but my wife is waiting outside in the car.'

" 'Well, don't leave her out there,' he said. 'Bring her in.' He stumped through the hall, opened the door, and said, 'Come in, my dear. Come in.'

"We had a glass of sherry, and then he suggested, 'Why don't you stay for dinner? Wait a minute, though. I'd better check up with the cook.'

"With that he put his head through the door and gave a sort of bellow. There were hurried footsteps outside, a few muttered words; then Churchill said, 'Oh! *He* won't know, anyhow. I'll see to it myself.' He stumped down to the kitchen and returned with the report that the cook could make the meal stretch to two more people. The only other guest expected was their daughter, Diana.

"At this point Lady Churchill, who had been dressing, came into the room, and Sir Winston told her proudly, 'I've fixed it. They're staying to dinner. The cook says he has enough.'

" 'That's very nice,' said Lady Churchill. 'I'm glad to hear that.' But as he went off to attend to some other matter, she sighed and told us, 'I *do* wish he'd leave it to me, you know. I do it so much better.'

"We sat down to dinner, not in the dining but in a tiny room at the front of the house. The butler handed round the carrots in a saucepan, and Sir Winston growled, 'Is that the best you can do?'

" 'Yes, sir,' the butler replied. 'We haven't got the crockery out yet.' And Lady Churchill cut in, 'Don't interfere, Winston. You're only making things worse.'

"They had only moved into Hyde Park Gate a couple of days previously, and the place was still at sixes and sevens. It was all delightful —just like having a family picnic."

Conversation during dinner naturally turned to the coming election, and Winston asked, "Do you think I could be unopposed?"

"No," the Colonel replied. "The Socialist will stand. He is only a youngster, and it will be rather an honor to be able to say he stood against Winston Churchill."

"Well, it's a bit of a waste of time," Winston commented.

"Of course," their guest agreed. "But casting your mind back to the age of twenty-seven or twenty-eight, given the chance of opposing the Prime Minister at the time, wouldn't you have taken it?"

"It never arose," Winston said. "I took good care to be on the same side as the Prime Minister!"

The house at Hyde Park Gate is the repository of John Napper's little-known portrait of Clementine. It was presented to Winston at a meeting of his constituents in the Girls' County High School at Woodford to mark his eightieth birthday. The painting depicts Clementine dressed in a lavender lace evening dress, with a triple row of pearls about her neck. Those who have seen it say it is a delightful likeness. Let Colonel Barlow Wheeler recall the presentation in his inimitable fashion.

"Sir Winston was not supposed to know anything about it, but I am darned sure he did. The meeting was public, and he made a political speech. It was at the time when the newspapers got excited because he claimed to have told Montgomery to keep the German arms carefully because he might have to reissue them to stop the Russians getting into Berlin. When the speech ended, the cunningly concealed portrait was turned round and presented to him.

"After thanking everybody and saying what a good likeness he thought it was, he said, 'I think the only possible thing on an occasion like this is to salute the sitter as I do the portrait.' And with that, he went across and kissed her in public. Everyone was delighted. They thought that was just the stuff. It was quite unaffected."

Clementine was obviously as happy as Winston with the gift, and they inspected the portrait hand in hand.

Their genuine affection for each other has not failed to impress the Colonel. He says, "I have noticed time and again at social gatherings that if he speaks she is looking at him, taking in every word he is saying. And when she speaks, he is looking at her and taking in every word. They might almost be a young, newly married couple, completely absorbed in each other."

It was perhaps unfortunate that the presentation of Clementine's portrait should have coincided with the presentation by the members of both Houses of Parliament of the celebrated Graham Sutherland portrait of Winston himself. It is no secret that both Clementine and Winston regard the latter with less than temperate enthusiasm. And, because of that sad fact, Clementine's picture has never been hung in public view.

"Mind you, there's a lot of sense in that," said a friend. "If it were hung on the wall, people would say, 'What a good picture of Lady Churchill! When was that done?' And then he'd have to say, 'For my eightieth birthday.' Then, of course, they'd say, 'What about the Sutherland? Where's that?'"

353

Winston likes the three portraits of himself done during the war by Frank Salisbury, who caught him in military moods. His favorite is a standing pose, and this one hangs in the Constitutional Club. When Clementine saw it, she said, "It has a fierce expression and one that I would not have chosen. It will make everyone terrified of you, Winston."

But he was delighted. "Surely, in wartime, that is all to the good," he said.

A happier story of another presentation relates to Clementine's visit to Epping in 1954 to accept an eightieth birthday present from the Epping Division Conservative Association. It was a seat made of teak recovered from H.M.S. *Ajax,* which took part in the battle of the River Plate. The seat had been inscribed with a quotation from a speech that Winston made shortly after he had been elected Member for Epping in 1924.

The inscription reads, "I have now found a resting place in the glades of Epping Forest."

Clementine told the Association, "When we sit on it we shall remember you.

"In 1924, you accepted my husband as your representative and he was determined to fight for his seat and gain it on his own merits. He wanted to be accepted as he was. Later, he joined 'the Old Firm.'

"It is a fact that you gave him his chance to reenter politics. From 1904, he had been in Parliament without a break and, in 1922, when he lost his Dundee seat, it was a great shock to us. Through everything, you in Epping have pinned your confidence on him.

"We had wonderful times in the old days. When my husband first came here, he was new and strange. He says that one of the greatest compliments that he has ever been paid was that a strong Conservative seat should accept a non-Party man. When he came here, he was intending to rejoin the Conservative party, but, before he did so, he was determined to fight the seat on his own merits. When he was approached, he was asked to stand as a Conservative, but he said he could not accept a gift like that.

"He was a lonely little boat floating in the political sea, and it was only some time after he won his seat that he rejoined 'the Old Firm.'"

That wooden garden seat now has its own resting place in the peaceful glades of Chartwell.

27

Happy Birthday!

THE great, historic Westminster Hall was a scene of bustling preparation. Chairs were being set out, flowers arranged, carpets unrolled,
for the following morning Winston was to receive gifts from, and the
acclaim of, both Houses of Parliament on his eightieth birthday.

Westminster Hall is a chilly place, so a thoughtful Ministry of
Works' official had ordered electric pads to be fitted to the backs of the
chairs to be occupied by Winston and Clementine.

There were to be two birthday cakes weighing ninety pounds each
before icing—one for cutting after the ceremony in the hall, the other
for the private luncheon party to be held at Downing Street. Iced in
pale amber, the first cake had eight giant candles, and colored badges
depicting milestones in the Prime Minister's career—Harrow, Sandhurst, the Order of the Garter, the Nobel Prize medal, the crest of
Bristol University, and the Churchill racing stable colors of pink and
brown with a jockey's cap. The cake also carried a picture of St.
Margaret's, Westminster, and a wreath of orange blossom. In gold set
in a circle was the phrase, adapted from one of Winston's famous wartime quotations, "A thousand years hence free people will say this was
our finest man."

On the eve of the celebration, Clementine went to a special exhibition of manuscripts and books being held in honor of his birthday,
and came home with her personal present for him—a large and heavy
volume, *Divi Britannici,* published in 1675, and authored by another
Sir Winston Churchill—the fervent seventeenth-century Royalist. When
someone opinioned that it was a very dull book, Clementine punning
the old Latin pronunciation commented, "I can't wait to dive into it."

She hurried back to Downing Street from the exhibition to complete arrangements. They were giving a dinner for Members of the Government and the House of Commons, together with the Speaker of the House and two Back Benchers chosen for the honor of moving and seconding the address in reply to the Queen's speech at the following morning's opening of the new Parliamentary session. Even with five absentees, over seventy sat down to dinner with Winston and Clementine that evening.

In the morning, the sun streamed through the windows of the ancient Westminster Hall onto the 2,500 people gathered to honor Winston as well as the woman at his side. He wore morning dress, and Clementine a fur coat and green feather hat.

As they were received at the St. Stephen's entrance, a bouquet of orchids was presented to her, then to shouts of "Happy Birthday!" they entered the hall. To slow drumbeats they walked forward to receive the welcome of the reception committee of M.P.s and their wives. Winston and Clementine shooks hands with each one of them. The portrait of himself painted by Graham Sutherland, and a commemorative book of the occasion signed by nearly every M.P., was presented.

When the ceremonies were over, they returned to Downing Street for a family-only birthday lunch. The birthday cake at this party measured a yard across—three inches less than the door of No. 10. Sugared in pink and white with white roses raised above the pink, it also had a round center posy with the quotation: "He is a man, take him, for all in all, we shall not look upon his like again." This cake had eighty candles.

Each year Winston's cake is Clementine's secret, shared only with the staff of the bakery that makes it. Every year the design, decided by Clementine, is kept a last-minute surprise. Clementine's own birthday cakes are likewise kept secret from her. One year, to depict her interest in gardening and croquet, the top of her cake was a representation of a green lawn, with croquet hoops and mallets. And, within a border of flowers, was the verse,

> You stand mayhap in the shadow of the man
> Who with your undoubted help our history has made.
> You stand demurely and becomingly
> And dignify that very shade.

On his eighty-second birthday they were posing for the customary photographs when a photographer, his work done, expressed the hope that he might be taking their picture on Sir Winston's hundredth birthday. Winston stared at him a moment, then replied, "I see no reason why you shouldn't, young man—you look hale and hearty enough."

April, 1955, brought Clementine's seventieth birthday. She had just recovered from a severe neuritis attack, but was back in top form, busily completing the preparations for her celebration. It was to be a small dinner party for the family at No. 10, to be followed by an evening with friends.

Her birthday cake arrived from Soho; it was a thirty-pound fruit cake, and again because of her love of gardens, the top of the cake had been fashioned into a garden of grass with flowers made of icing, and a big chocolate Easter egg in the center. The baker had taken the idea of this touch from the continental custom of hiding Easter eggs in the garden for the children to find.

It was a wonderful evening, and, although there was a houseful of politicians in the premier political home of the country, there was no talk of politics, yet there was one unspoken political question uppermost in the mind of every one of the guests that night.

For days, newspapers throughout the world had been speculating—"Will he, or won't he?"—in a great guessing game about Winston's possible retirement. There had been no hint from him, yet everywhere people were preparing themselves for the event.

M.P.s were even making unprecedented applications for tickets for the public galleries of the House of Commons for the following Tuesday, believing it to be the day of his final appearance in the Parliament as Prime Minister.

Asked on one occasion whether he would give an assurance that he was not on a slippery slope to "another place," he replied, "Provided the term 'another place' is used in a strictly Parliamentary sense, I will gladly give the assurance required." Beyond that he would not go. The secret remained secret from even their closest friends.

In February, 1955, Clementine and Winston had made one of their rare visits to a House of Commons evening reception. She seldom attended such occasions. As they walked that night throughout the corridors of the House, they met Sir Tom O'Brien and stopped to speak to him. Rumors of Winston's retirement were strong even then, and Sir Tom asked, "Well, Prime Minister, how long are we to address you as Prime Minister?"

"I'll answer that—later on," Clementine replied.

"And she wasn't, of course, referring to later that evening," said Sir Tom.

By the first weekend in April, 1955, the rumors were making world headlines, and expectant crowds started to watch in Downing Street—waiting tensely for something to happen. People filled the length of the Downing Street pavement, even stretching into Whitehall itself. Among them could be heard speculation and discussion of the retirement reports with a clear reluctance to believe them.

On Monday, April 4, a little before eight o'clock, the Foreign Office floodlights were switched on, transforming the façade of No. 10 into a theatrical setting. The stage was set for an evening without precedence in Downing Street. The Queen was coming to honor a Prime Minister and his lady as their guest at dinner.

Other guests were to include members of the Churchill family, and past and present statesmen associated intimately with Winston and Clementine's lives and achievements.

First to arrive were Captain Christopher Soames, M.P., the Prime Minister's Parliamentary Private Secretary and son-in-law, with their daughter Mary. By this time the crowd had swelled to about 2,000. A long black limousine glided to a halt outside and from it stepped Sir Anthony and Lady Eden to be greeted with applause and cheers.

Just before 8:30 the door opened, and two figures emerged almost onto the pavement. Clementine looked magnificent and regal in a white evening dress, a glittering tiara, and a corsage of spring flowers. Winston wore Court dress, and both of them were resplendent in the brilliant sashes of Royal Orders. This was the moment for which everyone had been waiting. Their welcome was affectionate and unrestrained. Within seconds the Royal car arrived. The Queen had come with the Duke of Edinburgh, and an excited crowd watched as Her Majesty, in a silver-beaded white crinoline dress, and the Duke, in Court dress, stepped from their car to be received by their host and hostess. As the Queen, wearing a glittering tiara and drop pearl earrings, alighted, Winston and Clementine stepped forward.

Winston held the Queen's hand an instant, and bowed low over it, silent, and clearly moved. The Queen then turned to Clementine. In a moment, the pavement reception was over and the door of No. 10 closed behind its host and hostess and their distinguished guests. It started to rain, but the crowd remained.

The dinner, for which Clementine had supervised every detail, was

358

held in No. 10's State dining room on the first floor. She had arranged pink carnations in silver bowls in the oak-paneled rooms, and spring flowers massed along the approaches to it—she had personally chosen some of the flowers she had nursed herself at Chartwell.

Guests included forty-six statesmen and their wives, as well as distinguished officials and their wives. The evening somehow had the atmosphere of a farewell party for close political friends of past years, as well as Winston's fighting team represented by the Earl and Countess Alexander of Tunis, and Field Marshal Viscount Montgomery of Alamein.

There was also one special guest. Mrs. Neville Chamberlain, widow of the last of the five Prime Ministers under whom Winston had held office, had been invited by Clementine.

In proposing the health of Her Majesty and of the Duke of Edinburgh, Winston proclaimed, "I have the honor of proposing a toast which I used to enjoy drinking during the years when I was a cavalry subaltern in the reign of Your Majesty's great-great-grandmother, Queen Victoria."

The Queen rose and said she wished to do something which probably few of her predecessors had had an opportunity of doing, and that was to propose the health of her Prime Minister.

At the end of the brilliant function, Winston and Clementine saw their Royal guests to the door. Winston bowed deeply, Clementine curtsied gracefully, and they stood together on the doorstep of No. 10 watching the Queen's car until it disappeared at the end of the street.

Not until the following afternoon did rumor resolve into certainty. The door of No. 10 opened to reveal Winston in black frock coat, shiny top hat, gold-headed cane, zippered shoes, and cigar in mouth. Behind him in the doorway, was the ever-present, smiling Clementine, plainly proud of his unusually smart attire. He waved his hat to acknowledge the cheers, signaled for his car, and got in. Clementine waved to him as it moved off almost surrounded by people eager to catch a glimpse of the great man with his jutting cigar and jaunty smile, eager to remember him as they had known him throughout the war. For everyone there was a feeling that a chapter of British history was about to close.

At 4:22, a cluster of sightseers outside Buckingham Palace saw the Queen arrive, followed ten minutes later by Winston.

At 5:12, Winston's car drove out. People outside were strangely silent, then, suddenly, they went mad. He was no longer Prime Minister, but he was still their Winston. Hundreds surged forward cheering and singing "For he's a jolly good fellow," and shouting "good luck!"

When his car arrived back at Downing Street, he looked flushed and excited. He hurried from the limousine to reach Clementine waiting to meet him on the doorstep. After giving the V sign, and taking a final public puff of his cigar, he vanished inside the shadow of the doorway. At 5:21, the official announcement of his resignation was issued from Buckingham Palace, and at 5:30, Ministers arrived at No. 10 for the final farewell.

The crowds still wouldn't go. Even after 11, they stood outside calling and singing. When, eventually, Winston and Clementine appeared at a first-floor window, the crowd roared appreciation.

The following afternoon, the Churchills said good-by at No. 10 to a hundred of the staff—private secretaries, typists, telephonists, cleaners, messengers, drivers, cooks, maids, Forces personnel—all who had served them at No. 10 and at Chequers.

Clementine had arranged a tea party for them during Winston's last hour at No. 10. In the first-floor dining room—the same State room in which the Queen had dined—they both received each of the guests. The servants were served ham sandwiches, cakes, pink and white ice cream, and laughed at the jokes in Winston's speech in which he also thanked them for the service and loyalty they had given both him and Clementine.

Then came the departure. Two cars were drawn up at the door. In a cage on the floor of the first car was Winston's pet budgerigar, Toby; his poodle, Rufus, sat alone on the front seat of the second car. In the hall, their office staffs lined up, and as they moved towards the front door, the whole staff began to sing, cheer, and applaud. The cheers were taken up by the crowd of a thousand outside as the door opened. Clementine didn't join Winston in the car, nor did she come out, as she usually did, to see him off. She had to remain another day to attend to many things and prepare No. 10 to receive its new master and mistress —Sir Anthony and Lady Eden. Winston drove alone to Chartwell.

At Chartwell, the sun burst through the skies as his car hurried through the lanes, and the sadness of his leaving Downing Street gave way to the simple warmth of a country homecoming. To the little group of thirty people, most of whom had waited from noon to greet him, he laughed and waving his hat, shouted, "Come in the grounds, all of you, and see my goldfish."

Asked whether he had any last message as Prime Minister, he smiled, hesitated, then said, "Yes—it is always nice to come home."

Weeks later, he made it publicly plain that he hadn't been "pushed out."

"I gave up my office because I thought it was my duty. Whatever one's feelings, one must not think only of one's self, especially after a long life such as I have lived.

"I thought I would go in such a way as would be right and proper for me, to leave my successor to choose, for himself, the moment of election and the program for which he would be responsible. Don't you think it was the right thing to do? I have no doubt about it."

When their old friend Sir Will Lawther, ex-President of the Miners' Union, asked Winston why he hadn't retired at the end of the war in all his greatness and glory, Winston replied, "You should know, because, like me, you were born into mischief, and, like me, you believe you'll be in it to the end."

"It was his wife who largely influenced his retirement decision," said Sir Tom O'Brien. "She could see that he wasn't doing the job any longer to his *own* satisfaction, and that this worried him. His hearing was affected, and he was not answering questions in Parliament properly—particularly Supplementary questions—because he couldn't quite hear what he was being asked. So she persuaded him to retire because she knew he had become physically unable to do his job in accordance with the fullness with which he himself wanted to do it. She realized that if he was allowed to become more and more dissatisfied with the manner and efficiency in which he was carrying out his duties as Prime Minister, this growing dissatisfaction with himself would have created a terrific psychological reaction both in him, and in her. She knew that if he carried on much longer in this way, he would blunt his past. It was for those considerations, rather than any feeling that he had done all he could do, that made her decide to press him to resign."

"What will he do?" Clementine asked, as his retirement began.

"Well," suggested one of her friends, "he will be able to paint to his heart's content; he will be able to travel; he will be presented with the freedom of a large number of towns and cities and many university degrees both here and abroad—wherever he goes he will be received with great honor."

"Yes," answered Clementine, "I can see all that, but that still does not tell me what he is going to *do.*"

She need not have worried. A few months later, M.P.'s crowding

361

the entrance to the Chamber of the House of Commons, stood aside to permit a familiar figure to stride through. The man paused at the traditional Bar of the House, gave a dignified bow to the Speaker of the House, and returned the many smiles of recognition and welcome. There was a hasty movement on the Government Front Bench below the gangway, and a first seat was vacated. Winston made for the vacated seat, lowered himself into it, and then M.P.'s and people in the galleries stood as one and cheered themselves hoarse. Winston blushed and wiped a happy tear from his eyes.

He was back in Parliament for the first time since his resignation as Prime Minister. But this was one outstanding moment in his career that Clementine missed. She had fallen down the stairs in their Hyde Park Gate home that day, and broken her left wrist.

28

Roses, Roses All the Way

"WHERE does the family start? It starts with a young man falling in love with a girl—no superior alternative has yet been found"—was Winston's comment on the secret of domestic bliss. He added, "Many things in life are settled by the two-staged method. For instance, a man is not prevented from saying 'Will you marry me, darling?' because he has not got the marriage contract drawn up by the family solicitors in his pocket.... It is hard, if not impossible, to snub a beautiful woman—they remain beautiful and the rebuke recoils...."

As for what the role of women should be in the future, he asserts, "The same, I trust, as it has been since the days of Adam and Eve...."

Closer to home was his comment on Clementine, "She has been the companion and prop of all my life in so many ups and downs and stresses, long and hard."

On September 12, 1958, the sun shone on the French Riviera for a golden day. Seated in the shade of the patio of Lord Beaverbrook's villa perched on the rich red hillside of Cap-d'Ail, Winston sat working on a canvas, spending a little of their golden wedding day on the pastime he loves most. Inside the villa, Clementine was opening hundreds of messages of congratulations. She wanted to open every parcel, telegram, and letter herself.

Never before had the tiny post office in the local village had such a flood of mail to handle. The post-office staff had to be augmented for the occasion from neighboring villages. All the world wanted to wish them well. Messages and gifts continued to arrive, and by midafternoon they had not been counted, let alone opened.

Red roses came from the people of Cap-d'Ail, and when Winston came downstairs, his eight-year-old granddaughter, Arabella, welcomed him with a special greeting for the occasion by reciting most of a classical Greek poem, with a rose garden as its theme. Clementine and Winston listened as flaxen-haired Arabella managed without stumbling, thirty of the fifty lines of "The Garden of Malagea of Gadera." Knowing roses have always been Clementine's favorite flower, admirers, known and unknown, sent them to her this day. Hour after hour, more and more roses were delivered.

First of the huge pile of telegrams Clementine opened, was one from the Queen and Prince Philip, and Winston and Clementine's first pleasurable duty of the morning was to send their thanks to Buckingham Palace. There were telegrams too from Prime Minister Harold Macmillan and his Cabinet; from France's President Coty; from General De Gaulle; the King of Norway; and a special one, from President and Mrs. Eisenhower, was brought by hand by the American Consul from Nice.

Randolph, who with his little daughter Arabella, were the only members of the Churchill family present, gave his parents the family's golden wedding present. He told them their gift was to be an avenue of golden roses, and that the avenue was to be planted the following month in the grounds of Chartwell. There were to be 146 standards and bushes in 29 varieties of gold and yellow. And, because the avenue could not bloom until the following June, they had prepared a souvenir book giving details of the avenue and embellished with paintings of the twenty-nine roses. Randolph presented them with the beautiful vellum book.

Together, Winston and Clementine sat turning the pages of the magnificent volume which had been produced in only five weeks. All the roses in the book had been painted by noted British artists, among them Augustus John, Cecil Beaton, Sir Matthew Smith, Paul Maise, Duncan Grant, and Mr. R. A. Butler, the Home Secretary—Winston's amateur painter "pupil." The box holding the book had been embossed in gold: "Sir Winston and Lady Churchill, 1908 to 1958," and the book itself titled: *The Golden Rose Avenue at Chartwell.*

Randolph, Diana, Sarah, and Mary had spared no effort to make the book perfection. All the script and illumination in it had been carried out by Denzil Reeves, of the Colchester College of Art, and inside it contained a simple dedication in raised gold lettering on a page decorated by Sir Winston's artist nephew, John Spencer Churchill. The verse, by the poet Paul Jennings reads, "Once golden words transmuted leaden gloom and fired all England to a golden age; now golden roses for you two shall bloom whose golden peace turns one more private page."

Beneath it was a water color of a single rose on a tree with Toby, Winston's budgerigar, perched on a branch. The inside of the cover and the front of the first page of the heavy, handmade, parchmentlike paper with deckled edges, had been backed with green watered silk, and the pages bordered with roses tooled in gold, symbolic of the avenue to be erected at Chartwell. A miniature Blue Garter Sash, with the initials "W.S.C." and the motto "Honi soit qui mal y pense" embroidered on it—a gift from the Garter King-of-Arms, Sir George Bellew—was the bookmark.

By now the volume of gifts had grown so great that members of the staff were stacking them in the corridors of the villa. There was a chocolate cigar weighing 25 lbs. from a Swedish Countess, a 5-liter bottle of Cognac 119 years old, from the restaurant on the Riviera where Winston and Clementine often dine; there were pictures from many amateur painters, dozens of bottles of champagne of the best vintage from champagne companies, and a box of cigars, brought to the villa by an old French tramp who had walked 1,500 kilometers to give Winston his golden wedding gift.

The tramp, Henri Marchand, had been one of thousands of soldiers standing around when Winston arrived in France after the war. "Suddenly there was Churchill, and he thrust one of those great cigars into my hand," said Henri Marchand, recalling the day. "Now I have walked all this way to give him cigars for his golden wedding. I begged the money for them."

While the world's congratulations poured in, excitement at the villa was deliberately restrained for eighty-three-year-old Winston and seventy-three-year-old Clementine. The celebration lunch was held on the vine-covered first-floor terrace of the villa. Winston sipped a little champagne and Clementine sat opposite him. Their sole guests were Randolph, Arabella, Mr. Montague-Browne, Winston's personal secretary, and two women secretaries. Clementine, who had arranged all the masses of flowers around the villa, also specially chose a celebration menu of some of Winston's best-loved dishes.

After lunch, on being told fifty photographers were waiting outside hoping to take a golden wedding photograph, Winston and Clementine opened the gates to them.

"Come in, come in," they called. Photographers crowded round to photograph them as they sat side by side in armchairs on the villa's sunlit terrace. He politely refused to walk across the terrace for newsreel cameramen saying, "No, I'm too old for that," adding, "Go and have a glass of champagne instead." Winston, Clementine, and little Arabella served the champagne. Arabella, copying her grandmother, behaved like an experienced hostess.

Winston turned a golden wedding smile on Clementine when she put a very feminine foot down and said in French and English, to the cameramen, "Don't come too close. I don't mind if there are fifty of you, but I don't want any close-ups. Don't forget, I'm not so young now."

As an additional tribute, the Mayor and citizens of Cap-d'Ail spent £5,000 to have the road that passes the villa where Winston and Clementine stay so often, widened and renamed "Avenue Winston Churchill." Commented Winston's secretary, Mr. Anthony Montague-Browne, "They spent a quiet and happy day, profoundly touched by the kindness shown."

Later, on the villa's terrace, Winston and Clementine sat together in the glow of a rose-tinted sunset. The day must have brought back memories of their fifty years—half a century unparalleled in a man's history. But their over-riding thoughts must have been for the deep and abiding love that helped each of them through.

Mr. John Napper, who painted her portrait, said, "There is a greatness radiating from Lady Churchill as well as from Sir Winston. I would call it a partnership in greatness. This is a case of seeing a great man and looking at his wife who is partly the cause of it."

Sympathetic, understanding, cooperative, encouraging, possessed of freshness and charm, "spoiling" Winston but never allowing him to spoil their grandchildren too much. There were many times when the changing emotions and moods of her husband made her feel like counting him among her children. An example of her motherly care of him was witnessed during the 1945 election campaign, by Mrs. Doris Moss, who was then one of their Woodford constituency committee-room helpers. Said Mrs. Moss, "They had been on a nonstop tour of committee rooms in the constituency and our place was the last stop. When they came into the room, he looked exhausted—he wasn't a young man then, and although he has remarkable powers of relaxation, he takes so much out of himself. As soon as they walked in, Mrs. Churchill came over to us and said, 'You know, Winston's tired. Do you think he could have a real rest for a few minutes?'

"She made him comfortable in a large easy chair; he closed his eyes, and was asleep in a few minutes—being able to go off like that is a gift he has. She went on chatting to us, keeping everything around her going in the extraordinary way she does while, at the same time, diverting attention from him awhile.

"After about ten minutes she went over to him, and it was just like a mother waking a baby. She roused him gently and said softly— 'Winston—time to go now.' He opened his eyes, and the smile that passed between them was something to see."

As Chairman of the Woodford Conservatives, Mrs. Moss presided over the last big public meeting Winston addressed. "We were a little worried about him," said Mrs. Moss, "because he hadn't done any public speaking for some time, and Lady Churchill was also obviously worried lest he should let his own high standards down in some way.

"I was seated on the platform next to her, and, as he began to speak, I could see her sitting tense; tying herself in knots. Knowing her well, I was very conscious of what she must have been feeling at that moment.

"He rose and moved to the high box on which he always rests his papers. He took a pair of glasses from his pocket, put them on, and Lady Churchill gasped 'Oh!—he's got the wrong glasses!—He must have put the wrong glasses in his pocket.'

"We breathlessly watched him peering through the strange glasses, then he removed them as they were obviously useless, and suddenly a great beam spread across his face.

" 'I can *read without my glasses,*' he announced to everyone.

"As the speech continued, I could see the knots untying, and gradually her nervous hands rested and relaxed peacefully in her lap—she could see he was going to be all right. Then, when he had finished, she leaned right across the platform behind him, and, unseen to the audience he was still facing, got hold of his hand and *squeezed* it in the way that young lovers would.

"When we met again some weeks later, and I asked about his glasses, she announced with delight, 'Oh, he's still not using them!'

"Invariably, she would always ask him before a speech, 'Have you got your speech glasses?' and he would pat his pocket and grin.

"She would never allow anyone to talk with him when he was about to make a speech. He insists on a period of concentration before he faces the microphone or steps onto the platform, and she makes certain his concentration remains strictly uninterrupted."

Good-humoredly, Clementine always managed to cope, always managed to inject a little discipline whenever necessary, such as the Royal Garden Party at Buckingham Palace, when she noticed Winston reaching for one too many cream cakes. She caught his eye, and he took his hand away.

She delighted in his successes, was downcast when things went wrong for him, but she never showed her disappointment in public. Whatever happened, she, a soldier's daughter, always remembered when she was "on parade."

Her own antidote for the poison of worry is, "Whenever you are vaguely oppressed by you don't know what, write down all the things you can think of as possible annoyances. Once they are down on paper, you can deal with them. This one won't happen for six months ... I know the answer to this one ... this—the only real and immediate difficulty, crying for an answer—you deal with.

"You make it all manageable the moment you break it into precise and concrete issues. The one thing the human mind can't stand up against is mystery."

Her counsel and opinions were always important to him. Whenever they had been unavoidably parted, he had longed for her to be with him. She had always been at hand when he needed her in a crisis.

It had been to her that this man—this tower of strength among men in fact—turned in so many decisive moments of his life. In moments of world tragedy, and in personal political defeat, he had literally run to his Clemmie calling for her, seeking solace in her smile, and in her words.

It was to Clemmie he ran with tears streaming down his face on hearing the early morning announcement of the death of King George VI. It was to Clemmie he ran, bewildered and wounded, when his political enemies branded him "warmonger" on the eve of the 1951 election. She alone had breathed strength and spirit into him, renewing his will to go on. In those moments they had stood alone, but together.

Wrote *The Times:* "He has been sustained through the ups and downs of his eventful career by great domestic happiness. In sickness and in health, in and out of office, through triumph and disaster at Chartwell, Chequers, and Downing Street, Mrs. Churchill has been his gay and understanding partner through all these exacting years."

One morning a telegram was delivered at their Hyde Park Gate home. It came from delegates attending a great political conference in London. It offered "greetings and thanks for your incomparable service

368

rendered to the nation and Empire." It was addressed to "Mr. and Mrs. Churchill."

Back came the modest answer, "We are so glad you think our services were of use." The reply was signed Winston and Clementine.

They had shared everything—glory and heartache, and continued to share great moments and little things like holding hands in public at a Buckingham Palace garden party.

"When he was in hospital in 1962, following his leg accident, I had to see Lady Churchill at Hyde Park Gate," said Mrs. Doris Moss. "We lunched and discussed all sorts of constituency matters. I asked how Sir Winston was, and she replied, 'Would you like to go and see him?'

"I said I would love to, but thought I'd better wait until he came home.

"'Well, I'm going this afternoon, how about coming with me?' she asked.

"Sir Winston's personal assistant, Anthony Montague-Browne, was lunching with us, when suddenly there was a domestic crisis in the kitchen.

"'I'm afraid this will mean, Doris, that I will be unable to come with you to the hospital,' she told me, and turning to Anthony Montague-Browne, added, 'You take Doris, and I'll come along later.'

"When we got to the hospital we had to wait quite a time because Sir Winston was doing his exercises, and that went on and on, and, as you know, what he wants usually goes on. Anyone who thinks the famous will isn't what it was doesn't know what they're talking about. As a result of his sudden enthusiasm for exercise we had to wait about twenty minutes. Finally we went in. He looked very well—it was only a few days before he left hospital. We had been there fifteen minutes, and I thought I'd better not outstay my welcome. I was about to leave when Lady Churchill came in. She was visiting him twice most days, and had already seen him that morning, but you would have thought they hadn't met for years. One felt almost embarrassed being there. She had eyes for nobody else, nor he for anyone else from the moment she walked through the door. She went to him, took his hand, and never let go.

"Few people realize the terribly worrying time she has had during the past few years. I asked her one day on the telephone, 'Why don't you have a holiday? You haven't had a real holiday for ages.' She replied, 'Oh, but I couldn't go away! You see, Winston needs me.' She wouldn't go. She has to be there when she is needed. It has been the same, I know, from the beginning of their marriage.

"When she and Lady Reading spoke at a function in Woodford during the year that my husband was Mayor, they were both resplendent in the colorful sashes of a Dame Grand Cross of the Order of the British Empire. In her speech Lady Reading said, 'You may have noticed that we are both wearing the same decoration. Now mine was given to me for doing what hundreds and thousands of women have done, but Lady Churchill's was given to her for what she is, and has done.'"

The Dowager Marchioness of Reading, who has known Clementine since 1931, and who is one of her close friends, had this to say of her, "I have the deepest personal regard and respect for Lady Churchill, especially as I think she has been able to do a thing that is rarely done—has kept herself quietly in the background, and always been the support, rather than the somebody that's always getting limelight recognition of what she's doing.

"She has a forceful strength, she never misses a single thing, she stimulates where necessary but never interferes. In other words, she lets people get the kudos for what they're doing and gives recognition to everyone rather than ever snatching it for herself.

"I honestly think she is the ideal wife. If a wife loves a husband enough to sink herself completely in him, in what interests him, and in his work, ignoring her own advancement except through him—that is the perfect relationship of husband and wife.

"As a woman she is ideal. By saying that, I mean she is practical, wouldn't obtrude her views at awkward moments, has poise and diplomacy, and knows how to do things.

"You expect a man or woman who has had background advantages to be able to do many things, but it is another matter as to whether they manage to successfully exert to the best advantage all the different strengths, all the contributory powers that have taken years of discipline to generate. It is a question of discipline, of observing what is necessary, and tailoring yourself to do it. This, I think, Clementine Churchill has done because she has known that it was a strength. After all, she has gone through all Winston's difficulties with him, gone through all the political upheavals, all the disappointments, all the elations.

"A husband with a flibbertigibbet wife very seldom reaches the zenith. Interference in continuity of thinking and irritation can do an awful lot of harm—you have only got to look at a machine to see what it does, and it does a great more to a human being.

370

"Clemmie Churchill's contribution to her husband is a very great one. She and her husband are absolutely devoted. She automatically felt that she should give him everything, and she has. She has also done it in the finest possible way because lots of people who give are very blatant in the giving. She has never been blatant in the giving. Her devotion to her husband shows the depth of true feeling.

"She was there when she was wanted, yet arranged to do things she had to do on her own. She has always been faithful to her friends. Those who were her friends in childhood are still her closest friends, and that is a wonderful thing to be able to say. She hasn't a wide circle of friends, but they are very close. It isn't a matter of loyalty, it is real friendship, and that is quite a different thing. Loyalty is something you command through discipline of your mind. Friendship is companionship—a natural thing. Her complete companionship is what I think is so wonderful in her. It's the greatest thing one can have.

"Her husband has always been the most important thing in her life.

"I have been dealing with women for a very long time now, and in large, large numbers, and when I express my really deep and sincere admiration of a person, it is not a light thing. It's a considered, a balanced thing, and I think that any person who aimed to have the perfect daughter would want her to be able to behave as Clemmie Churchill behaves. You can't say any more than that. It is the height of one's admiration for her.

"For any woman—especially a good-looking woman—to be selfless is a tremendous thing. She is a very good-looking woman, and always looks right. Even when she is feeling ill, she always mirrors whatever is needed in order to back her husband. She doesn't obliterate herself—she is simply, naturally there—where it is necessary for her to be.

"My admiration for her is so great that it knows no bounds at all. The reticence in her behavior is the quality that everyone admires. Discipline, reticence, not unselfishness—selflessness; courage to meet every sort of adversity—and she's had plenty—this is Clemmie Churchill."

The lasting quality of her thoughtfulness and friendship is something Sir Tom O'Brien has good reason to appreciate. He was attending an official reception connected with the War Office in 1962, when Clementine arrived escorted by Randolph. She saw Sir Tom O'Brien looking at some paintings on the walls of great soldiers of the past. He thought she was about to speak to someone else, but she went over to him instead.

"They can wait," she said, "I want to talk to you. Don't think that

371

because we don't see each other so often nowadays, and because I am no longer so much in the public eye, that I ever forget your great loyalty to Winston on that horrible New Year's Eve when he went, a sick man, to Bermuda, and you sent him that wonderful good-luck telegram. Nor do either of us forget that you were battered about because of it. We still remember that, as well as your many other kindnesses."

She was referring to the year that Sir Tom had been President of the T.U.C., which was also the year Winston was reelected Prime Minister for the first time after the war. He had just taken office again, Eisenhower had been elected President, Stalin was still around, and there was great agitation for Summit talks between the three former war comrades to sort out the urgent problems in Germany and elsewhere.

"Winston was going to Bermuda for a fortnight's rest, and had decided to call on Ike as well," said Sir Tom. "On the night of his departure from London, there was a terrible blizzard. It was shocking flying weather. Clementine was very concerned, but blizzard or not, he was going.

"The night before, I had sent him a telegram saying that he would carry the goodwill of everyone with him, and that we hoped he would be able to bring back to Britain a glimmer of light—things were bad at the time and people feared the danger of yet another war.

"One of Winston's secretaries phoned my office to say the Prime Minister was delighted with my message and asked whether I objected if he made the telegram public. I said no. He released it to the press. The following morning every newspaper carried it, and hell was let loose. One or two of the Communist branches started to send letters of protest to the T.U.C. I was censured, kicked upon, spat upon, my resignation was demanded, the agitation went on for months.

"As soon as Winston returned, Christopher Soames saw me at the House of Commons and asked me over to Downing Street for a drink. Both Winston and Clementine were there. She said, 'I do hope you are not going to get into too much trouble because of the telegram.' The trouble was only just starting then.

"I said, 'Don't worry about that.'

"That evening they invited me over again. We sat in his room, and he said, 'I've been reading the cuttings about what these people are trying to do to you, but it doesn't matter—they're only scratches and mauls —they can't *eat* you—just a few scratches, that's all!'

"Both Winston and Clementine were genuinely worried that all the hullabaloo would do me harm, which it finally didn't, as sensible people in the trade union movement knew my telegram had solely been a gesture of goodwill. Winston and Clementine offered me true friendship during that difficult period, and their friendship has remained. With them, the description 'friend' isn't just a word. It is something of deep value."

While Winston will go down to posterity as the most dynamic and impulsive of all of Britain's Premiers, Clementine will be known as the most gracious hostess 10 Downing Street ever knew.

In the years of their marriage Clementine accustomed herself to an extraordinary way of life, but of one thing she never could complain— she could never say her husband didn't appreciate her. Winston made no secret of the fact that he had adored her from the beginning. His dependence on her, his adoration of her had always been something to be seen. He loved to select a rosebud from one of the bushes in their golden wedding avenue of roses at Chartwell, and personally nurse it day after day until it was beautiful enough to present to her.

Their golden wedding anniversary gave great pleasure to people all over the world. This was one occasion when a successful marriage made front-page news. Said the *Sunday Times:*

"It has cynically been said that happy marriages are not news; it is those that have failed that make the headlines but here, to confound the cynic, is a marriage the success of which has never been in doubt which has always been news; for all the civilized world has known that for 50 long years besides the fighting, turbulent personality that has evolved into the much-loved world figure of today has been the serene and strengthening companionship of his wife, comforting and supporting him in good days and in bad.

"It is a tremendous tribute to Lady Churchill that, never seeking the limelight of public life herself, though always engaged in good works, she should have so impressed herself on the public mind by her perfect share in one of the most felicitous partnerships of our time."

Today, in the garden of Chartwell, a living and loving tribute to Winston and Clementine's golden years together stands for all to see. And, among the twenty-nine different varieties of roses making up the golden avenue, is that favorite in thousands of gardens all over Britain —"Peace." A sundial standing halfway down the avenue is encircled by ten standards of the magnificent rose "Peace," a yellow rose with strong shadings of cerise-pink on the edges of the petals. Outside this circle is another one planted with twenty trees of the bright yellow fragrant rose

"Lydia." All the famous rose-producing countries are represented, and the avenue in full bloom is a breathtaking vista of golden beauty.

On the occasion of a previous milestone in their marriage—their twenty-fifth wedding anniversary—their friend, Lady Desborough, organized the presentation of a "signed letter" to them, and asked another of their dearest friends, Eddie Marsh, to compose the message. He wrote:

"You are not among those who are happy in having no history, but from all the vicissitudes of your two distinguished lives, in which Fortune has shown you both her faces, you have emerged with unshaken dignity and courage breathing united force with fixed thought and have given your countrymen an illustration of faith and happiness in marriage."

But it is appropriate that Winston should have the final words in this book—this tribute to his darling Clementine:

"There is no doubt that it is around the family and the home that all the greatest virtues, the most dominating virtues of human society, are created, strengthened, and maintained. . . ."

Bibliography

ARNOLD, GENERAL H. H.: *Global Mission* (Harper & Brothers)
ASQUITH, MARGOT, COUNTESS OF OXFORD AND ASQUITH: *More Memories* (Cassell)
BABINGTON SMITH, CONSTANCE: *Evidence in Camera* (Chatto & Windus)
BARRYMORE, ETHEL: *Memories* (Harper & Brothers)
BIRKENHEAD, THE EARL OF: *The Prof in Two Worlds* (Collins)
BEAVERBROOK, LORD: *Politicians and the War* (Hutchinson)
BEVERIDGE, LORD: *Power and Influence* (Hodder & Stoughton)
BARUCH, BERNARD M.: *The Public Years* (Odhams)
BLUNT, WILFRID SCAWEN: *My Diaries* (Martin Secker & Warburg)
BRITISH RED CROSS AND ST. JOHN: *Official War History* (1939–47)
BROAD, LEWIS: *Winston Churchill* (Hutchinson)
BRYANT, ARTHUR: *Triumph in the West* (Collins)
    The Turn of the Tide (Collins)
CHURCHILL, JOHN SPENCER: *Crowded Canvas* (Odhams)
CHURCHILL, WINSTON SPENCER: *My Early Life* (Odhams)
    Thoughts and Adventures (Odhams)
    The Gathering Storm (Cassell)
    The Second World War (Cassell)
CLARK, GENERAL MARK: *Calculated Risk* (Harrap)
COOPER, LADY DIANA: *Trumpets from the Steep* (Rupert Hart-Davis)
COWLES, VIRGINIA: *Winston Churchill* (Hamish Hamilton)
CRIPPS, COLONEL THE HON. F. H.: *Life's a Gamble* (Odhams)
EDEN, GUY: *Portrait of Churchill* (Hutchinson)
EISENHOWER, DWIGHT D.: *Crusade in Europe* (Doubleday)
ELLIS, JENNIFER (edited and arranged by): *Thatched with Gold* (Hutchinson)
ESHER, VISCOUNT: *Journals and Letters* (Ivor Nicholson & Watson)
GRIGGS, G. P. (edited by): *Sailor's Soliloquy* (Hutchinson)
HALIFAX, THE EARL OF: *Fulness of Days* (Collins)

HASSALL, CHRISTOPHER: *Edward Marsh* (Longmans)

HOLLIS, GENERAL SIR LESLIE (with JAMES LEASOR): *War at the Top* (Michael Joseph)

HORROCKS, LIEUTENANT-GENERAL SIR BRIAN: *A Full Life* (Collins)

HYDE, H. MONTGOMERY: *Carson* (Heinemann)

ISMAY, GENERAL LORD: *Memoirs* (Heinemann)

KENNEDY, MAJOR GENERAL SIR JOHN: *The Business of War* (Hutchinson)

MARCHANT, SIR JAMES (edited by): *Winston Spencer Churchill: a Tribute* (Cassell)

MARSH, SIR EDWARD: *A Number of People* (Heinemann)

MASTERMAN, C. F. G.: *Lucy Masterman* (Ivor Nicholson & Watson)

MCGOWAN, NORMAN: *My Years with Churchill* (Souvenir Press)

MONTGOMERY, OF ALAMEIN, FIELD MARSHAL VISCOUNT: *Memoirs* (Collins)

MOSLEY, LEONARD: *Gideon Goes to War* (Arthur Barker)

NEL, ELIZABETH: *Mr. Churchill's Secretary* (Hodder & Stoughton)

NORWICH, LORD: *Old Men Forget* (Rupert Hart-Davis)

OLIVER, VIC: *Mr. Showbusiness* (Harrap)

PAWLE, GERALD: *The War and Colonel Warden* (Harrap)

PICKERSGILL, J. W.: *The Mackenzie King Record* (University of Toronto Press)

RIDDELL, LORD: *War Diary* (Ivor Nicholson & Watson)
More Pages from My Diary (Country Life)

ROOSEVELT, ELEANOR: *Autobiography* (Harper & Brothers)

ROOSEVELT, ELLIOTT (edited by): *The Roosevelt Letters* (Vol. 3) (Harrap)

ROSENMAN, SAMUEL I.: *Working with Roosevelt* (Harper & Brothers)

SHERWOOD, ROBERT E.: *The White House Papers of Harry L. Hopkins* (Eyre & Spottiswoode)

SMALLEY, GEORGE: *Anglo-American Memories* (Duckworth)

STEINBERG, ALFRED: *Mrs. R.* (Putnam)

TABORI, PAUL: *Alex Korda* (Oldbourne)

THOMPSON, WALTER H.: *I Was Churchill's Shadow* (Christopher & Johnson)
Assignment Churchill (Farrar, Straus & Cudahy)

WEBB, BEATRICE: *Our Partnership* (Longmans, Green)

WIART, SIR A. CARTON DE: *Happy Odyssey* (Jonathan Cape)

WINANT, JOHN G.: *A Letter from Grosvenor Square* (Houghton Mifflin)

Index

Index

379

380